VIVIENNE WESTWOOI

'Authentic and compelling'   *Times Literary Supplement*

'Everyone can have their say, fans of punk, the connoisseurs of sexual freedom, the fashion addict; Dame Vivienne has directed all the excitement of the past fifty years – and it is told here'

Die Zeit Germany

'The prevailing impression of Westwood that we get . . . in *Vivienne Westwood*, an autobiography written with Ian Kelly (rather than the usual ghostwritten celebrity tosh), is of a leader . . . As in her punk days, Westwood has tremendous influence on the way thousands of men and women choose to dress'

Bee Wilson, *London Review of Books*

'An entertaining mix of interviews and authorized recorded conversations of Ian Kelly with Westwood, her relatives and friends. In wonderful conversational pieces Westwood reveals her anecdotes and memories, [and] you get an intimate look at the life of a woman who likes to create scandal – a legend that is known as far as the East and as much as the Queen and Madonna'   *Deutsche Zeitung* Germany

'Packed with characters from the history of music and icons from the dazzling yet quirky fashion world. The book is a journey into the seventies and paints a picture of an idealist. Above all it is the work of one thing: A tribute to punk – the youth culture that was born in 430 Kings Road, according to Westwood . . . and a tribute to Westwood. She herself is modest: "You cannot take fashion too seriously." Long live punk.'   *Echo* Germany

VIVIENNE WESTWOOD

VIVIENNE WESTWOOD
& IAN KELLY

PICADOR

First published 2014 by Picador

This paperback edition published 2015 by Picador
an imprint of Pan Macmillan
20 New Wharf Road, London N1 9RR
Associated companies throughout the world
www.panmacmillan.com

ISBN 978-1-4472-5414-0

Designed and typeset by Clare Skeats
Printed in Italy by Printer Trento S.r.l.

Visit **www.picador.com** to read more about all our books
and to buy them. You will also find features, author interviews and
news of any author events, and you can sign up for e-newsletters
so that you're always first to hear about our new releases.

My duty is to understand. To understand the world. This is our exchange for the luck of being alive. From people who have lived before us we can rediscover different visions of the world through art – this is the true meaning of culture – and by comparison, we form our own ideas of a world better than the one we are in, the one that we've made a mess of. We can change our future. In the pursuit of ideas you will start to think, and that will change your life. And if you change your life, you change the world.

VIVIENNE WESTWOOD, 2014

CONTENTS

EVERYTHING
IS CONNECTED

*A child sees everything in a state of newness; genius is childhood
recovered at will.*   CHARLES BAUDELAIRE,
                                        The Painter of Modern Life

Never dance without a story in your mind.   RUDOLPH NUREYEV

Paris Fashion Week. Spring / Summer Collections 2014.
    'Don't talk to me now, Ian, I'm really, really busy.'
    I am sitting, typing this, beneath a clothes rack, under ninety thousand quid's worth of frocks. To one side, Vivienne Westwood, in beanie hat and frayed cardigan, is pinning glittery appliqués onto knitwear and evading my questions. On the other, a largely naked model sways on platform heels. We're somewhere in the 2nd arrondissement. It is three o'clock in the morning.
    A few things you need to know about Vivienne:
    She seems to be indefatigable. It'll be dawn soon enough, and she's still going strong, working as hard as interns fifty years her junior.
    She looks fabulous: 'skin like porcelain', as her friend Tracey Emin described her to me. She seems to live on apples and tea.
    She's super bright: don't be fooled by the ditzy-Northerner shtick, she's sharper than the pins in her sleeve.
    She is a tad hard of hearing. I suspect this to be a tactical deafness. It serves her well against the clamour around her.
    But mainly what I've learned about Vivienne is this: she has maintained the child within herself, against all the odds. Wide-eyed. Inquiring. Open. Stroppy. Mercurial. Dressing up sometimes. Rude,

some of the time. Heart-soaringly loyal and loving at others. She behaves, mainly. Sometimes she goes off on one.

At seventy-three, you might not think that's quite dignified. Not quite the thing for a Dame of the British Empire who is head of a global fashion brand and one of the most famous Englishwomen on the planet. Not very *grand couturier* here in Paris either, for a woman who might easily be admiring her own laurels or resting on them: 'the Coco Chanel of our times', a woman more famous in the Far East than the Queen or Madonna, and who is still cycling down Battersea Bridge Road to work every day in her eighth decade.

If so, this story may not be for you. If you think fashion can never be more than frippery or that seventy-year-olds have *less* right, not more, to lecture the world about its future or bear standards for its past, then you can lay aside this book. As Vivienne said to me the other day, 'it'd save on trees'.

If, on the other hand, you can go the rounds with this punk-grand-mother, who is still in the ring, fighting for what she thinks is right and thinks is beautiful when, let's face it, many of her contemporaries have settled for a Shackleton high-seat chair and their memories, then stick with her. You may be in for as much dazzle and as much unex-pected insight into the workings of a unique mind as I have had in my year with Vivienne. My Year of Magical Blinging. Because this is a story that is far, far more than fashion, though it is woven with cloth.

'Look: I only mean don't talk to me just *now*, Ian. I mean, I'm think-ing. Go and have a drink. They're free. I'm not.'

The other thing you should know about Vivienne is that she can be very funny.

26 September 2013, 2 a.m., and there are sixty hours to go. In sixty hours the new Vivienne Westwood collection will be revealed in Paris for the first time. The Gold Label collection is the flagship line for the Vivienne Westwood Group, and its biannual launches in Paris (spring / summer, then autumn / winter) are the highpoints of the design year for Vivienne. Although there are other collections – Red Label (ready-to-wear) and Red Carpet (as it sounds) amongst them, plus 'diffusion' lines like Anglomania that filter her ideas and classic

designs to other territories under licence, and also a range of menswear ('MAN'), showcased in Milan as well as shows in the Far East and elsewhere – these Paris openings are the mother of all shows for Vivienne. It is the same for all the other fashion houses that crowd out the hotels around the Place Vendôme this time of year. Chanel, Dior, Prada, Comme des Garçons: this week they are all showing their collections, Vivienne's being a partial 'couture' collection showing in Pret à Porter week. These high-end, loss-leader, identity-defining collections are still shop-windowed in Paris despite the rise of rival fashion capitals over recent decades in New York, London, Milan or Hong Kong. Most collections lose money, though Vivienne proudly tells me her Gold Label eventually goes into profit through special orders. Paris Fashion Weeks are the pinnacle of the fashion calendar, and every few hours one show closes and another opens and the pavements of Paris are crammed with matchstick women walking too fast in high heels while talking on cell phones. Seriously: don't get in their way. It is a fracas of fashionistas and trade press; a glossy posse of buyers and models, photographers and liggers, and the focus of many months of work for the London studio of Vivienne Westwood and its Italian cutters and shoe factories. This collection Vivienne has entitled 'Everything is Connected' – and it's the first time I've ever been in Paris except to eat or to try to impress a girlfriend. This time, damn it, I don't get to do either, but all round, it's quite an education.

In the decades during which Vivienne has been a designer, fashion has shifted enormously in the way it markets itself. Her story defines this seismic shift in what fashion is, and in what it means for Western economies like Britain's. Once upon a time the collections were aimed at an outrageously privileged cabal of women who needed outfits to attend galas and diplomatic functions, races and tea parties. What they wore filtered down into the mainstream relatively quickly, via magazines, patterns and rip-offs, but the grand houses made bespoke outfits in tiny, unaffordable numbers, the prices of which nevertheless more nearly reflected the huge number of craftspeople involved in making them. Today, a couture collection is sold at a major loss, though the prices involved are breathtaking. A single Vivienne Westwood outfit might retail off the catwalk at £2,000 to £6,000 – though some have been known to cost ten times that. Yet this is still only a fraction of the real cost of their creation and original marketing, as they are works of art that have the input of thousands of man-hours and dozens of highly skilled individuals. Fashion Week makes no sense. The goal is to grab the attention of a much wider public, increasingly via the Internet, who might buy versions of these styles, or buy into the name that is figureheaded here in Paris. Nevertheless, these Paris collections are in a sense Fashion at its purest: Fashion as Art. Fashion that reflects its moment in time. Fashion, as Vivienne now has it, that might even change the world.

So these collections draw crowds both in person and especially online quite out of proportion to the number of people involved in wearing or even making the clothes. During Fashion Week, Paris is the epicentre of a singular phenomenon of our age: the new global fascination with fashion, a novel language, mainly online, fusing design and marketing, fame, art, sensuality and politics that has no real parallel in cultural history but can be traced also to Vivienne's early punk work bringing together fashion, music, celebrity and the zeitgeist. So don't think this is frippery for rich bitches. Well, it can be. But it is also a major part of the global economy, and a vital story in what Europe now is. It is a shopfront. Paris during Fashion Week is a metaphor for one way the global economy is heading, a trade fair on an epic scale, but also a marketing happening for Old World style, fusing fashion, music and a new narrative about being. And selling, increasingly, to China.

Hundreds of thousands are following what's happening online. There are scores of professional fashion journos and bloggers at Vivienne's shows alone, representing the emerging markets of the Far East and Brazil and Russia and focusing the concentrated attention of vast crowds, in their bedrooms and offices and high streets, from Hong Kong to Sao Paolo to Moscow. Cable TV and now the Internet have revolutionized fashion, and nowhere is this clearer than in the story of Vivienne Westwood, whose name is known across the globe as a result of what happens and happened in Paris. Paris is the international huckster for all the accessories and perfumes and magazines that feed off fashion, all of them circling what begat them in the first place:

Vivienne and the much-anticipated running order.

couture. And here in the centre of it all is Vivienne, one-time King's Road punk and now a global luxury brand herself, maintaining her wry amusement at the business that is show, maintaining in the face of all this brouhaha her calm passion for beauty, especially beauty wrought in cloth. And all the while campaigning constantly, via fashion, for the higher goals of art and politics as she sees them, and the highest standards in what she makes.

It should also be noted that a Paris Fashion Week is one of the few times in the year when Vivienne Westwood, scourge of the British Establishment, grandmum, mother and eco-activist, turns her manxome gaze directly and to the complete exclusion of all else on that which has made her world-famous: clothes. A lot of the rest of the year, there is much else that occupies her days. But not in Paris. Paris is devoted to fashion. It is therefore perhaps the best place to begin to understand Vivienne, in this moment of creative calm, hectic though it is, and – oh shit – 4 a.m. though it now is, in this storm of activity that is Vivienne Westwood's regular rhythm of being. Paris Fashion Week ends this weekend, with Vivienne's Gold Label collection as one of its closing highlights. And there are less than three days to go . . .

Number 13 rue du Mail, just behind the Palais Royale and Paris's Bibliothèque Nationale, has been turned upside down this week. It's a swanky old building, much knocked around by war and corporate usage, but once home to Liszt, and later the Gestapo, and now housing the Paris showrooms of Vivienne Westwood in the building's former ballroom. For three days in September each year this space is transformed into the base unit for the creation of the Vivienne Westwood Gold Label catwalk show. The show itself will take place elsewhere.

Walking up the rue du Mail, it is clear to me which is the Vivienne Westwood showroom, and what's going on. Girls with unfeasibly long legs and limpid eyes traipse in and out and onto the backs of waiting moped couriers. They are the models. Newly migrated from Milan like feeding locusts, indistinguishably and implacably beautiful and all dressed in black, their faces nude of make-up and blank, they come and go on the back of motorbikes, casting to casting, their stilettos in their bags, their legs wrapped around the dudes who work as model-couriers. With two days to go to the main collections, it's casting day for the shows. I follow the girls inside.

The ballroom-showroom is divided by ten industrial-sized clothes racks from which hang maybe a hundred unique couture items: satin ballgowns, Grecian draped viscose, wool and linen tailored suits, cotton knitwear dresses. A million pounds' worth of frocks. On one wall, a display cabinet holds the entire range of Vivienne Westwood handbags; on another, the jewellery. Against yet another wall is a small encampment of desks and screens and mobile phones, the buzzing hive of event managers, presided over by Kiko Gaspar, sleek, efficient and Portuguese, and dressed head to toe in Vivienne Westwood. Another corner, and an impromptu studio has been set up, a cyclorama with nuclear-white lights, and a desk where a shaven-headed Italian graphics designer makes photos sharper, crisper, whiter. These are the images of the girls in catwalk outfits, to be printed and shuffled like a deck of cards into the catwalk running order.

The clothes, shoes and knitwear have just arrived from Vivienne's Italian factories and London studio. The jewellery for this collection has been impounded by customs at Calais. No one seems perturbed or alarmed at this last-minute glitch. Some of the clothes are less than half made, with pieces lying on cutting tables between sheets of her logo-stamped tissue paper. The casting session with the models doubles as a fitting for the couture items. No one seems bothered either that ten-thousand-pound outfits are in pinned segments on the floor, with two and a bit days to go before they are on view to the world. So I pick my way over them and through the queues of models awaiting their auditions. Shoes are lined up on the ballroom staircase, like glass slippers for a hundred punk Cinderellas. There is a low hum of mobile-phone conversations. I can make out five languages.

More and more people seem to be arriving all the time, with no one discernibly in control or clocking anyone in or out. The entry requirement appears to be at least one item of Vivienne Westwood design and an air of cool. A tattoo seems to help. In the centre of the room, commanding by a simple presence and the accident of great height, is forty-eight-year-old Andreas Kronthaler, Vivienne's husband.

A prized Gold Label invitation, printed before the collection even had a name.

What will be news to no one in fashion, but perhaps unfamiliar to those who know only Vivienne Westwood's name, is that her work today is co-designed by her husband and creative collaborator of two decades. When they met, she was a visiting professor of fashion in Vienna and he was one of her design students. Mr and Mrs Kronthaler have been together for about twenty-five years, which is also roughly the age gap between them. More on this later. For now, it is clear to everyone in the room that Andreas is the centre of things as much as Vivienne, and in the context of Fashion Week he has a certain advantage. He combines the looks of a rough-trade Jeremy Irons with the accent of Arnold Schwarzenegger. This, combined with a disturbingly mesmeric gaze and the build of a Tyrolean blacksmith (the family trade), makes Andreas an unlikely figure in Parisian haute couture. Everyone, including Vivienne, appears to be slightly in love with him. And one singular impression of this whole experience has been to watch at close quarters a couple at work together, in somewhat stressful circumstances, who nevertheless are conspicuously easy and happy partners in life, in art and in shared trade.

Less easy to spot at first is Vivienne herself, somewhere behind the clothes rails, wearing a headband sloganed, appropriately enough, *Chaos.*

'I can't talk to you just now, Ian – but I will.'

Each of the potential models is being photographed, some of them in the outfits that might be worn. Those who will be chosen are marked on a board with a red dot, like a sold work of art, by the model-booker Maiwenn. Maiwenn is working a Pearl-Harbor-geisha look with Vivienne Westwood Anglomania shoes and is the keeper of the gate so far as models are concerned. The red dots go on the girls' noses. Green dots mean they fit the clothes too. Which is an advantage but not an insuperable obstacle for those who do not, as the clothes have not all been made. Issa, who combines a Japanese ancestry with great height and strong bearing, may open the show. Ajuma, from Nairobi, a Vivienne regular, is back for the first time after the birth of her child. Marta, from Valencia, who won a modelling competition but should still be at school, is as excited as a puppy and as beautiful as the day, still alive to the drama of it all, the sheer little-girl dressing-up party that is a Paris catwalk show. Most of the others exude an air of glamorous ennui, accessorized with iPods.

When I leave them all to meet a *Vogue* editor, the line-up of both girls and dresses is beginning to emerge.

'It's availability as much as chemistry,' explains Maiwenn. 'Vivienne's is not the highest-paying gig in town; it never has been, so we may lose some of the girls. On the other hand, this is the party they all want to be at, even if their agents don't. That's how we all feel about Vivienne.'

Thirty hours to go, and I am again cross-legged at the clothes rail under a bolero jacket, this one apparently made of chenille and cobwebs. It is being pinned and restitched by Vivienne. Surrounded as we are by some of the world's most beautiful women in various states of nakedness, and fabrics and creations of both beauty and oddity in various states of unpreparedness, Vivienne nevertheless manages to concentrate simultaneously on a press release that explains the collection, scraps of paper like fabric samples arranged around her slowly coagulating into prose.

At this juncture I should introduce you to the Vivienne Westwood players dotted around the room. I can't see a chain of command here as such. There's no call sheet, no director. Things happen by stealth and by osmosis: word spreads. People whisper. These seem to be the main cast: there's Vivienne and Andreas, obviously. They loiter between the boards of pictures and the half-screened dressing rooms where the naked models change. Andreas paces. Vivienne sits, or works on a mannequin. As the hours tick by, the models are more often being dressed in full view of everyone. Christopher Di Pietro – head of marketing and merchandising – comes and goes, and is deferred to on all things non-design. Brought up variously in London, Paris and Ulster, ex French military, now sporting Vivienne Westwood ensembles so striking he is accosted in Paris restaurants and a beard that half masks his Gallic good looks, Christopher is a voice of clear intelligence and one of the many wise and loving presences Vivienne has arrogated to her business. Carlo D'Amario, CEO and Italian godfather to Vivienne Westwood 'Inc.', is also in and out. Looking like a Borgia pope, shaven-headed, powerfully built, Carlo likes to let it be known that he is responsible for the economic success story of the Vivienne Westwood Group, and on this Vivienne concurs. Certainly they go way back, he and Vivienne, all the way to the King's Road in the 1980s and a brief love affair in Italy. He is only to be seen properly at the Gold Label show itself and afterwards with the Italian lawyers and Far Eastern buyers. Likewise, the 'big three' in design terms, after Vivienne and Andreas, are absent until the show. Murray Blewett and Mark Spye, design managers who have been with Vivienne since the early eighties, and Brigitte Stepputtis, head of couture, are all intimately involved with the making of any collection and also its later dissemination. The teddybear presence of Alex Krenn, who does all the graphics on textiles, and the married graphics team of Joe and Beata De Campos, make up the visual language of Vivienne Westwood on cloth and paper. Kiko Gaspar, from Lisbon, is head of events, so this is his battle if not his war. He smiles at everyone while not quite making eye contact: a general benediction and a general admonishment to get the fuck on with it. He seems to be surgically implanted with a headset. In the showroom and later backstage, Peppe the super-on-trend design assistant and his friend Ilaria seem to be at the centre of things creatively, with stylists Yasmin and Rachel. Make-up is a separate command structure, as is hair, field-commanded by Val Garland and Sam McKnight respectively. Maiwenn Le Gall and Brice Compagnon sit at one of the few desks, casting models. They live on Planet Fashion, but it appears to be a happy place for them. Rafael, heavily bearded in the way of this year's menswear looks, beams constantly through the haze of sleep loss. Westwood archivist and assistant, Rafael solves all problems for all people while running coffees and food from the kitchenette to the showroom. His ready laughter and indeed his ability to explain what the fuck is happening make him my lodestar through the strangeness of it all. This is a role usually played by Tizer Bailey, Vivienne's PA, a woman who combines ethereal beauty – she was one of Vivienne's signature models in the nineties – with the soothing efficiency of the perfect Home Counties head girl and a rather dirty laugh. Then there is Benedikt, another six-foot-three Austrian, with blond hair down his back, currently held up by pencils. He is Andreas's assistant, and recruited, like so many others here – Georg, Alex, Brigitte – from some part of the Habsburg empire where all tempers and histrionics are banned. Truly, I've seen more drama and tantrums at WH Smith's than at Vivienne Westwood's. It's almost disappointing.

'You need to know, this is a great place to be. We want to be working here,' says Christina Nahler, an intern. 'I'm *paying* to be here, to get here, I mean, but I am learning much more than I would anywhere else. And it means something, you know; it's fashion for a reason, and with a story. I mean: this is *Vivienne-fucking-Westwood*. We're part of a legend.'

Twenty-eight hours to go and now it's the styling of the chosen models, the creation of the entire 'look'; which shoes go with which dress, and then the compiling of a running order – the much vaunted 'story' of this collection, along with hair and make-up tests. Andreas is fitting girls to outfits.

'We tell a story,' smiles Andreas from under his thick eyelashes and baseball cap, 'that's why people pay attention. What we are doing, it is fashion like it used to be. Vivienne is constant. You recognize what we make because it is not fashion; it is a story about her, and her reaction to the world.'

The temperature has gone up about ten degrees. The interns sew.

The models who have been booked for tomorrow turn up for fittings and loiter around, changing in and out of outfits and footling on iPhones, being photographed. Walls fill with glossy printouts of them in differing looks, their hair uniformly drab. The air is heavy with expensive scent and nervous laughter. The last of the shoes, mis-sent to London, arrive and take their place on the grand staircase, the cavalcade of heels. The collection's jewellery is still impounded, but otherwise everything is now here, and everything is unwrapped from a growing mountain of tissue paper, all of it stamped with the distinctive Westwood logo of royal orb and Saturn-rings. It looks like Christmas Day, sponsored by Vivienne Westwood.

Of the thirty or so models needed, fourteen are now booked: red dots on their noses and green dots on their bodies. Five are on standby. Many of the top girls are booked to other designers and catwalks through the afternoon, girls with names like Dasha and Iekeline – girls from every corner of the globe and of every ethnicity who have in common only their preternatural beauty, height and need for a good meal. Their average age is nineteen. My flirty conversation with Marta is broken up by her manager. Who turns out to be her father. Who turns out to be slightly younger than myself. As the day runs into evening, more and more models arrive. It's going to be an all-nighter, and the salads and fruits provided for the girls are replaced with butter cookies and chocolates and the constant burr of the espresso machine.

The creation of the look of the show is not just down to the clothes. It is a stage show featuring lights and music and themed hair and make-up. This is a specialist art form all of its own.

'I adore working with Vivienne,' says Val Garland, exponent of this rarefied art form, taking a pause from testing a Kabuki-white face paint. 'It's a creative holiday.'

'The girls love working here,' says the model-booker, 'because they are treated with enormous respect, and they become part of the story. Which is easy to forget. With Vivienne and Andreas, it's all calm and respect, and both are quite unusual in our business.'

To one side, Mr and Mrs Calm and Respectful are bickering over knitwear:

'It looks a mess, Vivienne,' says Andreas.

'No, look, Andreas, look: you can just stitch around and around and tie it here: that was my idea; there's plenty of room.' Vivienne demonstrates. Andreas shrugs.

'You just leave it on,' Vivienne whispers to the intern, 'and don't show him.'

Twenty-three hours to go. The press and marketing team from London arrive. Giordano Capuano, Laura McCuaig and Victoria Archer set up shop halfway up the grand staircase, scrambling for power sockets and Wi-Fi connections, stuffing envelopes with VIP invitations and 'access all areas' wristbands. Because I am used to seeing them in the London HQ of the Vivienne Westwood Group, all three of them invariably exuding elegant executive style and fashion savvy (though Giordano is keen to point out to me that he is as much a devotee of rugby as couture), it feels odd to see them huddled like students at a sit-in, fretting over their piles of papers and lists. It's every man and woman for themselves. They work harder than anyone I know outside of medicine, and, like stressed doctors, combine this with an enviable ability to party through the night when the job requires it. Which it occasionally does. The press teams from the Far East and from the International wing of the VW Group arrive and set up slightly to one side. The Taiwanese team produce a 'celebrity' profile of the Far Eastern stars who will be in attendance; Annie Chen and the rock star Wubai, 'one of the biggest in Southeast Asia', are illustrated with Google-images so that they might be treated with suitable deference.

Sometimes, not always, out of a Vivienne Westwood show one girl emerges who ends up being the 'look' of the collection. Naomi Campbell was it in 1993, in part because she fell off her platform shoes on the runway. Sara Stockbridge became the poster girl for Vivienne's late-eighties tweeds and crinolines.

'It may or may not be the first girl, or the last girl in the wedding dress,' Vivienne explains to me later. 'Andreas is a genius at choosing, at getting the perfect girl for the perfect look. I remember once Naomi Campbell in tears wanting to wear this amazing glittery dress, with metal flowers made by Andreas's father, and Linda Evangelista was going to wear it, and Andreas said, "Naomi, you'd look like Diana Ross" – in my opinion no one is better at choosing than Andreas, or dealing with models.' Ajuma, from Nairobi, and Marta from Valencia seem to be in the running for this year's girls.

'She's my biggest supporter in the industry,' says Ajuma, former Kenyan 400-metre sprint champion and one of many 'girls of colour' (as she puts it) chosen by Vivienne and Andreas. 'In New York and London and also in Kenya with our charity work, we work together. It's like a reunion when I see them. In the campaign we did there [Vivienne supports a charity that makes her bags in Kenya, through the United Nations International Trade Centre Ethical Fashion Initiative] I went with them to places I had *never* been – hard-core slums . . . they are brave people . . . but in Paris, I always want to be in their show. I've just had a child. But now I am back, so it feels like: let's see if I've still got "it"!' The running order, and the first and last girl positions remain, until the last moment, up for grabs.

Vivienne takes off her fake-crocodile pumps and pads around in her socks, arranging folds of knitwear over the semi-naked form of Silvia.

The loose hanging tabards of knit are tied and stretched into a ruched stocking, ablaze with appliqué and rumpled around the buttocks and below the breast in a classic Westwood line. Here she is. Beatific. At work. At one with cloth and needle and living body. 'Vivienne is at her happiest now,' whispers Christopher as he passes by. And so she is, working on into the night.

More staff arrive: cutters and design team members as well as more interns and press officers. In total, a workforce of sixty people, representing eighteen hundred man-hours over the course of these three days that will make up the Paris show. The numbers mount. Layer on layer of expense and industry, as well as art: the palimpsest of luxury in action: sixty 'looks'; twenty-nine models; forty hair and make-up professionals. Eight hundred and fifty-seven named guests. Two hundred pairs of handmade shoes. A million pounds' worth of clothes. A budget of over £200,000 on the event. It is costing the VW group directly a mere £120,000, but there are also sponsors to keep happy, along with the international press. Everyone involved wants constant updates and images for their respective blogs and PR teams, and Victoria and Laura dutifully feed snippets of information and a draft version of Vivienne's press release text – typed-up and almost ready now – gleaned from the notes and quotations strewn around the showroom.

Early in the wee hours, Vivienne's finished press release circulates. She quotes Shakespeare, references the Renaissance, the Enlightenment and Frida Kahlo, and, in her new-minted title 'Everything is Connected', makes allusion to E. M. Forster. 'I often think of the titles,' Vivienne tells me. 'I'm good at that.' 'Everything is Connected' invitations, still smelling of printer's ink, are pressed into envelopes in Kiko's corner. They sport a logo for the collection hand-drawn by Vivienne herself of two serpents eating each other's tails, an ancient emblem of aggressive symbiosis used to express the economy devouring the planet. 'This is the main message of the Climate Revolution and of my life now: that everything each one of us thinks or says or does can make a difference,' she says. Everything is connected.

The call comes to listen to the music that will accompany the show. Composer Dominik Emrich samples widely, from baroque

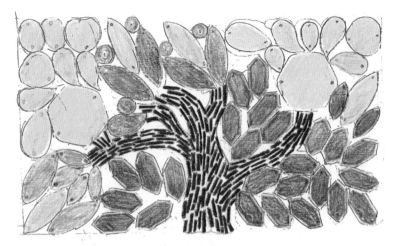

Embroidery design made from plaques cut from re-cycled reflective sunglasses & bugle beads 11½×20

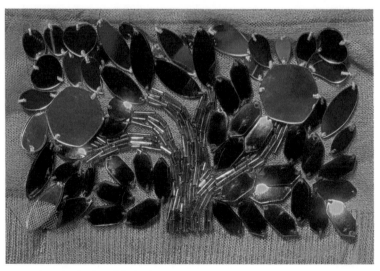

Vivienne's studio sketch, and the finished Gold Label detail.

court marches to English madrigals and folkloric Cretan pipes. There's a snippet of Alfred Schnittke and some Saint-Saëns underscored with an insistent beat both dancerly and portentous: 'like *bang* – it's the end of the world – *watch out!*' booms Andreas, beaming one of his high-energy smiles. He's a man having fun: either high on fashion or determined to fight sleep deprivation with laughter. Vivienne is more contemplative. She struggles to hear these days if there is a buzz of background noise. 'I can't hear what's being *said*,' she complains of Dominic's offstage mantra, '*the Oracles of Mother Earth . . . the trail of blood*', which would please her as a refrain, I dare say, if she could hear it. The conversation between Andreas and Vivienne meanwhile ranges from shoes to bags to hairstyles to confusion over how to describe the look of it all: 'It should all be *apposite*,' says Andreas, indicating lopsided hairdos. 'You mean *opposite*,' Vivienne corrects. And then Rosita Cataldi and Paola Iacopucci of the Westwood Italian factory arrive, bearing flowers and kisses for Vivienne, who lights up in the warm embrace of friends. The chatter turns easily and fluently to Italian, a softer sound in Vivienne's mouth than her native English, sensuous and light-filled.

Fifteen hours to go, but a long night stretches ahead. 'It has to be last minute – you have to have all the molecules in one place, and then *whoosh*.' Andreas gestures a tree growing or an atomic mushroom cloud, his physical theatre as expansive and indeterminate as his accent. 'We do it for ourselves, you see, Vivienne and I, making things as perfect as can be. It doesn't matter what anyone else thinks. So long as *we* know every girl looks amaaaazing.'

Fourteen hours to go. In fairness, I've been out at Café de Flore knocking back espressos and whisky while trying to keep up with the fashion talk – but Vivienne, when I return at 2 a.m., is up to her neck in the running order and the music and models. Do these people ever sleep? They are now trying the 'show pieces': that is to say, items that will never be made commercially, but which might feature in a *Vogue* editorial or could, perhaps, be ordered bespoke by a favoured and moneyed client. The main focus seems to be around a metallic knitted bikini, which may or may not be paired with drapes or a knitted vest in tomorrow's couture show. It is, it has to be said, very sexy. The house model is used for the final fittings and pinnings, and she is as unflaggingly upbeat as she is beautiful. A concentrated calm seems to have descended upon Vivienne, born of many years in the business and many Paris collections. She ponders snapshots of models, and mouths to me, or herself, or anyone who might be listening, 'I've no idea what we are going to do,' but she clearly does. There are twenty-nine pink-edged body bags laid out on the floor, with the names and mugshots of the booked models – the clothes bags that will hold their outfits. Two each. The names are mainly indistinguishable Middle European.

'It's been the way, this last decade,' explains Rafael, the assistant.

'Slavic cheekbones and cool manner – it's not what Vivienne is famous for, but models with attitude and sex appeal are more difficult to find these days. Perfection is easy,' opines the model-booker.

Finally the press release is ready, whittled down by Laura and amended by Andreas with a fashiony sign-off to his 'Darlings', which may or may not be tongue-in-cheek.

'I am going to call the show "Everything is Connected",' Vivienne has written, 'because that is the main message of the Climate Revolution and of my life, that everything each one of us thinks or says or does can make a difference.'

Thirteen and a half hours to go. It's three in the morning, and the collection and its running order are complete. Vivienne sits hunched in a chair, her legs swollen, she complains, her eyes a little bloodshot, sipping at a glass of red wine. Andreas drinks white.

'It's all about the order at this stage, really. We have to get it right, and especially what goes first. It sets the tone.' In the end, one of the Frida Kahlo-inspired ensembles is to go first, worn by an angular and androgynous Japanese model. The picture of her has been moved around the board numerous times, but keeps going back to the top. Ajuma will wear the white column dress; Marta, amongst other looks, the chenille lace. A lot of last-minute attention goes too on items of styling that will pull together the story – the idea of pilgrimage, the references to Kahlo – some of which are just now being made: headdresses with giant flowers and antique ribbon; garlands and walking staffs. 'There is no one better at this than Andreas,' reflects Vivienne, 'at styling. We carry on until it's right. It's about perfection, and when you see it, there it is, and then you can go to bed.' Vivienne and Andreas help finalize prices that have been argued over in London and Italy already, and that range from merely expensive to oligarch-unaffordable. It's late, and some of this can wait until after the show and the sales days that happen back at the showroom once it's all over.

Four in the morning, and apparently it's impossible to get a cab in Paris in Fashion Week. It takes me an hour and a half to walk back to my friends' apartment. What Vivienne Westwood shoes lack in obvious practicality they make up for, it turns out, in comfort and durability. The men's ones, anyway.

Five hours to go. I've slept a little. Most of the VW team have not. They moved at 8 a.m. from the showroom on the rue du Mail to the venue for the show itself, which had a team of builders and set decorators in overnight to create the show space and backstage areas. Normally 18 rue du Quatre Septembre, near the Bourse, is a bank. Its grandiose central atrium, part Victorian opera house, part futuristic hangar, gives it the air of a *Blade Runner* set revamped by Tim Burton. It's vast. You could fly a small aeroplane down its central hallway. You have to enter up a huge staircase, guarded by stentorian security staff sporting regulation dark glasses, Hugo Boss suits and a menacing manner, and through security barriers, all of which gives the right meet-the-queen ambience. Music thunders around us, a soundcheck for Dominik's music, and the composer himself is huddled over a computer console, chewing his scarf, trying to arrange the finale that will accompany Vivienne and Andreas for the catwalk curtain call. Beyond the atrium, and visible through a tangle of glass bridges and translucent floors, the bank drops away three floors underground. Escalators rise up from this subterranean vaulting, and it is via these that the models will rise, and then descend, looping around a hex-agonal catwalk with a phalanx of photographers – eighty are expected. Giant mirrors have been hung over this gallery space so that the models are reflected ascending and descending like angels on Jacob's ladder, but they also serve to reflect the audience, and indeed the press photog-raphers themselves, through the looking glass.

In the basement area, flooded with daylight, forty dressing-room stations have been erected, ablaze with lightbulbs and frenetic with activity. Val and Sam are recreating their mud-spattered look by flicking brown body paint off brushes. The girls blink.

Two hours to showtime, and Kiko calls a production meeting. Two dozen international staff of the Vivienne Westwood Group, speaking over twelve languages in total, all there to greet and seat the press, the clients, buyers and sponsors from their respective corners of the world. A third of the seating is given over to the Far East, with press and buyers from China, Taiwan, Hong Kong and Japan. 'It's an extraordinary venue,' Kiko rallies the troops. 'Let's make it a great show!' Such is the crush on the steps that Laura topples backwards off her Vivienne Westwood heels, a domino effect only just averted by one of the many men in Vivienne Westwood tartan suits.

There are three tiers of seating and a strict hierarchy as to who sits where. 'It's rather like Versailles must have been,' quips my French friend. The British and American and Far East press are all front row, up where they can see the models first. In another corner, but with prime view, are the couture buyers: the select women and men who buy Westwood Gold Label designs off the catwalk, to wear or to collect. One loyal customer has been known to buy every single outfit from the season's collection, an outlay of many hundreds of thousands of pounds. *Time, Harper's Bazaar,* the *Sunday Times,* the *Telegraph, Marie Claire,* the *New York Times,* the *International Herald Tribune* are afforded prime seats. *Vogue* is accorded a *lot* of seating, for its various international representatives. And there on the front row of the international glossies is Gene Krell of *Vogue* Japan. Gene Krell, former proprietor of Granny Takes a Trip and consequently a fashion legend as the man who sold glam-rock to London, was also once Vivienne's lodger – saved solely, according to his own account, by Vivienne from heroin addiction and early death.

Down below, the models wear T-shirts printed with 'VW GOLD LABEL SS [spring / summer] 2014', their elaborate pompadours in hairnets, looking like rockabilly Nora Battys. Most wear nothing else but thongs.

Ninety minutes to go. The Shoe Rehearsal. This is a ritual of couture shows, but of particular importance for Vivienne Westwood's as her shoes are famously high, and, after Naomi Campbell's notorious 1993

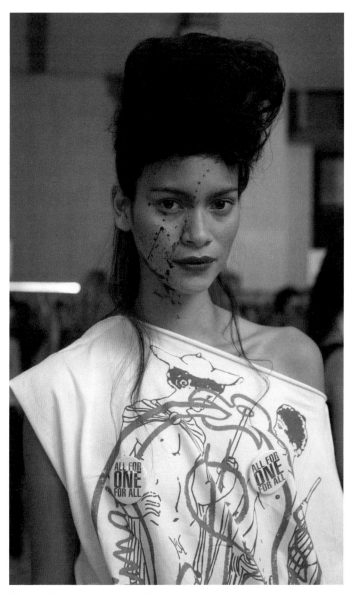

The model Juana Burga in rehearsal T-shirt.

fall from them on the catwalk, worth rehearsing in. Six-foot models, six-inch platforms, plus an arrival onto the catwalk from a moving escalator, demand an attentive dress rehearsal. The last of the girls arrive.

In theory we are now only half an hour away from the show. It's 4 p.m., and the call comes from the Paris Federation that the previous shows have overrun, so we are likely to go up at 4.45. There is a palpable sense of relief. Vivienne pulls gowns off shoulders, rearranges elaborate Frida Kahlo garlands and laurels, and photographers snap at everything. The girls are used to it, and pose against stark white and black backgrounds: perfect, serious, and then flirty and playful, hanging out in twos and threes and posing for the myriad smartphones and anonymous photographers who also have 'access all areas'. They are snapped between outfits and with their hair still in nets. They are snapped in their knickers and half naked. There is no place that is not on view, and about to be online.

Vivienne, in headscarf and glasses, has suddenly the air of a madam at a madcap bordello: 'I'm quite tired, actually,' she allows, 'but it's beautiful, isn't it, when it comes together?'

Five minutes to go. Apparently there is an emergency. There is a tsunami approaching, a moving tide of obsequious humanity and arc lamps, with at its centre the diminutive but instantly recognizable form of Pamela Anderson. Slightly under normal height, even in Vivienne Westwood heels, Pamela is nonetheless ablaze with big hair and celebrity wattage. A loyal, if recent, muse in the world of Vivienne, she has flown in from LA simply for this event, booking a bank of suites at the Plaza Athénée hotel. Dinner afterwards will be with Pamela and a former Westwood model called Carla Bruni who seems to be quite well known in Paris. 'Just a few friends: we're all very tired,' explains Christopher. Pamela, Carla and Vivienne have a lot to catch up on in their shared world of eco-politics and animal rights. Who knew?

And so, Suzy Menkes finally sits down and Pamela Anderson is in place, and the show begins, half an hour late and exactly three minutes before Vivienne would get fined by the Paris Federation. The lights dim and an arc lamp leers over the rig a hundred feet above us to pick out the first model as she steps onto the escalator up towards the atrium.

The giant mirrors reflect the photographers as well as the opening girl, and four hundred and fifty expensively perfumed necks crane upwards. The atrium erupts with flashbulbs, and like two hundred crocuses instantly coming into bloom, a field of smartphones are raised amongst the audience, everywhere but on the front row. On the front row, one doesn't take one's own photographs.

The long struggle over, the running order appears to have settled into a montage that begins with Frida Kahlo, moves into the colours and textures of pilgrimage and folklore, and ends up with some nods to serious couture and Yves Saint Laurent and the structured baroque tailoring that made Vivienne's name as a couturier in the years after punk. The girls all adopt the super-serious, super-sexy steeliness that is their professional armour. Twelve minutes seems a long time. In the absence of real narrative or language, and given the insistent rhythm of one girl after another every thirty seconds, the show does get difficult to ingest. That, and the sheer visual overload. The colours and shapes, the preternatural beauty of the clothes and the girls; it is occasionally as if the world has decelerated into slow motion. As they walk away and out of my view, the clothes move in gravity-defying billows, airy nothings that hold the weight of a fashion empire's expectations, but also manage to laugh a little at the beauty that can be wrought with cloth and the human form. Here I am; touched by beauty. Mark Spye, I see suddenly as we stand at the end, is in tears of rapture. Not what you expect of a burly man of fifty in a lumberjack shirt. 'It's one of her great collections,' he opines. 'It's what she does best.'

And it's over. There is a slight kerfuffle over whether Andreas or Vivienne will arrive first on the catwalk, and in the confusion the bouquet is lost that Vivienne should carry. And they hold hands around the catwalk, until Andreas breaks off to join the applause for Vivienne, who smiles shyly, as is her wont, to accept her ovation.

You've got to wonder. Quarter of a million quid. Twelve minutes. Sixty outfits. Eighteen hundred man-hours. You do have to wonder what the point of all that really is. As Lord Chesterfield opined (about sex, but it holds for couture), the spectacle is ridiculous, the price exorbitant, and the pleasure momentary. The world must be peopled, but

Vivienne and Andreas, the catwalk bow, minus bouquet.

surely it has been peopled with enough fashion? Anyone can see the sheer ravishing beauty of cloth moving over perfect bodies. There is everything to be said, here in Paris especially, for the perfecting of any human art form as a discipline, a craft, a religion. But in the cult of fashion, as opposed to, say, fine art or even food, there is a fetishizing of 'now' that works its own magic, to the detriment, sometimes, of the art form itself. It's about the economy, stupid. Which of these designs will stand the test of time? Why design more and more and more? How can Vivienne justify the expense, the air miles, the sheer concentrated focus of hundreds of supremely talented and largely underpaid individuals? It is to her credit that she takes on board these criticisms and suspicions, and addresses some of them head-on. My Year with Vivienne has taught me more than most men are ever blessed with knowing about why fashion might matter, and what it is that draws its devotees back to the altar of Vivienne's art, and what keeps her creating. There's the industrial imperative, of course – the economic one. A lot of people now rely for their living on Vivienne and Andreas's ongoing creativity. There is something more at work also: a passion for the importance of fashion at the centre of cultural life, and a passion to explain the world as Vivienne sees it, through clothes.

Vivienne is at the centre of a swirling mass of fashion journalists after the show. Cameras and live television coverage: the epicentre, albeit briefly, of the moving media tornado of Fashion Week. She takes it in her stride, perhaps the only woman in the room not greatly exercised about her clothes or her appearance, assured that her style will shine through. She parries brief fashion interviews in French, Italian and German, though mainly in the international language of fashion that is Anglo-American. Even the Taiwanese have Carrie Bradshaw accents. Thick Derbyshire cuts through all of this, nonetheless:

'I had a vision of a girl on a pilgrimage . . .'

The next morning, slightly hung-over, I sit with Vivienne in the showroom before the buyers arrive.

'Some places give birth to legends,' says Vivienne, 'like Venus from the island of Cythera.' This is not, of course, the sort of answer you expect to 'Do you like Paris?', but bear with her. 'Paris changed everything for me. Here's the thing. I get myself into situations. The reason I'm sitting here in Paris with you and am a dress designer is because I thought it was my duty to be one. For Malcolm, my boyfriend at the time, to help him out. I said, "Malcolm, either I help you in the music business or you help me in the shop. One or the other. You decide." He said, "Fashion every time." But then he went off into the music business! So that's when I made the decision to carry on, to prove something to myself, and that's when I did the first proper collections and that's when I came to Paris. And fell in love, really. And like being in love, it was as if I'd always known: I'd always known Paris was important to me, and I'd always known, in a sense, that I had things to say in fashion. People seem surprised still that you can have been in punk and then also be in couture, but it's all connected. That's why we called one early collection Punkature. It's not about fashion, you see; for me, it's about the story. It's about ideas.

'But we should start in Paris, because it is the centre of that part of my life that is clothes. The very first time I came to Paris was with Malcolm's punk band, The New York Dolls – they were going to do a gig in Paris. And it wasn't till years later that I came to appreciate it properly: its art and history. Because of my friend Gary Ness. I'll tell you about him later. But I'll say this now: there are things I can only say in this book because time has passed and some people – Malcolm, Gary – are no longer here. I think a lot about Gary when I am in Paris. We made incredible statements in Paris, with Gary's input, because he did know what he was talking about historically. My point is, I get my ideas because I'm interested in the past. I'm interested in geniuses of the past: the best selves people have tried to be before. I'm interested in people's vision of the world in the past. We can learn so much from what has happened before; their ideals and their hopes for the future. And you feel that very strongly here.

'It was Malcolm's idea that we needed to do a Paris show. It was the early 1980s and we had got a French PA, Sylvie Grumbach, who was very good. This was my third collection. We had done the Pirates, the Savages, and this was the Buffalo collection. The official title was "Nostalgia of Mud", along with the shop we then had. The start of New Romanticism. That was me! We had done Buffaloes in Olympia

Invitation to Nostalgia of Mud, the first of Vivienne's collections to be shown in Paris.

and we decided to do a repeat of it in Paris. The reason being I'd had the experience by 1981–2 over and over and over again of seeing my things copied and put on Paris catwalks. Punk stuff for instance got copied all over Paris.

'So we did a show in Paris, at Angelina's Café on the rue de Rivoli. Compared to now, of course, it was all done on a shoestring, but it was much more exciting. And not just because it was new to me or I was younger. In those days fashion magazines would see the show, and then the next day they would borrow your clothes and do a shoot. Simple. It was all done in one go. French *Vogue*. Italian *Vogue*. Even American *Vogue* used to do it like that. Italian and American *Vogue*: they made me. It was so immediate. So exciting. You knew the effect you were having. Instant feedback. Of course the fashion world was smaller then too.

'I wasn't nervous. Not a bit. I've never, ever been nervous. Not about the clothes. Ever. I say to myself, "I love them, and that's my best." The first Paris show, the Buffaloes collection in 1983, was a sensation. It was in all the newspapers, as well as the magazines. It was so exciting. But it took years and years before I felt that I was at all accepted in Paris like I am now or could really safely call myself a designer. The people who always mentioned me were the Italians. I owe Italy a lot. Italian *Vogue* and American *Vogue*: they were wonderful about me, my two main supporters early on, because of what they saw in Paris. So, even early on, Paris began to change everything for me. Less punk. Less tabloid. I began to be taken seriously. But not because of Parisians or the fashion press of France. The first people I got the real support from were the Italians, the Americans and especially the Japanese who came to Paris buying for boutiques. Because here's what was happening: it's funny, and I'll tell you this and I shouldn't, but John Galliano, at that time, for instance, he was such a fan of me and he copied the clothes very closely and I know this because he used to come into the shop. And I went with a friend of mine in Paris to see John's show, and she loved it, and rightly, and so did I, but that's because it was *my* show from the year before. I just thought, well, fashion: it's really weird. But it *is*. Weird. People wrote that I was unwearable, but then there it all was the next season and the one after that, copied by others, sold for

The Buffalo girl 'look', 1982.

much more money, with much more backing. I don't know. And that upset me at the time, definitely it did. I knew my clothes were great, though, and that I had time on my side. But it was weird and it was undermining.

'So that's some of my Paris story. Where it all began. You see, designing is about telling a story. I spent this morning in bed reading about Chinese art, trying to understand through their objects how they thought and how they understood the world. Or like I say in this collection: "She looks like she's going to Canterbury." It's the equivalent of opening a book and looking at a medieval manuscript. And it's the same with this biography: it's a story, what I want to say, in fashion, in activism, in life. It's not a *copy*. It can't be the whole of me. It's *inspired* by something. You make something by being inspired; like a breath drawn in – that here she is: a pilgrim. The cloak she is wearing has to be the best of all possible cloaks. It has to be Joseph's coat of many colours. It has to be the cloak of the Wizard of Oz. It has to be the troubadour's cloak. If you can breathe in those references, you have something that sums up the whole idea of "cloak". To sum up the whole idea of "Vivienne", not that I am sure I want to or that one could, you'd need to find the references; the ideas from the past and the goals for the future. Like this cloak. This is what gives clothes timelessness, you see. Weight. That there's something to relate to. Like a kind of nostalgia. Like knowing that you've always loved Paris. A sort of nostalgia for something that you already know. When you see it, you know. That's something I understand, I recognize. If I have a talent, I think that is it.'

Vivienne suddenly looks at me. 'Do you know *Pinocchio*?' she says, pronouncing it as an Italian would if they came from Glossop. 'The real one, not the film. I've never seen the film. That would be on the top of my reading list, with *Alice in Wonderland*. You have to be your best self. That's part of the story I want us to tell. Be your best self. And follow your conscience.

'It's like when you make a collection: you start to think of a story. A frame. Here it is. This is what's happening with me right now. The moment of attention I have off you, off anybody reading this book,

I have to use to the best purpose. You have to look for the beauty. In everything. In every moment. And everyone.

'"Once upon a time," as *Pinocchio* has it, "there was just this little piece of wood . . ."'

THE GIRL IN THE
UTILITY DRESS

The patterns which life assumes are not necessarily conscious ones in their inception, consciousness being oftentimes later achieved through the painful press of circumstance on the nerve of rebellious sense.

SAMUEL PUTNAM,
François Rabelais, Man of the Renaissance

I lived all my life as if I'm young, but now I'm old I realize not just that youth is precious but that it's actually something else.

VIVIENNE WESTWOOD

'The first thing you should really know about me is that I was born in the Second World War. Rationing. All of that. I didn't have a banana until I was seven. Didn't like it when I did. Things were scarce. And everybody was knitting. You can even find patterns for knitted wedding dresses. Hours and hours spent knitting. And we did things like collecting little nutshells and painting them and making little sprays of flowers. It was all about "Do It Yourself".'

Vivienne picks at her knitted skirt, and holds up a photograph of herself as a small girl.

'I'm a fashion designer and I'm what is known as an activist. And I suppose there were signs of that from an early age. I've been embarrassed sometimes at telling stories that give the impression I thought I was special or some sort of goody-goody person. That isn't right. I just didn't like people to know that I felt myself this kind of champion, even as a little girl. I think people behave according to their intrinsic character from a very early age. These things are definitely a sort of little key to understanding me, and the freedom-fighter side of my life. Not a little key: it's a very, very important indication. Here's an example, really, of how in my way I was ridiculous as well as passionate. At school dinner time – lunch – we would all wait until the supervising teacher came in and invariably she would say, "Stand up whoever was talking." This one time the head teacher, Mrs Booth, came and asked the regular question and I thought, "What would happen if I stood up?" – if I tested the rhetoric, as it were. I thought I might get praised for owning up, even though I had not been talking. I stood up and said, "It was me." It wasn't. I stood up alone, feeling safe as I knew Mrs Booth liked me, and enjoying the glamour of the self-righteous. Ridiculous. But also, I thought everyone else was going to own up as well. I really did. Like in *Spartacus*: "It was me", "It was me". But no one stood up. Mrs Booth did praise me for standing up, I remember – I knew she would. But I also recall thinking what a farce sticking your neck out can be. So I learned a sort of proportionality. I really did care about things a lot. I realized that I was unusual; I felt I was. I am not a stranger to that. And I recognized that about myself from early on: that I saw myself as somebody who was going to *do* things – that's what I felt. So there it is. My sticking my neck out is an instinct. But I know it is not altruism pure and simple. And at the time I thought, "Well, I won't do *that* again." But of course I have.'

The girl in the photograph looks four or five or thereabouts. The image, curled at the edges by sixty years' handling, is black-and-white but hardly the less arresting for that. The girl is Vivienne. She stares warily at the camera, posed in her new Fair Isle sweater, knitted by her mother for when she started school in 1945.

'I would have been four or five, yes.'

This photograph, which Vivienne picks up from her pattern-cutting table high above the rooftops in Battersea, and turns over and over between hobnail fingers, is one of very few images of her before her teens. This is no measure of her parents' reticence in recording their eldest daughter's early life. It is an index of the progress of photography in mid-century Britain. A working-class Derbyshire family like Vivienne's would only have photographs from holidays, weddings or christenings – or if they were for some reason in the newspaper.

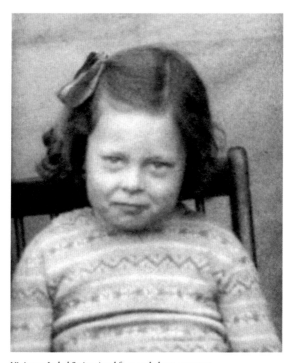

Vivienne Isabel Swire. Aged four-and-three-quarters.

Vivienne, by the time she was twenty-one, had had all those occasions marked and photographed. But this is one of the first pictures that is recognizably *her.*

The girl from the photograph, four and going on seventy-three now as I register her rueful recognition of herself, is instantly the same. Wary. Quizzical. Half shy and half defiant: a manner that has become Vivienne's trademark but one I suppose shared by many four- and five-year-olds as they step out into the world, was a pose forged, I surmised, by the mixed emotions of excitement at a new life-chapter and discomfort at new clothes.

'Actually, I hated making people laugh, or that anyone might think me silly or not grown-up. So I tended not to smile for cameras. Or to try not to. I was determined to be taken seriously!

'I remember mainly from that time a little dress my mother made too, for school. I think it really suited me, but, like this Fair Isle jumper, I'm not sure I liked it at the time. It was brown, this dress, with a little turquoise-and-white striped collar on it. And it was quite plain, like a little sort of orphan dress, in brown wool. And it probably really suited me, actually, but I didn't like it – I never seemed to get these really wonderful, pretty princess-type dresses that I wanted – like little Princesses Elizabeth and Margaret Rose – and I thought of this as a little-orphan-Annie dress, really awful, but of course, as you can see, it was very smart, actually, and nicely made. My mother was very particular about clothes and what she'd let me wear. She made it all. And we were lucky, because she worked in a factory that had material. She made herself ill, working extra hours for us kids and what we might have and wear. Anyway, I don't remember the dress because of mum. I remember it because of something else altogether. I wore it when I started school. And I remember I did the most awful thing. It was only a few days after school started, this day that sticks in my mind. I had to run home over the moor tops from school because we were outside the village – in the countryside, really, but on a main road between two villages – run home for lunch. It would be only probably about two-thirds of a mile, but I'm talking about when I was four years old. The houses where I lived had been carved between hills and there were these very steep banks on either side of the road, and then there were fields on the top. I'd just go up on this bank and walk along the tops; raspberries grew up there that time of year. Anyway, and you had to cling to this little wooden stake fence, and this boy, I remember his name but I won't tell you – all right, I will; it was Barry Swindle – his grandma lived very near us and he used to come and be looked after by her some of the time, and for whatever reason I was scared of him, really scared, and I was climbing up. He was there with Brian Marsden. I expect they are very nice men now. Anyway, it was all slippery and wet and clay and he was there in front of me, and there wasn't room for both of us on the path, and he just stood there with his stick and I had to go down in all the clay and mud to get round him and I was skidding and slippering, you know. Because I knew he would've hit me if I'd gone near him, so I risked getting the dress muddy and skidded down another route, and got scuffed, and was late back to school after lunch break. Anyway, when I was asked why I was late, I said he had pushed me into the mud, this boy, which wasn't true at all. I don't know why I lied. I've never told anyone this. And he was hauled over into our class. I felt so terrible about it. I'd like to apologize to them both now, really. So you see, I had quite a developed sense of shame and guilt at the time. And in the end, I found I rather loved and admired Barry Swindle and Brian Marsden. But the grown-ups at home never found out. I said I'd slipped. If I could talk to her now, that little girl, little Vivienne Swire, I'd say I suppose: "Don't be scared. Don't. If you tell the truth – the real and adult truth – people won't be angry. Well, not eventually." And I always think, you know – always listen to children. And that's why I remember that dress.'

From a blue file of papers and jottings, Vivienne takes out a small handwritten note on soft and yellowed wartime paper that Dora, her mother, sent to the local newspaper. Written in the distinctive confident curlicue that they share, it reads:

SWIRE.
On the 8th April 1941, at the Partington Maternity Home Glossop,
to Gordon and Dora; God's precious gift of a daughter. Vivienne Isabel.
First grandchild for Mrs and Mrs E. Ball.

SWIRE On the 8th April 1941, at the
Partington Maternity Home Glossop, to
Gordon and Dora, God's precious gift of
a daughter. Vivienne Isabel.
First grand child for Mr & Mrs E. Ball.

Dora Swire announces her daughter's birth.

'My mother was very proud of me. She was proud of me when I was little and I knew she was proud of me, of what I became. I remember my mother said to me that I could recite poetry at eighteen months old. I suppose she meant nursery rhymes. When I was around fourteen months old, she told me, the postman was at the door, and I said, "Good morning, Mr Venables," and he said, "G'dness, Mrs Swire, dun't that girl speak as good as you nor me?" I've never lost my accent. I remember when my mum was ill and was in hospital towards the end of her life and I'd visit her she'd call over to the nurses, "Do you know who this young lady is? This young lady – this is Vivienne Westwood, my daughter; she's a fashion designer, you know." One of the last memories I have of her was a nurse went by and Mum recognized her, and she waved. She was such a social person, my mum. My son Ben was with her at the end . . . and she said to him, quite clearly, she said, "I don't want to die." That was the last thing she said. "I don't want to die." Andreas – who really adored her, and she him – was in tears, and was with her too. I wasn't. I was at a rally. The Campaign for Nuclear Disarmament. I had arranged to leave early to come and see Mummy, but they phoned up and . . . you never know how quickly it's going to happen. So I missed her. You see. I missed her.'

Dora, Vivienne's mum, is someone I have come to know and rather admire but only second-hand: an impression from friends and family and Vivienne. One key to understanding anyone, of course, is to understand their mum. Dora is a constant presence still around the Battersea studio where we talk – for one thing, her little dog, Jackie, pootles about, now old herself. Dora died in 2008 and the dog has been with Vivienne or Dora's grandson Ben ever since. Dora is also a presence because Vivienne, now a mum and grandmother herself, is said to be increasingly like her: Vivienne's sons Ben Westwood and Joe Corré, and Gordon Swire, Vivienne's brother, all point this out to me. And in embracing feisty non-conformity, not so much raging against the dying of the light as brazenly ignoring it, Dora Swire and Vivienne Westwood seem both to have embraced older age:

'My mother, Dora Ball, came from the village of Tintwistle in Derbyshire. She was the second-eldest of five children. Her father, my grandfather, must have been a very unhappy and frustrated man. He was a spinner in the cotton mill and had left school at fourteen. He was very clever, as were his children, but he tyrannized his family: he once, in front of my mum and Beatrice, dashed out the cat's brains over whatever frustration it was – he had a fearsome temper. For all his faults, my grandfather had been a very good scholar and was always a reader. In 1928, Dora left school and eventually went to the mill as a weaver. Maybe as a result, Dora always wanted the very best for her children – for them to profit by education.

'Dora and my father Gordon were in bliss together all their lives. Or so it seemed to us children. He was as strong a personality as my mother, and very ambitious and enterprising. I remember he wanted to emigrate to Canada or Australia. It was Mum who insisted they stay near her mother. I was so proud of my dad; he was such a handsome man. They met dancing, and my father died in his early seventies when they were dancing. Dora said afterwards, "If we hadn't done the Gay Gordons he'd still be here." I simply had the greatest childhood. An idyll. I was born in the country, to parents who were just great and who just did everything for me and Olga and Gordon, and as well as that, my father knew quite a lot about nature. He was also quite a sportsman, my dad, and a very good dancer as well: very sociable and very popular, just the best possible dad. And they gave us the most brilliant childhood. We lived in Millbrook, a row of stone cottages in a hollow on the road half a mile from Hollingworth and a mile from Tintwistle. We had relations in each village and the short walk they had to make gave their many visits a sense of occasion which made my house and family, including me, seem centrally important. To me, anyway!

'It was all about family. We really spent a lot of time in the countryside, visiting each other, going on walks together, walking to and from Tintwistle and Hollingworth. It's very nice to go and walk and then go and meet your extended family and have tea with them, usually at Aunt Ethel's as she was the most well-off, and then go home. Our weekends were that kind of thing. I was very fond of my aunts and uncles. Some of my first memories are of listening to the gossip, "taking it all in", impressed by the affinities and the strongly differing personalities. Auntie Beatrice came in for the most criticism, because she herself was so critical and unbending, but she had a good heart and

I loved and admired them all. To them I was, and always remained, "our Vivienne".

'We had a coal fire set in a blacked iron range which took up nearly all one wall of our tiny living room. The settee and chairs were pulled up in front of it. My mum sang to us for hours – she loved singing and she loved Romantic poetry, Wordsworth and Walter Scott. In the evening she read us Grimm's fairy tales. We were surrounded by love. I knew little of the war except for rationing, which meant only that there were certain clothes and certain treasures I knew about but couldn't have: paper decorations at Christmas, for instance, so we used recycled chrome tops from the salt and pepper as Christmas tree decorations. And my most precious possession was a matchbox with bits of broken glass inside copied from a friend's make-up compact, which had fake gems and pearls. And I coveted the idea of a single peacock feather, but this seemed too exotic to ever hope for.

'Jelly and blancmange were the staple specialities of parties and I somehow associate their coldness, and the hundreds and thousands scattered on the cake, with childhood happiness – but also the quality of our distempered living-room walls, where my father had faked a wallpaper effect with a crushed pad of cloth dipped in green paint. And Mum made sure that we children had a birthday party every year – from the age of one – and we always had a summer holiday at the seaside. I remember when I was asked to write "My Autobiography" for school homework Mum insisted this information was in the introduction!

'I loved my home at Millbrook Cottages – the very stones. Every part was stone. The walls were eighteen inches thick and I used the window recess to play in. And I loved playing "tippling" – doing handstands on the walls and flipping over the other side. There were stone flags on the floor where we played marbles, a stone pantry, a stone sink and stone boiler for clothes with a zinc hemisphere inside. And when my parents got up I read in their bed for as long as Mummy would let me and as long as she would allow Olga to fetch me drinks and snacks. Then I transferred to the settee and she'd say, "Get your feet up out of my way," and she'd be round with the broom. She was very house-proud. But she'd say, while I was reading, "There's our Vivienne, she's in her glory." And she'd say to Olga, "You might as well leave her there: our Vivienne's in her glory." And she was right, I was.

'That's what Mum always said, and it wasn't meant approvingly. But I still use that expression when I find myself in my own bed with nothing to do but read. Reading is, always was, my sublime luxury. Eventually she'd get me out of the house and when she did I loved it. I used to be out all day. I used to make little gardens, miniature gardens with moss for the fairies in the woods. So I wasn't just some swot. I used to live for skipping. Skipping is fantastic. Two ropes. The best thing.'

Vivienne's brother Gordon, five years her junior, concurs: 'We were very free. No one ever told us when we had to come in. We'd just come in after dark having been playing in the fields with friends. My mum's theory was: plenty of fresh air and fruit and not too much reading, such that mum came to think Vivienne was too much in her books and it was bad for her. So when Vivienne would've been about eight or nine, our mum made her throw away her library tickets. She *paid* her to destroy them: five shillings, which was precisely five times our weekly pocket money. So, this is Vivienne for you: she took the money, which was quite a sum, and then she carried on getting books, borrowing with friends' tickets!'

Dora need not have worried. Vivienne alternated her 'glory' time buried in books – from Enid Blyton to Dickens to Walter Scott – with an increasing love of the wild countryside of Derbyshire:

'Millbrook Cottages were at the bottom of an old quarry and from the earliest age my mother lifted me over our back wall to play in a dell where bluebells grew. As I grew up I was free to wander in a countryside which was beautiful and intimate until you got to the moors. After that it was wild and a little frightening. But I was perfectly happy to be alone and have always needed to have solitude. It is only then that I can think. I climbed trees and jumped streams. I saw myself as a tomboy. Though when a friend, Norma Etchells, asked if I actually wanted to be a boy, I was shocked. It had never occurred to me there was anything better than being a girl. I never wanted to be a boy or to have the perceived freedoms of a boy. I liked being me, and I happened to be a girl. I wanted to be a hero and saw no reason why a girl couldn't be one.

Dora and Gordon Swire, holding Olga and Vivienne respectively. September, 1944.

'The changing seasons were the panorama of my world; of my fantasies, my home, my loves and my sense of self. One morning in May – my favourite month, perhaps because of this memory – my mummy had dressed me in a gingham frock and turned me out of the house, saying, "Get some fresh air!" I sat reading in the meadows beyond the upper quarry where the ground was still damp with the dew rising through the long grass and the air was full of birdsong and the smell of may blossom and dew from the hawthorns, and I said to myself, "I am happy." These are the main colours of my childhood. Picnics at Devil's Bridge with our cousins. All the visiting relations. Or the times when we would walk over the fields with our dogs. Over the fields on black winter evenings playing ralio with torches. Harvest Festival. Lambs born in the snow. Getting snowed in. The "subtle and melancholy beauty" of the English countryside, as Huxley has it.

'But it wasn't all idyllic. There is pain in growing up too. Firstly, there was the birth of my sister Olga – which wasn't her fault, obviously – it was just the beginning, for me, of realizing how much adults can lie. Here's the story: my mother never told me she was having a baby, and I never noticed that there was anything wrong with her, getting bigger or anything. I was three. I probably would have loved the idea of having a sister, but my mother said to me, "Would you like to go and spend a week with Auntie Ethel for a holiday?" And of course I said, "Yes," and it was really nice, and then a week later my Auntie Ethel said, "Your mummy's coming to collect you today and she's bringing you a new baby sister." And that was that. And I actually said, "I'll dead her and put her in the dustbin," I was so angry. And then when my brother Gordon was born when I was nearly five; the only thing I remember about that is that I was very disappointed because he was a very big baby and I thought he was just too big to be *my* baby brother! And I remember being very angry when I saw my brother sitting on my mother's knee, and knowing I wouldn't get to be a baby any more. But I was also determined to be taken seriously, and never to admit to my ignorance. I remember for instance I had always wanted to be a bridesmaid, but missed my chance because when my Uncle Ed and Aunt Alice were getting married they asked me to 'carry the horseshoe' and I didn't know what they meant, and my pride wouldn't let me admit to my ignorance, of not knowing what the horseshoe was all about.

'So there was Olga and there was Gordon, but the other truly memorable impression upon me from my early childhood was to do with religion.

'When I saw the Crucifixion for the first time, it was a huge, huge thing in my life. I've talked a little about this before, and it can sound pi or pretentious, but it was, at the time, simply deeply shocking. Partly this was because it proved, it seemed to me, that I had been lied to by adults. I remember it like it was yesterday: I was with my cousin Eileen, who was about twelve, in the back of my auntie's greengrocer's. I remember the tap dripping and remember the taste of the pop my aunt gave us, and I was staring at her calendar on the wall. Maybe it was Easter. There was a picture of the Crucifixion.

'"What's that, Eileen?"

'"Don't you know who that is? Silly. That's Jesus when they nailed him to the cross."

'I didn't say anything else. I was so shocked. And moved. I was supposed to know about this and I didn't. I only knew about little baby Jesus: "Away in a Manger". I could not believe that there were people in the world who could do this. I knew with all the fervour of a child that I would stop them and I would die if I had to, to stop them! I never told anybody how I felt. Because I was ashamed even then of my ignorance – that other people knew about this injustice and hadn't explained it to me. Ignorance was a crime. So was indifference. Nobody was talking about it: why weren't they shocked?

'So you see, as a child I became very tied emotionally to the love of Jesus. Not to be a Christian would have been a betrayal equal to the acceptance of his torture. And the truth of it is this: I became Derbyshire's only five-year-old freedom fighter! Dedicated to opposing persecution!

'Somehow the younger sister and brother got mixed up in my young mind with the business of the Crucifixion and I thought, you know, adults didn't tell me anything important! They should be fighting injustice and not letting these things happen. And in my mind, this got quite mixed up in terms of my fear, as I saw it then, of Catholic churches and their art, which in truth was more a fear of the Big Ideas in life – fear of death and sex and babies and politics and all the things that grown-ups wouldn't explain.

'I've always been a bit careful about admitting all this, until now. It feels still like a very private experience, this sensation of being different, and I used to feel embarrassed about it, that I felt so strongly about things even when I was little: who does she think she is? But to be a little kinder to myself now I am older, it was simply very genuine, my heart then, and I hope it is now. I often protected the victims of other children's spite – or tried to. My need to attack injustice and my aloofness were the things which as a child were part of my unorthodoxy and my need to think for myself, to form my own opinions, but it hardly made me "popular", obviously! One mad example: there was this boy at school who was very dirty – he was a sweet little thing and he was always isolated in the playground, in a circle of space no one else went into, moving his body and his head in a sort of dance. He smelt and his blond hair was so dirty, poor little Edward, that I thought, you know, I would rescue him. So I decided I would do this by announcing he was my boyfriend. (We were six.) He was horrified. I can still see him now, pink beneath the grime: the worst day of his life. Everyone laughed at him. And me. But he was so upset. I realized you can't always do the best.

'The winter for us in Derbyshire could be magical. When I was between five and six years old, I remember the school being hung with paper chains for Christmas – we had been given black sheets of paper because we were doing a snow picture. This was the winter of 1947 in which we had so much snow in Derbyshire that prison convicts had to cut a pass through the drifts in our hollow to clear the road. I remember stopping to listen to the dot-dot-dot-dot of the wax crayons as the snow was falling, a good foot deep by the end of the day, and the whole room filled with every child's contented concentration, with the silent descent of snowflakes outside the windows laying a snow carpet on the ground for us to try to get home. But if you looked up through the window and focused as high as possible on the falling snowflakes you had this impression of travelling to heaven.

'I remember I went with my daddy far afield over the snow because he wanted to find holly berries in Robin Wood. It must have been Christmas, and my mother and he made extra money for Christmas by making wreaths which sold in the greengrocer's shop. He made the best sledge for miles around too: the best and fastest, so that the other children called the Swire children's sledge "The Stagecoach".

'Olga followed me around a good deal. In the woods she helped me to collect moss and bits of twigs and I made my miniature gardens with ponds and trees like fairy grottoes. This Olga loved, but the thing she loved most was if I would make a house, and we made a doll's tea set from rose hips and acorns and elderberries. And when I was that age, I had a fantasy of being a grown-up alone in the caves made of beech-tree roots until one day I would emerge from there in a wonderful tulle dress with pink ribbons (so I was thinking ahead!) and happen by chance on this very handsome farmer's boy. I was never sure of the boy. It could have been Ben Timperley. He would be instantly smitten by me in this dress, but I would merely reply that it was, in fact, just for everyday.'

The post-war years of British austerity are rightly signalled by Vivienne as the essential background to her childhood, along with the Derbyshire landscape that was and is a liminal space between wild countryside and the long impact of early industrialization: Vivienne's childhood world straddling moorland and mill. The war had, in truth, been relatively kind to the villages of Tintwistle and Hollingworth, to much of Derbyshire, and especially so to Vivienne's family. Only one bomb fell near Millbrook Cottages, missing its intended target of Manchester, inexplicably, by ten miles. But there was clear impact from the war on Vivienne's immediate family, some of it far from bad news. Her father, Gordon, got work in a munitions and aircraft factory at Trafford Park when war came, and as a result of this he was never called up. His firm, A. V. Roe's, made Lancaster bombers, and Gordon told with pride after the war stories of the Dam Buster bombs that were tested on Derwent dam beyond the factory gates. Shopkeeping was in the blood through several generations of shoemakers and grocers on both sides of the family; Dora had worked as a weaver in a local cotton factory from 1928 onwards, but the business converted

Vivienne in Scarborough, 1949.

after 1939 to making uniforms and parachutes, along with camouflage and webbing and tents.

The Swires' marriage had been and remained a strikingly happy one. Friends, relatives and Vivienne herself have this as their main memory of Dora and Gordon, along with their shared good looks. They were dedicated to each other and to their children, Vivienne, born in 1941, Olga, 1944, and Gordon Junior (not that anyone called him that), born in 1946. The childhood Vivienne describes – Lawrentian, romantic, vanished – is perhaps most remarkable for its freedom. Out till late at night on summer evenings in an era when that was considered normal, free to explore the natural world, Olga, Gordon and Vivienne were encouraged in a utilitarian approach to education: it would be useful for their job prospects. 'I never really thought I would pass the eleven-plus, but I knew it was important,' Vivienne says. 'It was why Dad had transferred us to the church school, with its marked adherence to monarchy and the Church of England; it was because they had a better record with getting children into the grammar school. I say children – it was nearly all girls that passed!' For some parts of the British economy, Derbyshire included, the Second World War forged a route out of economic depression. The war certainly had a clear impact on the textile trade, and on the progress of British fashion. Derbyshire and parts of what became Greater Manchester prospered. Munitions was one large part of this story, but also heavy textiles for army and other use, and the Swires, with two incomes and grandparents running the local greengrocer's, lived and ate relatively well. When the bomb fell near Tintwistle, in their house at the edge of the parish, ceiling plaster fell into the truckle bed where Vivienne slept – not that she remembers. Even so, the air-raid warden came to *their* house to call the nearest hospital. It was the only phone in Millbrook Cottages. But there were few books.

'We were encouraged to make, more than read. My father had given us a blackboard, you know, to chalk on, and I used it as a base for models, and I remember sitting outside one day and I made this little cardboard farmhouse with real earth and chickweed that looks like a miniature potato plant and miniature cabbages from little leaves all rolled around and planted. I would have been about seven. I thought it was a lovely little farm, but the point is actually I wanted to impress Mum and Dad, and I did, even though I'd ruined his chalkboard. My father was very good with his hands – making the holly wreaths at Christmas to sell, and mending anything, and my mother, though she never thought she was very good with her hands, was this demon sewer and knitter.

'So I knew I was good at making. Honestly, at the age of five I could have made a pair of shoes. I only realized that I was at all unusual when I went to school. The example that really sticks in my mind is this: when I went into the class of Mrs Turner, we used to make models every so often. We had shoeboxes and she showed us how you could make a little hole in one end and put a scene in there, like a camera obscura, and then you look through the hole and see it all. Oh, and I loved making those! You could even hang Dad's flashlight inside and you could make this moonlit glen. But this one time Mrs Turner wanted to make a fairground scene, with maybe a roundabout and everything, and she got the children to try and make things. They had to make little people as well. And I remember her saying to me, "Now, Vivienne, how do we make the swing boats? – you know, those old-fashioned fairground swing rides." And I just knew. Instantly. I said, "Well, get a matchbox and then get some cardboard – then you draw the swing boat on the side of it. You make two of them and stick them on either side of the matchbox and then you get a strip of paper, like about as wide as the matchbox and then you just get the ends and you just twizzle them and then you can put this in the middle of the match-box." And Mrs Turner just said, "Well, Vivienne, I think you know what you're doing: go and make them and show the others," and I just made her this whole fairground scene, with these little swing boats. And when I was eight and Dad transferred Olga and Gordon and me to Tintwistle Church School I had proper sewing classes for the first time. It was a very small primary school with only three teachers, three classrooms and three iron stoves. Each had a coal monitor – I was one! – the point being a church school like that in those days had less to spend per pupil, so we had less heat and fewer teachers. But once a week we would have sewing class, setting a cloth over the table, and that's where I learned chain stitch. So these are some of the early clues to what I became. I drew and I studied nature and I read and read, and I sewed. But also I made things – constantly. And increasingly so at school. We had traditional instruction in embroidery like previous generations, with a bag for our work and an apron to wear during the lessons, and a petticoat even. But the very special treat for me would be the lesson where we had some felt with which to make dolls. We sewed these in Mrs Leeney's house. She invited us once a week for tea. You learn most about making in the process of making. You have to be good with your hands in what I do.'

Clothes are the warp and weft of social history. They are part of what makes Vivienne's story so compelling – so intimate and feminized, but so clearly at the centre of a story of tumult. Long before she was in 'fashion' in any sense, her clothes and her memories of them tell the story of a changing Britain.

'You've got to understand that in the war and afterwards, the British wrote their own history of fashion. I know it's not exactly the usual V for Victory and Churchill story – but people forget: clothes were politics long before "fashion", and in a very real sense when I was a girl. Every day you knew there was rationing and there were utility clothes – how many pockets you could have and no turn-ups – and you knew it, even as you pulled on your navy-blue utility knickers; you knew there was war and there was want and that you were part of it. But we were lucky. I don't know how my mother did it but we were never made aware of the restrictions – on elastic, for instance – never.'

The Second World War is the Book of Genesis for modern British culture. The films and stories that shape the way Britain thinks about itself and its place in the world date from the middle of the twentieth century – to the Depression, the War and then the years of post-war austerity that formed a background to the NHS, the welfare state, the Queen – and Vivienne. For some, the most shocking image of the May 2000 anti-capitalist riots in London was the punk Mohican hairstyle fashioned out of turf and placed on the head of Winston Churchill's statue. It neatly linked, however, some key elements in this story and that of modern Britain – the man who 'saved Western democracy' and the protest of those who felt the victory and its sacrifices had been wasted. The era that shaped the great institutions of this country, and some of the individuals who still head them, also gives Britain its sense of its place in the world. This is alluded to in terms of 'Blitz' and 'Dunkirk' spirit – an indomitability that borders on intransigence and pig-headedness. It has become part of the way Britain is perceived abroad: its eccentricity, its bullishness, its pride in its history and its bomb-scarred modernism. It is the spirit alluded to in the symbols and songs that crowd football terraces as much as Olympic opening ceremonies. And Vivienne's story begins here too, in the war and its aftermath, and is woven with fabric and fashion as much as politics and social history. Her story is intimately political, because for her clothes always have been. Even from her earliest days.

To some degree Vivienne's highly informed eye on fabric can be traced to this familial awareness of cloth: the utility-wear gabardine raincoats or the starched cottons, worsteds and tweeds that were woven in the mills around her before the war and again after. They have remained staples of her designs. During her childhood, however, fabric became part of the war but also part of the regular business of being a girl.

This world of austerity, of DIY and 'make do and mend' and of ingrained expectation of recycling necessarily has its impact on Vivienne to this day. This much she shares with her entire generation and even her Queen, who recall, with both pride and nostalgia, the heroic intent behind the drabness of austerity Britain. 'Buy less. Buy well and make it last' – a mantra of Vivienne Westwood and her company in the twenty-first century – could have been coined by the Attlee government. It was all meant to be practical, and the Ministry was nothing if not eco-evangelical about the savings to be made by centralized control of what women wore. But of course it was political too. People noticed. They applauded each other's sacrifice and recognized joint endeavour by becoming uniform in the grand national cause, through what they wore, or didn't wear. Which is also in its way a Vivienne mantra: clothes for heroes, clothes that state intent. But utility wear was a political and propaganda coup played out primarily on women's bodies. Take underwear. The *Elastic (Control of Use) Order* of 1943 is little studied in histories of the Second World War or of the

The Westwood family. Back row (L–R): Joe Corré holding Olga's granddaughter Hannah, Peter Watts (Olga's husband), Ben Westwood (holding Jackie), Gordon Swire, Andreas. Front row (L–R): Cora Corré, Olga, Lucy (Olga's daughter), Oliver (Olga's son), Geraldine (Gordon's wife), Vivienne.

social progress of British womanhood. It should be. It prohibited the use of elastic in all garments except in the corsets and knickers of women directly involved in the war effort, as determined by the Ministry of War itself. 'When your suspenders wear out,' Whitehall advised, 'cut away that elastic worn part and replace with an inch or two of strong twine.' It took a personal appeal from Nancy Astor to have the Ministry repeal such intimate parsimony, and the women of Britain fought on with recycled rubberized suspenders – a small knicker-flick of defiance in the face of Hitler. Not so for girls. Vivienne's knickers should have been buttoned, as became commonplace as the elastic of wartime Britain simply wore out. But somehow Dora, who 'made herself ill' working extra hours for her children, found elastic and struggled on.

We all have our stories of where we began. We tell stories to each other, and to ourselves, about our pasts: as individuals and as a nation. Vivienne traces her life as an activist and as a humanitarian to the shocking image of the Crucifixion – a positively Damascene revelation that there was terrible suffering in the world and that she was personally challenged to help alleviate it:

'I knew my reaction was exceptional, but it was, and is, also private. I was aware as a child that others were spiteful and I knew I didn't want to be part of that.'

Meanwhile, her work as a political fashion designer has its roots in the politicized clothing of wartime and austerity Britain, just as much as her eco-politics can be dated to a place and time where the shared responsibility to recycle and avoid waste became ingrained.

'I think, in talking finally about the past, it's important to think afresh, not just tell the safe stories, but tell it as it was as best as I can. I wouldn't want to limit what we have here, in this book, to the things I've said already. I know now that even the Crucifixion story, which embarrassed me for years, has no power to embarrass me now. There are some consolations to being older – and to being thought of as eccentric in the first place. Everybody knows that their past life is like a series of different little scenes. It's a story and you've selected from your memory the things that you think are important. Nothing from the past is entirely true. But you are only in those scenes properly when they are put together. That's what we should do, you and I, Ian: sew together all the life scenes. I look back and it's me, but it's not me – do you know what I mean? So I look back now and I hardly recognize myself, or I recognize just this tiny piece of what I have become and I think, "You silly, silly little girl, how could you be so naive?" But then again, of course, naive gets you places too, and it gets you hungry to learn. That's what I'd say to the girl in that photograph, actually: don't be afraid. Keep reading. Say it like it is. And then think for yourself.'

LET IT ROCK

The real start of youth culture? – it was rock 'n' roll.

TOMMY ROBERTS
of Mr Freedom – Vivienne's landlord

I started making rock 'n' roll things when I was at school. Immediate 'Do-it-Yourself' kind of things. DIY became my motto. In the summer we used to make quick tops, like little bras out of two scarves and sew them together, at a corner, behind the shoulder. Stuff like that. It was the best possible time to be a teenager. VIVIENNE WESTWOOD

It rained all over England on 2 June 1953, Coronation Day. The many planned celebrations and street parties were a washout. Twenty-five-year-old Elizabeth Windsor was crowned Queen, and twelve-year-old Vivienne, newly started at Glossop Grammar, attended the wet celebration tea party at her old school in Tintwistle. The entire Swire family, along with dozens of others, then moved on to a house nearby – the house that had a television. Like 'New Elizabethans' the country over, they huddled around a novel domestic intrusion, the telly, to watch the ancient ceremony in Westminster. The image had a profound effect on Vivienne, as did her royalist church school. Our personalities are fixed at a young age, she tells me. So too were some of her design motifs. The sounds and the looks of the 1950s have infused her work in fashion. So have images of Englishness, and queenliness, that also date back to a particular moment in British cultural history. All the Churchillian rhetoric about a new era of hope and aspiration was one thing – but messages are often better delivered visually, theatrically, even ritualistically, and the ancient coronation ceremony of dressing and anointing, rendered in fifties technicolor and centred on a coterie of overdressed young debutantes and a twenty-five-year-old queen, delivered its punch. Vivienne has played with the image of royalty, tradition, history and aristocracy ever since – from the 'God Save the Queen' T-shirts to, most notably, her Harris Tweed and Anglomania collections and the orb that became her company logo. The Coronation is characterized as a splash of vibrant colour set against the drab greyness of austerity Britain. But it was also a moment centred upon clothes, upon ceremony, and upon a queen. Perhaps it was inevitable, then, that this shaded Vivienne's vision of the world, and gave image and metaphor to what she was already learning: the singularity of being British, and of being a woman.

'Everything shifted for me around that age. There were eight children in my year at primary who took the scholarship exam to the grammar school. Six of us passed – all girls – the year before the Coronation. We moved from Millbrook, from the cottages, and lived for one year in a new council house estate in Hollingworth, and then moved into Tintwistle, as my parents had put together enough money to buy Tintwistle Post Office and become its joint postmasters.

'We were bang in the middle between Hyde and Glossop at Tint-wistle. It was the same distance on the bus, but children up until then had gone to Hyde Grammar. But the year before me, these two girls a year older than me had the choice of going to Glossop and they chose there, and that's why I ended up there too. Of these two girls above me, one was the top of the class and the other one was second, out of the whole grammar school, so straightaway there were great expectations of us. But here's the thing: despite these two older girls being really bright, they left at fifteen to go and work in the cotton mill, both of them, even though they were really clever, highly intelligent girls who did very well at school. But even those two wanted to leave. Girls just did round where I grew up. The new headmaster tried everything to persuade them not to. But they left. We didn't really know what we wanted to do. But then it came to me: I was very good at art at school, and I liked art, and the idea formed in my mind, little by little, that I might go to art school at some point.

'I had hoped to find a bosom companion when I went to grammar school – the kind of utterly loyal relationship I had read about in schoolgirl novels. I thought I had found her in a friend called Julia, but she preferred another and I was in misery! I only got over it when I started going out with boys. I was still wonderfully silly at fifteen, playing children's games at playtime, but of course the difference was we now wore pencil skirts and white socks and velvet bopping shoes. And we girls risked being told, "Lower that ponytail three inches!" as this older, cheeky girl, Ena Porter, had had happen to her – rather than having it spring out of the top of our heads like bobby-soxers. I thought pencil skirts were probably the most exciting garment ever designed. I made myself very tight skirts and dresses copied from a girl I saw on holiday at Butlins. And the change for me, mid teens, with high heels and make-up and wearing *that* skirt to go dancing – it was like changing from a child to a woman overnight. It is a thrill I'll remember forever. But there was nothing very racy going on. I remember my first proper kiss: I was fifteen and this boy kissed me in the park. I was deeply shocked: not because of the kiss, but because he said he loved me, which I thought was ridiculous, aged fifteen.

'And as for shoes – well, it was such an exciting time in shoe design, not that I knew that at the time. I had to go into Manchester to buy shoes and I'd save some money in case I saw something wonderful to buy. This one time I couldn't believe what I saw, something of which I could never have dreamed: stilettos. So new that there were only two pairs in the whole shop. And only one by the time I'd left. On Monday I took them to school and placed them on my desk for all to admire. I remember I was in such a reverie that I didn't notice Mr Scott, my history teacher, come in. I adored him. He saw these shoes, and I remember him saying, "Well, well, Vivienne Swire, if God had meant us to wear pins on our feet, He would have provided us with them." I was in heaven. I was glad I had caught his attention and he had caught me – because I liked him.

'I'd arrived at Glossop Grammar School with not much exposure to anything one might call "high art", and by the time I left I could only say I had had a hint. My world at Glossop Grammar was all English Literature and History – that's what I really loved. I got 95 per cent in

Vivienne, aged fifteen.

English Literature O level and 90 per cent in History! I read Dickens at home, and at school we had *The Wind in the Willows*, *Morte d'Arthur*, *Macbeth* and *Henry V*. I loved Keats, and *A Passage to India* touched me, and Maupassant and Chaucer. They seemed to talk properly about life and sex and the human condition: the universal in the particular.

'The advice about careers and prospects was of its time and place. Especially for us girls. It wasn't exactly the school's fault; in fact the headmaster was ambitious for us, but in a very restricted way. When we were sixteen he came round to make sure we would carry on into the sixth form. He made some enquiry as to the career we were considering. I had no idea. My friend Maureen Purcell wanted to be an architect but her mother said she must be a hairdresser because she was artistic. Another friend wanted to be a journalist, not just on the *Glossop Chronicle* but a real paper! Even the headmaster thought this wildly unrealistic so she was told to be a nurse. If I had stayed up north I probably would have carried on into the sixth form because I loved school, absolutely loved it, but the point is there were only four jobs that we ever knew about. There was being a schoolteacher, a hairdresser or a nurse, or more likely a secretary. I think that was it. I can't think of anything else that was ever discussed for anybody.

'That's how it was at my grammar school and sixth form. I, for example, thought that a librarian was just somebody who just clicked the books out. If I'd known what they really did – do – I would've probably been very interested in being a librarian, actually – all the research and stuff. And great literature.

'Mr Bell, the art teacher, was quite a dramatic presence at the school. His health had been undermined during the war: he'd spent a long time in a Japanese concentration camp, and he lisped because he'd been tortured and had his tongue cut. In our school we did art, but I simply didn't know of the existence of art galleries. I'd never looked at a book of reproductions. I'd never seen a sketch reproduced in a book, anything, until Gordon Bell. Somehow the books I read were not illustrated. I came from a place where you didn't have this visual language. Just before I was seventeen, just before we came to live in London, rather, about a month or so beforehand, Mr Bell told me that there was this art gallery in Manchester and so I went. It changed my life, really. I'd never been to an art gallery before. I'd heard of painters, of Michelangelo, but I just thought they were in private collections or in Catholic churches. In theory I was studying art, so it's bizarre really that paintings and galleries had not been part of it. We studied architecture, castles, the Perpendicular period, a bit on Elizabethan and eighteenth-century buildings. And posters. That was it. Industrial graphics, really; font design. It wasn't a great education. To give him his due, Mr Bell used to let us do sketching from life, but it was never about letting my spirit and my hand connect and really draw. But it was Mr Bell who saw that art lit something up in me. Then in my last term Mr Bell showed me an art book, which was of the Impressionists. He got me to do some scenes from photographs in this Impressionist style. And he talked to me. He showed me some stippled Seurat and he showed me other techniques of Impressionism and he said, "Don't do it with a little brush, don't be safe," and so I did these landscapes and things with a large stencil brush. Free. And he saw me drawing some fashion sketch once and he was the first person to say that I had real skill. He thought that I should go to art school. He helped me put together the folder, but more importantly, he gave me the courage. He was the one person who said it: "Go on, go." He had a son, Ivan, who I knew later on, and he told me that at home it caused some upset, Mr Bell talking about me. His wife got fed up with him going on about me!'

Slightly less glamorous of background than Gordon Bell, but younger and passionately political, was Mr Scott the history teacher. He taught Vivienne in her last term at Glossop and fired his pupils with his own proud liberalism in special classes that he entitled 'Civics'.

'The first thing he explained to us was the fundamental rule of law embodied in habeas corpus. He spoke with pride of civilization and of democracy and a hatred of arbitrary arrest, for instance under the French monarchy that caused the storming of the Bastille. "We can only take democracy for granted if we insist on liberty," he used to say. I knew this when I was sixteen, thanks to him.'

Even had the family not moved south, Vivienne would have applied to art school with the folder she had prepared at Mr Bell's suggestion. Though her confidence in herself as artist wavered a few years later,

Glossop Grammar School, 1957.

the impact of Manchester Art Gallery and the faith of Mr Bell were what separated her for a while from her girlfriends, along with a conviction, born of Dora's example, that a woman's destiny could be in her own hands. But this set up a tension in Vivienne's world – one which remains even in the day-to-day business of 'Vivienne Westwood' – a tension between the concerns of commerce and the business of being an artist. Vivienne's expectations of herself were confirmed by the prejudices of her schooling: an expectation of finding a trade that would earn her a living. At the same time, her world was lit up by literature and by Mr Bell's belief in her talents as an artist. But what could be done with that?

'Everything that has happened subsequently for me: London, Malcolm, fashion, art and politics, I can date to 1958. I was nearly seventeen, and everything in my world changed. My mother and father decided we children would have a better chance in life if we moved to London and they bought a post office in Harrow. I would have been seventeen in the April of 1958 and we moved to London about February or March. So I didn't leave school at sixteen like so many of my contemporaries at Glossop Grammar. I went into the sixth form for a couple of months, but then we came down to London, and I applied for Harrow Art School with the folder I had prepared with Mr Bell, and I got in.'

Vivienne's brother Gordon remembers the move south as a dramatic turning point in the story of the family, and a time of bleak decision-making. No one else in the entire extended family had left the Tintwistle–Hollingworth area – many are still there. The move was looked on with suspicion by some, and the children, Olga, Gordon and Vivienne, were equivocal about being moved away from the schools and friends they knew. But the Great Depression still haunted the Swire parents, and the British economy was suffering one of its many post-war recessions in the late 1950s. Dora and Gordon saw more secure prospects in the relatively prosperous south. 'People didn't flit down to London that easily, back then,' Vivienne's brother recalls. 'People discussed going to Australia or America or something for a better life, but not London. There wasn't a master plan with Mum and Dad but I suppose they were ambitious, and for us kids as well as for themselves, so when they saw an opportunity, they took it.' It was explained to the children in starkly pragmatic terms: 'Dad was affected by the Depression and he figured if you worked for the government you would have a salary, and that running a post office as well as a grocer's meant customers had to walk all through the shop and buy something on the way. Mum and Dad worked that out and went from one post office to the next. And eventually that took us to London.'

Vivienne has spent all her adult life as a Londoner. By dint of her fame and her famous looks, she is one of the few celebrities of modern London life about whom it can sometimes seem every Londoner has a brief anecdote, usually involving having nearly run her over on her bike. But to begin with, she found the city claustrophobic and hated the 'cliquey' ways of young Londoners. She had found herself not in London itself, but in the leafy suburbs near Harrow-on-the-Hill, very much at the bottom of the hill, as part of the service economy of what became known as Metroland. The post office that Dora had been asked to run and which precipitated the family move south was at 31 Station Road, Harrow. They all travelled down together by train. Number 31 was the local general store as well as post office, and there was a large three-bedroom flat over the shop. This meant Vivienne sharing a bedroom with her twelve-year-old sister Olga. Vivienne, sixteen going on seventeen, had completed her School Certificate at Glossop Grammar, applied to Harrow Art School exactly as Mr Bell had suggested, and ended up on a jewellery-making and silversmithing course. It remains her only formal training in design.

Vivienne did not settle well or quickly into suburban London life. One reason for this was an awkward teenage readjustment into a new social scene. Another was that she had started seeing a boy back in Manchester, and used their 'love affair' ('though it absolutely doesn't warrant that name') as an excuse to keep heading back at weekends to her old stomping ground.

'The truth was there was this boy. And I liked him, and I liked it there, up near to Manchester. It wasn't a big love affair or anything, really, and I wasn't, you know, that committed to him, really. I'd only known him a few months. He was ever such a lovely, sweet young man. So even to say I wasn't that heavily committed to him seems a bit, I don't know, disloyal. He was so lovely. Very handsome. One of those people who always looks friendly. I hope he wouldn't mind my saying. He was called Jimmy Grant and he was a police cadet, and he lived quite a long way on the other side of Manchester at Chadderton. And we'd met because I had been working at Woolworths in Manchester – just a Saturday job. There would always be young lads walking through, trying to pick us up, my friend and me: "You want to come to a dance tonight? There's a dance at such and somebody's school." And we'd just go. And that's how I met Jimmy Grant and his friend. They were both police cadets. They didn't tell us, mind you, not straight away, that they were police!

'On our first "date" he insisted on taking me home. He lived twenty miles away. He said he'd get a lift back. And he *insisted* on taking me home on the last bus to where I lived. And it was pouring with rain and he would not borrow my umbrella because, of course, it was sissy to have an umbrella. So that sticks in my mind because Jimmy Grant walked all the way back home in the rain. I don't know, his suit must have been ruined – soaked – he must have been able to wring it out. But I can see him now, walking all the way, with his collar up. I don't think it was love. I think I knew there and then. Because I didn't know *why* he wanted to take me home. I kept telling him not to, but then he so wanted to. That was Jimmy. And moving to London ended it, really. I only went back about three times.

'Here's the thing: I just didn't like London to begin with. What I first noticed when I came to London was that people had to plan to meet each other – you couldn't just turn up and do things like we used to do around Manchester. And I remember I went to a dance on my own because I liked dancing, and I danced with somebody, just one dance, but then nobody would dance with me because I didn't dance like them – we had different types of dance really. It had been really a very nice protocol we had had in Derbyshire and Manchester for dancing. The band played three numbers, then they did a long chord and you said, "Thank you very much," and you went back to your girlfriends or whatever and that's what it would have always been for me. But when I first came down to London, things were beginning to change in music and dance. So I felt embarrassed and left out. And

sort of homesick. And soon after I moved, it became the fashion for clubs rather than dance halls with bands and "partners", and you started, well, dancing on your own in these dark clubs. You couldn't even see what people were wearing – which I never really liked. And I always liked to *talk* to people. I don't like to just dance in the dark and not see people. I didn't like Ronnie Scott's at first and places like that and I didn't really like modern jazz, either. I liked rock 'n' roll. I loved that. But in London then it was migrating to this modern jazz, and I was never mad about that.

'So two things changed London for me, really. I gave up on Jimmy, back in Manchester, and I got into Harrow Art School. So I'm seventeen and it's the spring of 1958 and I am now in Harrow Art School. I went there in the April, but by the summer I'd jacked it in. I was there for one term. I was doing the foundation course. On Fridays I did dress design. That was my choice of subject. The dressmaking teacher was quite famous. She was called Maggie Shepherd. And I saw the girls who had been exclusively with Miss Shepherd for two or three years and were doing their diploma and they made these dresses. These beautiful dresses. And I knew I was just dying to make dresses. That's what I wanted to do.

'I had made my own clothes before – everything apart from coats, but I wanted to be making clothes for myself in school, getting something really fashionable together and wearing it. But you weren't allowed to do it like that. You had to sit there and make drawings and the truth is I just got bored; I couldn't stand not *making* anything.

'Meanwhile, I became a "Trad". I kind of reinvented the way I looked, dressing in full skirts with a great sloppy knitted jumper over the top, a scrap of a headscarf, a big basket for my art materials, and bare feet. Like an artist! Nearly everybody in Harrow Art School was a Trad fan [traditional jazz] but I was never into the music of the Trad boys. But I was walking round Harrow in bare feet with a little headscarf and a long skirt: me! For my special subject I did dress design, but I was completely frustrated, for I was only allowed to draw and I wanted to be shown how to make myself a dress in a perfect way, so I transferred to the silversmithing course where I made beaten copper bangles and silver rings.

'I did make some new friends at Harrow but they seemed very unworldly to me. If they had a boyfriend, then they hung on to him. They went to parties or jazz clubs. I didn't find any sexual vitality amongst the beards and the cider of this "alternative" crowd. I was used to dance halls up north where you'd get asked out by a different bloke every Saturday, maybe having a date once for the pictures where the course was to snog all night on the back row. But I met a good friend at art school, Sylveen Bugg (she pronounced it Boug), who was also working-class, and she got me interested in the new London urban fashion which revolved around modern jazz: "mod" boys wearing short boxy Italian jackets, known as "bumfreezers", and girls wearing pencil skirts just on the knee. And Sylveen and I got beehive hairstyles and ordered winkle-picker shoes from Stan, a Greek shoemaker in Battersea, with pointed toes which extended three inches beyond the end of the foot. We called ourselves "mods" from modern jazz – which was neat to dance to – which was not the same as the slightly later mod look – young Mick Jagger and Roger Daltry. Through '58 and '59 me and my girlfriends from art school were all getting into mod clothes. And Sylveen became really keen to find a mod boyfriend, like an accessory for this look! And she found one; he was called Rob, I remember, and she married him. I hope they're still together because when she found him she thought he was perfect. He had the right haircut, the right everything.

'Once weekly, our course at art school involved travelling to the museums in South Kensington to draw. I read the *Kon-Tiki* story and was fired to find out about the Incas, and I visited the British Museum, but in all this I hadn't started to appreciate beauty, though as must happen to everyone, my imagination was set alight when I saw the plaster model of the great blue whale and I followed the evolution of the horse from its primitive beginnings. And in the British Museum, the pure gold of ancient jewellery, buried with the fire of a brighter and earlier sun which had shone on people who held in common with us the human potential for genius and yet whose ideas must have been so different . . . so you see I browsed in a bookstore across the road from the British Museum and remember being struck that anthropology was a subject you could study – at university, even.

Vivienne and her friend Ann on holiday in Jersey.

It had simply not occurred to me before that such a fascinating discipline might exist.

'So I did learn things because of Harrow, but the reason I left that summer was that I did not think – and this is really crazy, it just shows you how stupid I was – but I thought, "How do you make your *living* as an artist?" I knew I could do things. It wasn't that. But I was set on the idea that the only way to make a living in the arts was to sell paintings. I was just too working-class to see beyond that one stereotype. And then one day that summer of 1958 I got on the Tube and saw these advertisements for Pitman's to learn to be a shorthand typist. I thought, "That's it – that's making a living, unlike art. I'd better earn some money." So in order to do that, I went to work at the local Kodak factory in Harrow, to earn money to pay for a Pitman's typing course. And that's what I did. For a year.

'I soon realized that I did *not* want to be a secretary! So I thought about it, and I thought what I would do – I'd have been nineteen – was go to teacher-training college and study art with the idea that then I could perhaps find out whether I could live by painting, and, well, if I couldn't, I would be a schoolteacher anyway.

'So I applied, and I got in. My specialist subject at teacher-training college was art, which was a two-year course and I got a distinction for art in that, so I could have taught art if I'd wanted. However – and this shows you I didn't have much of a clue – I just took the first job I was offered, which was in an infant school, so that was it: I went and taught infants – five-, six-, seven-year-olds. And that was in Harlesden. "Miss Swire", that was me. I found it very easy teaching infants, because they're good and they like school and they're allowed to play and you can take little groups and teach them things, and it's very, very creative – no real discipline problems.

'There was a certain pressure, because in that first year you're under supervision to see whether you're going to be allowed to be a fully fledged teacher or not. A probationary period. The inspector always seemed to have problems with my appearance: "Miss Swire, your petticoat's showing", "Miss Swire, is your skirt a bit short?" (It was – I'd made my dress myself out of furnishing fabric, and then it shrank in the wash. I had to pull it down. It was the early sixties!)

'Stuff like that always made me feel that I was going to get into trouble with people for not being a good teacher. But I really did love the kids. I just loved them – the infants, that is. I taught only infants before Ben was born, and then later, after I went back teaching when I had Ben and Joe, I ended up teaching huge classes of juniors. "Supply teaching." Sometimes two classes at once: eighty kids! Imagine! I wanted to teach them by force of personality and didn't really insist on discipline, which was a very hard choice but a good one. I mean, if you've got a big class, forty children, you have to do it with rewards and discipline, to get them to behave and everything, and I just somehow wouldn't do it, with the infants. So when I was teaching juniors, I was *not* a good teacher! But to begin with, I was two years at the same school, my first job, as an infant teacher. And I was very, very happy, and I knew I was good.

'One other vital thing happened for me just then. When I arrived at teacher-training college – late as usual – for the first dinner, I caused a little stir in this all-female, Christian establishment, because I looked so stylish. I had beehive hair and a mod suit I had made. I looked around the room, and I sat down next to Susan, the most glamorous and beautiful girl there. I've worked in fashion all these decades and yet Susan, for me, is probably to this day the most beautiful girl I have ever seen. She had a wide mouth and a lovely pointed face and almond-shaped hazel-coloured eyes and an aquiline nose. And she had a nobility about her, and the self-irony that goes with it. I thought she was splendid and we were immediately friends. She had this affectation: when she said things – and she was very witty – she'd have her head down to one side, beautifully poised, with her cigarette, and she had burned her eyelashes through doing it! But what was typical of Susan was that she made a big joke of having burned her own eyelashes by being perfectly poised! She knew books that were worth reading and something about the theatre, and we became inseparable . . . until, that is, I met Derek. With her, and with Derek later, my social world returned to being about what I'd loved up in Manchester: it was all about dancing. It was all dancing, and the clothes of rock 'n' roll.'

*

Vivienne's adolescence and early womanhood, on the fringes of Manchester and then in the suburbs of London, coincided with a transformative moment in British culture, fashion and popular entertainment. Rock 'n' roll crossed the Atlantic to a welcoming British population, one that had been seduced into Americana, just as Vivienne's parents had been, by a generation of Hollywood films and the tumult of the Second World War. Musically, rock 'n' roll followed in the wake of wartime American music and culture, and offered, to austerity Britain, a similar promise of liberation. In 1948, 60 per cent of Brits polled said they wanted to emigrate. Huge numbers did, and often to America – and Dora and Gordon discussed but rejected the idea. The return trade from the Americas was in music. There was certainly very little to compare or compete in Britain with the American records that arrived in the UK after the war, and increasingly from 1954, in terms of explosive energy and Afro-American beat. The whole 'Be-Bop-a-Lula' soundtrack of Vivienne's youth came to coincide, oddly, with the hoopla of a coronation and a country beginning to look forward as well as back. A passionate dancer, a flirt and an instinctive positivist, Vivienne warmly embraced rock 'n' roll music and the aesthetics of mid-Western fashion that followed in its wake. She made little summer bra tops out of gingham, wore bobby socks and her ponytail too high. It was, of course, the era that gave a name to the 'teenage' phase of life, which was in part an acknowledgement of a new consumer body, but also an awareness that Vivienne's postwar generation was writing its own rules, forging its own culture, and dancing and having sex to a whole new beat.

Vivienne, like many of her generation, will tell you that music has never been quite as good since. But rock 'n' roll then was much more subversive than it now appears – or appeared to Americans at the time. And it was about fashion as well as sounds. The BBC didn't play rock 'n' roll until well into the 1960s. You had to tune in to the American Forces Network – broadcasting all over Europe in the Marshall Plan years – or Radio Luxembourg. As a result, the energy and promise of personal and sexual liberation that was part of this American sound took on a furtive, underground tenor in the context of Britain. This has its impact on Vivienne's story too, partly because rock 'n' roll was stated and referenced with almost everything she later created, first with Malcolm McLaren ('Vive le Rock', 'Let It Rock') within the context of the 1970s revival of rock 'n' roll, and later on her own. But also because 1950s rock 'n' roll became a cult not just about the music, but about the only way teenagers like Vivienne could pay court to this new craze – with clothes.

'I was not a rebel, but it was a great age to be a teenager, because the look was all about rebellious youth versus age. This all, later on, appealed to Malcolm. I had a certain devilry about me, and in that sense I was very suited to rock 'n' roll.'

In Britain, unlike in America, rock 'n' roll came to have a look. For the boys, a cultish uniform of brothel creepers and slicked-back hair, and a new silhouette and new attitude for the girls. The principal means by which the British absorbed the powerful new youth culture of rock 'n' roll – one which was self-consciously alien – was to consume, dress, shop and make, and turn it into a 'look'. The temple in this new mysticism of rock was less the record shop or dance floor: it was the boutique.

Vivienne was a teenager at one of the great moments to be such, the late 1950s: if not in terms of real sexual emancipation, then certainly in terms of revolutionary new music and fashions. Dancing alongside the rock 'n' roll look, however, there was a rival youth-cult dress scene spawned out of the immediate post-war period, that was first described as neo-Edwardian, and thereafter became known as 'Ted'. It fused elements of Edwardian dandyism with American drape material that was being imported by Cecil Gee, amongst others, and gave a nod to both the American zoot suit and the Edwardian overcoat in its long-bodied box-cut jackets. 'Because Teddy Boys [(the working class incarnation) later became] associated with teenage violence' – Bank Holiday pitched battles at British seaside resorts – 'the idea of fashionable clothes as a threat to society was born,' said costume historian Colin Woodhead. It was a significant moment in fashion history, not lost on Vivienne. Not just one, but *both* the youth-cult fashion forms that feed into Vivienne's early work – the Teddy Boy suits she later made for Malcolm McLaren and the T-shirts and jeans that were the mainstay of her Let It Rock creations – had their origins in the demob

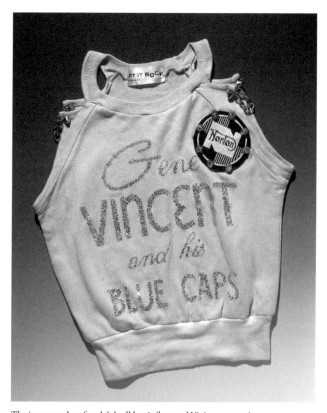

The iconography of rock 'n' roll has influenced Vivienne ever since.

fashions of her teenage years, reworked as urban guerrilla wear in the seventies. Teddy Boy fashions, as worn by her brother Gordon and her early boyfriends, were one large part of the British rock 'n' roll fashion scene. Meanwhile the T-shirt, leathers and jeans of Brando and James Dean and Elvis Presley were the essential American uniform of teenage rebellion through the rock 'n' roll years that fed directly into the British rock 'n' roll look, and this too has roots directly out of World War Two. They are the first ingredients of the Vivienne Westwood look, and the early designs along the King's Road. And it was, like so much in Vivienne's story, a handmade, do-it-yourself story.

'I started off like all girls my age, trying not to wear my school gymslip, buying skirts instead. I was always interested in extremes, and making an impression. Aged fifteen I went to Butlins on the Isle of Wight with my friend Norma's family. I adored it: the ballroom, the whisky, the fashion for stoles and the feel of the sea breeze in full petticoats. And there was this fashion for large plastic daisy earrings, but I made enormous earrings out of giant marguerites and I remember the band leader stopped the music when I came in and said, "Look, everyone, at that amazing girl in those earrings."'

Ian Dury, who knew Vivienne later, once reminisced about his 1950s teen years in a similar suburban milieu to hers: 'grey worsted trousers with 12-inch bottoms done on my mum's hand-driven Singer, yellow-and-black check shirt.' It was a new urban dandyism, the beginnings of 'fashion as challenge to society', yet, ironically to modern ears, it was often run up by mums and girlfriends in suburban front rooms. Like Vivienne herself, the rock 'n' roll and Teddy Boy years tended to fuse Do It Yourself with the accidentally radical, with historical reference (the Edwardians) and the perceived classless glamour of America and bikers. And beyond even this, the period saw the origins of a new trope in the business of business as well as fashion. There was a fusion of apparent creative autonomy, music, fashion and identity that has become known as the first era of 'teenage', but it had become one model of how to sell. Vivienne may have been one of the first-generation teenagers. For marketeers, be they hucksters of clothes or music or political ideologies, we are all teenagers now.

As Malcolm explained, and as Vivienne still concurs: 'just look at what people like Jack Kerouac were wearing after they had left the marines and the army and went on the road. White T-shirt, jeans, leather jacket. When Hollywood looked around for rebellious images which would suit stars like James Dean and Brando, they settled on that. And when kids in Britain saw it up on the big screen, they wanted it too.'

Somewhere between the 1956 'Rock Around the Clock' year-of-the-Ted violence that saw sleepy Orpington Town Hall trashed by marauding Ted gangs, and the 1959 murder of Caribbean carpenter Kelso Cochrane that led to the Notting Hill riots, Ted fashion became imbued with an idea of danger, with violence, and with racism. It was an essential repositioning of fashion, in that it came to represent, as it repeatedly would in the late twentieth century and partly because of Vivienne's work, disaffected youth cults and everything that an older generation might despise. But also, in a pre-echo of what would happen with punk, Ted fashion had a life cycle in notoriety that was not lost on Vivienne either. It was a fashion of white, urban, excluded youth – for all that it had its earliest origins in Savile Row. After its first incarnation, it was then adopted by the merely bored or aggressive – Bank Holiday teens looking for trouble – which in turn sowed the seeds of its own demise because it was also, and consequently, adopted by the simply racist. It was a trajectory later followed by punk – without, it has to be said, the Ted attention to tailoring. First-wave Ted style had its apogee in 1958, just as Vivienne came down to London. Its essential emblem, the brothel creeper, a badge of radical dissent in an era when the colour of shoes was one essential desideratum of what it was to be a 'gent', was replaced by Italian-style pointed shoes – the male equivalent of what Vivienne bought so proudly in Manchester. This became the one unifying look of teenage Britain in the late fifties and early sixties, 'sticking-out winkle-pickers'. But the Teds were all over by 1960. The look was referenced, as it later would be by Vivienne, as something 'deliberately archaic', but the Ted thing was hopelessly tainted after 1959 by the Kelso murder that gave rise, eventually, to the racially mixed Notting Hill Carnival of today. This explains some of Vivienne's fashion and dance discomfort as she moved south in 1958-9 – the whole scene, in music, in fashion and in dance, was shifting under her winkle-pickers. Rock 'n' roll as a fashion trope and the Ted look merged, and they did so, coincidentally, just as Vivienne was moving down from Manchester. And at the same time, for a while, music moved also and contrapuntally against rock 'n' roll and back to its origins in 'traditional' jazz.

And for girls like Vivienne, attachment to a particular 'tribe' of fashion- and music-conscious young men became a key element in what it was to grow up. The electric thrill of the pencil skirt, not to mention the conical bras of the era, signalled a vital moment in fashion history: the commercialization and visualization of sexual maturity, the marketing of clothes and music together around the creation of a cult of sexy youthfulness.

Perhaps it was inevitable that a look as overstated as both the Teds and the (jazz) mods – there were even proto-Mohican hairstyles called an 'apache' forged out of enormous quiffs and Brylcreem – could not exist without a music to dance to. That music was rock 'n' roll, a world away from the Savile Row and Humphrey Lyttleton of the original neo-Edwardian look. But, as Vivienne recalls with her keen ear for music and keen eye for fashion, the main issue of the era was that the clothes marched in time to the music styles. They even adopted each other's names. In the late 1950s there was a reawakening in Britain of traditional jazz. The acceptance of rock 'n' roll had opened British hearts and ears to earlier jazz styles, ones that soundtracked French new wave film as much as Soho clubs and Harrow pubs. The style of dress that accompanied this, the 'Trad' look, was the one adopted by Vivienne as she entered art school in 1958: a statedly unstructured and quasi-intellectual look suitable for Paris's Left Bank or Greenwich Village or Ronnie Scott's. ('Though I should point out,' Vivienne tells me, 'Ronnie's was all modern jazz, and I ended up hating that as much as trad.') Baggy trousers, huge jumpers, duffel coats and scarves in emulation of French existentialists or New York beats, and dirndl skirts. Dirndl skirts have featured in almost every Vivienne Westwood collection ever since, somewhat under the radar. They were what she wore as a 1959 'Trad', along with necklaces she made out of melon seeds ('I had never even seen a melon before!'). The look, along with the cider and the very English jazz of George Melly and Humphrey Lyttleton, was the British reinvention of Black American jazz, and a fashion to go with it. In *Absolute Beginners*, Colin MacInnes's epoch-defining novella, a 'Trad' girl is described who could have been Vivienne in 1960: 'Long hair . . . with long fringes . . . big floppy sweater, maybe bright-coloured, never floral . . . smudged-looking's the objective.' It was a look that blurred the problem of how to be a Ted or rocker in the American style, and it was a look that bridged the era from the end of the first wave of Teds but before mods were much on the scene.

But 'Trad', the style that solved Vivienne's sartorial dilemma in coming south and trying to fit in, was a remarkably brief moment in the history of fashion and for Vivienne too. As Vivienne's friend the late Tommy Roberts once said: 'Trad became corny in about two seconds. All these bods jumping about in college scarves . . . Trad was really a bit naff.'

Vivienne concurs. 'My Trad phase was very, very brief. I copied what Sylveen was doing, I was inspired by her look, and I liked the full petticoats. There's a photo of me taken in Jersey when I went to visit Derek when he had a summer job there as a barman. I didn't look like that for long. Trads were middle-class and arty. Teds were more my thing. And later mods – but by then I was a mum.'

Nevertheless, these looks all told a new kind of story, expressing a synchronicity between fashion and music that had not happened before. And again, as with the British rock 'n' roll scene that begat it all, it became an issue of clothes as much as anything.

Vivienne, as she left her teens, had therefore already lived through and had direct experience of four interconnected shifts in fashion and music that have impact to this day: rock 'n' roll, Teds, the early (jazz) mods, and Trads. But by 1962, her life was taking a radical turn into marriage and motherhood that might have seen her move away from fashion entirely had it not been for a Ted-dressed London art student called Malcolm Edwards McLaren.

Vivienne Westwood

MRS WESTWOOD'S
WEDDING DRESS

I became very interested in working-class sharp dressers. Mods. I did not want to go to university. I thought the boys who went to university were poncey effete intellectuals. They carried umbrellas and had pineapples-and-sherry with the French mistress after school. Sexually, I wasn't interested in them. I don't know why. I liked blokes on building sites.

VIVIENNE WESTWOOD

'I don't want to talk about Derek too much,' Vivienne says.

But then, of course, she does. 'You see, the thing is, I feel I've not been very nice to Derek. In the end, it's just that you grow apart ... but to begin with, it was ... well: here's the thing...'

Vivienne is sitting at her cutting table with her thick glasses on, occasionally shuffling a piece of paper – a sketch of some appliqué that will one day grace the Paris catwalk, and a picture of the son she had with Derek, Ben Westwood, at his recent wedding in Japan. Ben is a wry and lithe fifty-year-old who is in and out of the studio where we talk. He would look like a man in his thirties had his long hair not turned prematurely grey. Tomoka, beautiful, Japanese, constantly at his side in the manner that marks them as newlyweds, is adjusting slowly to England and to life as the new Mrs Westwood (Junior).

Vivienne has been reluctant, over the years, to talk much about her first marriage. Out of a loyalty to Ben, perhaps, and to Derek – a man for whom she has maintained a constant affection and respect – and out of an innate reticence about exposing either of them to the glare of an attention they never sought. She has, however, kept Derek's name, and she has made it world-famous – something Derek, a retired airline pilot, is on record as saying he did not always appreciate. Theirs was one of those marriages that today, perhaps, would just not happen. Based on an assumption by others that they would marry, and in an era when, as Vivienne says, 'you weren't allowed to experiment', it had its own inevitable momentum and its own all-but-inevitable potential for minor domestic tragedy.

'You know in 1961 if you were going out with somebody, you had this problem of coming in late and "What have you been up to?" from Dora – all that judgement stuff. So you sort of got married. That's how it was. I don't think Derek would mind my saying that. I don't know if I'd been in London even a year before I met him. So I would have been eighteen or nineteen. We were both so young. We were a crowd, you know. We all went out together, and you know there were no drink-driving laws in those days. We'd go to a pub in Elstree where we'd meet everybody or they'd all show up there, and we'd go to the same dances. So we'd maybe arrange to go to pubs in Harrow and Kingsbury, or Ronnie Scott's or somewhere in town, but normally we went to this ballroom in Queensbury, the Ritz.

'Before then, you see, I had loved best in all the world going dancing and I used to hang out with the people who were all dressed up, to dance. These were my friends. They were the kind of people I was attracted to: outgoing people. Dancers. So all through teacher training, this gang of friends and I used to meet to go out dancing – sometimes church dances, even – and we'd have parties and we'd meet each other round each other's houses, and that became for a while the focus of things for me. It was all about going out – dressing up and going out. And sometimes the gang would go out a bit further, to somewhere a little bit in Middlesex or somewhere, Aylesbury or whatever, and just go to a pub out there. That was my social life: cars and pubs and dancing, and I didn't – at that point in my life, I don't think I'd met, ever, anybody that I'd had any kind of intellectual conversation with at all. Never. Apart from with Susan. And I was quite happy about that to begin with, but because of Susan, I was changing . . .

'And then, one October night, I went to a dance on my own. No one would dance with me at first. And then Derek asked me for a dance. And we liked each other and I thought he was very attractive. He was.

March 1963, Hillingdon Heath Masonic Lodge; Vivienne, aged 21, with Gordon and Dora.

He is. He's a very, very nice person. A fantastic person. He was lovely and warm and friendly and funny and sweet, and I don't know – I just liked him. But he liked me as well, which was even more important to me, probably, at first! And he was such a good dancer. We were just dancing. I don't really know almost how it happened.'

It was late 1961 when Vivienne met Derek Westwood. Like her mother before her, she met her husband on the dance floor, and, as for her mother, it was a certain dancerly skill, athleticism and worldliness that attracted her. Derek was two years her senior, and a southerner. His family lived on Belvedere Way in Kenton and at the time Derek was an apprentice in west London's famous Hoover factory. His dream, however, which he was on his way to realizing, was to train as an airline pilot. He and Vivienne Swire had much in common, not least the same tastes in music and dance styles. He dressed like a mod and listened to the Modern Jazz Quartet.

'Derek was an apprentice toolmaker when we met but wanted to be a pilot. To pay for his training he ran dances. He ran bingo halls, but also gigs at places like the Glenlyn ballroom in Forest Hill and the Dominion cinema at Harrow. He put on The Rolling Stones and The Ronettes at different stages, with his friends from the Hoover factory, Bob Druce and Barry Funeigh, and eventually even The Who . . .'

'I remember Derek was a really good dresser with nice mohair suits,' recalls Vivienne's brother Gordon. 'He'd come and collect her and they'd both look amazing. So glamorous. So I rather hero-worshipped Derek, and always had Vivienne. They were running pop groups. Derek used to work for an outfit called Commercial Entertainments, running dance halls. They used to manage The Who, way before they were called The Who. They were called The Detours and then The High Numbers and then someone brilliant – and I always thought it was Vivienne but it turns out it was Rodney, Derek's brother – thought of "The Who?", but they were managed by Derek Westwood, with Vivienne Westwood – as she became – taking money on the door! This is in Stonebridge Park on the North Circular Road near to Wembley where Carpetland now is! We were all interested in clothes in those days. Teds, then mods. And The Who were our group. But they were obliged to play these dance halls, and I think the nightly rate in those days was about thirty, forty quid, but Derek could rehire them out, The Who, for about a hundred and fifty or something, you know, when they were getting really popular. So he and Vivienne made quite a bit of money!'

'Mainly what I remember,' continues Vivienne, 'is Derek getting very cross with me because I was always, always late. I was so late. Because of my clothes. Mind you, I never paid to get in anywhere – even if it was nothing to do with him. I looked great. I'd be supposed to meet him there, at the Queensbury, say, but I would get there about a quarter of an hour before closing, because I'd be finishing my outfit! And he felt humiliated in front of his friends that I, his girlfriend, never showed up on time, because I was making things.

'You have to understand as well that Derek, like Malcolm later, was great fun. I used to love going to this pub with him where he used to sing; get up on stage and sing all those old cockney songs, "What a calamity / Three old ladies locked in a lavatory . . ." And we'd all join in. I used to just love all that stuff. And then we just, you know, agreed to get married.

'But this is how it went. When I first came to London it was all about being a teenager and getting a job and doing stuff, and then when I was eighteen I went to teacher-training college for two years, and that's about when I met Derek. And the idea of going to art school had been that I would like to do art and possibly be an artist. But I realized I wanted more. And then I met Susan, and just really, she was my best friend. She was the perfect friend: good-looking. You have to be interesting-looking to capture my attention! I don't know; you're always attracted to people who are really good-looking. Aren't we all? And she was lovely, I thought. And we became great friends. But she stirred something in my head and heart. I definitely loved her. I would've done anything for her. I thought she was just great. And also, you see, this comes from what you read. And I used to read all those books about girls at boarding school and their friends, and everything they got up to, and I wanted a friend: a bosom pal. As a young person I was more interested in my own sex than the opposite one; children are. Although I always liked boys as well. I think if I'd had a stronger relationship with a girl, that would've been OK. I should have. But I met Derek.

(L-R) Derek's brother Martin, Derek Westwood and Vivienne, summer 1962.

For instance, I had really wanted Derek to go to the theatre with me – I'd never been in my life. He took me to see the comedy *Boeing-Boeing* and I was so bored. I thought, "If that's the theatre, I don't need that!" But then Susan took me to *A Man for All Seasons* with Paul Scofield, and then we went to *The Crucible* by Arthur Miller, and I just was amazed. Knocked out. So, you see, my association with her was getting me thinking. There was such stimulation in my relationship with Susan. She had come from a different background and she was interested in these things, and she had a nice boyfriend who could tell us all these things as well. Susan was intellectual, my first intellectual friend. She had a boyfriend too who was quite intellectual and he exposed me to even more things: poetry readings with the Beat Poets at the Royal Albert Hall – Allen Ginsberg, Lawrence Ferlinghetti – everything I thought I was hungry for. But in our group, it just became all "This is Derek and Vivienne, they're getting married." And yet I knew I was changing already, partly to do with Susan.

'That's how I'll put it, Ian. I'll say this much and you can figure out the rest: my choices have always been intellectual. That was a different sort of decision, and it didn't work out. Derek and I had met because we were interested in being "mods" or "Teds" or whatever and in being part of a crowd. Our social life was very good. But it was a teenage thing. It's what teenagers should do. I have great respect for him as a person – a good, good person. And I think it's an incredible story, how he became a pilot, I really do. But even though I stuck with the engagement to Derek, in the end I knew I wanted to go outside of that relationship to find other things. And for some reason your sexual life, in those days anyway, was tied up with that. And so I did eventually fall out of love with him. It's so obvious now. But then it was all tied up with my mother's attitude to sex. Because in those days there was such a pressure put on girls to be respectable. Virginity. And all that kind of stuff. Not getting pregnant, and all that. I was a virgin when I met Derek. And more than that, even, at some stage I just realized that if I'd been older, well, I think you know what I'm saying. Nowadays you could live with somebody. And at the time, maybe I was frightened to hurt Derek; 'Del', everyone called him, but I was more interested in my girlfriend, Susan, because she was intellectual and I just adored her, really. Put it like this: if I'd had to go and live on a desert island, I would've gone with her.

'And I don't want to spell this out particularly, because of the people involved and because, despite everything people think about me, I am quite a private person, but there is something else I should explain about me and about then. Regarding boys and men. Up until then, until I married Derek, I would have to say I'd always cared about my girlfriends more than any bloke I went out with. That's what I wanted, thinking back – the closeness and complicity of a woman. A soulmate. And eventually, when I went to teacher-training college, I met Susan. My whole emotional world was her. People misunderstand: the fact was that was where I felt alive and understood. And then Susan got a job in Canada after teacher training. And that was that. I do think my mum should have known and if only my mother had thought of suggesting an adventure, getting away – teaching in Canada, I don't know – I would've gone like a shot. That's something that I could have done and not hurt anybody's feelings. I wish my mother had talked to me a bit more about it or had the sense to say, "Why don't you get a job in Canada with Susan for a year and then come back and *then* see how you feel about Derek?" That would have been perfect, and would have saved everyone a lot of pain. But then again, I wouldn't have Ben.'

Despite all of this, Vivienne, just turned twenty-one, began planning a small wedding and a dress to suit. Derek would have settled for a register office, but Vivienne and Dora insisted on a church wedding, and on 21 July 1962 at St John the Baptist, Greenhill, Vivienne Swire became Vivienne Westwood.

'And that's that, really. I was late. I made my wedding dress myself. Not very well – and it wasn't even finished. It was still all pinned together and it wasn't finished properly. I made it to the church on time. Ish. Just.

'I shouldn't say this, but when else would I? I think in those days I had this idea – maybe we all did then – that "the man in your life" ought to be "The One"; you know, that somehow you wouldn't ever need anybody else in the world but that person. So if you *did* need someone or something else – and I knew I did – that meant it was all wrong. I knew by then, and partly because of Susan, that I needed an intellectual complicity, a meeting of minds. So I did a great deal of thinking around that time, and I think I changed. Don't think we were unhappy: we weren't. I was very happy and we were fine for a time. I got pregnant very quickly. You do quite a lot of thinking when you are pregnant, and looking after a baby, even though you are exhausted. But I was changing. In quite quick succession I became a teacher, I married Derek, and my son Ben was born. And I lost my faith in God. I was only twenty-one. My brother Gordon at this time had a lovely American girlfriend, Lesley, who was staying with me some of the time and helping out. This was 1962. She was strongly opposed to the Vietnam war. She didn't stay long but she punctured my political naivety, and when she realized that I was a practising Christian she challenged me to defend my position and I found that I couldn't. I had already ceased to believe much of the dogma, but as soon as I acknowledged to myself that the whole thing was held up solely by my emotional commitment to an idea formed when I was a child – my personal commitment in the face of Christ's suffering, all that – it all just collapsed in front of me like a house of cards. Little Dolly Daydream was beginning to wake up. I didn't know what I believed – I only wanted to read and read and read and find out.

'Lesley had a profound effect on me. Gordon had met her in Ibiza – on the hippy trail, as it were – and we went to the theatre together in London I remember, and even went hitch-hiking to Devon one time, talking all the way about Vietnam. On royalty, on religion, on politics, she was very challenging. She wouldn't stand for the National Anthem. She helped change me. And the question became, if you marry young and then your passions diverge, is it fine and right to end things?'

In 1963, the choice to end things, as a young mother, was considered shocking. Many of those around them – Vivienne's parents and siblings, Susan and the dance-hall friends – were shell-shocked when Vivienne announced, only months after Ben's birth in 1963, that she was leaving Derek. Some assumed it was post-partum depression, or the pressure of their divergent careers and a young baby. But Vivienne was adamant. A hunger for further intellectual and cultural exploration had awoken in her, and it held out the promise that somewhere

Vivienne and her baby son, Ben.

(L–R) Olga, Dora, Vivienne (with Ben on her knee), Gordon and Gordon. 1964.

there would be people – or one person – with whom to go on that journey of exploration.

'It was about my steps towards politicization. Of course this all connects to my childhood, ideals and experiences. And that became the difference between me and Derek. What Del did do – the direction he went – was skywards, literally. He was a glider at the time. I remember one of our happiest times was when he was gliding up over Dunstable Downs. It was thrilling. He was amazing and exciting. Such a sociable man. When he did become a pilot, you know what he used to enjoy most? His announcements to passengers. Those were his passions. And mine became politics. We just grew apart.'

Derek Westwood gave Vivienne her name, and her first son, Ben. Their marriage and its ending also endowed her with a self-determination born of this early experience of societal disapproval and the break with the past and with the expectations on young women of her era. Derek also exposed her to the world of professional music and the new London bands that were closely linked to the art-school scene Vivienne already knew. The other vital contribution of these years to Vivienne's story, along with Derek's name, was her experience of a new nexus in youth culture. In early 1960s Britain, the worlds of dance, music and art school were closely intertwined. It was part of what made London swing. Album covers, fashion and bands were to become the essential manner in which Western youth expressed itself (until computers). Pop, and for that matter punk, both of which evolved out of rock 'n' roll through the latter half of the twentieth century, were phenomena that could only have happened through a powerful constellation of ideas and influences that have left their imprint all over modern Western culture, but which oddly loop back over and over again to London in the late fifties to mid sixties, and to the dance clubs and art schools that Vivienne and Derek knew. From rock 'n' roll's British genesis in the seminally influential *Blackboard Jungle* of 1955 (a film Vivienne finally saw in Christine Keeler's flat on Gene Krell's television years later) all the way to the anarchy of punk, the popular music of the later twentieth century found its initial evangelists and fans in the new art schools which mushroomed all over urban areas of the UK as part of the post-war education reforms. Many leading figures in the industry had studied graphic design (which the art schools taught at the expense of fine art), most of them originally working-class kids who had been the first of their families to benefit from tertiary education. This is the story of Pete Townshend of The Who, briefly managed by Derek Westwood, but also Charlie Watts, Keith Richards, the artist Peter Blake, not to mention Blake's pupil, Malcolm McLaren, John Lennon, Eric Clapton, Roy Wood of The Move, Ray Davies of The Kinks and Freddie Mercury of Queen a little later. All came from art-school backgrounds and most of them were grammar-school kids too, exactly like Vivienne. But, as with Vivienne and Malcolm and indeed Gordon and others around the Harrow scene, there was crossover from art to music and from graphics to sales and marketing – as they might now be termed – into running businesses that fused pop iconography, fashion, music and 'happenings'. For instance, Nigel Waymouth – owner of the Granny Takes a Trip shop later run by Gene Krell and muralled by Michael English – was simultaneously the leading graphic designer in the then pop scene and formed the psychedelic design collective and band, with English, Hapshash and the Coloured Coat. Similarly the London-based design co-op The Fool (who were actually Dutch) were commissioned by The Beatles in 1967 to design clothing and murals for their Apple store. But they too were, at one stage, a band. Like Malcolm, who ended up in retail with 430 King's Road, but managed The Sex Pistols, or like Vivienne herself, who wrote songs for the Pistols and art-directed the Sara Stockbridge band and advised Sid Vicious on clothes while also designing graphics for T-shirts, there was intimate cross-pollination between the spheres of fashion, music, art and graphic design.

Pop musicians, pop artists, pop designers and the fashion and boutique scene burgeoning all over Britain, but especially in London, gave a context and reason for the creation of youth cults and the sales that they could generate. There was nothing commercially sinister or pre-planned in this, though – as Vivienne and McLaren would later point out – it has become rare for anything in fashion or popular music to remain un-exploited for long. The opening up of the educational franchise that hit Vivienne's generation – giving access to grammar schools and student grants to art colleges – allowed working-class kids like her, with all their agenda of non-conformity and indeed social indignation, to give expression and image to the rise of consumerism and mass-marketing. Vivienne, who was noted in her teens by Mr Bell for her skill in design and who proudly boasts that she could have been a copywriter, has also been at the forefront of the new agendas in graphics. The post-war generation, bombarded with the 'non-stop distraction' of advertising like no generation before, were many of them schooled in its techniques at the newfangled art schools. British pop culture was not just accidentally attached to the art schools; the one could not have happened without the other. The public displays of musical taste and 'tribe' membership did more than just sell records and clothes; it became part of a new language of belonging. 'It was the best possible time to be a teenager,' says Vivienne. 'We made up what it meant, and how it would look. Or, as Malcolm later said, "we were searching for identity".' Graphic art, fashion, music and identity: Vivienne's generation of Londoners were the first to sew it all together. It was a story as old and as British as they come – the creation of insider and outsider groups with clothes.

Derek, Vivienne's dapper mod husband, followed his aspiration to be a pilot, and left London. For much of Ben Westwood's childhood, he was based in and around Luton airport, and after a few years he remarried. He never gave up on being the best father he could to Ben. After the marriage break-up Derek remained intensely loyal to Vivienne, reticent, as her fame grew, about commenting on the brief years they had spent together or the reasons for the split. They formally divorced in 1966.

Get a life

life

Art Lovers Unite! ♥

THE
DIRTY-TURQUOISE
SKIRT

*When I met Malcolm and I fell in love, I thought he was beautiful and
I still do. I still treasure the experience of Malcolm. A world without
Malcolm would have been like a world without Brazil . . . he was
charismatic, talented; I really liked him. And even though he was crazy
I knew I wanted to find out more about him.* VIVIENNE WESTWOOD

*Malcolm was like a small boy, lost in a forest. The forest is dark and
foreboding, and the dark trees represent the forces that subjugate and
repress our freedoms. Because Malcolm can't find his way out, he realizes
he must let in the light. So what does he do? He burns the trees down.*

STEWART MCLAREN
at his brother's funeral in 2010

'I can talk very freely about people who are dead, including Malcolm,'
Vivienne tells me, glancing sideways and out over the Battersea skyline
in the manner that I now know signals her departure from reticence.
'I can say certain things that I wouldn't have said when he was alive.
It's like they say: "To the living we owe respect and to the dead we owe
the truth." I would protect Malcolm while he was alive. But not any
more. Not that I like washing dirty linen in public. I don't. But the dead
deserve the truth.

'I've had very, very few romances. Very, very few. I could tell you my
boyfriends on these fingers.' Vivienne flutters a jewelled hand in my direction, which might indicate five fingers or ten, and, before I can ask,
she carries on: 'I never had a lot. Of men. I've always been very loyal to
one person. And I certainly never wanted more than one at a time.

I expect it was Malcolm who was the first "intellectual" man for me. I can't say I'd had one, before then.'

Intrinsic to the legend of Vivienne Westwood is Malcolm McLaren. Theirs was the partnership that some say changed the world. It shaped punk: its look, its most notorious band and its philosophy, so far as it had one. It is this relationship that links Vivienne to The Sex Pistols and to the jubilee summer of 'God Save the Queen': the record, the image, the debacle. It is also the relationship that gave her her second son, Joe Corré, who himself tells me, 'Whichever way you look at it, Mum's credibility is derived originally from punk rock, because, simply, it was a revolution. No one had ever seen anything like it.' Punk rock, the eruption of incandescent outrage, with matching look and sound, can be viewed now from many angles. It iterates constantly in fashion – from allusions to fetish-wear to distressed clothing to T-shirt slogans – and it resonates still with every new wave of popular music. It was arguably a brief moment, involving a surprisingly small number of accidentally influential people, and it was a revolution without obvious result or ethos. Some, like Westwood executive Christopher Di Pietro, will tell you punk changed business practice to this day and even political discourse, lending voice and urgency to ending orthodoxy and allowing creative dissent. Some credit punk with godparenting, variously, changing attitudes to unorthodox sexuality, or dress-down Fridays, or individualistic fashions. But if many are confused (especially after the fast submission of punk to the forces of commercialization) about what it truly contributed to Western culture beyond an inarticulate snarl, there is unanimity that its London epicentre was the mismatched coupling of Vivienne and Malcolm. Their importance in shaping the look of punk as well as its London beat is one theme of this book, and Vivienne stated quite early on in its inception that the business of setting the record straight, so far as one ever might, on who made what when, was part of her motive for having it bound in hardback. Setting the record straight has proved to be an elusive task, even for her, and she was there. To misquote Tolstoy, most relationships that work out, work out for similar reasons. Those which fall apart (and Vivienne and Malcolm's did, artistically and personally, in explosive style), fall apart for reasons too complex to untangle even for the protagonists themselves, even at the time. The controversial impact of their creative and personal partnership, from the late sixties to the early eighties, refracts down the decades in the memoirs of punks and pop stars, in the weary bitterness of their son, in Malcolm's arguments at the V&A over top billing on garments in their collection he did not create, even to the extent of Vivienne being heckled at Malcolm's funeral in 2010. It is as complex to pick apart as Vivienne's most elaborate knits. But it all began simply enough with a chance meeting above a Ruislip post office, between a mercurial art student and his best pal's elder sister . . .

'I knew Malcolm first as Gordon's friend, my little brother's friend. It was 1965. My only income was from making jewellery and selling it in the Portobello Road, and I was living back with my mum. That's how I coped. Malcolm was in and out of the flat above her post office, visiting with Gordon. He came and helped me for two or three hours at a time, and I was very impressed by his designs. They were very mod. I thought straight away he was really good. And so I got to know him because usually he would come there when my mother was in the shop downstairs – she didn't ever like him – and, which surprised me, sometimes when my brother Gordon was at college. Or he'd just hang out in the flat with Gordon and they'd both sit there chatting while I was there making jewellery and looking after little Ben. And, little by little, I got to know Malcolm . . .'

Malcolm Robert Andrew McLaren had been born in 1946 and was brought up in Stoke Newington and Highbury, within crowd-roar of the old Arsenal stadium. His childhood was dominated by his dramatically eccentric grandmother, Rose Corré Isaacs. Rose, whose family were part of Stamford Hill's Sephardic Jewish community, had wanted to be an actress, but ended up a theatrical landlady, small-time art-fraudster, and insistently pushy stage-grandmother. More shockingly, perhaps, her daughter, Emily, Malcolm's mother, is described by members of the family as a 'prostitute', though her 'career' was perhaps rather more *grande horizontale* than that, insofar as her most acknowledged partner was Sir Charles Clore, who installed her in his apartment in Monte Carlo. The family is more open about all this now than was the case in earlier years, but the manifold dysfunctions of the extended Corré-Isaacs-McLaren family are neatly summed up by Vivienne: 'Malcolm never knew real maternal love as a child, which was the root of all his troubles.' Joe, their son, is more forthright: 'Well, his mother rejected him, and Rose was fucking insane.'

Peter McLaren, Malcolm's father, a Scottish engineer, bequeathed his son his complexion and colouring ('puce and cream', as memorably described by Sid Vicious) but little else. In fairness, there was red-headedness on both sides of his family: the Corrés were Portuguese Jews 'who looked down on all other Jews', according to Vivienne. 'Malcolm looked like his grandmother Rose, who always liked me and I liked her. But they shouted a lot in Malcolm's family – ever such a lot. That's where Malcolm got that from.' There was a second son, Stewart, who went such a different path in life that Cora Corré, Vivienne's granddaughter, was unaware of his existence until her grandfather's funeral. And Rose Isaacs Corré began a family tradition, followed by her daughter, grandson and now great-grandson, of picking a surname apparently at random from the various ones on offer, and then returning to another alias according to whim, circumstance or the evasion of the tax authorities. Rose Isaacs was rarely known as Mrs Corré. Emily, her daughter, seldom went by Mrs McLaren. Malcolm spent his early life as Malcolm Edwards, after a local fabric business with which his mother's second husband was involved. And Malcolm's son with Vivienne, Joseph Ferdinand, was given the surname Corré in honour of the eccentric Rose, as if to turn the clock backwards, just as it does at Vivienne's Worlds End shop. His daughter, Vivienne's only grandchild, rejoices in the name Cora Corré, at Vivienne's suggestion. It's like some multigenerational disavowal that it is a family at all. 'The effect of growing up in a family that never wanted to be a family,' McLaren later remarked, 'is that it is very, very difficult for you to behave in a normal way.' Yet his affection for his domineering grandmother remained intact and in some respects, an upbringing with Rose Corré was some of what would prepare Malcolm for life with Mrs Westwood. 'Rose was a woman who created her own world and everybody else had to live in it or live without it,' Malcolm wrote. 'This world was far better than the world we live in, because it had a lot more soul and a lot more passion. It was a world that had brilliance. It shone.' It is the world Vivienne lives for too.

The presence of Malcolm McLaren in the writing of this work was and is as strong as that of Dora and Gordon Swire. You can't really understand Vivienne – her place in the cultural pantheon or her progress from primary school teacher to punk couturier – without trying to understand Malcolm, any more than you can understand her strength without the backstory of her inspiring parents. 'Vivienne was very, very influenced by Malcolm; he changed her life,' recalls the man who introduced them, her brother Gordon. 'No matter what else you might say about Malcolm, he changed lives: he changed my life; he certainly changed Vivienne's. He probably changed the lives of everyone he came into contact with.'

Malcolm's background, before he and Vivienne met, closely informed his personality and his work with her. At its simplest – as noted separately by Gordon, Vivienne and Joe – Malcolm was both deeply inspirational and deeply scarred. It was what made him fascinating, as well as dangerous. The Great Pretender, the mercurial fashion maverick and rock 'n' roll swindler, the Svengali behind Vivienne and The Sex Pistols, was a man at once exploding with self-confidence and deeply needy. It was part of what drove him in the first place, no doubt, this need to overcome the profoundest rejection by a constant dazzle: dazzling the media, dazzling his grandma, dazzling Vivienne. But his neediness inspired a vast jealousy of others' success, be they punk rockers, his own partner or his own son. It was a neediness that led to his hunger for Vivienne's constant affirmation of his talent, to the complete abnegation of her own. And it led too to their volcanic rows, as well as to the altercation that reduced one V&A curator to tears, and to his threat to sue his own son for copyright infringement or destroy the company and legacy of the woman with whom he changed fashion history. Vivienne, gracious to a fault in giving credit to collaborators, makes therefore this subtle revision of what has come before. There is no need, any longer, to cater to Malcolm's neediness, and a certain rewriting of the record on her own input is the just deserts of a woman, and a creative partnership, wronged. Yet if in researching this book I have felt a sense of his pugnacious ghostly

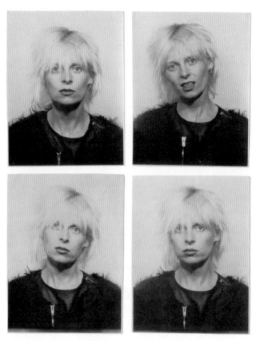

Vivienne with the style that became 'coup sauvage'.

presence, I have also gained an idea of what allowed him to inspire and manipulate, through the way people laugh and smile when they tell stories about him. 'Just being alongside him you would realize how "possible" the world is – and you'd be laughing, laughing all the time,' remembers Gordon. 'He was the funniest, wittiest, cleverest man I ever met. It's a funny thing when people hit the jackpot of success like Malcolm and Vivienne did, because, beforehand, it can look like a great big wall between your life and your dreams, and you look over the fence and think, "Oh my God: the difference" – it's like another world. But this was Malcolm's gift: he would take people into that world, because he had never really lived in reality himself. He showed Vivienne what was possible, and allowed her to dream. And no matter what happened later, that is the greatest gift you can give anybody.' It's a clear enough summation of Malcolm's singular talent and attractiveness, but what Gordon said next was almost as arresting: 'And you know what? Vivienne used to laugh. A lot. Especially early on, with Malcolm. She can be terribly serious these days. But I always remember her being very funny when we were kids. And Malcolm brought that out in her. For a while. She's got a very, very, very good laugh.'

'Malcolm's family were cosmopolitan Jews,' Vivienne explains, 'but I came from a cultural backwater. For Jewish people to leave home and community – like Malcolm did to go to art school – was shocking in its way. But I liked his ideas, and the journey of discovery he was on I wanted to join. It was about potential.'

Malcolm had a background in mad storytelling, a hazy relationship with the concept of truth, and a compelling urge to entertain a crowd. Most of this, it seems, was down to Rose. His wildly unconventional grandma, whose mottos included, 'To be good is bad,' and 'If you have enough neck, you can get away with anything,' always told her grandson never to have a fear of not working. Accordingly, she barely sent him to school at all. He is recorded as having attended William Patton School in Stoke Newington. He always claimed he went for one day only, but this was untrue. Rose's attention to her grandson's education, erratic at best, was punctuated by occasional bursts of forceful didacticism featuring *Jane Eyre* and a large dictionary, and, yet more bizarrely, the occasional appearance of Agatha Christie, a distant family friend. So perhaps it was to be expected that Malcolm would stray away from conventional education, and have a suspicion of those who had ploughed its furrows. He had a lifelong hatred of authority and managed to skid through education and past the bare minimum two O levels and thence to art college, and thus lived off the then mandatory art-school grants through all his early adulthood. This was one reason he and Vivienne never married: he would have lost his student grant if they had. And so, from the age of seventeen to twenty-five, Malcolm managed to play the system adroitly, bouncing between, variously, St Martin's, Croydon College of Art, Goldsmiths, South East Essex and Chiswick Polytechnics and, for a while, the lesser-known Harrow Art School. He was there more than a year after Vivienne had left – but exactly as her brother, Gordon, was accepted into Harrow's sixth-form college, with which it shared a canteen. Malcolm fitted in well there, certainly according to the slogan of its charismatic tutor Mr Fox: 'Better a flamboyant failure than a benign success.'

This, according to Gordon, is what happened: 'Vivienne met Malcolm through me. He was nineteen. I can remember the very first day I first saw him. The canteen in the technical college in Harrow. Vivienne was just splitting up with Derek. Ben was a baby. Our parents were living in Ruislip, their latest post office. I signed myself in to do A levels at the technical college – like a sixth-form college then – and it shared a canteen with Harrow Art School and that's where Malcolm "Edwards", as he was then, went. He was very striking-looking: red hair, white face. You couldn't miss him. He used to put talcum powder on his face to accentuate his paleness – which I thought was hilarious. No one else I knew did anything like that. He was this very, very funny guy and we became great friends, hanging out with a load of mods. I was seventeen. He influenced me quite a bit. And Malcolm was very inspiring, about how to go about living. Everything that Malcolm did was always couched with a political overtone. It was the sixties; it felt like the world was going up in smoke and there was the Vietnam war and the Troubles in Ireland and there was just an air of revolution. So there was all that with Malcolm, but mainly, at first, I just thought he was this very, very funny guy. And we used to go round to parties and stuff, arguing about politics and how the world should be. And soon I got involved in his art projects; they weren't called "happenings" in those days – they were "installations". I just knew nothing about all this stuff. So I thought it was really exciting. But what happened was this. Malcolm had this bedsit in Hendon that his granny had got him but a while after I met him he became homeless, because she'd not paid the rent. So he moved into my car, outside. He'd slept in it a bit before, after parties. He wasn't living in it for weeks. But long enough for Vivienne to notice. And that was when she first began to feel sorry for him, I guess. But what happened was I left home and ended up sharing a flat in Clapham, and Malcolm moves into the box room because it was cheaper than everyone else's room. So there's me, there's two or three slightly older American draft dodgers – mid twenties – and Malcolm. But then one of these draft dodgers left – he'd been caught dealing drugs. And I bumped into Vivienne at Mum's and said, "Look, there's this empty room." So she moved in.'

'*No way* was I attracted to Malcolm,' says Vivienne. 'Not to start with. Not at all. But I did like him. I wasn't sexually attracted: not at all. And I thought, anyway, he was much younger than me – which I suppose in those days I thought of as a bad thing! But I really did like him. Always. Right from the first. I thought of him as Gordon's friend, but then I moved into the flat where Gordon was installed and Malcolm was there and that's when I really got to know him. We'd spent time together before, when I was making jewellery, and I found I liked him very much. He had this crazy energy. He was very charismatic, extremely good company to be with, very lively. And a very good artist – he really could draw. The thing about Malcolm was, he made your world seem livelier, just by being Malcolm. And he told stories. Stories that he just made up. They weren't true. Well, maybe some were true . . .

'This is what he looked like when I met him: he had a big red hole in a white face; that was the impression of his mouth. And when he opened it he could be scary, but at the same time it gave me the feeling that he was fragile, vulnerable.

'Malcolm chased me. I didn't want him. I didn't want him for my boyfriend. I liked him tremendously – he was vital, shocking, informed and he was such fun to be with – and I felt sorry for him. He didn't look after himself. And I started trying to cook for him a bit and stuff like that. And, well, that's how it started. He wasn't well one time and he didn't have a bed. Malcolm's room was completely bare except for a mattress, I remember, and then I suppose he even used that for an art project. He slept on anything, because he'd used all our landlord's furniture and broke it all up to make art – sculpture-type things. So I made him sleep in my bed in the daytime to get over a fever, and he stayed in there for days and then he wouldn't get out. And that was how we ended up having sex. The point is, I didn't want Malcolm at first, but I did in fact end up getting pregnant by him. But even then I didn't really want him. But here's the thing: does this make sense? I felt, you see, that somehow I'd been so kind to him that maybe he'd got the wrong idea, and it was my fault, and that I'd somehow misled him, led him on without knowing. So I had to get involved with him. That's the truth of it. And then there was this other guy – nothing serious, just someone else I was set to go out with. And Malcolm called me a whore. And that's when I realized he was obsessed.

'But then he organized an event, a "happening" in a gallery in Kingly Street. He had a sort of try-out in his room one evening and when I came home from teaching with Ben, who was a toddler, Malcolm had this big cube of white balloons stuck together and a ten-foot mat of red ones. Ben was so happy – it was a wonderful sensation to pat the balloon shapes and keep them in the air. The next evening Malcolm had a six-foot-high roll of corrugated cardboard which he unwound a little to make a maze for my little boy to get lost in. He was magical like that, sometimes. And very talented. Well, next night at the gallery I went along to see this "installation" after school, and I entered the cardboard maze which was now completely unfurled, in the dark, filling the room; there was sound and flashing light and I really was trapped with lots of other people going round and round and never meeting. People tried to tear it down but it did no good; there was too much of it. We were scared but we finally got out. Malcolm's art was always alarming, but also, in a way, childlike. So in that way, too, as an artist, I found him very interesting. Very endearing.'

Malcolm, ungallantly, insisted that this was not the story at all. His spin on things, on how a twenty-year-old art-school slacker ended up having a child with an older schoolteacher, reeks of overstated machismo as much as a vague embarrassment that a radical artist should become a father at all. He claimed he was appalled when Vivienne moved into the shared boys' house with 'this little kid who I hated and loathed', but that because of her 'northern stubbornness' he couldn't persuade her to leave. 'After three or four weeks I decided to feign being sick,' he later alleged, in order to wheedle his way into her bed for reasons of idle 'curiosity at the thought of being inside a woman's bed . . . a schoolteacher . . . there was something harmlessly perverse about the whole notion.'

Malcolm lost his virginity to Vivienne, which was a fact it seemed to pain him to admit, perhaps for its mixture, in narrative terms, of gaucheness on the one side and conventionality on the other, in that it appeared to trap him into accidental fatherhood. It was a role he never embraced.

Ben, who remembers little of the earliest stages of the relationship, is sanguine about it all: 'Malcolm was a hyperactive kind of person and he was young. The way I've started thinking about it is that if I'd been a twenty-year-old starting out with a twenty-five-year-old woman who had a three-year-old child, and I'm kind of a virgin and it's all kind of sexy and you want to kind of do your sexy things – well, you don't want this kid around, do you? I can completely see that now, and that's how it was. But as a matter of fact, he was all right, Malcolm.'

Gordon was shocked. 'I suddenly realized that they were an item. It had simply never occurred to me to even *think* of them in those terms – my big sister and my mate. And lo and behold, they'd got together. And Malcolm hadn't had a girlfriend at all before then. So it was quite strange altogether. I mean, Malcolm was like a contemporary, a lad, my best friend; and to complicate things, I'd liked Derek and looked up to him, and felt for him. Look – it's like this and it's not an uncommon story: it was upsetting for me at the time, because it was like my sister and my best friend. And, for a while, I lost them both.'

If Gordon was rueful about it all and Ben, a mere three-year-old, was happily bouncing balloons with art students and hanging out with American draft dodgers, Rose Corré was pragmatic. When Malcolm told her that Vivienne was pregnant, Rose immediately offered to solve things by paying for an abortion: an option which was to be made legal only six months later.

'I was actually on my way to get an abortion. We were going to Harley Street with Rose's money. I changed my mind on the way. I hadn't been pregnant very long, and I looked at Malcolm and I suddenly realized. *What are you doing?* I thought. He's amazing. He's such a fantastic person. You'll never meet anybody like him. What are you doing? He's not your type or whatever, no, but he's . . . he's just fantastic. And I just completely changed. It was a very dramatic moment. I completely changed. I thought: you are CRAZY. Not to see that this man is wonderful.

'So here's what I did: we went to South Molton Street instead of Harley, and I bought a cashmere sweater and a matching piece of fabric made out of the same yarn, and I made a skirt. A little suit, really, in dirty turquoise with a matching dirty-turquoise tweedy little skirt that went with it. It was fantastic. I loved it. That's what I did. I kept Joe and I made the beautiful tweed suit and I just decided that Malcolm was great. Unfortunately, by that time, almost immediately, really, he had lost his amour for me, to some quite large extent. So we didn't start off very well, and apart from which, he then got alarmed at this idea of being sucked into being a family man. But nevertheless, he could be crazy – in a good way. He wanted me there all the time. I remember coming home one day. I'd gone to the doctor by myself, I can't remember why; I was pregnant. And I was late home because I was teaching. And I'd picked up Ben from the nursery and I was late home. Malcolm was in the middle of the road, walking up and down the white marks in the middle of the road, out of his mind wondering where I was. He thought I'd left him or something had happened to me because I was late. So, I don't know; it was full of contradictions from the start.

'But I tried to concentrate on the good sides. Malcolm was fascinating. He had so much information that I didn't have – even the fact that he knew London like the back of his hand. I knew I was provincial, without perspective, ill-equipped. I so much needed a way to gain

Vivienne and Malcolm in Let It Rock, 1971.

some insight, and through Malcolm I was able to look at society and politics and culture. He introduced me to the writings of John Berger, the Marxist art critic; of the anarchist Buenaventura Durruti, who, when he and his gang blew up a building, left the sign of a black hand and who said, "We are not afraid of ruins. We built the buildings. We can build them again." I don't believe any of this stuff any more. Malcolm was heavily influenced at that time by the work of the French Situationists, and, in a sense, to understand what we ended up doing with punk, you need to know about Situationism. But I'll tell you about that later. And he influenced the way I dressed and thought about clothes too. He began to spend most of his student grant on clothes for me. He cared passionately for clothes and he transformed me from a dolly bird into a chic, confident dresser. It wasn't for love of me. He loved clothes. I remember once he bought me an outfit, very naval, coarse navy-blue with white pleats. He was very clever like that. And John Lewis school department sold schoolgirl uniforms and he bought those for me – blue dresses, white collars and red tights. I wore them with rubberized cotton macs from Cordings of Piccadilly. After my previous Dolly Bird look, this Malcolm style got me a different sort of attention. And sometimes it was happy; I was happy that he was excited about his life and college, and I loved it if he came home with his friend Fred Vermorel, to stay the night. I'd sit up listening to them. Fred was half French, romantic, and their conversation was of artistic events and international politics. And I felt a long, long way from Tintwistle.

'Once I had made the commitment, in my mind, that we would be together, that was that so far as I was concerned. I was utterly committed and that's what mattered to me. It was like seeing him differently; willing him to be the best he could be. And he did know an awful lot more than me about everything and I began to think he was very brave. Now, I'm not so sure: I don't know whether he was that brave. He always sent me to do everything, when I think about it. He once wanted me to go to Madame Tussauds and set The Beatles alight in there – some "Situationist" stunt. A "statement". He wouldn't go himself. I wouldn't do it either, in the end, because I thought it was dangerous – but that's what he tried to get me to do. Just because he hated The Beatles. But on the other hand, he had ideas and he introduced me to all kinds of things I wouldn't have discovered otherwise: what was happening with the hippies, Compendium Books in Camden where he had discovered all these books and magazines on Situationism, and what was going on in Argentina – Pinochet, all of that; I wouldn't have known any of it. It's laughable now, but I was *so* impressed by his urban know-how and cosmopolitanism: I was thrilled to bits when we went to Chinatown to find decorations for our first flat together. And he got Chinese lanterns and then he went to the army surplus store and got the table that I still work at – it's just there, look – which was our table, and a cactus plant! Imagine! How artistic! But you see I had lived in outer London all those years and not even known that Chinatown existed, you see?

'But it was not a good start. Being pregnant never can be, I suppose. And I was so tired. Malcolm became more talkative the later the hour – and his favourite subject was himself. And long before we had sex or anything, when he'd been ill and was sleeping in my bed, he'd kept me awake every night, telling me his life story. And this carried on. And I was teaching the next day! I'd be exhausted. I couldn't concentrate. So it wasn't exactly a happy time, when we got together. I was really, really worn out, and Malcolm led his life at college, being an art student, and came home, not necessarily every night. And we discussed what to do, but the thing was that I was still married to Derek and so, Malcolm and I, had we wanted to live together properly, we would not have been able to get married. He was a college student on a grant and couldn't claim for me as a dependant. We couldn't claim dole, social security, because they said he would have to support me if he was the father, which would mean that he would have had to leave college and I couldn't have done that to him. So the only answer, it seemed to me, was for me to carry on teaching – right up to Joe's birth and then as soon again afterwards.

'So it's November 1967, I'm nearly a month overdue and I am going to be induced, and Malcolm knew I had gone into hospital. In those days one spent a week in hospital, and I didn't mind when all the husbands came to visit that my man didn't come, because he was special and not like other men. On the sixth day after Joe was born he came in.

Malcolm's table, in use today in Andreas's office . . . still with cacti.

I can see him now in his second-hand tweed coat with snowflakes melting on it. And the ward sister said, "Where have you been? Are you a long-distance lorry driver or what?" But I didn't mind: I was full of joy at having little Joe, and to me, Malcolm was like an angel, covered in snow. A few days later it was still snowing when I came out of hospital, and do you know what we did? This is typical of Malcolm: the first thing we did as new parents was to go to a Socialist Workers Party meeting to join some Trotskyist intrigue. It was all very cloak-and-dagger, up over a fire escape and across a snow-covered roof and in through a hatch. We didn't join the group. Malcolm thought the leader was too bossy! One thing he did do: he had found us a flat near the Oval. Beyond this he had no intention of getting trapped into family life. The big cactus he had bought which I so loved he started calling "Joe's dad", and when Joe was a babe he made a point of telling him it was his daddy. He refused, always, to be called "Dad".'

Joe was born on 30 November 1967 and given the names Joseph Ferdinand, after the Velázquez *Fernando de Valdés y Llanos* (King of Portugal) in the National Gallery, and the Portuguese surname Corré in honour of the great-grandmother who had sent money for his abortion. Vivienne accepted it all, and dedicated herself to putting her new little family into a routine that would allow all the men in her life – Joe, Ben and Malcolm – to prosper in their different ways. They moved into Aigburth Mansions, very near the Oval in Kennington, which made for an easy commute for Malcolm from Vauxhall to Croydon College of Art, and back into his newfound world of radical politics and Situationist art. While Vivienne struggled with the feeding demands of a voracious new baby, as well as a febrile four-year-old, and decorating their little flat with Chinese lanterns and cactuses, Malcolm began in earnest his long flirtation with radical politics and the allied shock tactics of the late-sixties student art scene.

'Thank goodness Ben and Joe were both very easy babies. I looked after all of them. All three. Little Joe, and Ben – and Malcolm, who was a student. I used to take Joe to nursery school. Ben had a place in the same school where I taught. And Malcolm didn't help at all. He wouldn't help. He refused, because he had said it was my decision to keep Joe. I said to him, "Malcolm, you've got to at least take Joe to nursery for me in the morning. It's too much for me to drop him off every day." I was late for work nearly every morning, being threatened with the sack, and Malcolm's still in bed. Do you know how long it takes a kid to feed and everything? Joe took so long, and you think, "Hurry up, Joe, *please*, will you?" I was feeding him with a bottle – I had to because I was taking him to the nursery. Poor Joe – I'd be cramming milk and food at him and running down such a long road to the nursery with his ever-heavier weight – we couldn't afford a pram – then back on the bus with Ben to my job. My life and the life of my children was very, very hard. Luckily they don't remember. And in the evenings, there'd be washing and sorting and cooking and cleaning, and I did a lot of school preparation in the evening. I was exhausted. And I'd ask Malcolm for help and Malcolm would look at me and he'd say, "You could give him to me" – meaning Joe – "but if you do, I'll take him straight to Dr Barnardo's." And I knew he would have – he really would have. So I couldn't ask him for help at all. I know people will think this is mad. But that's how it was. Malcolm was horrible at that time. And he reserved a special "horrible" for anybody who was a mother. He hated my relationship with my children, even with his own son, even Joe. He always pretended that he wasn't Joe's father at all. "No, your daddy's the milkman," or "Your daddy's the cactus in the corner," whatever. And so, unsurprisingly, my mother and he weren't at all able to get on and I therefore couldn't see my mother at that time of my life either. It became too difficult for me, because I was very loyal to Malcolm, for all kinds of reasons. I believed in him, absolutely, as an artist. And that he needed me. So I wouldn't see my mother. And meanwhile she was very good and she looked after Ben after school such a lot. She loved Ben. She probably loved Ben more than she had loved me and Olga and Gordon when we were little, because she felt that he was really neglected and that he needed her. And she was right. But it was this huge, frightening love for her, almost. She used to say that the room lit up for her when Ben came in. And when I had Joe, she said, "I'll never love Joe as much as Ben. I can't let myself." She said, "I'll never ever invest so much affection in anybody as I have done for Ben."

'So though it may seem that Malcolm was a bastard because he wouldn't help, that was the extent of his bad treatment – to begin with. My position was simple. It was about commitment. I loved him. I believed in him. I could learn from him. My children would benefit in the long run, and still, sometimes, he would organize very creative things for the boys to do. And I think it's because, simply, I valued so much what I could learn from Malcolm. I think what I want to say is this: I know people will think I was a doormat, because I put up with his cavalier attitude to me and the boys, but I knew at the same time how much he depended on me. I told myself so. He needed me. I needed him for what he knew, and he needed me because someone had to need him – and I could talk to him and I could develop by talking to him. Ideas are more important than everything, don't you see? So I stayed with him. I would stand for anything in Malcolm. Because I'd committed myself to him.'

The founding document in terms of what later became punk could well be said to be Guy Debord's *La Société du Spectacle*. It was an enormously influential text for art students of the time. Debord was the original theorist in what became known as the Situationist International, founded as early as the late 1950s, but finding voice and agenda by the late sixties all over Europe and in parts of American campus life. It was part of what gave voice and theory, ultimately, to the *événements de mai* in Paris a few months after Joe's birth. Not since the revolutions of the 1840s had students and artists felt their power to rock governments and fan the flames of change. The Situationists declared that artists and thinkers were morally obliged to break down the definitions between art and 'real life' in order to evade the commercialization of the former. In other words, artists and activists were emboldened to deliberately flummox their viewers and audiences, and act, ideally, as agents provocateurs in creating ridiculous, potentially risky 'happenings' as an absurdist comment on the status quo. Art, as well as protest, was to be on the streets and know no barriers. Taste and structure went out of the window, along with accepted media or the strictures of gallery or press or academy. One descendant of Situationism is immediately recognizable now in the joyous absurdity of flash-mobbing, arranged through fast new social networks. In the late sixties, things were a little more difficult to set up. Malcolm

Vivienne and Let It Rock, 1971.

became fascinated with a fusion of surrealism, Dadaism and the drug-fringed pleasure-seeking of the times, in Situationist 'happenings' that defied categorization as protest, art or street theatre. For instance, he hit upon the idea of dressing up as Father Christmas along with Fred Vermorel and other art students, storming the toy department of Harrods the month after Joe was born, and giving away all the toys. Few young fathers have dreamed up quite so anarchic a comment on the commercialization of childhood. It took the security guards half an hour to break up the happy melee. Christmas came early for a few fortunate shoppers, if not for Joe, and Malcolm inhaled for the first time the head-lightening oxygen of media exposure, controversy and art-world infamy.

As Vivienne struggled with life at Aigburth Mansions, Malcolm, by virtue of his hair as well as his politics, became known as Red Malcolm and attracted a crowd of like-minded politico-artists. Jamie Reid, the graphic artist behind much punk iconography, and Fred Vermorel, Robin Scott and later Helen Mininberg, were at the time devotedly radicalized and insistent that their agenda should be revolutionary in its scope and ambitions. While Reid founded a community press in Croydon, Vermorel went to Paris and encouraged Malcolm to follow him, despite or because of Vivienne and little Joe. Though Malcolm was unable or unwilling to head to Paris until after the tumultuous events of May 1968, he picked up via Fred a number of the slogans that would become iconic mantras of punk, on Vivienne-designed T-shirts, but which had first been seen splashed across the École des Beaux Arts on Paris's riot-pressed Left Bank: 'Be reasonable: Demand the impossible', 'Under the paving stones lies the beach', 'It is forbidden to forbid'.

It was a time of feverish excitement in politics as in the art world, and Malcolm was besotted with being part of it, with or without his partner and baby. 'I was excited by this idea of taking culture to the streets and changing the whole way of life, using culture as a means of making trouble, really,' he said. It was a mantra that Vivienne took up and which has its echo still in a lot of what she does and proclaims: make people think and change the world by making art publicly. In her case, her 'Situationist' art became clothes.

Much of this has become mainstream as an idea, an inherent part of what contemporary art has come to mean, long before the shock tactics of Damien Hirst or Vivienne's friend Tracey Emin. Definitions of art have shifted, for good or ill, and ideas and protest are expressed in as many media as invention will allow. And though Malcolm and the whole pretentious, hedonistic world of late-sixties student politics has become the stuff of easy ridicule, the legacy of the Situationists, via Malcolm and Vivienne and punk, is difficult to overestimate. It brought street fashion into high fashion. It allowed many forms of expression and protest to be discussed as art, and it helped fuse the already related worlds of pop music, art, graphic design and fashion into one insistent roar of defiance called punk.

This period coincided with a violent moment in Western arts and politics, the build-up to 1968 when 'anarchy, agitprop and radicalism were heard continually . . . and . . . a violent revolution in Europe seemed not only possible, but . . . likely'. This restive atmosphere also saw a revolution in graphic design that would have huge impact on Vivienne's later work. How much she was able to take it in at the time she is unclear about; her memories are of quotidian worries over rent and baby-feeding. All of which afforded Malcolm the time to pick up on the zeitgeist and collect political 'comix' and porn from Compendium Books in Camden, or create posters in emulation of what was being done in Paris and for that matter in San Francisco. All of this would in time inform Vivienne and Malcolm's work in fashion, graphics, music and marketing.

But while Malcolm was contemplating revolution, and briefly heading over to Paris (he later greatly exaggerated his involvement, even down to fictionalizing an account of having met Guy Debord), Vivienne taught.

Vivienne and Malcolm and the two boys did not play house for long. Vivienne, exhausted and overstretched, reverted at school to the title 'Miss' but kept 'Westwood'. Malcolm kept house, poorly, between his commitments to art, politics and Situationism. Miss Westwood is remembered as a wonderful, if unconventional, teacher – one described by a colleague as 'potentially the greatest primary-school teacher' they had ever known. 'I wasn't,' protests Vivienne, 'here's how it was: I was supply teaching down the Old Kent Road, one time, in Brixton, in Streatham – up to eighty kids. I liked them and they liked me. But not a lot got learned. I remember sometimes there were children dancing on the tables. There was little Tony Hogan, Irish, and more trouble than anyone. Mainly they were Jamaican kids. I was very political, so I didn't discipline the children and thought the naughty ones were right. There was Leroy, I remember, who sat there chanting "ya bitch ya bitch ya bitch", but he got all his sums rights. I loved him. And when I took them out into the countryside, he was terrified. He'd never seen long grass.' In those happy days before the imposition of a National Curriculum, Health and Safety or Child Protection measures, primary-school teachers had enormous creative leeway in what they taught, what they did and where. Vivienne took a class of eight-year-olds to see the silent Russian classic *Battleship Potemkin*, frequently marched them out to the nearest parkland hedgerows to forage and learn about nature, and even managed to inveigle McLaren into taking them all out on a bus into the countryside proper. While McLaren stuck to his teen-age Stoke Newington diet of chips and roll-ups, Vivienne increasingly turned to vegetarianism as a life-choice and economy drive. She even sent McLaren and the little boys out foraging for dandelions to make 'coffee' in the manner she had known during the war. By the middle of 1968, however, the pressures on her as a working mother were straining things to breaking point:

'Here's how I ended up living in a caravan. In 1968, Joe and Ben spent a month with their grandma. When Malcolm and I got back from a summer in France, camping on the beach, Joe didn't recognize me. I had to go straight to work for the start of term. He went into a nursery. Two weeks in, I go to collect him and he is catatonic. He had shut down emotionally, completely. It was hours later that Malcolm managed to get him to smile. And I collapsed onto my knees and gave thanks to God but the next day I went into work and handed in my notice and said I was leaving instantly to look after my children. So we had no money. No income. We couldn't afford Aigburth Mansions. I tried living with Dora, but our parenting was very different. She wanted to smack Joe if he broke things – and she had lots of little knick-knacks at his height she wouldn't pack away. So we rowed. And it was Dad who suggested that we live in the shed – which turned into the idea of living in their caravan, up in Prestatyn.'

Vivienne must surely be one of the very few people in the couture and fashion business who has known true poverty. Her family were consistently supportive, and not without small means, but Vivienne insisted she should stand alone with her little boys and with the choices she had made, and that meant, in the short term, accepting the offer of the tiny caravan in windswept Prestatyn. She took Ben out of school completely, and determined to live on family allowance ('six pounds a week, plus foraging in markets'), on her wits and on her own with her little boys. It is a salient character point, and perhaps a key to her later fearlessness and lack of concern for critical or commercial success, that Vivienne took off and found self-sufficiency – and some creative positivity – out of dramatically straitened circumstances: 'I can only do my best,' as she says. 'Sometimes that is really all you can say or do . . . I remember Joe learned to walk by holding on to the sides of that caravan . . .'

The park, at Tan y Rogo farm near Prestatyn overlooking the Dee Estuary, was bleak. Ben remembers the caravan as seeming tiny, even to a seven-year-old boy, without running water or separate bedrooms. But to him it became as magical as any gypsy wagon, an adventure written and set-dressed by his mother. As a registered teacher, Vivienne could legally keep Ben out of school, so they lived together, the three of them, with Vivienne taking Joe and Ben on impromptu nature walks and rambles into the fields and foraging for wild fruits and vegetables. 'I remember when it was my birthday, my grandma, Dora, sent a cake,' recalls Ben. 'It was the most exciting thing ever. Mum ate most of it. But I didn't mind. I'd have to say, she never made me feel it was a struggle. I just always knew: life with Mum was so interesting.' Although life was fraught financially, and it was unclear how long the arrangement could possibly last, Vivienne was relieved to have the countryside around her and some time, again, to think. She read Hardy novels and knitted, she spent more time with her sons than any career or regular life might afford, and, on two occasions, she welcomed Malcolm up to North Wales to visit and to talk about the future.

Let It Rock clothes and styling, 1973 rock 'n' roll revival.

While Vivienne was struggling as a single mother in a caravan park, Malcolm, unbeknown to her at the time, had married. It was a visa scam, he later explained, arranged for a fellow student who wanted to remain in the UK and who paid him the unprincely sum – even then – of £30 that he needed for his student film *Oxford Street*. 'I wasn't bothered,' says Vivienne, 'we both disregarded convention and I am not sure I even believed him.' It seems likely that his ulterior motive was to prove to Vivienne again his mixed feelings about family life, and even when, later that year, he and Vivienne got back together, he told friends that he was only doing so for Joe's sake, 'so he wouldn't be brought up in a narrow, working-class way, as Vivienne had been'.

Vivienne accepted Malcolm's invitation back to London, first to a bedsit in Cavendish Road, Clapham, and then to an art deco flat that he had secured, near Rose's, in Clapham South. Vivienne, Joe, Ben and Malcolm all moved into 10 Thurleigh Court, Nightingale Lane, in the early spring of 1969. It would remain her home until relatively recently and it is still kept in her name and as she and Malcolm decorated it. The ménage at Nightingale Lane was brokered gradually by Vivienne, trading conventional partnership for the things she felt she could learn from Malcolm. 'It was actually quite happy for a while,' she says, and Vivienne returned to teaching, supporting the £3 10s. a week rent on the two-bedroom flat. It was, and remains, cramped, and despite his radical politics Malcolm soon raised the prospect of both boys being sent off to boarding school. With one failed marriage behind her and an instinctive and decisive loyalty, Vivienne willed herself to make it work, and in a sense it could. There were relatives on both sides able to pitch in from time to time – Rose was round the corner and Dora and Gordon had the boys every summer from their earliest days. In the tiny green-tiled deco kitchenette, Vivienne perfected her skills at her macrobiotic and vegan cuisine – disdained by her boys almost ever since. And Malcolm came and went. Joe, their son, now a major player in the fashion world himself, explains, 'Over the years Malcolm tried to excuse himself for the dad he'd been, and to explain those years. And I don't think he ever really managed to do that properly to me. But I think he went through lots of different realizations about what he thought he was trying to be, which I didn't fit into, and nor did

Mum always, and I think most of it was tied up with his own child-hood. I do see that now. I think he was always trying to come to terms with his own messed-up childhood. He'd fuck off a lot, and eventually he never came back.'

Perhaps the most emotionally destructive issue was precisely Malcolm's commitment to bigger ideals, as he saw them, than par-enting or partnering. Vivienne granted him complete freedom, and gave him a constancy in love and faith that ultimately replaced his codependent bond with his grandmother. But it came at a cost that is obvious still in Ben and Joe's equivocal attitude to their father / step-father. And it came at a cost to Vivienne too, who accepted, as she repeatedly has, a conditional love, based often around shared interests and creativity, and also on her detached ability to give love in the expectation of little return.

If Malcolm was fickle in his attentions to domestic life at Thurleigh Court, he was also a restive presence. 'Malcolm *had* to row,' says Vivienne, 'he tried to give the impression that he hated you. He tried to wound me.' Things were complicated too by Malcolm's art-school friends who lived intermittently at Thurleigh Court as well: Robin Scott, Jamie Reid and Fred Vermorel. Ben, a gentle and shy boy, unlike his ebullient younger brother, recalls the fiery rows: 'I used to be quite scared of Malcolm, certainly. He had a temper, so you used to be care-ful. He hit me a couple of times. Mum looked after herself, mainly, not always. He'd just snap, was the thing with Malcolm. So I do remember that I wasn't at all worried about the idea that Malcolm might one day not be in my life. If my mum had split up with him at any point it would've been all right with me.

'Me and Joe used to hear the rows, up and down the corridor at Thurleigh Court, outside our bedroom. We'd go to sleep, Joe and me, but then quite a few times we'd wake up at eleven o'clock and hear some music going on and I used to be able to hear what they were say-ing as well. I remember them having an argument one night and Mum saying, "I'm going. I'm leaving." And I heard her going towards the front door. I mean, if she'd actually gone out the front door I think I would've jumped out of bed to go with her. But I heard Malcolm suddenly calm down and go, "Don't leave me. Don't leave me,

Vivienne." And then there was a pause and then I heard him say, "I need you. I need you." So, again, she stayed.'

'I would never have left without the boys,' says Vivienne, 'never.'

Warring couples often find some safe terrain where they can coexist – some spark of the sex or romance that first brought them together, some shared interest that is without dispute or holds the prospect of ongoing creativity. For Vivienne and Malcolm, as a contrast to the rows or as respite, there were clothes. On clothes and fashion, they found a safe island of creative complicity. On Saturdays, often without the boys, they walked the King's Road, in and out of the new boutiques that were beginning to drag London's fashionable centre of gravity westwards. 'Mainly I loved Mr Freedom, their velvet things. Malcolm would be wearing a knitted tie and check Viyella shirt and corduroy trousers – looking like a smart art student. And I remember I was into a navy look, with pearls.' Vivienne began to experiment, with Malcolm's encouragement. She cut and bleached her hair, and, in contrast to the flouncy blow-dried look of the times, found that it held its shape. It may have been her first gift to an emerging youth cult, in that David Bowie copied this look. 'I'm sure [he] got it from Vivienne,' opines style guru Simon Barker. 'She had that look a full year before *Ziggy Stardust* . . . "coup sauvage", the hairdressers ended up calling it.'

They already made an arresting couple on the rare occasions they were out and about together along Nightingale Lane – Red Malcolm and the Brixton primary-school teacher with the radical dress sense and savage hair. 'Everyone knew them – you couldn't not,' recalls local resident and ex-con Louie McManus. 'She looked amazing.'

'You have to remember,' Gene Krell tells me, 'Vivienne was, is, just dazzling. But then: her attitude, her body language, her look – it took your breath away.' With her domestic world falling apart around her over and over again, Vivienne was learning an important lesson – one not lost on Gene Krell, who lived with her slightly later, or indeed on Malcolm, who had taught her some of the trick: clothes can give you confidence. In contrast to the shifting currents of her personal life, Vivienne found strength in dressing fearlessly.

'If you wear great clothes, you have a better life,' Vivienne is often quoted as saying, but there may be clues here too to Vivienne's ongoing quest. We can be as much a hostage to our future as to our past: artists often strive towards an ideal 'best self', or as Vivienne has it 'a better world', as a way to ignore the compromises of the present. Perhaps a love affair could never live up to the exacting potential of what Vivienne could create and what she could imagine for the world. She projected her positivity, her creativity and her love into fashion. Analysts are often keen to point out that the past can be a weight dragged into the present. It is something biographers think about a lot. But the future is alive and weighty in the present too, especially for Vivienne; just as positive and just as damaging. I think the future seems always to have been more alive to Vivienne than the present, which is a gift to her as artist and campaigner, though a curse of sorts personally. The future is something she is creating, that in turn created her. The future was and is a fantastical place that shapes her every day. And it was her escape and solution, the blessing and curse of life with Malcolm. As the sixties turned into the seventies, and as her relationship with Malcolm tottered from one crisis to the next in rhythm with the flailing British economy, Vivienne returned to the idea of a market stall. Whereas she had previously manned a stall on her own, selling jewellery, now she and Malcolm hit on the idea of selling vintage records together.

'That's all it was, to begin with,' recalls Vivienne. 'We had got into the clothes – fifties things that we got from Brixton Market, but you could see there was this second wave of Teds who'd hang around the Black Raven pub in Bishopsgate. Malcolm started collecting old rock 'n' roll records, some memorabilia as well, and we could see there would be a market for it all. Patrick Casey, this James Dean lookalike, wore all this fifties stuff. There was a place called the Emperor of Wyoming, I remember. It was just all coming together. But all we were looking to do was have a market stall and sell records – and at that time, I actually wanted to go back to university.' Instead, Vivienne took one of those leaps in the dark that has characterized her life. It was her most decisive one. She handed in her notice at the last of her primary-school placements, Santley Street Primary in Brixton, at the same time that Malcolm finally left art school, and with some of the money from her final wage packet she bought a Singer sewing machine.

SEX AT THE
WORLD'S END

Invention does not consist in creating out of a void, but out of chaos.
MARY SHELLEY,
Introduction to *Frankenstein*, 1831

*There was no punk before me and Malcolm. And the other thing you
should know about punk too: it was a **total blast**.*
VIVIENNE WESTWOOD

'Punk' – Vivienne spits out the word with the added weight her accent
gives the vowel – 'punk was everything to me and Malcolm. I don't
speak about it now as much as people seem to think I should, but it's
not because I'm ashamed or think it's passé or anything. I am more
interested in what I am doing now, but what I need to explain is this:
what I am doing now, it still is punk – it's still about shouting about
injustice and making people think, even if it's uncomfortable. I'll
always be a punk in that sense. Punk, for me and Malcolm and at the
shop, became a sort of bricolage: collecting ideas. Collecting people . . .'

She sighs, and adjusts her 'Chaos' headband. She takes a deep breath
and a sip of herbal tea and allows sagely, 'There are things you can never
escape from your past. I tried to run away from it all after Malcolm,
but I am now proud of my role as a punk, because I think it contributed
to the stance many young people take to this day: Don't Trust Government. Ever. Climate Revolution is punk. And what I did at the
Paralympics was totally punk. Punk lives! Same attitude, but with
ideas more developed, more solid, and hopefully more earth-changing
than we managed first time round.'

Malcolm hit upon the idea of selling rock 'n' roll stuff – 'It was all about records, to begin with,' says Vivienne. 'There was Harold the Ted who worked at Mr Freedom on the King's Road, he was part of the second-wave Ted thing. This would be the autumn of 1970, and Malcolm was sourcing records through *Exchange & Mart*: Larry Williams, that sort of thing, and that's how it began.' Hip Londoners, disillusioned by the failed optimism of sixties hippydom ('hippos', Malcolm called them), were turning to retro-chic in the first of rock 'n' roll's many revivals. According to Malcolm, it was all planned to be less a market stall than an art installation, making small statements about the capitalist system by selling 'retro-tat', playing music and indeed refusing to sell key items of stock. There were to be no premises and no agenda, and there was very little money. But some synchronicity between Vivienne, Malcolm, music and mayhem was born.

'It wasn't about clothes at first. Malcolm was very influenced by Patrick Casey and he started buying up EPs and 78s. He got the idea that we could collect records and sell them but we met these second-wave rockers like Tommy Roberts, of Mr Freedom, and he suggested we look for a stall out west – maybe Portobello again. I had been a regular customer there, but it wasn't about clothes. I loved what I bought there. I felt like a space princess, in velvet leopard trousers and troubadour shirts, with hearts and spades on, I remember, or long T-shirt dresses with stars on and a Woolworths' headscarf in glittery lurex, and purple lipstick! So I say it wasn't about clothes, but of course I was interested. The clothes sequence was simple, really. First Malcolm bought some Teddy Boy jackets from Sid Green the tailor, and I customized them with different-coloured velvet collars, that sort of thing. Then Patrick Casey sourced some vintage zipper jacket with bat wings and a stripe, and I made a copy. And then I made some stripy T-shirts for women. But that was all slightly later, once we had more than a stall . . .

'I think I'd say it started properly in 1971. Clothes and me. There was an event at Wembley Stadium: rock 'n' roll. They invited Chuck Berry, and Little Richard and Gary Glitter were all going to play, and there were all these Teds, this second wave of Teds. Now, they didn't like Gary Glitter, the Teds, and it all went haywire: they were all throwing beer cans at him and stuff. We had invested in these T-shirts. But they didn't sell. It was a disaster. And because they didn't sell, we started experimenting with them. Putting holes in them, remaking them. First thing we did, I made some into knickers. We didn't sell many of them so we put little studs on them. Then they sold. The knickers were mostly black with a white image and it would say, "Let It Rock", and have a picture of Little Richard, either on the front of the knicker or the back of it. And in some of the white ones we ended up making holes in them. Next with the T-shirts I tried sewing the sleeves so they were rolled up, and that started a bit of a copying craze for T-shirts with a kind of capped, rolled sleeve. A bit fiddly. But that was me. Then next we took all these pin-up girls, photos of them, and that became part of the T-shirt too. Very fifties. These Raquel Welch-looking girls. They were always posed looking sort of shipwrecked or stranded on a beach or, frankly, violated in some way or other. And we added these pin-up girls – like cigarette cards, you know, that they had in those days – and they went in a little plastic pocket on the T-shirt. So we started to put holes in the T-shirts and bought some plastic, sometimes coloured plastic, and made these little pockets on the T-shirts and cut things out of books – mainly pin-ups – and stuck them in there. I did that. Then I was supposed to put these Situationist slogans on the T-shirts. I thought they were really good at the time – I remember one was, "Under the paving stones lies the beach", which is a good line, and that would be written on top of one these pin-up women with her breasts and pout and then we'd put holes in the T-shirt and machine the holes back down with coloured threads or turn up the sleeves and made them all look tight and little, which was very typical of the fifties things that I got made.

'So it was part Teddy Girl, part beginnings of punk. I was doing these things, and of course I was wearing them – like these little blouses that buttoned up the front with a little scooped-out neck and no sleeves. But there again, you see, things were on the turn and we had to rethink and remake. People didn't like stuff that was too fifties and they were beginning to be into more seventies stuff – or at least a new slant on what we had done, so I remember that we cut up these tight little blouses and made them all look like the fifties pin-up girls – which is to say fifties, but on a desert island or something. Ravished. We did that. I remember sticking bottle tops on the T-shirts, the ones that you could get in those days with a little crinkly edge. And eventually we realized we could make stuff covered in these bottle tops. And then finally we ended up burning holes with cigarettes in the shirts, and cutting holes in them. And you wore a pair of these three-quarter-length little pedal pusher trousers with them, so you looked, you know, like a little beachcomber woman – on a desert island.

'And on from that came some of my earliest bras in the street! I've never been to Puerto Rico. I don't really know anything about Puerto Rico. But somewhere I'd seen Puerto Ricans wearing their bras in the street and people who dressed in a little pair of shorts with a bra, and then just went to the shop with Coca-Cola cans instead of rollers in their hair. So it became a look not only of a beachcomber or somebody who'd been raped or whatever, it was also a feeling of the poor. But more than that, it reminded me too of when I'd been fifteen: I had a friend who was twenty-four, Marjorie Naylor, a weaver in the cotton mill, and she used to go with her curlers in and keep them in all day, and then, when she went out in the evening, if she went out, only then would she take the curlers out. So the ingredients of punk are various. The idea of people wearing clothes that were a bit too big or a bit too small – like hand-me-downs and everything. That was all part of a look. And distressed clothes. And people who've had a harder life and more dramatic experience than we have. I analyse it in this way: the poor have status, the status of having more experience, and therefore a patina of prestige attaches to their clothes. They were heroic. It's all about stories.'

The early years of Vivienne and Malcolm's partnership were remarkably fecund, creatively. These were the years that gave rise to a new language in clothes that eventually transcended punk: torn and ripped T-shirts and old jeans, 'retro' sampling and mixing of styles, slogans, appliqués and 'bricolage' (things stuck on to clothes in a manner copied from contemporary art) – ideas that would have been unimaginable in previous eras of fashion. Perhaps it is fitting, therefore, that one of the most interesting commentators on it all is the other product of that fecund partnership: Vivienne and Malcolm's son, Joe. Joe Corré has

430 King's Road, World's End, 1974.

gone on to enormous success in the fashion world himself with Agent Provocateur, the high-end lingerie business wittily named in honour of one of his father's favourite Situationist terms. Joe combines wry humour and warm bonhomie with a certain guarded bullishness, and has grown now, via years modelling on his mother's catwalks, into a bloke you wouldn't want to mess with. His summation of the situation is accompanied with a typical smirk: 'People think I'm scary but I'm not: I make frilly knickers for a living and my mum still dresses me! Their victory, Mum and Malcolm, was that they found each other. No matter what happened later, you have to give it to them; they changed everything and it's difficult to say who inspired who. Malcolm was brilliant at the manipulation of the media and the whole Situationist teaching that allowed him to be this kind of anti-manager with Mum, and do everything in a counter-intuitive way. Malcolm was always interested in those ideas from modern art – more interested than Vivienne ever was. Vivienne was more interested in technique, and really knowing how to make something. So here's the fusion: Malcolm had ideas for statements like "No Future" and "Cash From Chaos", but the thing that made it all work is Vivienne's technique and in making that idea work, graphically, *and* on something that you want to wear, something for the body. But when people say Malcolm was the "ideas" man and Vivienne just sewed it up, it's just not true. Ideas are nothing if they aren't expressed. And I think her ideas and the way that she made them work made the whole thing happen. On some level Malcolm recognized that completely, was scared by it, and didn't like to admit it. I think he absolutely realized it when he left Mum and found out that there wasn't anybody else that he could find in his life that he could have such a collaboration with. Only Vivienne could manifest his ideas into something. He never found anyone else after that. And I think that's the truth, and his tragedy.'

In October 1971, as punk legend has it, Malcolm wore a baby-blue suit down the King's Road. It was modelled closely on the one worn by Elvis Presley on the cover of the 1959 album *50 Million Elvis Fans Can't Be Wrong*. In it, Malcolm, accompanied by Vivienne, had walked the King's Road looking for fashion inspiration. The World's End, named after the pub on the kink in the road as it veered towards what Dickens describes as the 'barbarism of Chelsea', was and is a bus destination known to most west Londoners. But it was also a joke and a metaphor. It was about as far as fashion and shopping extended along from Sloane Square and was just on the fringes, in the late 1960s, of profitable retail. In Evelyn Waugh's memorable phrase from his review of the 1937 novel *World's End* in *Night and Day* magazine, World's End was populated by people 'economically, politically, socially and theologically, in a mess'. So perhaps it was the perfect place for Vivienne and Malcolm to be. The mess, however, had got a lot hipper in the years immediately before they arrived.

Mary Quant is often credited with 'discovering' the King's Road, or rather with exploiting its potential as a shopping street. She opened her first shop there as early as 1955. It was far flung from the traditional shopping nexuses of the West End – Knightsbridge or Bond Street. But it became the focus of a new form of shopping, born of the late 1950s and the newfound affluence and sartorial adventurousness of the British. And this new form of shopping was based around 'the boutique'. Over the course of the decade that would bring Vivienne and Malcolm onto the King's Road, boutiques – expressing different styles of cool – took over from the grocers and ironmongers that had once served the local community. Granny Takes a Trip had 'an American car that appeared as if it had crashed right through [the] window', recalled McLaren, Tommy Roberts' Mr Freedom had a window display 'which at one time sported a giant gorilla covered in bright-blue fake fur', and John Lloyd's Alkasura was presided over by its owner dressed as a monk. Trevor Myles, whose Paradise Garage was at 430 King's Road, 'was noted for selling the first used blue jeans'. 'I didn't like jeans in those days, or distressed anything,' says Vivienne. 'My favourite dress was a Mr Freedom ziggurat dress, in red and blue. All that comic-book futurism: I loved that.' 'All of these stores,' Malcolm wrote, 'were the street's visual answer to an authentic musical pop culture' of the era: the King's Road was where music and fashion met.

Number 430 stood beyond the initial florescence of boutique culture down the King's Road. For one thing, it was just beyond sight of the main kink in the road. For another, it lay in a small parade of functioning shops and next door to an unprepossessing Conservative Party club. 430 had been a pawnbroker's, and a grocer's. Its roof sagging, it had had an iron support inserted at the shop level. To this day the shop is ill-lit by the small front window and would hardly be credited as the likely epicentre of a global fashion revolution. It was part of the local economy of small businesses and cheap rentals all the way to 1967.

The first fashion outlet that had opened at number 430 went under the banner 'Hung on You'. It crashed financially through the course of 1968: the result, it was said, of the unwillingness of its posh owners' friends to traipse quite so far down the King's Road, and of the owners' overspend on the promotional materials. In any event, the lease was taken over in 1969 by Tommy Roberts of Mr Freedom, which in turn was the beginning of 430's relationship with Vivienne.

Tommy Roberts' Mr Freedom fashion empire extended by the end of the 1960s all the way from Carnaby Street to Kensington Church Street. Along with Trevor Myles, Roberts had supplied kaftans for Hung on You and waistcoats for another of Roberts' boutiques, Kleptomania. His clients, who would migrate to Vivienne in time, included Jagger, Sammy Davis Jr and Twiggy, amongst many others, and his style, which greatly informed some of Vivienne and McLaren's later designs, was often known as comic-strip-Hollywood-vulgar. It sampled, without historical exactitude, garish fashions that had largely penetrated British consciousness through technicolor films – and the look of the boutique matched the clothes: deco, diners, ice-cream sundaes – the clothes and styles of fifties B-movies. 'Trevor Myles was really, really clever,' says Vivienne, 'completely ahead of the game. Trevor ended up taking over the Mr Freedom that had been at 430 and turning it into Paradise Garage. I never thought at that time that it would end up mine.'

With Hung on You and then Mr Freedom and Paradise Garage at 430, the building was well on its way to becoming a London landmark for those who cared about clothes. By the time Vivienne was there, people already had expectations of, for instance, imported distressed jeans and leather, studs and biker-wear, Disney pastiche and rockabilly American. There were other expectations of the address too: 'It opened at maybe one o'clock. A couple of people would put on music and [someone] got a cup of tea. Models maybe would come for a photo shoot – Justin de Villeneuve or Twiggy: the King's Road was like a film set then, a kid's dream. It was where it was all happening. There'd be people looking out for the pop stars who came by: Jagger and Bianca, and Keith Richards and Peter Sellers, Rod Stewart, Freddie Mercury, Marianne Faithfull, Jerry Hall, Lulu, Britt Ekland, Elton John.' Everyone knew the address. It had a pretty druggy reputation – shop assistants would pose in the window smoking joints – and a louche and cliquey air, fuelled by its clientele: Mick Jagger, Ossie Clark and Pink Floyd founder Syd Barrett. It had also begun a long association with shop assistants boasting serious attitude. Jay and Bo, who worked there in the days of Hung on You, and came back after Malcolm and Vivienne took over, had been known to shout out at potential customers 'Are you cool?' to which the best riposte in foggy London was, 'Actually, we're fucking freezing'. So they let them in.

Roberts had taken over the lease on 430 King's Road in 1969, but, despite its attractions for the fashion cognoscenti, it also failed to thrive under his control. This was partly because his interest was shifting towards music – he went on to manage Ian Dury in the Kilburn and the High Roads days – and he handed over control of the World's End shop to Trevor Myles. Myles changed its name to Paradise Garage and also struggled. 'It was very good, the Paradise Garage,' says Roberts. 'American clothing and old jeans, but Trevor was too fickle-and-muckin'-about – but the rent was still for me to pay, so he rented out the back of his shop, when he could.' 'Malcolm and I knew Tommy Roberts well by then,' Vivienne says. 'I could always tell when Malcolm had been hanging out with Tommy because he'd come back talking like him, ending every sentence with '"n-that-'n-that"'. What happened, just in time for Vivienne and Malcolm to invade as squatters at 430 King's Road in 1971, was this. Trevor Myles fell in love with a Swedish model, 'as you do, or certainly as you did then', married her and headed off to Jamaica with (unbeknownst to him) a stolen credit card and another 'very wealthy girl who had just split from her man'. As you do – as you did then. By the time the tripped-out threesome returned, Myles found that Malcolm McLaren, his art-school chum Patrick Casey and

Vivienne had moved in. As Malcolm later told it to *Swindle* magazine, 'some American guy [had seen me] and invited me into 430 King's Road.' 'Where are you going, man, I dig the drainpipes,' were apparently the opening words of the American, one Bradley Mendelssohn. He had popped out of the shop for a fag. Subsequent to this unorthodox commercial takeover, number 430 has remained the retail home of Vivienne Westwood ever since.

In truth, McLaren knew exactly what he was doing: he knew the premises already as he and Vivienne were habitués of the King's Road, and as he had shot some of his student film *Oxford Street* at Mr Freedom. Myles was keen to sublet the back of the shop to help bring in the rental money he owed in turn to Tommy Roberts, and this Malcolm readily if disingenuously claimed he could pay.

'Malcolm and I searched markets for old rock 'n' roll records which we bought for a shilling [5p]. His idea was that we would be able to sell these in the back of 430 to trendy people who shopped there. "Let It Rock" initially was all these second-hand clothes and bits and pieces you could find in those days, left over from the fifties; fluorescent cardigans from Brixton Market and a market in Wales, I remember, rock 'n' roll things and suburban fifties things. Charles Saatchi and Paul Getty – the young one who'd been kidnapped – were among our first customers. And I was going to help him make fifties clothes. We wanted action; we searched for motifs of rebellion and focused on rock 'n' roll . . . but everything we did we were designing together.'

Malcolm and Vivienne set up in the back of the shop, a shop less and less frequented by Myles. Their success there was almost instant. McLaren felt able to import more and more fifties ephemera: magazines and postcards, furniture even, that lent authenticity to their recreations of fifties clothes. Patrick Casey, a speed freak, was less and less of a presence too, and eventually Vivienne and Malcolm were told they 'could have [the keys] . . . Tommy didn't have any financial interest there any more,' says Myles, Vivienne and Malcolm 'paid [Tommy] a few quid to take it over. But whatever the series of events, I just walked away.' Vivienne, with shopkeeping in her blood, was determined to fare better and was diligent in the early years about paying rent and suppliers on time. Along with her business partner,

Vivienne in Let It Rock, 1971.

Malcolm Edwards, now obliged to revive his long-neglected legal surname, McLaren, in order to sign a lease, Vivienne took over 430 King's Road. Malcolm reconditioned Myles's old jukebox and stocked it with his records, so that he could blast out Eddie Cochran hits and put off any passing hippies. Paradise Garage, with its vaguely South Pacific decor and corrugated hoardings, was rebranded, restyled and reopened as 'Let It Rock'. Vivienne recalls too that the seeds of later acrimony were sown straight away. 'My mother loaned us the money – £100 – to take over the shop. I didn't want to. Dora insisted it was all official, so we went to a notary and formed a partnership. That was the hold Malcolm had over me ever after: it was a huge mistake.'

Vivienne set her sewing machine buzzing back over the river at Thurleigh Court. She found fifties suits and trousers and carefully took them apart in order to create patterns she could replicate. She started to make mohair jumpers, in an approximation of the New York beatnik look, to be paired with tights as if you were 'wearing your boyfriend's sweater'. In canary yellow, it is a look she sported in early photographs, and is one of the oldest items still nestling at the back of her clothes archive. Meanwhile, old hoardings were painted black and large baby-pink letters spelled out 'Let It Rock', 'and inside, Malcolm made it look like a suburban Brixton front room in the 1950s'. It was also, immediately, a place to hang out. Steve Jones, later of The Sex Pistols and a close friend of Vivienne's, said, 'You felt, you know, that you could go in there and stand there and no one would bother you . . . it was just like being, not in a shop but a hang-out.' The front part of the shop, nearest the King's Road, was 'dominated by Odeon wallpaper', pictures of Billy Fury and Screaming Lord Sutch, and a suburban fifties display cabinet customized by Vivienne with pink taffeta and displaying Brylcreem and paste earrings that might or might not be for sale. The whole deal was a mixture of vintage and reconstructions, in terms of the clothes and the decor. Vivienne's first products into 430 King's Road were the Teddy Boy suits from Sid Green customized with velvet detailing. 'It was at first a question of changing things. Our first customers were men, who sometimes bought for their girlfriends. Like the customized T-shirt, where I took the ends of long sleeves off and made them into detailing around a low-cut V-neck. I had to sell my Singer sewing machine to get a telephone at Thurleigh Court, but then soon enough was able to buy a small industrial one.'

As she and Malcolm stated, 430 was both an art installation and a shop. This was in part because it attracted a specific cultish gang of rock 'n' roll revivalists – the new-wave Teddy Boys who attended Shakin' Stevens gigs. But it couldn't have lasted just on that brief revival, and that wasn't the point. McLaren had an instinct for fusing fashion, music and coltish cult that was an art form in itself. 'Entering the shop felt like entering the set of a fifties B-movie,' recalled one visitor. 'The place where music and art come together,' proclaimed McLaren, 'is called fashion . . . creating clothes is like jumping into the musical end of a painting, and number 430 became a natural extension of my artist's studio.' It was quite a pronouncement from a man who did not have a studio, and who had not made the clothes at all. He could be more measured about what it had first felt like for him and Vivienne: 'I [had been] counting on an unexpected moment of glamour and I found it at number 430 King's Road. In this black hole at the World's End I changed my life, in the shop's various incarnations – Paradise Garage, Let It Rock, Too Fast to Live Too Young to Die – I made clothes that looked like ruins. I created something new by destroying the old. This wasn't fashion as a commodity, this was fashion as an idea.'

'Well, that's all true,' says Vivienne, 'except he didn't make anything. Malcolm would get very excited,' she says. 'He would be in the shop late on a Friday night, decorating the shop, and he was very good at that. I remember once when he got this stepladder and just folded all these T-shirts on it, all these T-shirts with chains on and glitter saying things like "Elvis" and "Eddie", "Gene Vincent and The Blue Caps", with little rolled sleeves and studs, and it looked incredible, all cascading down this stepladder. He would just decorate the whole shop and he had these Teddy Boys and the shop was supposed to open at ten on Saturday and at twelve-thirty there would be ever so many of these Teds outside and they'd say, "Come on, Malc, let us in." Thirty to fifty people waiting outside the shop, smoking and drinking beer. But he wouldn't let them in until he had got the design of the shop just right. Meanwhile I would have been up all night doing things for the shop – studding or painting leather jackets or whatever. I've been told since that I am a disgrace to Women's Lib for letting him take credit, when I was making it all, not him. But it took two, at first. Malcolm and I were equal.'

The American boutique manager down the road at Granny Takes a Trip, Gene Krell, was instantly curious. 'In those days,' Krell recalls, 'at 430 King's Road there wasn't a "facility", a "toilet", I should say. So I first saw Vivienne going to the public one, opposite the pub, on a pee break. We had a huge window. She was fine-looking, you know. I just fell in love. Not only the way she dressed. Her body language and her sense of authority, and she just walked with this kind of confidence, you know, bordering on arrogance. And I wanted to get to know her. But I thought there was no way, you know, being she might have regarded me as a rival, because Granny Takes a Trip was kinda bourgeois; we catered to pop stars.

'Music became the conduit in our relationship. Vivienne was particularly interested in doo-wop music back then, which was the punk of its time in that it was the voice of the street. We talked about music and became friends. And in those days, well, I led a fairly salubrious life. Granny's was doing well. I was living at 13 Shawfield Street, where Christine Keeler lived. I rented it from her. And we had this huge TV. And I remember Vivienne didn't have a television, so quite soon after I knew her I invited her and Malcolm over to the house. We decided to look under the floorboards in case Christine Keeler had stashed anything there – and do you know what? She had. She had all these secret documents under the floorboards that Vivienne and I discovered. We were frightened we'd indict ourselves in some way or other – though this is years after the Profumo scandal – so we never read them and eventually Keeler came over and picked them up. But from then on, Vivienne and I established this special relationship. I just grew to be fascinated with Vivienne: everyone was along the King's Road when she arrived, because of what she represented. She really played against the character of the place. She wasn't a punk in those days. There was the punk *imagery* and there was this punk attitude long before the actual culture existed. And the attitude was Vivienne. Vivienne enjoyed creating a polemic. She enjoyed challenging you.'

Soon enough there was media attention, as well as the attention of Granny Takes a Trip colleagues. There was an article in the *London Evening Standard* and a mention in *Rolling Stone,* a photo shoot with Vivienne's friend and fan Louise Doktor for *Club International,* closely followed by a commission to provide the clothes for Ringo Starr and David Essex in the 1973 movie *That'll be the Day*. It was a super-charged start in the fashion world for a woman operating on cash-till to market-stall budgets with one sewing machine in her flat. It was super-fuelled however by Malcolm's hype and 'agent provocateur' style stunts. Vivienne would be persuaded out of an evening to clubs frequented by Teds to hand out 'Teddy Boys for ever! The rock era is our business' flyers, and to enter the fracas at Wembley concerts. Through late 1971 and into 1972, Vivienne and Malcolm surfed the latest wave of rock 'n' roll revivalism, but (as described by Vivienne) the tide was swirling under them. A younger generation wanted something subversive along with their rock 'n' roll music and clothes, and Vivienne and Malcolm began to give them T-shirts and knickers that might not have been recognized as such, but were in fact the first essential deconstructing of rock.

Former landlord Tommy Roberts visited from time to time, and helped rearrange the lease in Vivienne and Malcolm's names. He was immediately impressed by Vivienne. 'Trevor Myles had gone broke so I said to Malcolm and Vivienne to have it. I was concerned 'cos she didn't have a design background, though Malcolm had been to art school, but I used to talk to her . . . she was so interesting – had this little baby, I remember, in the shop sometimes . . . and she was a little bit difficult sometimes, but *clever*, really clever. Teddy Boys' clothes I remember, at first – they had coach parties of Teddy Boys visiting! No one knew if it was going to work, but it did.'

Let It Rock did not last long as a name. Ironically, it was a health and safety issue. The corrugated hoarding was crumbling and had to come down, along with the pink lettering. At the same time, by the summer of 1972 Vivienne and Malcolm were aware that the Teddy Boy thing could not sustain them creatively or commercially – and there was an appetite to subvert. 'Malcolm was a bit bored of the Teds by then and we became more interested in rockers. Chris Bedding was a customer, and Red Baron, a Clapham rocker – one of the ones who

Bricolage, chains, nipple zips (functioning), rolled sleeves: punk is born.

Boiled chicken bone appliqué: 'it was very fiddly actually'.

met on Chelsea Bridge in sleeveless leather: a biker look.' The shop was renamed as 'Too Fast to Live Too Young to Die' or TFTLTYTD, in reference to James Dean, and though they continued to sell brothel creepers and Vivienne's restyled zoot suits, her innovative new designs began to find shelf space – and a fascinated clientele. One shop assistant from this era, Glen Matlock, recalled being hired (at £3.50 a day) and being bemused to find himself selling both Teddy Boy suits and oddly customized T-shirts. The cash flow was dictated largely by shoes – a signal lesson for Vivienne: 'On Saturday mornings, you'd turn up late and there'd be this queue of people wanting to buy the creepers which had been delivered from Cox's the night before. They'd all be gone by the middle of the afternoon.'

For TFTLTYTD, Vivienne and Malcolm delivered first a series of sleeveless black T-shirts, bought en masse and customized in a manner that subsequently has become mainstream. VENUS was picked out in studs across the chest on one; another had the legend SCUM over the front (Valerie Solanas's Society for Cutting Up Men). Others had sleeves replaced with short arcs of bicycle tyre and the most revolutionary had small zips inserted over each nipple. Whether or not they functioned (they did) was immaterial: the idea was instantly subversive. All of this was outflanked by the T-shirt that has become the emblem of these first stirrings of punk chic: a black T-shirt decorated with bleached chicken bones, chained and sewn into lettering, the most iconic spelling out ROCK.

The clothing deviated ever more radically from Teddy towards something aggressively rocker. 'We bought old stocks – we introduced black jeans, super-tight ones.' *Let the Good Times Roll*, the stage version of *Grease* and the film *American Graffiti* all nodded towards a new understanding of the fifties as rather more leather-clad and sexually deviant – fascinating through being dangerous. *The Wild One*, as much as *Rebel without a Cause*, became the touchstone image, but the fifties leather-and-T-shirt got dirtier in the era of Hells Angels, referencing gothic film (bones, shrouds, purple lips) as much as gleaming motorbikes. And because no one had quite done leather, danger, death and shock like the Nazis, elements of their iconography crept into Vivienne and Malcolm's designs as well.

The flat at Thurleigh Court began to smell of leather and glue, of dyes and fabric glitter, and the shop at 430 King's Road was embellished week on week with designs that freely cross-referenced Elvis, Himmler, biker / fetish-wear and skulls and crossbones. The clothes, and the shop, stopped traffic. T-shirts were sold that had words and slogans picked out in studs, in glitter, or with tiny chains, sewn on by Vivienne and further customized with kinky balls and chains. The corrugated hoarding was emblazoned with a white skull. 'Let It Rock' was kept as one label and 'line' and 'TFTLTYTD' introduced on other stock. It was the beginning of a practice McLaren and Westwood repeated often: reinvent, rebrand and sell the old as well as the new.

Gene Krell was not the only American attracted to the store, and to 'the happening couple', as Vivienne gleefully recalls. Gerry Goldstein, half-American pal of McLaren's from Stoke Newington and a friend of Lenny Bruce, came to work in the shop along with Roberta Bayley, a Californian Vivienne met in a Chelsea vegetarian restaurant. They in turn helped attract a classless and international crowd of film-makers, artists and singers who looked to London for the next thing in pop and fashion. Iggy Pop and James Williamson headed for the shop in the middle of recording *Raw Power*, Marianne Faithfull was a regular, and Jimmy Page, and The Kinks. Vivienne's costumes for *That'll be the Day* caught the eye of Ken Russell, who asked her to create something suitably shocking for the climax of his film on Mahler. She and Malcolm devised a Valkyrie dominatrix leather suit, with a glittery swastika and appliquéd crotch-top Christ. The ensemble was completed with a Nazi helmet and whip. Not an easy look to carry off on the King's Road or anywhere, but exactly the sort of thing to light up the tabloids and garner yet more attention for the shop.

Where had it all come from, this look? And who was going to buy it? McLaren seemed unperturbed by the position they fast found themselves in of generating notoriety quite out of proportion to their retail profile or ability to capitalize. Vivienne put her faith in him and his ability to reinvent and rebrand the shop, and meanwhile went on with the simpler but vital work of making more and more shocking clothes. It was a revolution in that simple thing, the T-shirt. Vivienne is sometimes credited with 'inventing' the sloganed shirt, but this was more accurately Tommy Roberts and in a sense predates either of them in that it was an idea born of Second World War military branding and American advertising campaigns of the 1950s. Nevertheless, that which has become commonplace: jokes and ideologies splashed across our chests – 'No philosophy that can't be printed on a T-shirt', as Tom Stoppard witheringly described sound-bite fashion – was popularized by Vivienne and by punk. It is one of her singular and specific claims on posterity. What was absolutely new as well was Vivienne's 'bricolage' customizing of T-shirts and then other clothing items. Pockets made of plastic into which cigarette cards could be inserted. Studs and chains and even rubber inner tubes. And then the astonishing idea, in fashion if not in contemporary art, of taking detritus like chicken bones and bottle tops and rendering them fashion. 'It was very fiddly. Trying to get Araldite [glue] into tiny chicken bones that crumbled inside. Fiddly. But worth it.'

It should be said too that Vivienne, long credited as one of the vital fashion designers and couturiers of our age, was and is also a profoundly influential graphic designer. From 1969 to 1979, she, Malcolm and their collaborators created images, mainly on T-shirts, that have become part of our shared visual language. For one thing: text on clothing. Text in contemporary art had been a trope within art circles for years; it was known as Lettrism. Whether anyone said such a thing at 430 King's Road Vivienne doubts, but she and Malcolm, back at Thurleigh Court, began to experiment with written designs that were then printed. Vivienne's clear primary-school teacher handwriting was put to a very different use writing out song lyrics and extracts from soft porn. One highly influential idea was the division of the shirt into a list of 'ins' and 'outs' of 'hates' and 'non-hates'. The idea dates back at least to Nancy Mitford or earlier, but it had never been done in a fashion context or certainly on a T-shirt. McLaren, typically, later denied that Vivienne had anything to do with it, and some say it was Bernie Rhodes, but the top tag line 'you're gonna wake up one morning and know what side of the bed you've been lying on' is remarkably akin to Vivienne's handwriting. The list of 'hates' included obvious targets of mass media and commercialized pop: Leo Sayer, David Essex, *Top of the Pops*. It also included *Vogue, Harpers & Queen* and

Vivienne's once-beloved C&A. The 'loves' referenced her whole rock 'n' roll background but also Jamaican rude boys, Jimi Hendrix, Iggy Pop, and a band no one had yet heard of, Kutie Jones and His Sex Pistols. It was the grandmother of all the 'in' and 'out' lists that have cursed or blessed the style and fashion press ever since. It was also an effective in and out, 'U' and 'non-U' statement of the tribalism that helped sell early punk designs.

Lettrism, however, was only one part of Vivienne and Malcolm's graphics universe. Priced and sold at 430 King's Road at between £2 and £7, 'which was very reasonable, actually, it took hours and hours to make some of those designs,' shirts were printed in high-contrast colours, ripped, sometimes outer-seamed and often customized with cigarette burns and zips. The few that survive are of inestimable worth and value in the history of fashion. They were items that challenged the eye and the mind, and had impact quite out of proportion to the relatively small numbers first sold. They also helped set the agenda in graphic arts and in the ongoing identity of the Vivienne Westwood Group as innovators of printed fabrics and accessories. Take an idea, maybe from high art, maybe from existing popular culture; juxtapose it closely with that which challenges the original intent of the image or which merely shocks. Arrange centrally across the torso or so that some detail will emerge only on close inspection. Sell. Shock. And wait for the column inches to induce more sales.

As the years went by the designs became more outlandish and outrageous. What Malcolm patronizingly referred to as Vivienne's 'potato printing' – a technically accurate description in some cases – took on icons and taboos. One of the more enduring – it still sells in the Worlds End shop – is a plain T-shirt printed with a naked breast at chest height. 'A favourite of Paul Cook' of The Sex Pistols, it achieved further notoriety too when Alice Cooper wore it on a 1973 magazine cover. Others took icons of Vivienne's childhood and adolescence – Mickey Mouse, Snow White, Marilyn Monroe – and subverted them in a manner both ridiculous and shocking. The Disney logo character had his ear turned into an anarchist 'A' and the Disney princess was redrawn in sexual congress with her eponymous dwarves. These images the Chelsea police impounded after a complaint from a King's Road

Brokeback T-shirt. Obscenity is in the touching, allegedly.

resident. 'It was ironic really. They never impounded our "How to Make a Molotov Cocktail" T-shirt. But anything where we could be accused of "holding an indecent exhibition" they were after. And Disney objected, so we had to stop. They couldn't now: it's all out of copyright. One time Jordan hid all the stock in bin liners and put them in the entrance hall to the flat above, where we went to pee. It was annoying, actually, to lose the stock. I got fed up with it: but I felt all the more duty-bound as a result to carry on.'

The images retain their power to disturb. A gay punk gang bang, quoting the Joe Orton pun 'Prick Up Your Ears'. Two cowboys, naked from the waist down, facing each other, their flaccid penises almost touching. A work straight out of gay porn (Malcolm liked to leave plenty of vintage and hard-core porn around the shop), the cowboy T-shirt has caused outrage ever since. Disturbingly tender as much as sexual, it is typical of Vivienne's elliptical attitude to sex, requiring us to ponder intimacy between men as well as the power of the phallic in fashion. It also led to the arrest of Vivienne's friend Alan Jones on grounds of 'exposing to public view and indecent exhibition'. 'We knew Alan from the Portobello Hotel. Young Paul Getty used to stay there and Malcolm and I would drink there late at night, so we knew him quite well. He loved our clothes.' Even more 'out there' would be the Sex Pistols T-shirts, featuring the band's name in condom pink, and featuring a naked prepubescent boy smoking a cigarette. Oddly, it is one of the few images that is probably more shocking and less marketable now than when it was first produced. The infamous 'Piss Marilyn' mixes the obvious iconography of the rock 'n' roll years – James Dean and Marilyn Monroe's estates both profited hugely in the early seventies from the fifties revival – with hard-core porn. Ejaculating penises adorn each arm, vaguely aiming at the screen goddess depending on how you wear the garment, Marilyn's face Jackson-Pollocked with urine-yellow cum ropes. Ben, Vivienne's small son, saw her make it: 'I'd be doing my homework in the corner while she was making things and when she did the Piss / Marilyn Monroe I said, "Mum, I'm confused: do you like her or not?" And she said, "Yeah, it's not about that, I'm just trying to shock people by putting piss on." And then when she was pencilling in the cock of Jesus on the inverted cross on the swastika / Destroy T-shirt, I was doing my homework and I do remember thinking, "My mum's quite eccentric."'

Because it was neither screen goddesses nor the Messiah who had died but rather recent female graduates, it was perhaps to have been expected that the Cambridge rapist T-shirt should have caused most controversy. It still does. 'It's the one thing I regret,' says Vivienne, and it is one of the few design statements Vivienne has ever apologized for. The serial rapist in question had been described as wearing a fetish gimp mask, such as was sold at the shop at the time. The then manager, Michael Collins, was interviewed by the police. 'Malcolm had just come back from a trip to the US where he wanted to start a band, and the first thing he suggested we do when he got back and heard about this was this rapist T-shirt.' Vivienne created a T-shirt featuring the mask, a picture of Beatles manager Brian Epstein who had recently died, allegedly in sado-masochistic circumstances, and the legend 'It's been a hard day's night.' 'It was all part of Malcolm's "Defend the Pervert" campaign and idea that "England is the Home of the Flasher", giving kids "sexual autonomy" by letting them see the hypocrisy around them. Malcolm was a shock merchant first and foremost, not into politics as such. I think it's maybe fine to shock the Establishment, say with a swastika, ideally inverted so it doesn't look like you are supporting Nazism. I don't think it was right to do the rapist T-shirt.'

Vivienne muses: 'The shape of a T-shirt is simple and beautiful. You are aware of the cloth, of the body, but also of an image: it is a canvas.' And like a canvas, the T-shirt was open to experimentation of all sorts. Pop art. Lettrism. Found objects and bricolage; the T-shirt was the place where fashion, sex, politics and art met. As Vivienne says, 'My job then and my job always was to confront the Establishment to try and find out where freedom lies and what you can do: the most obvious way I did that was through the T-shirts.' This politicization of clothing is another gift of Vivienne and Malcolm to contemporary culture. It set the scene for what others, notably Katharine Hamnett, would do. It also set the scene during the early seventies for what would become punk, fusing anger and outrage or just boredom, through the prism of sexual outrage that will always appeal to the libidinous and youthful. So it was only a matter of time, in a sense, before Too Fast to Live too

Young to Die got rebranded, and the obvious name was the central selling point too: SEX.

Sex, or at least the idea of sex, was enormously important to Malcolm. Vivienne denies it was to her, at first. The sexual impulse and the iconography of sexual behaviour and sexual deviance (chains, rubber, fetish-wear, not to mention heels) became icons of liberation for them both, at odds with the simple vegan domesticity of their home life and what Vivienne says was never a sexually charged relationship. 'The sexual morality that inhibits the will to freedom,' Malcolm wrote, 'as well as those forces that comply with authoritarian interests, derive their energy from repressed sexuality.' To liberate sexually was to liberate politically, which was where Vivienne felt involved. It was as simple as that. The imagery of repression and of kink were all part of a broader propaganda designed to appeal to those who sought freedom. Which is why and how Vivienne can sit knitting in her studio now, aged seventy-three, explaining a clear trajectory from nipple clamps to Climate Revolution.

'The only reason I am in fashion is to destroy the word "conformity". Nothing is interesting to me unless it's got that element. So we began in our shop "Let It Rock" with a look from the fifties. The walls were covered with pages torn out of fifties pin-up porno magazines – these ravaged or shipwrecked temptresses. The fifties also inspired me to have a crew cut. My hair was fine so I dyed it blond [*sic*] to make it more coarse so it would stick up. Then I took pleasure in letting it grow longer but still sticking up, and this hairstyle caught on. People had never seen this before.' And then the changes progressed through chains and leather (Too Fast to Live) to rubber and bondage and high stilettos to urban guerrilla-punk. Sex was in the air, and so it became the name.

1974 saw the shop acquire its third identity under Vivienne and Malcolm. Though Tommy Roberts' old corrugated iron survived in part underneath, the facia became dominated by giant pink rubberized letters spelling out in capitals the new name, SEX, with Thomas Fuller's aphorism below, 'Craft must have clothes but truth loves to go naked.' The interior was again remodelled, spray-painted with pornographic graffiti (the flying penises still sell as earrings and cufflinks), and strewn with the trappings of hard-core kink: padlocks, rubber curtains, chains, whips, handcuffs. 'It didn't look, inside or out, like a boutique at all; it felt deviant to even go in – like some sex-dive off Times Square or down some Soho alley.' Marco Pirroni of the group Adam and the Ants recalls, 'Vivienne used to be in the shop wearing leatherette trousers and purple make-up. She looked fantastic.'

'I thought I looked like a princess from another planet,' says Vivienne. 'I thought I couldn't look any better. I particularly loved my SEX look; my rubber stockings and the T-shirt with pornographic images and my stilettos and spiky hair. I'd have to say Mr Freedom had been a big influence on me in terms of confidence in looking "intergalactic". I stopped the traffic in my rubber negligee . . .'

SEX deliberately intimidated. It was part of McLaren's brilliant 'anti-managing', as his son puts it, to sense that this dark sexuality and cocky attitude would inspire its own in-crowd, its own loyal customers. Clothes from SEX were worn as much as anything else as a badge of honour that you had been there. And as such they were indeed statements as much personal as political: the fashion corollary to the contemporary output of Germaine Greer or Camille Paglia: an angry shout of sexual defiance. The clientele was very mixed. Prostitutes and flashers and voyeurs were drawn to the shop – to the occasional horror of Vivienne herself. 'One time somebody asked where the girls were, and I had to say, "This isn't a BROTHEL, you know." But I became great friends with some of the prostitutes and supposed "deviants". Linda Ashby, a dominatrix and lesbian, became a great friend and I used to go with her to Louise's, the lesbian club in Soho.' Described by Adam Ant, who became then an habitué of 430 and remains so, the shop was simply 'one of the all-time greatest in history'. It is remembered widely and fondly by punters as diverse as Jerry Hall, Bryan Ferry and Jonathan Ross for its astonishing and revolutionary fashion embrace of the deviant, and its flagrant use of sexuality. It was also widely remembered and indeed photographed because of two assistants Vivienne recruited at the time: Chrissie Hynde, who later fronted The Pretenders, and the 'shop-girl goddess' known simply as 'Jordan'. Jordan became an attraction in her own right, becoming every bit as much the poster girl for early punk as Vivienne herself. 'Andy Warhol was disappointed when he met me,'

(L–R) Shop regulars Danielle, Alan Jones, Chrissie Hynde, Vivienne and Jordan spelling out their favourite emporium.

recalls Vivienne, 'because he had thought I was Jordan – or rather had seen pictures of Jordan and assumed that was me. She was amazing. I had been distressing clothes, thinking others would follow suit, but no one did till Jordan ripping her tights, and later Johnny Rotten.' Jordan, originally Pamela Rooke, bottle-blonde, ballet trained, curvy and confrontational, was unabashed at posing in SEX-era 'looks': see-through rubber 'condom' dresses, black leather, tea-stained knickers and rubber lingerie. It was a dominatrix devil-may-care dishabille that got teamed by her and Vivienne with more and more outlandish eye make-up, gothic lipstick and electric-shock hair. Jordan's toilette took over two hours before she commuted in to the World's End from Seaford in Sussex. British Rail granted her her own first-class carriage, to calm her fellow passengers and prevent fights, proving Vivienne's point that extraordinary clothes might give one a better life. Club owner Michael Costiff recalls that Jordan 'eclipsed every other thing in sight. She was like a goddess.'

When Reginald Bosanquet, the newsreader, and other showbiz figures made ill-judged passes at her, Jordan rebuffed them with an acid tongue. The clothes could appear to be a come-on, but were not intended as such. As staff or as customer, SEX attracted a number of strong female personalities who both reflected and helped shape Vivienne's personal style. Bella and Rose Freud, daughters of the painter Lucian, were recruited in part for their striking looks. 'I've always been fascinated by strong and beautiful women,' says Vivienne. During Chrissie Hynde's brief stint working in the shop she posed in stilettos and bondage gear for a series of photo shoots, including one where S.E.X. is spelled out in lipstick across her, Vivienne's and Jordan's arses. Siouxsie Sioux, later lead singer of The Banshees, Margi Clarke, the Scouse actress and presenter, Toyah Willcox, as she moved into her version of punk-pop, and Gerlinde Costiff, the club promoter, all became regulars. To be accepted into the shop in the first place took commitment and self-confidence, so the group became self-defining. 'That was what was attractive about them,' wrote one member of the Adam and the Ants coterie of Vivienne then, 'it was 100 per cent – or nothing.'

SEX's range of fetish and bondage fashion was nearly all black. When I asked Vivienne about this I quoted Malcolm McLaren to her: 'Black expressed the denunciation of the frill' he claimed, 'Nihilism. Boredom. Emptiness . . . Sex translated in fashion becomes fetish, and fetishism is the very embodiment of youth.' 'Well, yes,' mused Vivienne, 'I do still say that a lot and believe what he wrote, that the "fundamental belief in [youth's] own immortality" is what "it needs to assert over and over again . . . fetishism . . . is its necessary razor's edge, the exhilarating border between life and death." Yes, I do believe that. I say that a lot.' Perhaps it was inevitable then, to again quote Malcolm, that a shop and designers with such radical new responses to the era should 'act as a catalyst for the musical tastes of the time'. Malcolm and Vivienne had already lived a decade between them on the fringes of London's music scenes. They were designers in want of a band.

'My best look then, which sold in the shop as well, was a little rubber skirt that we sourced via *Exchange & Mart*. Tight on the bum, and puckered into a waistband, it could have been couture it was so well made. Rather Chanel, actually, but in rubber. And my favourite outfit then was that skirt with a turquoise T-shirt, with text on it – one of the ones that I had written with a bamboo cane like lots of those Seditionaries T-shirts – in violet ink with some porn quote on it, and slit through horizontally just above the breast, and then men's winkle-pickers in pale blue faded to grey and flesh-coloured tights. That was me.'

This, then, was the true beginnings of punk as a highbred fusion of fetish, bricolage, Lettrism and attitude. Though Vivienne and McLaren joked that they were selling 'rubber-wear for the office', the clothes sold to a relatively small clique of young London clubbers, notably the 'Bromley Contingent' of South London ne'er-do-wells, arrant blades like Simon 'Boy' Barker, Billy Idol, Philip Salon and Steven Severin, as well as that constant hidden clique of sexual fantasists and rubber fetishists. The genius in marketing terms was the notoriety the shop and its assistants generated, and the T-shirts that could be sold merely alluding to the extreme sexuality of the shop's other goods and decor. At the darker fringes of urban sex Malcolm and Vivienne found illumination for a potential design future as well as for Malcolm's own agendas on sexual confrontation: 'It had started with an interest in any form of youth revolt; Teddy boys and rockers. We brought the sex element into it.' And that lit the fuse.

NEW YORK DOLL

Rimbaud would write about the monstrous city . . . and here it is in 1973.
That's what my songs are about.   DAVID JOHANSEN
of The New York Dolls

I don't think Punk would have happened without Vivienne and Malcolm.
Something would have happened, and it might even have been called
Punk, but it wouldn't have looked the way it did, even in America.
And the look was so important.   CHRISSIE HYNDE
of The Pretenders

'We should go back a bit, so I can explain. I'll tell you about The Sex
Pistols later, but I wanted to explain about New York.'

Vivienne thanks Tizer for a cup of tea and a letter she has to sign –
something for Amnesty – and then turns her attention back to punk.

It really depends who you believe. Punk began either in New York
or in London, either in 1974 or 1975. For some it was all about music,
for some, mainly Londoners, it was largely about a 'look'. For others it
was art. But undeniably it was a New York–London story – a style and
scene born of the angst of city living. The American capital of punk
was Manhattan, and the centre of it all in the mid seventies was two
downtown nightclubs, CBGB and OMFUG (Country, Bluegrass and
Blues, and Other Music for Uplifting Gormandizers), that mirrored
TFTLTYTD in style terms. Punks seemed to love acronyms. Perhaps
it was easier to spell out on T-shirts. Or it was the sheer thrill of explaining – or not explaining – to the ignorant. The New York venue with
the best claim to be the cradle of punk there was founded by Hilly

Kristal at 315 Bowery in the East Village. In London at the same time punk was indisputably centred at 430 King's Road. It was for this reason that the recent punk exhibition at the Metropolitan Museum of Art in New York faithfully recreated both venues as if they were the twin studios of a great artist or the scene of some infamous act of violence. In a sense they were both. The connection between the two, the skein of creative energy that stretched between the Bowery and the King's Road, London, was Vivienne and Malcolm.

In August 1973, several King's Road shops were invited to show their wares at what was then an annual event at the MacAlpine Hotel in Manhattan: the National Boutique Show. It was a trade show by any other name, but predicated on an awareness that boutiques were necessarily niche-market. Business would never be department-store sized. Nevertheless, the splash made at the event could have publicity value far outshining the worth of orders taken. Vivienne started plotting in the spring of 1973 to be there, and arranged for Ben and Joe to spend yet another summer with their grandparents so that she and Malcolm could make their first trip to the States.

'1973 was the first time I had been to America. I went with Malcolm and our friend Gerry Goldstein. Here's a picture of him outside the TFTLTYTD shop and that means it was 1973 – we were called Let It Rock but we were in the middle of changing the name of the shop. I was so very excited. I liked America very much in those days but when I got there it was so dilapidated – not like the gleaming Gotham of the Batman comics at all! And it was incredibly, incredibly hot – and I just kept the bath full of cold water, and I was just in the bath and out of the bath – there was no air conditioning anywhere. But the first thing we did, on the very first day we were there in New York, before we even unpacked or started selling anything, we paid a visit to Andy Warhol's Factory. We just thought that's what you did in New York. Mostly on that trip I wore this catsuit in stretch lycra that looked like tweed – like a dogstooth tweed, and it had a bra knitted out of mohair that was attached to it, the bra part, with diamanté straps over the back, and I wore it with these boots like Robin Hood and the top was cut like a jester, like a castle, and Malcolm had seen these boots in the windows of Freed's the ballet shop – for some sort of principal boy, and so I wore those boots all the time in New York, I loved them . . . that was my best outfit for the New York trip but also I had some little torn tops and things as well . . . it was really hot . . .'

In the mid seventies, there were still ocean liners arriving from Europe every single day into the Mafia-run docks of New York's Hudson river. Vivienne and Malcolm flew into LaGuardia with Malcolm's art-school chum Gerry Goldstein and enough samples suitcases to have more than justified taking the more leisurely sea crossing. But they had not intended to be away long from the King's Road shop, or from the boys. They nevertheless had a lot to carry. They set up in the MacAlpine Hotel with a stall in a bedroom – an installation involving T-shirts, Teddy Boy and rocker clothes as well as rock 'n' roll memorabilia. From a small portable record player bought downtown, they blasted Jerry Lee Lewis and Bill Haley hits. People came and went. No one bought anything.

'We went first to the MacAlpine Hotel, just across the road from Bloomingdale's – I remember even one of the letters of Bloomingdale's was missing, that was what New York was like then – and the way that the clothes were displayed in there, it was like a bargain basement. And I was walking around the foyer because I looked good, and Gerry Goldstein was there in his Teddy Boy clothes, and I don't know where Malcolm was but probably not walking around the foyer – and we were trying to attract people but we were in completely the wrong place. We didn't sell a thing.

'But about six months before, The New York Dolls, the band, had come into our shop in London, and they came to visit us at the MacAlpine in the bedroom where we had this display of clothes – so we went out with them to Max's Kansas City club, dancing with them, and to parties. I think I had had this idea that American youth was where it was at. They had the first teenagers. And more than that, I'll tell you – I had a thing about American men – their bodies. My parents had had a post office in Harrow and then Ruislip and near there was an American army base, since the war and into the fifties, and they had a swimming pool – and I thought American GI's were really, really something – something very powerful and sexual, for me, the idea of an American . . . I had a romantic idea of American men, even American soldiers; you know, Elvis in his army uniform, and I still felt America was very inspiring during and after the trip – because of the films, and the men, and the Andy Warhol films – Joe Dallesandro – he was really, really something . . . but, you see, it was an *idea* of America, not, as it turned out, the real thing.'

There was already enough crossover between what was going on in the alternative music scenes of early seventies London and New York for some New Yorkers to be aware of Let It Rock on the King's Road. Alice Cooper and Sylvain Sylvain, rhythm guitarist for The New York Dolls, came to Vivienne's hotel room 'installation' at the MacAlpine. Sylvain and his fellow band member Johnny Thunders knew Vivienne from 430, and if nothing else, it was obvious to them that Vivienne's clothes were band attire: shocking, theatrical, in-your-face; they also tended to flatter the lithe-to-lanky bodies of those who partied too hard. 'We loved to dress up,' says Sylvain. 'In America nobody gives a shit about clothing, but in Europe, somebody will go, "What the fuck are you doing with those crazy pants?" That might get you to be cool.' Sylvain suggested to Vivienne that they move out of the MacAlpine, and into his favoured hotel: the Chelsea. This was where their real New York adventure would begin.

Sylvain was one of the three key members of The New York Dolls, and, along with Johnny Thunders and Billy Murcia, was both clothes-obsessed and a sometime visitor to London. They all knew 430 King's Road. The group had been formed during 1972, with Arthur Kane on bass and David Johansen on vocals, and their look and style took elements of glam rock and the androgynous theatrics of Jagger and Bowie, but gave it a particularly downtown-Manhattan, Warholesque twist. The Dolls set out to shock and to play with gender stereotypes and ideas of revolt, so they had plenty in common with Vivienne, but they also inhabited a world around the dying embers of the Factory that gloried in transvestitism and was populated by drag queens, gay and straight. Johansen, when asked if he was bisexual, replied: 'No, man, I'm trisexual: I'll try anything.'

The screeching half-harmonies and the leering stage antics were new to Vivienne and Malcolm. They have their place as ingredients of what later became punk music in the UK. The New York Dolls, along

Vivienne, aged thirty-two, Gitanes in hand. 1973.

with that other fan of 430 King's Road, Alice Cooper, gave McLaren some essential new keys for the punk revolution Vivienne was dressing back in London, and he began his long courtship of the group as unofficial manager, or 'haberdasher' as Johansen cuttingly put it, Svengali and stylist. 'It became my *raison d'être* to be in New York,' McLaren later explained. 'The New York Dolls were an adventure I wanted to have.'

Meanwhile, the Dolls suggested Malcolm and Vivienne move into the Chelsea Hotel. There, amongst the ghosts of past residents Frida Kahlo and Dylan Thomas, Jimi Hendrix and The Doors, Vivienne and Malcolm unpacked their samples and settled in. It was in every way the more appropriate venue for what was about to unfold. 'The Chelsea Hotel does not belong in America,' Arthur Miller once said – having lived there for six years following his divorce from Marilyn Monroe. 'There are no vacuum cleaners, no rules and no shame.' Vivienne loved it, despite the heat.

The Chelsea, on West 23rd Street, was by the early seventies perhaps at the nadir of its respectability and accordingly about to enter its gory glory-years. It became legendary for its violence, eccentricity and gothic excess. Jack Kerouac had once booked into the room where Vivienne and Malcolm stayed with Gore Vidal, the only recorded account of Kerouac spending the night with another man. Vivienne recalls Malcolm claiming he saw the chalk outline of a murder victim in a room nearby, 'but it may not be true; he had a very active imagination'. It was wild and violent, but it was also a place of artistic endeavour and experiment, and one linked with a strong literary and artistic tradition. Rothko had worked there and Larry Rivers too, and they had paid, in part, with their work, so that when Vivienne moved in it was a cross between an avant-garde art gallery, a rock 'n' roll club and a badly run crack den.

The presiding eminence of the Chelsea at this time was Stanley Bard, who managed it for more than fifty years. Just like Vivienne, 'Stanley really did believe that art transformed the world and that it was a force for civilization,' the British writer Barry Miles (who bumped into Vivienne in the corridors) remembers. 'I think he saw it as his duty in a way to provide a home for these people. And he was ripped off by a lot of people but he ran the hotel as a sanctuary for waifs and strays and those who could not pay but might enhance the reputation of the place.' Vivienne and Malcolm immediately fell into this category. Other residents at the time included Gene Krell's girl-friend Nico, and the Andy Warhol 'superstar' Viva. Quentin Crisp would live there too, and George Kleinsinger, the American composer, who shared his apartment with his collection of reptiles – a twelve-foot python and a pet alligator – and his twenty-something girlfriend. Kleinsinger, in the 1970s, was as old as the century. So Malcolm and Vivienne had the perfect address to enter into the downtown scene with Sylvain and Johnny Thunders of the Dolls. They largely gave up on commerce in favour of anarchy, party and culture, with the Dolls as their guides and no one, seemingly, footing the bill for anything. They were interviewed by Andy Warhol's *Interview* magazine, went clubbing with the Dolls at CBGBs and saw performances there by Richard Hell (Myers), Patti Smith and The Ramones. 'There was a lot of cocaine,' says Vivienne, 'a lot – it just got passed around. Eric Emerson was there and Viva, and Warhol of course – all the gang from his Factory films. And a lot of cocaine.' Vivienne's friend Debbie Harry, later of the band Blondie, recalls nevertheless that some clothes were sold, if in unconventional settings: 'I was hanging around with the New York Dolls back then and one of the other girls that was in this circle of friends / fans was Eileen Polk, who lived on West 13th Street in Greenwich Village. One day some of us were on her street and Malcolm McLaren pulled up in a rented station wagon, parked, opened the tailgate of the car and started pulling boxes out and selling all of this wonderful rubber clothing designed by his [then] partner Vivienne. It was a sort of feeding frenzy, or as it were, a "fashion frenzy" on West 13th Street!'

Fashion frenzies notwithstanding, Malcolm had decided by 1974 that his next Situationist coup would be less as fashion huckster than as a band promoter. It was an exciting moment to be clubbing in New York. The Dolls wore rubber and dog collars of the non-clerical stamp, and hung out with Iggy Pop and Lou Reed as well as the heroin-chic teenage clubbers who formed their core audience. Hilly Kristal, the club promoter who booked them, introduced Vivienne and Malcolm to Alice Cooper and Michael J. Pollard, who came to visit them at the

Chelsea that hot summer, and Bob Colacello asked if he could do a film interview with them and Andy Warhol at Warhol's *Interview* offices in Union Square. They agreed. Malcolm talked. Vivienne posed – and Warhol was silent. They went to private Dolls' parties along with the poet Patti Smith, and found themselves late one night at Johansen's apartment when the new Dolls' album was to be played for the first time. With Vivienne and Malcolm's taste still running to rock 'n' roll, it was a shock 'so awful that it crashed through into the other side, into magnificence . . . it was this inverted aesthetic [that] rekindled Malcolm's interest in pop'.

While downtown New York was providing Vivienne with new ideas for her fashion eye – the real as opposed to the filmic America – New York for Malcolm was a turning point in his career in pop. Music became his obsession that summer, as if the Let It Rock boutique fair had been no more than an excuse to start reinventing himself as a band stylist. But through the Dolls he and Vivienne first became aware of the man who would subtly shift what Vivienne was thinking about clothes just as the band was shifting Malcolm's ambitions within music. His name was Richard Myers, he was also a musician, and he was always known as 'Hell'. He is the essential lynchpin, in stylistic terms, between New York, Vivienne, Malcolm and punk.

'I just thought Richard Hell was incredible . . . here was a guy all deconstructed, torn down, looking like he's just crawled out of a drain hole, looking like he hadn't slept in years, and looking like no one gave a fuck about him. And looking like he didn't really give a fuck about you! He was this wonderful, bored, drained, scarred, dirty guy with a torn T-shirt. I don't think there was a safety pin then, though there may have been, this image of this guy, this spiky hair, everything about it – there was no question that I'd take it back to London. By being inspired by it, I was going to imitate it and transform it into something more English.'

These words are Malcolm's, but they have the distinct stamp of a conversation he had had previously with Vivienne, and Vivienne claims now that Hell became a sort of poster boy for a look that they had already assembled. Like Vivienne, Hell drew his inspiration from literary history, in his case the self-destructive aesthetic of the French

New York's Chelsea Hotel, 1974.

poets Verlaine and Rimbaud. His ensemble of mussed hair, fifties shades, torn T-shirts and leather was entirely within the orbit of what Vivienne and Malcolm were already doing and wearing. But he helped bring together the look for men, with its sexually ambiguous fusion of world-worn, drug-worn aesthete, razor-sharp mod, threatening rocker . . . and safety pins.

It has become controversial exactly who – Hell or Johnny Rotten or Sid Vicious or Vivienne or Malcolm – first used a safety pin, which was to become such an iconic part of the semiotics of punk. Vivienne shrugs about it all now, and claims it was Sid and Johnny. 'Johnny wore a safety pin in his ear. Sid had these pink gabardine trousers – I can see them now – and they had been destroyed, ripped to pieces by some junkie looking for drugs, and when Sid came round his trousers were slashed, so he pinned them back together again with safety pins. He turned up at the shop, I remember, in those and some toilet roll round his neck as a tie. It was like that, then. These Irish girls using kettles as handbags and this guy who walked around with jam and toast on his head. So safety pins weren't so very extreme.'

But Malcolm saw in those early Hell experiments with deconstructed clothes, and in the safety pins and kettle handbags aesthetics of London, that fashion could be bricolage. Richard Hell, whom Vivienne does not remember meeting, became Malcolm's touchstone of what punk could be: urban guerrilla-wear, incandescent outrage in clothes and attitude. The look of punk began to take proper shape. If McLaren was the 'Diaghilev of Punk', as he was described by the activist Caroline Coon, Vivienne was his Nijinsky, and the first person ever to wear the full 'look', back in England, was her.

Johnny Rotten (John Lydon) immediately latched on to the reworked Vivienne style when she came back to the World's End. Part of the gang who frequented the shop and who would become The Sex Pistols, Rotten is unequivocal that it was Vivienne who put it all together – while in turn she acknowledged him as the originator of safety-pin fashion. He castigates her now for selling a look that, by its very nature, was meant to be both creatively DIY and anti-capitalist. But then, some rockers refuse to move on.

Ironically, it was America and the Dolls that gave Vivienne and

'The Dolls were an attitude. And if nothing else we were a great attitude.'
Johnny Thunders of The New York Dolls

Malcolm their most controversial motif: the swastika. The band, Johansen claimed, had doodled the Nazi badge along with skulls and crossbones since high school: historically neutered, like the pirate flag, of its original power to terrify. It was part of the semiotics of shock for a generation distanced from the realities of the Holocaust. 'When you want to make a statement about how BAD you are, that's how you do it,' said Johansen, and so it was added to the collage of revolt. For many, and certainly Vivienne's father when he first became aware of it, the swastika was an emblem too far, still specifically allied to the politics not of freedom but of repression.

'When I was with Malcolm,' explains Vivienne, 'he wanted to shock – I was worried . . . about the swastika, for instance, but Malcolm, being Jewish, had his reasons for wanting to do that kind of thing. We weren't only rejecting the values of the older generation, we were rejecting their taboos as well.' On the whole it was served with irony and humour – the studded dog collars that were made for real dogs, for instance: 'you put that on, and basically you are insulting yourself, but you're also clearing yourself of all egotism.'

Something shifted after the New York trip, but it was not a simple infusion of a New York look. Let It Rock had been founded on a reinvention of Americana; so too was the James Dean world of TFTLTYTD. By the early seventies, Vivienne and Malcolm were working with images of America based on films and music that explored the violent implosion of American city life. References would include *Taxi Driver* and *Cruising* and the whole sex / death cult look of Hells Angels, fused with the ghoulish make-up and frenetic violence of Kubrick's *A Clockwork Orange*. Vivienne began to deconstruct these looks, literally unpicking the pieces to keep up with demand by making hybrid copies. And New York had made her realize the impact her ideas were having abroad: Warhol was interested, the Dolls wanted her clothes and Richard Hell had presented a full synthesis of what was shaping already in her mind; adding to the poetic nihilism of urban-warrior-chic, an element of classless American masculinity that Vivienne had always found attractive. New York also signalled a shift in her and Malcolm's interests and interest in each other. Vivienne had seen the potential of what she was doing in fashion to shape the look of a generation, while Malcolm had been drawn ever closer to the idea that a band might be the best fusion of art, music and Situationist 'happening'. It was the real beginnings of the punk revolution, but it was also the beginning of the end for the two of them.

Vivienne came home first, responding to the parallel demands of the shop, the school term and the end of Dora's babysitting goodwill. Malcolm stayed on in New York, and indeed would go back and forth over 74 and 75. It was a taste of what was to come and what he wanted. In the Dolls he had found a marriage of rock and attitude that suited him perfectly. When they came to London and to Paris shortly afterwards, playing Biba's Rainbow Room and *The Old Grey Whistle Test*, he trailed them like a groupie, with Vivienne sometimes in tow, expressing his yen to manage, style and dress them. He started to hang out more with the Americans in London – with Marty Breslau and Gene Krell, back and forth to Granny Takes a Trip, where Keith Richards was a regular. And Vivienne's work became infused with the darker hues of Gotham and the arch-machismo of Richard Hell. 'You started to see the early stirrings of a real artist as well as activist,' Gene Krell recalls of her work at the time. 'With Vivienne, the philosophies and the references were always so deep, so diverse. Rimbaud. Rockers. Brando. Gotham. Modern-day pirates. Who thinks like that in fashion, now?' Meanwhile, New York had fuelled an idea already in Malcolm's head that their whole combustible pile needed more than Vivienne's extraordinary designs or his media savvy. It needed music, and a band, and a singer. 'I've written lyrics for a couple of songs,' he wrote to a friend back in New York when he finally returned to London, 'one called "Too Fast to Live Too Young to Die". I have this idea of a singer...'

In late August 1975, Bernie Rhodes, sometime manager at 430, spotted a lanky rotten-toothed youth called John Lydon, dressed like Richard Hell and adjusting his safety-pinned trousers on the King's Road, and suggested he come into the shop...

GOD SAVE THE QUEEN

*They really did mean it, you know, The Sex Pistols, and I loved the lyrics
– not just the ones that I wrote, although I love writing lyrics [Vivienne
has joint credit for some of The Sex Pistols' songs] and I'm good at it.
They were brilliant, The Sex Pistols. I met someone the other day, quite
old, but I knew he'd been a punk before he told me. Give me a punk and
I'll show you the man.* VIVIENNE WESTWOOD

'Maybe punk came in part from New York, but the punk "look" evolved
in our shop at 430 King's Road. Malcolm and I changed the names and
decor of the shop to suit the clothes as our ideas evolved. But punk
didn't mean anything more than that at first. I did not see myself as a
fashion designer but as someone who wished to confront the rotten
status quo through the way I dressed and dressed others. Eventually
this sequence of ideas culminated in punk. The way I thought about
"punk" politics was this: at the time, we were just becoming aware of
these terrible politicians torturing people – I'm thinking of Pinochet,
for instance. I mean, the world is appalling. It's cruel and corrupt and
dangerous and there are awful people running the world. And so, first
of all, punk was about contempt. I don't know whether that's a strong
enough word for it, really. Contempt for the older generation because
they hadn't tried to do anything. The idea was that kids would try to
put a spoke in the wheel of this terrible killing machine.

'And that's more or less it. That's when I did the anarchy sign. I put
this "A" on everything, that we were anarchists. It was me. Malcolm
wasn't terribly interested in the politics of it all, or in us standing up as
anarchists. He just hated everybody. He particularly hated anybody in

authority – but it was very general. He'd hated all his schoolteachers. He hated anybody who told him what to do. He had a problem with Richard Branson because Richard had power. He hated record companies. Malcolm hated all that. Like Richard Nixon, he kept a list of those people he thought of as a kind of enemy. And so it wasn't surprising, I suppose, that he hated me on one level as well. He hated the idea of family. He hated mother figures. He always tried, whenever I was with him and the boys – The Sex Pistols, as they became – to pretend that I was this mother-figure-nanny who would tell them off if they did anything naughty or swore. He was all "Don't tell her." He was horrible, sometimes, Malcolm. It's not that I resented it exactly – but it was – I think the word would be "wearing".'

Too Fast to Live Too Young to Die lasted from 1972 to 1974 at 430 King's Road, and SEX from 1974 to late 1976. The year of the Queen's Silver Jubilee, 1977, saw the shop boarded up in final recognition of the regular window-smashing from passing Chelsea FC fans. The hoardings next had graffitied across them 'Seditionaries' – 'which is my position anyway over all those years,' says Vivienne, 'making clothes for heroes and encouraging sedition – seducing into revolt.' McLaren had described the shop over those years after New York as 'a haven for the disenfranchised which, in turn, helped to create the phenomenon known as punk rock'. In the mind of the public and the increasingly fascinated media, 430 King's Road was the place to look for the emerging meaning of punk, and year on year, Vivienne never failed to make headlines. 'Seditionaries' became the synthesis of her sartorial experiments. Some elements – the ripped and sloganed T-shirts – were a constant, and the oddly placed zips segued easily via the fetishism of SEX into the essential language of punk. There weren't a lot of buttons involved. Rubber and fetish, on the outer limits of wearable, nevertheless shaped key concerns for Vivienne as a designer and polemicist. It forced her to embrace the strong reactions to proactive female sexuality, and it taught her the value of research: 'I got so intrigued when I started to make clothes in rubber-wear by all those fetish people and the motives behind what they did . . . I wanted to make exactly what they wore . . . that's where all the straps and things came from.' Fetish, which grew out of Malcolm's Situationist desire to change through

Seditionaries, 430 King's Road, 1977: 'always go through any door that looks like you're not supposed to enter.' Malcolm McLaren

shock, in turn taught Vivienne about restriction and about straps, and has its place therefore in understanding not only the intricacies of her later corseted tailoring, but the whole world of underwear as outerwear. 'The look,' as Jon Savage later wrote, ' – both in the original and the imitations – spread throughout the world.'

Chrissie Hynde says that some form of punk might have happened anyway; Vivienne disagrees. Perhaps the slow decline of British self-confidence along with its economy and the specific ignominies of the three-day week and the fall of the Heath government; perhaps what was all around would have thrown up some riotous dissent. What was unique about punk was that the clothes were so integral to the meaning of the times. The music, in effect, followed in the wake of a 'look' that Vivienne and Malcolm assembled. 'We didn't rip off anybody, or exploit some street thing: there was no punk before us.' They were so interested in cults that, Vivienne claims, 'we invented one of our own. It wasn't invented from the streets, it was the other way around.' Vivienne designed a new concept in trousers as part of this aesthetic. Increasingly over the years they were made in her long-favoured tartan. She put a strap between the knees at Malcolm's suggestion, binding one knee to the other, in a manner they had seen in bondage-wear straitjackets. She stitched a zip on some that went right under the perineum, again, as a reference to the crotch-access agenda of fetish and kink. The trousers, 'bondage kecks', became 'a declaration of war against the consumerist fashions of the High Street', according to Malcolm, and 'an explosion of the body' through its confinement. 'I made the bondage trousers in cotton sateen,' Vivienne recalls, 'and Malcolm came up with the strap. He also said we should attach this little flap on the back. He just thought it was right. But then I said it should be terry towelling. He wanted the suggestion of something tribal, like a loincloth. That's how we worked.' The idea echoes down Vivienne's designs to this day in terms of the paradoxical empowerment of constriction in fashion. More broadly, of course, buckles and straps of no practical purpose have adorned street fashion almost ever since. It was Vivienne who started it. The look was strong enough to serve as its own fanfare: the zips and fetish and references to porn as well as politics were added to by Vivienne with even stronger elements

Debbie and Tracey in Seditionaries bondage suits, 1977.

Vivienne, 1977. 'I do remember thinking [when I saw her wearing that], "My mum's quite eccentric."' Ben Westwood

of implied violence: razor blades as jewellery (ground down in part by nail files); chains and safety pins and the use of 'distressed' and apparently dirty fabrics – 'damage-driven clothes' as Malcolm called them, 'clothes for modern heroes' as Vivienne said, for a shop where 'modern was destroyed every day'. It was a deliberate inversion of the usual rules of fashion: it was an idea of 'street' created in a boutique. The cult grew. Punks felt safe in the shop. By the mid seventies, 430 King's Road was internationally renowned to a certain fashion and music cognoscenti, but was known to every London teenager as the centre of the new, dangerous look, irrespective of whether they chose to wear it. Many did. 'The police used to have to wait at Sloane Square,' recalls Vivienne, 'and round up all the punks as they got off the Tube. Once they had about two hundred of them, they would escort them in a procession down the King's Road to the shop. It's a twenty-minute walk. It was really wild.'

Vivienne was settling into the sort of creative conversation that would become her signature style, 'though I actually began to prefer it when Malcolm went away'. In New York with the Dolls, Malcolm picked up a new lexicon of imagery and shock tactics: 'fist-fucking, things like that: that came from Malcolm and New York clubs', and the imagery and vocabulary found its way into his T-shirt designs with Vivienne. But when he was in London, Vivienne explains, 'he had an affair with one of the shop assistants' and would often stay with Helen Wellington-Lloyd in Marylebone. 'She was very funny and intelligent, a great person,' Vivienne allows. 'Malcolm said they only had sex once.'

Vital to the story too would be the intensely photogenic nature of a lot of what Vivienne created. From centrally placed slogans and images to revealing and restructuring forms, Vivienne has always had an instinct for what the camera will appreciate. In an increasingly visually literate age, and living with a master of media manipulation, it was a gift that kept on giving. Though neither she nor Malcolm vocalized it at the time, they were also pioneering a new way of creating and marketing: where the image went ahead of the music and the cult itself. It had never happened before with the clothes first – or via a single shop. 'The clothes needed the groups,' McLaren later noted. 'When I went into

the music business, no one wanted to know about the fashion connection. Now it's the biggest plus you can have.' In an age familiar with
Madonna and Gaultier it is difficult to imagine that fashion and music
were once unmarried, but this was McLaren's essential claim on the
times: he locked the two concepts together, and now punk seems
impossible as an idea without Vivienne's clothes, and what became
Malcolm's band: The Sex Pistols.

'I really liked the Pistols,' Vivienne reminisces, smiling sadly. 'They all
hung around the shop, of course. That's sort of how it started. My
favourite was Steve Jones. I really liked Steve. And I got on very well
with Sid [Vicious] as well. Even though Sid was a very, very bad person.
He simply didn't know the difference between right and wrong, so you
couldn't really be that much of a friend to Sid. But he was very clever.
Very bright and interested. And interesting. Which is the sort of person
I like: if you can have all of that and look great in interesting clothes,
you'll capture my attention.'

Legend has it that John Lydon walked into Vivienne's shop in its
SEX incarnation just as Malcolm had given up on persuading Richard
Hell or Sylvain Sylvain to front a punk band for him in the UK. Like a
lot of Malcolm's stories, it's not quite true. 'He asked me who should
be the singer,' says Vivienne, 'and I said Sid, but he couldn't be found.
Johnny came in, Malcolm was there; it was his first week back from
New York and he was in the shop this Saturday, with Bernie Rhodes.'
Lydon, that summer of 1975, was wearing a Pink Floyd T-shirt, defaced
with 'I hate' and with cigarette burns in a familiar Vivienne style. With
his spiky, green-tinged hair, arresting pallor and attitude, he was a
likely poster boy for the Seditionaries clothes, but Malcolm was looking for more than a model. When asked if he could sing, Lydon snapped
back, 'What for?' but, again according to legend, he was persuaded to
sing along to Alice Cooper's 'School's Out' on the shop jukebox. 'After
the shop closed, he auditioned,' according to Vivienne. Lydon wasn't
the first to have been invited into the shop – or the pub opposite – for
an impromptu audition. Midge Ure and Kevin Rowland, who would
later front Dexys Midnight Runners, had also been 'talent-spotted'
along the King's Road by Bernie Rhodes for the stand-out feature of

not having long hair. From the get-go, the look was key. Not only was Lydon's T-shirt Vivienne-styled with holes and graffiti, it was even held together with safety pins. 'And then,' explains Vivienne, 'he started ripping everything, just like Jordan.'

Steve Jones and Paul Cook had met at school in Shepherd's Bush, and had teamed up with bassist and art student Glen Matlock via McLaren. Matlock was briefly a Let It Rock shop assistant. As QT or Kutie Jones and His Sex Pistols they appear on the 'List' T-shirt fashioned by Vivienne and Malcolm the year before, but they were missing a front man or two, as well as the signature input that would make them, properly, McLaren's band. John Lydon – renamed Rotten after his classically British teeth – and his friend John Simon Ritchie, later known as Sid Vicious, would become the lead figures, though Sid did not join till after the first tumultuous year of Sex Pistols exposure. Vivienne was instrumental in suggesting both 'Johns', whom she knew from their time hanging out at 430 with others of the Bromley Contingent. Vivienne had told him he should 'get the guy called John who came to the store a couple of times' to be the singer. When Johnny Rotten was recruited for the band, Vivienne told Malcolm 'he had got the wrong John'. But the idea of an 'anti-band' formed: one which made up in bile and pose what it lacked in conventional musical ability. As McLaren proclaimed, he 'launched the idea of a band of kids who could be perceived as being bad'. Matlock began creating melodies, riffs and beats; Lydon provided lyrics, aided by Malcolm and by Vivienne and Jamie Reid.

'I just don't remember too much about the Sex Pistols thing. I was very busy. I had two kids. I only went to gigs if I really thought they needed my support. John Lydon was brilliant. Steve was a wonderful guitarist. But their first gig was awful. By the time of their Screen on the Green gig, with The Clash, we all thought The Sex Pistols would blow them off the stage. It was, as a result of their competition with The Clash, their best ever gig. The force! The power! Amazing. I think I danced – maybe on stage, even – other times I did, as a sort of Sex Pistols cheerleader. I looked amazing. And we had this sort of cred or cachet with the punk scene, because of the shop. I was aware of the impact I made – the rubber short skirts, and the haircut by Malcolm, not hairsprayed or gelled. It was astonishing to look at. I got quite used to people stopping in cars. Though this one time, this guy shouted at me about my hair; he said "Is your bush the same?" I was *so* embarrassed.'

It was on 6 November 1975 that Vivienne attended The Sex Pistols' first gig, at St Martin's School of Art on Charing Cross Road. The Pistols, from the start, played very loudly. They did covers of the band Vivienne had known since her days with Derek, The Who, before attempting to move on to their new material, Pretty Vacant and other songs, but had no chance as the plugs on their amps were pulled when it became clear the borrowed equipment was getting trashed at the hands of the high-energy band. A fight broke out – only the first of many that became a feature of Sex Pistols gigs.

Vivienne and Jordan became responsible for the boys' look. It wasn't easy. 'They got very into it, mutilating the clothes. They thought they didn't have to pay for them.' In fact Malcolm deducted the costs from their royalties. Their second big gig was at Ravensbourne Art College in South London. Simon Barker was there, and Siouxsie Sioux (Susan Ballion) with her *Cabaret*-inspired make-up, and Billy Idol, Soo Catwoman and Philip Salon – later club promoter and Westwood aco-lyte – plus Debbie 'Juvenile' Wilson, who went on to work in the shop. The core 'Bromley Contingent', as Bernie and Malcolm dubbed them. Some of them were still at school, and it became a feature of punk concerts and the punk look (distressed school blazers, ties worn as nooses) that the style addressed an explosion of sexual and political frustration in a very youthful crowd, though of course Malcolm had dressed Vivienne in school uniforms for years. They were younger than the first fan base of Bowie or Queen, and they were poorer than most of the clientele who had, until then, shopped at 430. But the Bromley Contingent gave meaning and coltishness to the look, and a follow-ing to the band, even adopting a new style of dance, 'pogoing', that expressed both the energy and individualism, and the threat of vio-lence, that were typical of punk.

Vivienne was not immune to the violent tides around her, or averse to lashing out herself on occasion. 'She was quite punchy,' claims Steve Jones, 'she'd lock Malcolm in a cupboard . . . but Malcolm got a kick out of that.' 'That's a lie,' says Vivienne, 'we didn't have a cupboard. I'd

Debbie Juvenile, also arrested after the Jubilee Sex Pistols debacle.

lock him in rooms or slam a door at him. He goaded me – he drove me into a fury.' She also got into fights herself on occasion. 'It was at the Nashville pub, a Sex Pistols gig, and someone said to me about this stool near the stage, she said "You can't sit there," (her boyfriend had gone to get a drink) and at the time I thought, "Well, that's not very punk, I'll sit where I like." I was arrogant and stroppy. I was. I wouldn't move when he came back, so he picked me up, and the stool too, and Steve Jones came over to protect me. Then Sid took off his belt, which was covered in studs, and hit this guy around the head. I immediately regretted it all. Caroline Coon said I did it deliberately – a terrible thing to say – but it was my fault.'

Joe Strummer of The Clash was there, who said, 'That fight at the Nashville: that's when all the publicity got hold . . . I think everybody was ready to go and The Pistols were the catalyst.'

'Then at the 100 Club,' Vivienne continues, 'it all turned really violent. Sid hit Nick Kent – the *NME* writer who was Chrissie Hynde's boyfriend. Chrissie was a really, really close friend. I apologized to Nick and Malcolm told me off and said I was being bourgeois, so next time when I saw Nick I was unsympathetic. I followed Malcolm slavishly like that. I was wrong to be convinced by him. But I was fanatical, I do get that now: I was young.

'Johnny Rotten gave me a black eye. This is how it happened. It was Valentine's night, 1976; there was a party at Andrew Logan's warehouse apartment at Butler's Wharf. He knew all the "trendy", beautiful people. We were invited, but Malcolm got out his entire address book and invited everyone – I think it was meant to be a gig or a publicity stunt for The Sex Pistols. So it was chock-a-block, you couldn't get in. Derek Jarman was there and Duggie Fields and the Costiffs, Michael and Gerlinde. It was going to be "The First Miss World" – partly gay, partly transvestite – but not just that. Andrew Logan was made-up half man, half woman, and his girlfriend Luciana Martinez – she was so beautiful – was bare-breasted, and Michael Costiff was all painted blue, like an Inca god – he had the most amazing body. And Derek Jarman, I remember, for the "swimwear" round, didn't have a swimwear outfit, so walked down the side of the pool – there was a small swimming pool – and then fell sideways into the water. Deliberately. It was an amazing party, but then I got a message sent to me that Johnny Rotten couldn't get in. So I went to the door and Rotten was so angry he punched me in the face. Everyone held me back – I was quite drunk – from hitting him. He never did get in.'

Violence, or the potential for it, was some of the 'edge' that Vivienne has always played with in her designs, but in the mid seventies she was undoubtedly at her punchiest. 'Punk violence was theatrical,' recalls one contemporary, 'but at the same time McLaren and Westwood were complicit in inciting acts of violence.' And Vivienne, who had already flirted with the death-cult imagery of the Third Reich, looked for inspiration in the language of violence as well as its imagery. She loaned Sid Vicious, 'who really didn't know the difference between right and wrong', the memoirs of mass murderer Charles Manson. If she ever felt unsafe or ill at ease with the frisson of violence that attended The Sex Pistols and the imagery she created for them, she never let on. 'I've never been afraid of anything, or anywhere,' she claims, 'the punk slogan was "nobody's innocent".' 'I don't think [punk] was intentionally offensive,' says Gene Krell, 'nor was it born out of cynicism or trying to exploit the things that you hold to be true. It was really quite genuine. Vivienne doesn't have a cynical bone in her body.'

The look, the idea, the style spread fast through Britain's sultry summer of 1976 and into 1977. The high noon of punk was really remarkably fleet – an eruption of inchoate creativity, a handful of records and bands and Vivienne and Jamie Reid's seminal designs. 'Early punk was just so creative,' says Vivienne, 'really only six months of all these mad visual styles.' Steve Jones, quoting Vivienne, explained helpfully, 'Actually, we're into chaos, not violence.' The music and live performance agenda was a complete contrast to the rest of the mid seventies pop scene: stadium rockers and Abba and Rod Stewart. It played to a different agenda within Britain, and, it turned out, within Western culture, of revolt against consumerism and pop. It played well to urban teenagers in particular. The look and style spread fast to the North, to Manchester first and thence to two Bolton Institute students who headed down to London in search of the SEX shop, saw the Pistols and immediately formed their own Pistols-punk-style band, The Buzzcocks. As one of them put it, 'My life changed the moment

I saw them.' Meanwhile America's primary punk band, The Ramones, launched their UK debut album in the spring of 1976, which alerted the music industry to the untapped potential of an audience for punk music. It was moving fast out of London art colleges and the King's Road and into the mainstream, partly because of the strength of its image. So striking were Vivienne and Malcolm's designs that the band and its followers were instantly recognizable, drawn into the tribe by the immediate opprobrium their look provoked. When the Pistols played Paris later in September 1976, the first concert was a disaster, but the second was packed with French wannabe punks in improvised bin-bag punk outfits and home-razored hair. Vivienne's cultural references were easily copied and readily personalized. The Roxy club on London's Neal Street, which opened that year, regularly had to replace its loo chains: they were part of Vivienne's design semiotics, and were swiped every night. 'I loved that it was copied,' says Vivienne. 'When Soo Catwoman would turn up in a towel with a spider web painted on her, and then in a bin liner – I loved that DIY was really happening.'

For Vivienne and Malcolm, despite the tensions in their home life, it was a moment of creative togetherness and excitement, and the one time after rock 'n' roll when Vivienne allied herself completely with a popular music style: 'Malcolm was brilliant at what he did. Since then and since him and since The Sex Pistols I've not really been interested in pop music. I thought at the time that the Pistols really were protesting, but after a while it was beyond them and they sort of collapsed under the pressure of expectations, but it was very genuine at first. All the other pop groups since, pretending to be hard and tough and everything, people like The Clash, were just so poor next to The Sex Pistols. Joe Strummer was a lovely man and he did mean what he wrote and sang. With The Sex Pistols, their songs were outrageous. Archetypal. If you listen to "Anarchy in the UK" today, your hair stands on end. It's absolutely blood-curdling. Or Rotten, as a Catholic, singing, "I am an antichrist . . . I want to be anarchy . . ." And Malcolm was at the front, on the barricades with the flag, if you like, or pushing at the back of them from behind, depending on how you look at it! I loved Rotten's lyrics. "The future dream is a shopping scheme" – I thought he was really clever and talked to him a lot about politics.

You see, politically I had been such a late developer. I don't like what I think of myself then. I wanted it to be about heroes. Sex was going to break the hypocrisy of England. I am no longer a fanatic but I am proud of the shocking imagery. Some of it. Not the Cambridge rapist, but the boy smoking, I think that makes you think. I found that image, and then Bernie Rhodes turned it into a T-shirt, even though he didn't want to.'

Things moved fast and in various directions. Malcolm began to seek a serious record deal for 'the boys' and himself while the business at 430 (as it segued from SEX into Seditionaries) required Vivienne to take on extra outworkers: 'Greek and Turkish tailors mainly, real artisans, and small factory suppliers.' Jordan recruited her then boyfriend Simon Barker as McLaren's assistant, and via his crowd Vivienne first met Murray Blewett and Mark Spye, stylish designer-maker-tailors who have worked with her ever since. Vivienne began to arrogate to herself and to her shop a charismatic, if volatile, coterie of outsiders and creatives who were attracted by her and by the ideas she encompassed. 'We all, in Blondie, loved to go down to Worlds End to shop', recalls Debbie Harry of her times visiting London 'back in the "King's Road days" of the seventies'. Another close friendship that dates from that time and place was with the Texan model Jerry Hall: 'I first met Vivienne at SEX, while I was shopping there,' she tells me. 'I was living in London with my then fiancé Bryan Ferry and working as a model with English [sic] Vogue. My first impression – which turned out to be true – was of this earthy, sexy and eccentric person – just my kind! Vivienne and I got on immediately and I bought a LOT of clothes and was a frequent shopper at SEX. We have worked together and been friends ever since.' Vivienne laughs at the memory of Jerry then: 'She was shy, so very shy back then.' As Gene Krell, who began to manage the shop, recalls, 'All the characters I met at 430 King's Road were just as fascinating as Jerry. They looked at the world and they articulated themselves. People forget that punk was enchanting in its way: I remember I would be sitting in the pub with Vivienne and the grannies that went to the World's End pub in those days. And the punk kids would go in and they'd say, "Here, Bess, would you like a drink?" And some old nan who'd survived the Blitz would say, "Yeah, I wouldn't

mind." They would interface, from completely different worlds but they always found a common language, and that was one of the huge things that Vivienne initiated in my mind with punk: you can't be judgemental. She would embrace even those that rejected the things she believed. And I always thought that she was one of the people responsible for opening up this whole idea: you needn't define yourself in one way: you don't have to be afraid of the dark.'

On 8 October 1976, McLaren secured the first record deal for a band that was already a minor cult. EMI signed them for two years, McLaren leased them a flat on Denmark Street, and they went immediately into a recording session with Pink Floyd and Roxy Music supremo Chris Thomas. It wasn't an easy mix. Nevertheless, the band's first single, 'Anarchy in the UK' ('The idea and the title were mine,' says Vivienne), was released on 26 November 1976. 'From Steve Jones' opening salvo of descending chords,' wrote the music critic John Robb, 'to Johnny Rotten's fantastic sneering vocals, this song [is] a stunningly powerful piece of punk politics; a lifestyle choice and a manifesto that heralds a new era.' Another review called it 'the clarion call of a generation'. The Pistols' style was angry, euphoric and careless all at once: the perfect adolescent pose such as had not existed since the headiest days of rock 'n' roll. Vivienne and Malcolm had the soundtrack for their 'total blast' of a cult.

The packaging and visual promotion of 'Anarchy in the UK' also broke new ground within the record industry: Reid and McLaren came up with the notion of selling the record in a completely wordless, featureless black sleeve. EMI was appalled. A compromise was reached with an 'anarchy flag' – a ripped and safety-pinned Union Jack that would also feature in the artwork and T-shirts of the Jubilee. This and other images created by Jamie Reid and Vivienne for the Sex Pistols albums, posters and clothes have become the altarpieces of punk. 'You have to know, though,' says Vivienne, 'there was no masterplan with Malcolm. He just wanted Trouble. Nothing was planned. I mean to say, he actually wanted a real singer!'

Malcolm's Situationist philosophy involved all media being exploited for creative discourse, with no regard for convention or conventional outlets. At the same time he was motivated too by the

Vivienne and Malcolm, 1979.

ability of his media campaigns to generate cash out of chaos – 'though that slogan,' says Vivienne, 'that was mine.' To this end, he gleefully accepted on the band's behalf an invitation to appear on live TV in December 1976, after fellow EMI band Queen had had to pull out. The Bill Grundy interview catapulted The Sex Pistols, and by extension Vivienne, Malcolm and the whole punk hoopla, into the national consciousness. It was an early-evening TV magazine programme, Thames Television's *Today*, shown only in the London area and with declining viewing figures until the Pistols, plied with drink by Malcolm in the green room, hit the screens with a snarl of disdain for their pompous host and a willingness to be goaded into full-on expletives on live teatime telly.

It was a slow news week and it was a different world. The newspapers went crazy over the 'four-letter words that rock TV' (*Daily Telegraph*), and expressed 'Fury at filthy TV chat' (*Daily Express*). But it was the *Daily Mirror*, guardian of the nation's prissiness, that gave Malcolm the headline he longed for. 'The Filth and the Fury!' it boomed. 'This is the filthiest language ever heard on British television,' then going on to print it all in full transcript. 'Who are these "punks",' demanded the *Mirror*, 'who turn the air blue and cause uproar as protestors jam TV phone lines?' The question was answered all through 1977, as The Sex Pistols, and their apparent godparents, Malcolm and Vivienne, found themselves cast as Public Enemy Number One, besieged by press and brick-throwing locals at Thurleigh Court, but also at the eye of what turned out to be a very lucrative media storm. Vivienne, who was inured to the ways of 'the boys', nearly missed the interview because, appropriately, she was at home being Mum. 'I was in the flat hoovering, and I had to stop and turn the telly sound up when I saw it was them. But I thought nothing of it. I just carried on hoovering. All that "ol' fucker" swearing, I didn't think anything of it because that's just how they were. It was only when Malcolm came home, and was worried. That's what he told me: how worried he was.

'Malcolm was less a dictator than a leader of the gang. That's what he wanted to be. To be a schoolboy and have his own gang. Like when he was six years old and made a camp or den and he said, when the teacher came over and split it all up, he said he had never hated anyone more in his entire life than that teacher. Wally the guitarist [Warwick Nightingale, of The Sex Pistols' original line-up], for instance, Malcolm just thought was too professional. He hated professionals and teachers, so would sometimes cast me as the teacher figure. Though actually when he came into my class and took over a lesson it was all about "found objects" and he was very good. But anyway he sacked Wally, he decided Steve Jones was less a singer than a guitarist – he sang at the back of his throat, he was really, really good, actually. But that first gig of theirs had been what we called an "unhappening happening" and that's when Malcolm took things in hand. He nearly asked Chrissie Hynde to be lead singer, but in the end, for Malcolm, his "gang" had to be a gang of boys. You have to understand, there was no plan what-soever. Malcolm would create a situation and then sort of brazen it out. Try to win. Try to beat the system. And he cast me as an aider and abettor, the one schoolteacher who ever helped him, but he always cast me as the old woman, the mum who spoilt the fun and stopped the pranks. He changed his view a bit when I came up with the "Cash from Chaos" slogan for a T-shirt to help raise money for his film. By that time he was sticking to the marketing idea that The Sex Pistols couldn't play. As for Rotten, as Malcolm always called him, here are my thoughts. He and Malcolm were both jivers – they danced towards you and they danced or pushed you away. Malcolm loved Rotten's attitude, "the kid with green hair", and when he came back from that first audition he said Rotten couldn't sing at all, but he loved that and he loved that Rotten was loud and defiant. But they never really got on ever again. It was a battle of egos. And I know it's a cliché but Rotten was very Irish – fighting with mates and then a few bottles later arms around each other in consolation. And I remember I'd be outside the Thurleigh Court flat door with Rotten trying to get in to punch Malcolm, being the go-between, being the reconciler. He was only comfortable when he was at the right stage of drunk, Johnny. So in the end, I became the one teacher Malcolm fancied. That is how it was. But I am not sure he was ever political. I was into anarchy then because I thought I could get young people to challenge things. His idea of anarchy was just that: there was simply no plan.'

The storm around the Grundy interview and the subsequent

notoriety of The Sex Pistols raises a number of questions in the Vivienne story. Some artists and commentators have a sixth-sense sensitivity to the shifting currents of a culture, to the potential of expressing, even before the feeling is articulated by politicians or the press, the changing pulse of a civilization, and the agenda as it shifts from one generation to another. Malcolm and Vivienne seemed to have such an instinct, picking up on currents in American music and film and in British urban subcultures and recognizing that a band could be 'sold' or could articulate emerging truths about youth culture by not playing the usual game – indeed by not being a band at all in the normal sense, but by how they dressed and behaved. For some the Grundy interview only served to confirm what they thought they knew already: that popular culture was degenerate, puerile and wilfully ugly. It made The Sex Pistols, and by extension the design agendas of both Vivienne and Jamie Reid, look like nothing more than the commercial exploitation of shock, a brick through the plate glass of civilization, wrapped in logos, paid for by those stupid enough to want to pay for rancour. But for many others, who woke to the morning papers with real surprise that anyone would commit what appeared to be commercial suicide on live television, there was also a sense that this accurately reflected an angry truth. Society was changing. It was therefore as exhilarating a moment in popular culture as Elvis's first TV appearances or the premiere of *The Rite of Spring.* Vivienne, like those who look to punk as violent birth pangs rather than some end point of empire, notes her association with it as the first great proof of her worth as an artist. She helped express a moment, realize it, shape it, create it and dress it. And it was a moment that, at the time, was barely even understood.

'You have to understand I had a horrible life in those days. My therapy was work. There was no fashion pressure on me. It was therapy. And as for fame – or infamy – it just felt difficult. I saw it as a crusade, clothes for heroes. I NEVER wanted personal glory or attention. As line, shape and form, we were making what we believed. I was. I felt like I was fighting a cause. And when things I had created started appearing on catwalks I thought, again, "Wake up, Vivienne – make sense of what you are doing." But as for punk, well, we were against the

The Sex Pistols on stage, 1977. Johnny Rotten wears Destroy muslin, from Seditionaries.

older generation. Sexual liberation was the thing. Anti-conformity. For me, it was real. We wanted to be followed and to make changes. But in the end, I don't think it was saying anything other than jumping and spitting and being angry about the world.'

The crumbling British economy and British urban social structure of the 1970s has its own drab specificity. It is also now used as an image for what urban decay looks like. If Britain was the first industrial nation, it was also the first post-industrial wasteland, and the visual language of punk is now routinely used as a metaphor for post-modern grunge. Not that Vivienne terms it such; she speaks, as Malcolm always did, of a look 'for the "dispossessed"'. The mid seventies saw unprecedented OPEC oil price increases, a resultant devaluing of the pound, the fall of the Heath government, and the beginnings of the end of the Trade Union Movement as a central political force, which amounted, in a sense, to an end to the socialist positivism of the post-war years. It had all gone horribly wrong. But, as continues to be the case, the brunt of the monetary and economic crisis was felt in the UK very disproportionately. It was felt most by the urban poor, and the young.

The Situationists had long spat in the face of consumerism and decried all art that sought profit – whilst, in Malcolm's case, happily pocketing any that came their way. As is often said in marketing these days – such is the ongoing impact of punk – there is nothing that sells better than authenticity. If you can fake that, you can sell anything. And the punk sound and look felt, indeed was, originally, authentically angry and frustrated at the broken dreams of the sixties. Youth was suddenly a problem again, as it had been with the mods and rockers, which made it all the more exciting to be young and to be associated with the inchoate revolt. Vivienne admits to being greatly influenced in later designs by the post-apocalyptic vision of Ridley Scott's *Blade Runner*; it, in turn, and Vivienne, have their debt to Kubrick's *A Clockwork Orange*, which inadvertently gave wide screen appeal to 'punk' make-up and theatricalized violence and fetish-wear even more alluringly than the camped-up *Rocky Horror Show* had done. 'But the influence is everywhere and unexpected,' says Vivienne. 'Take

Star Wars, for instance: that design simply could not have happened without punk.'

The Pistols and their ripped and deconstructed clothes, not to mention their ability to rip through the proprieties of live TV, hit a resonant note. 'It was hilarious,' said Steve Jones. 'It was one of the best feelings, the next day, when you saw the paper: you thought, "Fucking hell, this is great!" From that day on, it was different. Before then, it was just music; the next day, it was the media.' It was the moment when the whole phenomenon spilled out far beyond the bounds of the King's Road, and, for some, that spoiled the party. But it also gave Vivienne, albeit briefly, the sort of exposure no money can buy and a platform the likes of which she has not enjoyed again until relatively recently. For some, punk, a word now instantly understood, had the seeds of its own destruction already planted because the media now dictated its own agenda on a subculture it had decided was better ridiculed than attended. Vivienne says she doesn't recall whether she or Malcolm were aware of the 'movement' fracturing through the sudden pressure of infamy and pending record sales. She was too busy in the shop and Malcolm in planning tours, record releases and the long-plotted EMI contract. 'It was just business as usual for me in the shop. There were requests for interviews and foreign press, that sort of thing. I wasn't greatly impressed. I do remember someone coming in to sell razor-blade jewellery – I could see the spread of it all in those terms, and that I liked.'

430 King's Road was restyled yet again, this time with a gleaming, high-tech Ben Kelly design and two giant black-and-white cityscapes; one, inverted, of Piccadilly, and one always taken to be a bombed-out Dresden but recently revealed as an unidentified find of Malcolm's from the Imperial War Museum. 'For soldiers, prostitutes, dykes and punks', read the clothes labels, with anarchist 'A's and the co-design credit of Malcolm McLaren and Vivienne Westwood. It was less and less the truth. Malcolm's time was devoted to the Pistols. The press began to pick up the fissure between the two of them. The Seditionaries clothes that were featured in all the magazine shoots for the Pistols after the Grundy interview had rival quotes from Vivienne

and Malcolm: journalists talked to Vivienne about the clothes, and Malcolm about the band. It only made sense. It was the clear division of labour.

The Grundy interview was in early December, and by the turn of the year into 1977, Vivienne and Malcolm were less at the centre of a party than in a bunker. The windows at Thurleigh Court had been smashed by local skinheads, the route from there to Clapham South Tube was a daily assault course for Vivienne, and Malcolm kept to his desk at the Denmark Street office of 'Glitterbest', the company he had founded to manage the Sex Pistols, writing manifestos on what it all might mean. 'What punk can do,' he said, 'is inspire fans to think and act for themselves.' It was a clear enunciation of the higher aspirations of punk, before it all blew over in a sea of gobbing and recriminations. 1977 was going to be quite a year.

'I would go along with what Malcolm said about the meaning of it all, but it never really happened. The way I saw it, it was about trying to put a spoke in the wheels of the status quo. For the kids it was a chance to engage and to form opinions. But they didn't. They just jumped around. But the look: that I thought was special. So I went to see Grace Coddington at *Vogue* to say that Soo Catwoman should be on their front cover. Grace was embarrassed. She said I should go and talk to *Ritz* magazine. I've got the scars from that time to this day: Debbie Juvenile knew this bloke who was called "Pete the Murderer" – a real narcissist – and he came into 430 one day with an axe and threatened me. He said I was a bourgeois capitalist ripping off kids. I was so angry and I told him so – and worse. So he came back with a gang of punks the next week. It didn't scare ME. Stupid Michael Collins, the shop manager, locked the door with me on the outside, but then got worried about me and opened it up and kids all rushed in and stole everything. Everything. I tried to force the door against them and look' – Vivienne holds up her middle finger, '– I have this damaged finger still from trying to hold the door against a mob of punks.'

The first months of 1977 were a steep learning curve for Malcolm and Vivienne in terms of public opprobrium and The Sex Pistols' position in the music industry. EMI dropped them, and they became aware they needed a smaller independent label and a way to use their

Vivienne on the *Queen Elizabeth*, 1977.

notoriety to their advantage. Between the end of their promotions of 'Anarchy in the UK' in the autumn of 1976 and the 'Secret Tour', as it became known, in 1977, because no venue would risk booking them for fear of riot, the Pistols played only three times. It all generated press coverage, but not sales, income, or, at first, a new record contract. And meanwhile, the band began to fall apart. Glen Matlock left or was ousted by Malcolm, and Sid, long-standing fan and possibly the originator of the Sex Pistols' pogoing dance, was taken on as the new bassist. '[Glen] had been growing apart from them for some time,' says Simon Barker. 'You can see it in the photos – at the start he always used to wear Vivienne's clothes from SEX, but then his hair and his clothes got really neat. He was letting the side down.' He also made the cardinal error of saying he admired The Beatles. So Vivienne got her preferred choice of 'Johns' into The Sex Pistols, albeit late, with a man rechristened 'Sid Vicious' who would be the other poster boy for the look she and Malcolm had created.

'I was instrumental in Sid being in The Sex Pistols,' says Vivienne, 'it was me. It was very naive of me. He was an addict. And if I'd known, what it's like to be a junkie and to be around a junkie, I would never have pushed for him to be in the band. People say it was Nancy [Spungen] who introduced him to heroin, but it wasn't. He said his mother had given him his first fix when he was fourteen. He was a junkie. That's why he was in the shop in torn safety-pinned trousers in the first place.'

In February of 1977, grandma Rose died while Malcolm was briefly in LA trying to secure an American recording deal. 'It was two weeks before they found her,' recalls Vivienne, 'in the flat in Clapham South.' In March the new line-up of Pistols signed with A&M Records outside Buckingham Palace, for the purposes of a Malcolm publicity stunt, and a week later one Nancy Spungen of New York arrived in London, headed straight to 430 King's Road, and set about trying to find a Sex Pistol to have sex with. 'She was a fairly typical suburban girl,' said Richard Hell, who had had a brief affair with her in New York, 'in that she worshipped rock stars.' She set her sights on John Lydon but ended up with Sid, with whom she immediately scored some heroin.

March 1977 also saw the first recording of Lydon's song 'God Save the Queen', always imagined by Malcolm as a perfect inversion of the intended fandango to celebrate Elizabeth II's twenty-five years on the throne, and originally titled 'No Future'. It might have proceeded in the usual fashion of the industry at the time, with a release date set once the single went into production. But during March A&M Records panicked at the title, the violent behaviour of the group and the laissez-faire 'boys will be boys' attitude of their supposed manager, and pulled their support. Twenty-five thousand copies of the single had already been pressed. By 16 March, the Pistols and McLaren's company Glitterbest were £75,000 richer but with a terminated contract and no immediate recourse on how to put out their record. The phone in Thurleigh Court rang through the night and McLaren eventually gave a quote to the *Evening Standard* that the Pistols were 'a contagious disease: I just keep going in and out of doors and people keep giving me cheques'. It was a great line that stole all the headlines the next day, but seemed to prove that Malcolm was better at generating opprobrium than at actually getting things made or said.

Vivienne attended Sid's first outing as front man, at Screen on the Green in Islington. The occasion was to prove damaging for the group: Sid went out to score heroin with Nancy down Camden Passage, and ended up with hepatitis that put him in hospital for more than a month. Malcolm eventually found a record producer willing to risk 'God Save the Queen', in the form of the young Richard Branson of Virgin Records. And the single, with its treasonable sleeve image, went back into production just as celebrations were gearing up for the June Jubilee. 'It was the beginning of a long friendship – Richard Branson and me,' recalls Vivienne. 'Malcolm hated him, because they were contemporaries and Branson was already an authority figure. "Never trust a hippy," Malcolm used to say about Richard. But I liked him, and my opinion of him was confirmed years later when he offered to take over the National Lottery for no profit. He is a good man.'

That summer of 1977, as the international press converged on London to cover the royal pageants, the image created by Reid and expanded at Seditionaries as a 'God Save the Queen' T-shirt was to be seen around the world. A postcard was launched featuring both the T-shirt and a gaggle of King's Road punks. The Cecil Beaton portrait of

Vivienne and Malcolm, 1979. Calm in the storm in a teacup.

the Queen with a safety pin through her lip has become the essential icon of the hit summer of punk – the Summer of Hate, as it became known – because it, and the Vivienne uniform, began to be seen all over Britain and across the Western world. The T-shirt, or its various sloganed cousins, teamed with bondage-wear and Vivienne's much-loved kilts, studded leather and dog collars, razor blades and chains, Situationist slogans, *A Clockwork Orange* make-up and Mohicans, became a tribal motif from Tokyo to California. And the song went straight into the charts, and indeed to number one, despite, or because of, a national broadcast ban.

The Summer of Hate had its emphatic emblems and it also had its dramatic climax. It was a simple enough plan. Hire a boat, cruise up the Thames, moor up somewhere near the Palace of Westminster (you could do that in those days, despite the IRA), and blast out 'God Save the Queen'. The Queen wasn't going to be there, though it was the week of her Silver Jubilee celebrations. The boat, however, was called the *Queen Elizabeth* – it was old enough to have been named after the Queen Mother. There was to be a royal flotilla later that day, and fire-works too, so Malcolm had plotted a publicity stunt to rival everything that had gone before. It was, after all, the Pistols' first real hit.

McLaren, Vivienne and the band all boarded the *Queen Elizabeth* at Charing Cross pier at about 6.30 – along with eventually over two hundred liggers. This was in the days before Health and Safety or the Thames boating disasters that would outlaw such overcrowding, but even so, it was immediately apparent that the stunt had the potential for disaster. Sex Pistols gigs were by habit and design chaotic, over-crowded fire hazards. But it was altogether more alarming when the only escape route was the silty river. The bar staff were immediately wary and insisted on selling only singles, not doubles, so alarmed were they by the raucous punk crowd. Johnny Rotten tried to play, despite a crowded band area under an awning on deck, and feedback problems. Someone else blasted out The Ramones in competition. Vivienne, dressed in black leathers that reside to this day in the Elcho Street archive, pitched in as designated hostess and enthusiastic dancer. It was one of those hot summer nights that went down in English legend

– the sultry summers of 1976 and 1977 – and it started out both magical and mad: the sort of occasion Vivienne loved. But then the police were notified. *God Save the Queen* was splashed down the side of the barge in lurid Day-Glo pink and yellow (paint provided by Vivienne), and the whole enterprise had been designed to get up the noses of the Establishment and attract press attention for the Sex Pistols. McLaren and Vivienne were no more or less anti-monarchy than many of their generation at the time: it was more about selling records than making a personal attack on Her Majesty's big day. What they had not bargained for was quite how over-policed central London was that day, and how much unwarranted police attention their stunt on the Thames would attract.

The *Queen Elizabeth* was boarded by river police before sunset, and escorted back to the pier. Fittingly, they cut the power on the boat (hardly an act of Health and Safety in the first place) just as Rotten was about to launch into a cover of 'No Fun'. Fights broke out, and by the time the two-hundred-plus passengers were being walked back up the gangplanks, darkness had fallen, chaos reigned, and there was an excuse for plenty of arrests. Vivienne can clearly be seen in the footage from the time (Malcolm and Julien Temple had arranged for a small film crew to attend) being manhandled into the back of a police van in her leathers. The papers the next day were full of it all: 'Sex Pistols Manager led away in handcuffs'. It got them the headlines and a de facto number-one slot for the banned single, but at the expense of a decent party. And Vivienne spent the night in Bow Street police station. 'They weren't arresting me, actually,' explains Vivienne. 'I just jumped in the van as I was so worried for Malcolm. It quickly became quite funny. I think I did a cartwheel when we got to the police station. I remember there was a somewhat prurient interest from the police. Debbie Juvenile's nipples were showing and I had on my usual lipstick and there were these written police descriptions, 'full-lipped', 'protruding nipples'. It was funny. I was put in a cell with Debbie, this girl called Tracy and there was an Irish girl who was freezing because she had been arrested dancing in the fountains in Trafalgar Square and was wet. So I mainly remember it being very nice to get away from the hard brown plastic bench, and away the next morning, just to wash. And more to the point, I had been very worried about the boys, as they were alone in the flat and didn't know where we were . . .'

It was the morning after the high noon of punk. The Pistols would go on to further attention-grabbing media bans with *Never Mind the Bollocks*, to tours of Scandinavia and even, disastrously, the US – but they never regained the high watermark of the Jubilee. And for Vivienne, it all ended with the deaths of first Nancy and then Sid, all within eighteen months. 'Sid killed Nancy,' states Vivienne emphatically. 'He admitted it to Malcolm, who told me. He stabbed her. He was out of it, and when he came round, she was dead. Malcolm used to say that Sid would have got off. But of course he was dead before it all came to trial. When it all blew up with Sid, I said, "I'm going to go to New York to see Sid and help. Go to Riker Island or whatever, I'm just going to be there," and Malcolm said, "You and Sid's mother! What use are you going to be with two junkies in New York?" because Mrs Beverley, his junkie mother, was going to go over and try to "help". Our leather man at the time was a spiritual medium, and he said, after Sid died, he said that Sid had contacted him from the afterlife and said when he came out of custody and saw his mother waiting for him, he knew, he knew then, he was seeing Death. I should have gone.'

The band struggled on in various guises and line-ups only as far as early 1978, eating up more and more of McLaren's time and Branson's money, with recording sessions in Rio and Paris and London when it proved impossible to have the volatile mix of personalities in one studio. Seditionaries, meanwhile, went from strength to strength. The King's Road shop became a pilgrimage site for those interested in the 'New Wave' fashions and sounds, and the rest of the street woke up to the potential of Vivienne's designs in slightly less avant-garde form. In April 1977 Zandra Rhodes put punk on the catwalk for the first time, having the grace to credit the 'movement' and indeed Vivienne for her 'torn clothes, chains and safety pins', and Debbie Juvenile and Jordan in the shop found themselves catering for a crowd that spanned high-end fashionistas and street louts. Another 'punk' outlet, known as BOY, opened nearer the Sloane Square Tube. 'These clothes are about survival in London in 1977,' the proprietor told the London *Evening News*. They were supposedly about what was happening every day on the streets, which was true enough if what happened on the street every day included hypodermic needles and contraceptives as appliqués and more bondage and swastikas. Beaufort Market, just before the kink on the King's Road, moved from antiques and collectibles to retro ephemera and punk clothing and jewellery, presided over by one Marianne Elliot-Said, better known as Poly Styrene.

The explosion into mainstream and the refraction into others' work has been a regular experience for Vivienne ever since. 'I didn't mind Zandra copying the punk thing because she did it in her own way,' says Vivienne – and she relished the extent to which her design ideas resurfaced on the street in improvised DIY forms. Though Vivienne thought of it as 'urban guerrilla-wear', fashion historians have pointed out it was also the beginnings of countercultural fashion – of putting on the outside what had been thought, or hidden, on the inside. Seams, bras, sado-masochistic fetish-wear, and 'Third World'-style reconditioned detritus from safety pins to bottle tops to, infamously, a red-inked tampon, all found their way from the literal inside to figure on the out.

One early effect therefore of the designs was the licence punk gave to women to dress assertively and to own the former tools of subjection. What started out with rubber-wear and stockings came in time to include a fashion lexicon for punk women that was just as strong, assertive and individualistic as the style created for Malcolm's 'boys'. This had not been the case with previous music / fashion cults, even those with which Vivienne had been involved, like rock 'n' roll, mods, Teds or Trads. Punk was almost unisex, and indeed for some was perversely asexual. Vivienne and Malcolm had succeeded by the end of 1977 in their intended and stated cause: to create and style and try to control a youth cult, for purposes that spanned politics, art and commercial cupidity. Vivienne also began to establish a constituency that has remained hers. Not only did her clothes attract and cater for assertive women, or women who wanted their clothes to lend them confidence, they also attracted an outsider in-group, a core constituency of those who felt themselves slightly to the side of normality. In 1977, just as Malcolm and Vivienne's relationship took its final and terminal slide into the abyss, Gene Krell, her friend and shop manager, moved into the spare room at Thurleigh Court. He tells this story of what it was like to be one of the shopping acolytes at the height of punk, a tale far from the usual spit-and-bile of the punk legend:

'The majority of the kids that came in were not, frankly, terribly attractive. They weren't the Coco Rochas of this world, you know, they weren't all Linda Evangelistas. They were, kind of, misfits. Very often they had weight problems. Some had physical deformities. We had a boy come in with no feet. He was a regular customer. He had wooden, kind of, stumps on his – and he would make these sounds as he came across the floor at the shop. I see him with such remarkable clarity, because I remember him coming in and he had these black-leather half-legs covered in gold studs and he really struggled. Life was just such a struggle for him. That kid came out of Vivienne's shop and he felt special and cool and accepted. One of the pre-eminent virtues of punk and of Vivienne is that she became an enabler, and punk demanded acceptance. And we did that on a regular basis. Those kids were, in many cases, abused. They were social rejects and, you know, they came in there and they left with something really quite sacred, for them. And people are always dismissive of what we did and they just look at it as being, sort of, one-dimensional and hateful. But, you know, for a kid to come in, like that, with no feet and lose his inhibitions and leave that shop feeling that he was part of something that was more worldly and more universal, you know, that's a very, very rare opportunity that's presented to us, and Vivienne knew that. To make someone feel as relevant or as significant as anyone who walks this earth, that's a rare and cherished gift. Punk could do that. Fashion can do that – rarely. Vivienne does it always.'

'When I turned round, on the barricades,' says Vivienne, 'there was no one there. That was how it felt. They were just still pogoing. So I lost interest. And it finished it completely, for me, when Sid died. But I am proud. If I had been made a Dame just for creating punk, I would have thought "fair enough": just with that, I've done more good than Mrs Thatcher. But it didn't change my life – or it didn't feel like it was doing at the time. It felt natural, and a continuity.'

Yet it did change Vivienne's life. For one thing, it brought her valid-

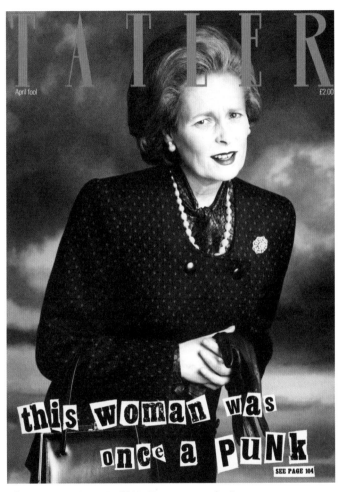

'This Woman was Once a Punk'. Mrs T was not amused. 1989.

ation as an artist and designer in that punk was discussed and written about globally, and she and Malcolm, as designers and 'curators' of a new way of dressing and behaving, have their place between the make-do-and-mend origins of Vivienne's earliest exposure to 'fashion' and the cultural impact of her subsequent designs. 'We just got these ideas, and we put them together,' she shrugs. Punk brought her nevertheless the sort of fame that even a family might notice: people turned and pointed at her in the street, and they knew her name. 'I remember when I first thought "My God – she's world famous," recalls her brother Gordon. 'I knew this guy working for the New Zealand TV station from my days in film school, and he called to say he was coming over doing a story on these people in the King's Road with this shop and I said, "that's my sister". It was just as The Sex Pistols blew up in everyone's face, but he was doing this big story not on them but on Vivienne. And that's the first time I knew. I hadn't noticed exactly. Who does? Of a sibling? But that was the moment I thought, oh God, she's known all over the world. Instantly.' In that regard alone, as her son Joe has said, her life was never the same again.

Punk, Vivienne tells me, began with a feeling, a spirit born out of London and New York that self-evidently resonated all over the world, and a look created by her and Malcolm. And it returned rock music to its rock 'n' roll function: namely to be rebellious, distasteful to elders, critical of the status quo, and to tell the important truth that it is each generation's prerogative to imagine and describe its future. But it didn't feel like that at the time. 'It's about identity,' she says, 'you can't be a designer without ideas. Talented people sometimes just do things for themselves. But I concluded very early on with punk that it was an immediate marketing opportunity. I approve of people's individual artistic freedom, and punk is to do with an aesthetic, but I sometimes think the only good thing that came out of it was that "Don't trust the government" idea and that meanwhile I do think I looked great! But is it really that important? It gave people a complacency, and the idea that "Nobody has the right to tell me anything." And one bastard child of that was an element of Thatcherism. When I posed for *Tatler* dressed as Mrs Thatcher – and I do look a little like her – it was like an acting job: "Put a little doubt in your eyes and you'll look like Thatcher." And it's true.

'Johnny Rotten's songs really were very clever, weren't they?' says Vivienne as I am packing up one day, and she starts to hum. '*No future. Your future dream is a shopping scheme.* We need to stop educating people to be consumers and educate them so they are capable of thinking with their own minds, as Noreena Hertz says in her books: you can look at economics from the *other* side, from the people it suppresses. That is what punk was all about.'

THURLEIGH COURT

There is no more sombre enemy of good art than the pram in the hallway.
                                                    CYRIL CONNOLLY,
                                                    The Charlock's Shade

*I was very lucky to have children. Meeting them was one of the greatest
things that ever happened to me. I'm proud of my boys – they'd never shit
on anybody. The best thing you can do for children, I think, is to give
them ideals.*   VIVIENNE WESTWOOD

Turn left out of Clapham South Tube, where Sid Vicious and Johnny
Rotten once loitered waiting for Malcolm, and along the Common past
where grandma Rose used to live, and you get to a low, cream art deco
building. Thurleigh Court, Nightingale Lane. There is a broad bay window on the first floor that used to overlook an evergreen oak and open
space. And behind this window is the light-filled 'front room' where
Vivienne lived and worked, designed and sewed for over thirty years.

Thurleigh Court doesn't have a blue plaque on it, but doubtless
one day it will. It is one of London's seminal addresses because this is
where punk was made, quite literally, on one Singer sewing machine,
and where Vivienne and Malcolm lived, rowed, split up, got together
again, and agreed, one winter night, that he would go his way towards
music and Hollywood and she would go hers in fashion. It is where
The Sex Pistols' contractual terms were screamed down a Bakelite
telephone, where the 'Marilyn' and 'Anarchy' T-shirts were hand dyed
and stencilled, and where Ben and Joe were brought up. And it is
where Vivienne would doubtless still be living were it not for the

reasonable disinclination of her young husband to live always and forever in the shadow of her past. 'It was very hand done to begin with, it's true, and it was mainly done there. When Malcolm found us that flat it felt like a godsend. The caretaker was lovely and let us have it at a discounted rent because it had been wrecked by hippies who painted it all pillar-box red. So we got it very cheap, £6 a week, and Malcolm painted it black.'

Number 10 is now looked after by a close friend of Vivienne's, Louie McManus, former south London drug dealer turned figurative artist. His canvases, created in and out of prison, are arranged around the cramped flat and his reformation through art has been supported by Vivienne and Joe and Ben. A long time ago he took a protective and avuncular interest in the boys and now he is part of the family, and the ideal curator and guide to this unusual cultural site, still painted the colours Malcolm and Vivienne chose, still crowded with art, half-finished projects and the colourful detritus of chaotic, creative lives. One long ill-lit internal corridor links two small bedrooms and a galley kitchen and a bathroom, still tiled as it was when Rose and Malcolm first found it, and off this is the little balcony where Vivienne dried the clothes she had dyed in a giant pan kept for that purpose in the kitchen. The large 'front room' with the bay window, actually at the back, was where Vivienne slept and sewed. The windows have long since been repaired after bricks were thrown in the furore at the height of punk, but the siege of Thurleigh Court after the Grundy interview remains Joe's most salient memory of being ten:

'The oddest memory I have is being locked in the flat for a week, unable to get out. It was like suddenly my parents were Public Enemy Number One . . . peeping out the window and seeing all these kids I used to play with – Pakistanis, West Indians, Chinese – and they were laughing along with the racists. They thought it was funny, us getting our windows smashed. That's when I changed. After that I became a lot more careful about who my mates were, who my real friends were.'

The same years that saw Vivienne sow the seeds of international fame and a fashion empire saw her also bringing up two boys, largely alone, at Thurleigh Court. Her life as a working mother is an unsung part of her story, partly because, as Shami Chakrabarti of Liberty

Joe Corré, Malcolm McLaren and Vivienne at Thurleigh Court.

said recently, 'Vivienne is a *practical* feminist. She gets on with it. She doesn't bang on about the fact that perhaps, as a woman, it's been a bit complicated.' It is an unsung part of her image as well, and an intriguing one, that in those years when she was striding down the King's Road in rubber and purple lip gloss, or for that matter the years when she was hoiking herself into platform shoes and uplift corsets, she was also doing the school run some of the time, or dealing with teenage sons disinclined to walk on the same side of the street as her. Either way, it intrigues many of Vivienne's admirers and detractors alike that she appears to have had it all, and balanced the conflicting demands of career, fashionability and motherhood, and come out the other end with two well-adjusted and successful sons who clearly adore her. 'Not at all,' she protests. 'I was not a good mother. I thought to myself, the best thing I can do for my children is the ideas I have, what I know, what I learn, and so I did not concentrate on family life. I didn't do what other mothers do. I neglected my children because I had to do certain things which meant that I couldn't be there for them. In order to do "fashion", because, at that time, I thought that fashion was a kind of crusade. At the time of punk it felt that it was. We needed to show the world that we're serious. Now, as a mother and a grandmother, I regret that. I got the balance wrong. But I was doing the best I could, as I saw it, at the time.'

Vivienne's boys strongly disagree. 'Did I have a happy childhood? Yes,' says Ben. 'The thing is, we didn't just love her, Joe and me, we *liked* her.' 'With punk, for instance,' says Joe, 'I just felt part of it, in the middle of it all the time, really. I really liked the shop girls, I really liked that my mum was so different, and I was quite happy to be there in the middle of it all. I don't ever remember not being into what Mum was doing.' Ben concurs: 'I was never worried and I enjoyed myself. We never seemed to have any money but Mum made it all quite fun. All these people working in the house and all these sewing machines and Hells Angels coming in for leather fittings. I loved it. There was a lot of extended-family support from my mother's mother and father. Joe and I spent a lot of time with them from an early age. But here's the thing: I remember one time, I was about nine and was staying back with Dad, but I spoke to her on the phone and she arranged to come and meet me one day and I waited at the end of this big, long road. So I saw her coming, about a mile away. This is Luton: Plastic Land. I can see her now, with her bleached spiky hair, and I just thought, "Wow. My mum's great. She looks different to everyone in this bloody place." And I just loved her.'

'I couldn't have coped without my parents,' says Vivienne, 'they were wonderful. And that was just how it was: boxes of studs and pliers, rolls of fabric in the corner and patterns and scissors and samples, and every day an Irish seamstress married to a Turk, Anne Alli, used to come and help, and Sid Green came by, and Mr Mintos the tailor and Red Baron the biker would be there and these Scandinavian leather-workers, and that's how it was for the boys.'

When the boys moved to Thurleigh Court, Ben was six and Joe two. The long corridor became littered with children's clutter, and as the years went by with the paraphernalia of their shared obsession with bikes. Vivienne was and remains a magpie creative force, accumulating fabrics and clippings, artwork or books that might inspire her. It drove Malcolm wild, and at times threatened to overwhelm Thurleigh Court, as every bunk bed and every surface was recruited in the service of designing or bike repairs. 'Mum did need space to create,' says Ben. 'She would have that, you know, "Go out and play, I'm busy," attitude; she was doing something all the time. But that's inspiring in its way, for a kid; in the end it *was* interesting.'

'Neither of them censored us from any of it,' Joe recalls. 'I remember one time, it must have been the era of SEX, and Malcolm had gone and got these bollock weights that you had to strap on your bollocks and then lift them off the ground, and I remember he showed me and Ben and we were laughing our heads off with Malcolm trying them out at the house. And we were just all of us in hysterics, Mum too.'

There was a free-ranging attitude to parenting that reflected some of Vivienne's own Derbyshire upbringing but would be anathema to modern city parents. 'We were brought up to be very adventurous,' recalls Joe, 'out and about all the time. Like travellers. Ben and I were going off to France when we were ten and twelve, on our own, camping on the beach. Come the summer, if we weren't at Dora's, Malcolm had always been full of "You can get out now," or more like, "It's the summer holidays – get those fucking kids out of the fucking house." The first time we went off on our own, and I think I was probably about nine, we rode on our bikes to Devon, where our grandparents had retired by then. It was Malcolm's idea. It was all accepted, and off we went. Malcolm had told us we had to do it and I think it took us about ten days to get to Devon on our bikes. We took a tent. And nobody stopped us, and off we went, with everything on our backs. Next year, we cut the time down by half because we knew what we were doing then a bit more. So our childhood was very free, or the holidays could be, anyway.'

In point of fact, Vivienne is keen to say in her defence, these were different times, and Dora and Gordon were sufficiently impressed with the idea to make a chequered flag with which to greet their grandsons on arrival. It was only on the first night that a worried couple who met the boys phoned to check that their story was true and they weren't runaways.

But Dora and Gordon, called upon to pitch in as grandparents, were sometimes critical of Vivienne's parenting. 'Not critical enough to think that the authorities should be involved,' says Ben, 'but almost. They hated punk and they hated Malcolm. They disagreed with things that Mum did but they backed her up 100 per cent. There were the usual things with parents and grandparents, like Joe would be dressed up in leather and a "Killer Rocks" T-shirt and Grandad would say, "I'm not going out with you tonight to the RAF club with you wearing that." And of course they didn't like Malcolm, Dora and Gordon. They thought that what Mum was doing was shocking, you know, putting safety pins through the Queen's lip and the word "fuck" which was every other word between Malcolm and Mum, and my grandfather would say, "I'm really shocked at that, Vivienne, you know, really, that you use language like that and let your boys," but then that was nothing compared to her support of the IRA. Grandad was really, really shocked by that. So in a sense nothing seemed quite as bad afterwards. He didn't live to see Mum's huge, huge success. He just wanted her to make some money!'

'We never ever had Christmas there,' adds Joe. 'The only thing we celebrated in our household was Bonfire Night. That was the big thing.

For weeks and weeks before Bonfire Night Ben and I would be doing "Penny for the Guy" up at Clapham South Station – all times of night. Mum's old clothes. Whatever we could find. We used to get a lot of money. We would make these huge bonfires. And throw bangers through people's letter boxes and fireworks at each other. It makes sense, really; for our family that was the Big Deal: the chaos holiday. Birthdays, no one really cared that much about. Though I do remember grandma Dora always remembered your birthday and sometimes she'd even send me or Ben a cake in the post – knowing that Mum or Malcolm weren't likely to. She used to make nice cakes, Dora.'

The bonfire nights became legendary and the date, if not the place, remains a fixture in Vivienne's work diary, with an annual party. Her friend Robert Pinnock recalls though that in the Thurleigh Court years, the evening descended into wild dancing and music back at the flat. 'You know, Elvis, that sort of thing, and Vivienne drinking whisky and dancing – Jameson was always her thing, and dancing until the morning . . .'

In both Ben and Joe's case, boarding school beckoned once the parallel career demands of their parents, with The Sex Pistols and Seditionaries, meant Malcolm and Vivienne could not be relied on to be at Thurleigh Court much at all. Scourge of the Establishment though she is, and one-time anarchist, Vivienne warmly embraced the idea of private boarding-school education for her sons, out of a love of pure learning perhaps, but also as a practical solution to her failing personal and professional partnership. It proved disastrous all round.

'When we first came to Thurleigh Court my mum asked if I would be interested in going to boarding school or to live with my father for a bit,' recalls Ben. 'I had nothing particularly against this and she said that it would be useful for her. And for Malcolm, I suppose. So I thought, aged eight, I was helping my mum. Derek was living up in Luton with his second wife. It was a year and a half later that I came back from living with my dad, and then Mum and Malcolm sent me off to boarding school for two and a half years. On open days Mum used to come down. Not with Malcolm but with Gene Krell, all dressed in black with long wavy black hair and about twenty rings on his fingers, and Mum with her spiky bleached hair. I remember she'd be there

with her hair and a rubber miniskirt on, and my schoolmates would tell me how much they fancied her, after she'd gone. And she came down to school one time with Chrissie Hynde – she wasn't famous at the time but she was very sexy, and my mates liked her as well.'

For Joe, too, it is the boarding-school experience that he cites as the failing of Vivienne and Malcolm's parenting, and even of that he is sanguine and forgiving: 'Boarding school was a trauma because I went when I was five or six. Malcolm tried convincing me it was going to be this fantastic big adventure but I turned up, for instance, at this one place and it was like the fucking House of Whipcord: they used to put soap in your mouth. And well, after that, nothing could faze me at all. I didn't resent it. I knew Mum and Malcolm were trying to do the best thing. And I knew we had my grandparents for holidays, for instance, which was nice. I used to also like hanging about in Clapham and stuff. But boarding school affected me quite deeply. It was a cruel place, though I don't think Mum and Malcolm meant it cruelly. And pretty much the first visit they came to see me, this one place, they realized, and they took me out, and then put me in another, which was actually much better. I just went from one school to another. They never lasted long. I always had the impression that Mum and Malcolm would put me in these boarding schools without ever having any intention of paying the fees. I remember quite regularly being asked to go to the bursar's office and the bursar would say, "Your parents haven't paid. Are they going to pay?" And eventually it just became a routine I was used to: first term, new school, then halfway through the second term the call to the bursar's office about the first term's bill. End of the second term: two bills unpaid. End of the third term: move to a different school. Now my mother says they always paid, and Malcolm said he had, but he hadn't.'

The couple once described as the Bonnie and Clyde of fashion had only one real getaway incident (Vivienne drove; Malcolm never learned). They arrived at one of Joe's schools with Ben already collected, found him on the drive, shouted, 'Get in the car,' drove off and did a runner. Malcolm howled with laughter at the subversive thrill of it all as the boys cowered in the back with embarrassment. Vivienne later paid back the money, and further claims the boys have misremembered

Vivienne at home at Thurleigh Court, by her son Ben Westwood.

the simple issue that Michael Collins was stealing her money; she was cash-strapped, and was sometimes late with fees. 'And he was very, very nice, that headmaster at St Christopher's in Letchworth. Both of them were there at one stage, and we were late with the fees, but he was very nice about it all.'

Unsurprisingly, perhaps, the memorable issue of growing up as Vivienne Westwood's sons had less to do with the hit-and-run schooling or lack of it, than with the business of dealing with her increasingly high profile and dramatic appearance. Most adolescents rebel against their parents' dress codes and sense of decorum, but when your mum is in the vanguard of extreme taste, it throws its own challenges at being fourteen. 'Your mum dresses you as a kid: I didn't even really think about clothes growing up,' recalls Joe, 'but I do remember hanging out with these kids in Clapham and them all suddenly pointing and laughing at me. And I just couldn't understand. I had on this semi-transparent pleated thing that Mum had made, and it had a pin-up soft porno "girlie" picture in the pocket. It was one of these shirts from SEX, but I just remember I really liked it because of the way it felt on me. So when I finally twigged that they were laughing at my clothes I just thought, well, that's stupid. Why would you laugh at anyone's clothes? But when we went out with Mum, even shopping, my brother Ben went through a stage of hiding behind trees. A hundred yards back. He was going through puberty, and he'd be dying with embarrassment. I was younger, I didn't give a fuck, and I loved that she didn't either. Ben was different, or rather punk and everything hit at a different time for him – he's four years older than me, so he was just coming into being worried about how he looked and all that kind of teenage angst and everything. I went through that too, but later. I mean, there were some fucking embarrassing clothes at some points. And I was going to new schools all the time and eventually I thought, you know what? I've got to buy some straighter clothes; I've got to have some normal clothes and not something fucking outrageous that my mum has made. I don't want to go to another new school and be this mad-fuck mad punk rocker. I think I was into pirate stuff at that point, early eighties, so I remember going to Marks & Spencers and buying utterly square things that would've appalled my mother.

But generally speaking, I would say I was pretty much always into what she made.'

Neither of the boys flourished in the school system, perhaps unsurprisingly, and Vivienne nags them to this day – along with Joe's daughter Cora, her only grandchild – about their reading. 'From a very early age,' Vivienne recalls, 'Joe assumed the responsibility of being head of the household. That was his manner, even as a toddler.' It became apparent with both boys that orthodox schooling might not be appropriate, and after Ben ran away from one school and before another could be found Vivienne found herself again home-schooling. 'I wasn't at school for a whole six months,' recalls Ben, 'and Mum sent me off to a different London museum every day, which I loved to do, but she was meant to be teaching us –she was allowed, legally, because she was a teacher. So after I'd decided which museums I liked, I spent three months in the Natural History and three months in the Science Museum. Every day. I didn't go to the V&A or the art museums. Of course the worst bit of that at the beginning was her giving me lessons at home. She'd sort of give you this really hard thing to do and then just leave you in your bedroom to do it and then come back after hours of making something. So she gave up on that, and she sent me off to the museum.'

The threesome of Vivienne and her two sons has become a familiar one from the press cuttings and news coverage over the years: at fashion events and Paris catwalk shows, and posing proudly outside Buckingham Palace when Vivienne received first her OBE and later her DBE (more on the knickers later). They are fiercely proud of each other, and loving. Physically and in spirit her sons are greatly different from each other, with traits perhaps of their respective fathers: Ben smiling easily, a gentle, calming presence; Joe a restive, watchful man, loud-voiced and strong-willed. But their love as brothers is as evident and oft-stated as their admiration for their mum, their pride in her, and their protective desire to repeat constantly that no matter how bizarre their upbringing, 'it was the best, for Joe and me – I wouldn't wish to have changed anything'. Given the strength of their relationship, the family tradition behind Vivienne, and Ben and Joe's indecision as young men as to where to head in life, it was perhaps inevitable that they would end up helping out 'at the shop'. It is a pattern that has remained in place. 'My personal involvement in the shop began in the eighties,' says Ben, 'when I was in my teens. Mum was doing the Punkature and Witches collections; her first Paris shows. So I went. I worked for my mum, mainly with Tom Binns, who was dipping all these bits of metal into ammonia to make it go green, verdigris – Vim tops, oxidized with ammonia. All of that. And then going to the dyers in Clapham Common to get all this wool dyed. I remember making the "Fuck Your Mother Punk and Don't Run Away" T-shirt, and kinda thinking "this is weird". But sometimes it felt like I was properly involved: I remember Mum got interested in *Blade Runner*, and I was a real science fiction buff, being nineteen, so I took her to Forbidden Planet. And funnily enough, Forbidden Planet was run by Alan Jones then, who had worked for Mum back at Let It Rock and had been the first person arrested for wearing the [naked] "Cowboys" T-shirt. So Mum and he had a good old chat – which was good of him, as she hadn't turned up in court to help, as I recall the story – and he gave us loads of stills of *Blade Runner* for free.'

For Joe and for Ben and for Vivienne, Thurleigh Court represents the punk years as well as the boys' childhood. It is part of what makes both boys fiercely nostalgic about punk, for all that their respective sartorial tastes have taken them in many other directions since. The crucible of creativity that was number 10 Thurleigh Court was also a lesson in family, in its ability to be both a comfort and a threat to the individual. 'By '85 punk was everywhere. It was in Teignmouth in Devon, for fuck's sake, where Dora and Gordon lived by then.' It felt to the boys as if something that was at the heart of their parents' partnerships and destructive relationships had gone very public, so that, for them, punk can only mean the mad years at Thurleigh Court and an idea of the future that never quite was. 'By the time punk started spreading it had died already,' says Ben. 'It died with The Sex Pistols splitting up because that was the big political side of anything. But the political side of it died when Malcolm changed and when he and Mum both changed their minds to get into something else, basically. They were the beginners and enders of punk and that's all you can say about punk.'

Vivienne, early 1980s.

Vivienne, like every parent, has her regrets. She is extremely close to Joe and to Ben, and the pattern set in their late adolescence of working, when the need arose, for and with their mother, remains in place. Ben has his own range of clothes sold through the Worlds End shop, whose website he also manages. An accomplished and respected photographer, he has contributed work to this book and many other publications about his mum. Joe helped rescue the business after the debacle of his mother's split from Malcolm and now has a parallel career in fashion, having co-founded the lingerie firm Agent Provocateur with Serena Rees, as well as now running the Jack Sheppard and Child of the Jago clothing ranges. Vivienne says she 'deeply approves'; she and her sons remain tied to the fashion business and thus it remains as it was at Thurleigh Court, a family affair. But Vivienne relates to the people around her through and with her work and her creativity. The *idea* of parenting, or grandparenting for that matter, is perhaps more apparent to her than the reality. In her Tree of Life – a pictogram published on the foundation of her Climate Revolution campaign in 2009 – 'parenthood' and two children figure strongly. 'Our parents are GAIA the Earth Mother and Science,' she writes, and their child is 'the better world which we could create – if we would stop and listen to our parents before it is too late . . . stability is necessary – comfort and freedom from worry and suffering, only then can we yield to our higher instincts, instincts that define us as human . . . This is our world . . . this is why the art lover is a Freedom fighter for a better world.' And, she might have added, makes the better mother.

As Ben walks Dora's dog Jackie Onassis with me in a London park near Thurleigh Court, he has no truck with the idea that Vivienne could have been a mother in any other way. As a plane overhead threatens to drown out his soft voice, he tells me this story:

'I remember when I had gone to live with my father for a while and things were really bad, so bad, with Mum and Malcolm – and Derek had got me my own room. He decorated it for me with framed pictures of aeroplanes from *Flight* magazine, and he'd done a really, really nice job. He was a great dad. And when I came back to Mum's the bunk bed that me and Joe slept on was completely full of fabric. The bedroom was full of boxes. And there was Mum in this cave of boxes, completely buried in rolls of fabric and stuff with a forty-watt light bulb by her sewing machine and she looks up and says, "I haven't had time to clean your room out or anything. I am sorry." And I started to cry. But it was all right; it was a kind of happy-crying because she sat with me, sewing, and she said she was really happy, and I could see that she was. And that made me so happy, to see her doing her thing. And then she said she was really happy too, to have me back.'

worlds
end

McLAREN WESTWOOD

BORN IN ENGLAND

Vivienne Westwood
& Malcolm McLaren
invite

GRACE CODDINGTON

to the
Worlds End Collection
Autumn · Winter 81 Show
at the Pillar Hall Olympia
12.30 for 1.00pm
Tuesday 31st March

R.S.V.P.
Marysia Woroniecka
89 Marylebone High Street
London W1
Tel: 01·486 3251

PIRATE PRINCESS

Vivienne, in those days: she was like a grenade with the pin pulled.

CARLO D'AMARIO,
CEO and former lover of Vivienne Westwood

Leave everything to me. I plunder for you. Stick with me and you might get a share of my bounty. My name is Progress ... There is hardly anyone left now who believes in a better world. What is the future of unlimited profit in a finite world? 'The Pirate' and 'Active Resistance'
in *Active Resistance to Propaganda* by Vivienne Westwood

'The reason I became a designer all connects, really, with the need just to get up and get on with it. I had started helping Malcolm simply because I could. But then there came a point with The Sex Pistols, and Sid had died, when everything had to change. The Sex Pistols had stopped and the lease was up on our little shop in the World's End and I really had to make a decision to carry on or not. I could have given up. At that point I was losing a lot of money in the shop – what I didn't know at the time was that that was because of the shop manager, who was stealing everything for his drug habit. It was a big problem for me. And meanwhile, things just completely fell apart with Malcolm. So Malcolm began it for me, designing, but then I ended up going it alone. The "Pirates" collection, I did *everything*, I knew every piece of clothing like my own children because I made *every little decision on them all*. I don't do as much of that now.'

In 1979 Margaret Thatcher's Conservative government won a landslide victory. It swept to power on a raft of contradictory ideals mixing

nostalgia for supposed wartime values – self-reliance and moral recti-
tude – with a stated distrust of the poor or disenfranchised. 'One
Nation' Toryism was consigned to the backbenches in favour of radical
free-market economics and an assertion that there was no such thing
as Society, only the individual and, for some, the family. By the time
Lady Diana Spencer was stepping out with the heir to the throne,
British fashion was also in the grip of a full-blown romantic affair
with the past, and indeed the royalist past, that came to suit rather
well what Vivienne worked on after punk. The country appeared to
be reinventing itself, for good or ill, and so too did Vivienne. But the
late seventies and early eighties were more, for her, than the transi-
tion from punk-boutique owner to mainstream fashion guru. They
were also the years that saw her definitive split from Malcolm and her
assumption of full creative control as a designer. 'All through The
Sex Pistols and punk rock, I'd never thought of myself as a designer.'
Thereafter, she did.

'Here's what happened. When The Sex Pistols finished we closed
the shop [Seditionaries]. The lease was up and I had to make a decision
to continue or not. I said to Malcolm, "Either I help you in the music
business or you help me in fashion," and he said, "Fashion every time."
Malcolm told me where to look; he said, "It should be romantic." I was
shocked: that was the last thing I expected to come from him. When
people asked me what we were going to do next, I said, "Romantic."
Soon after, these people were suddenly calling themselves New
Romantics. They were buying theatrical costumes from Fox's sale.
One of them looked really cool – Jeremy Healy, the DJ, who was very
handsome and skinny and he bleached and then dyed his hair grey
and tied it back in a queue. He looked like the rake in Hogarth's *Rake's
Progress*. I think he started off the whole thing, really, and that Malcolm
thought of "Romantic" from looking at him. Soon after Jeremy
switched his look to Hobo / Tramp. I thought, "OK, this is what other
designers do." So I bought myself a book on fashion history.

'Meanwhile Adam Ant asked Malcolm to manage him and The
Ants, his band. The first thing Malcolm did was to get rid of Adam
and look for another singer, and eventually he found one in young

The Pirate collection and the Westwood print that has become iconic.

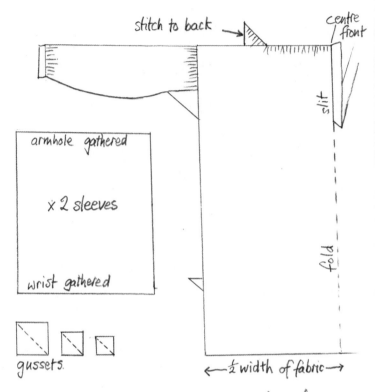

stitch to back

centre front

slit

armhole gathered

x 2 sleeves

wrist gathered

fold

gussets.

← ½ width of fabric →

Traditional shirt based on rectangles
+ using full width of fabric (≈36")
The gussets give 3 dimension e.g. the
Shoulder gusset opens up the neck +
it becomes round so you don't need to
cut it round. A slit fitted with a gusset
opens up the fabric + gives volume —
you can also use them to make a
flared skirt for example.

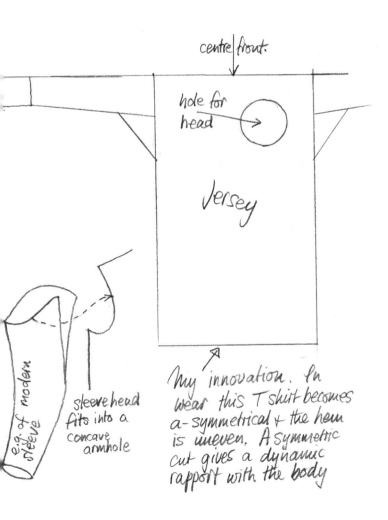

centre front.

hole for head

Jersey

e.g. of modern sleeve

sleeve head fits into a concave armhole

My innovation. In wear this T shirt becomes a-symmetrical + the hem is uneven. A symmetric cut gives a dynamic rapport with the body

Vivienne explains her cutting technique, both historical and revolutionary.

Annabella who was working in a dry-cleaner's, and that band became Bow Wow Wow.

'The look I was attracted to – and I have found this happens with students I have taught – was the dress and paintings and engravings of the French Revolution, of the *jeunesse dorée*, the Incroyables and Merveilleuses. They wore their wigs and coats back to front and a red ribbon tied around their throats in memory of The Terror and the guillotine, and the Merveilleuses cropped their hair in a style called 'à la victime' and dressed in long slivers of muslin tied under the bust which they wet to make them cling – trying to look like Greek statues. I included this dress in the Pirate collection and Malcolm got me to paint a Nazi helmet to go with it instead of a Greek one. However, the main hairstyle from Pirates was chopped around exactly like that of Rod-the-Mod Stewart, and the eighteenth-century frock coats with their narrow shoulders were too close to current 1970s fashions.

'Malcolm just wasn't around. He'd got interested in mixing music – making music out of other people's music: pirating. He wanted me to get a pirate look so I went back in history to the musketeer feeling of seventeenth-century garments. I copied some of the historical cuts as exactly as I could, delighting in my discoveries, and I always tried to catch the epitome of that period jacket, say, or breeches. I am the only designer who has tried to do that. Inevitably you adapt the patterns, embellish and / or simplify, according to what you're after. There were one or two ideas inspired instead by tribes and the Third World and prints from painted saddlebags of the Native Americans. We were able to style the collection as if the pirates had incorporated into their dress the exotic garments of tribal people.

'I started work on the Pirate collection, eventually "launched" as a proper collection for autumn / winter 1981, utilizing a shirt pattern that had not been used for centuries. I had thought, to do what I wanted to do, I would have to go to the V&A with a tape measure! Instead of which I found and bought Norah Waugh's *The Cut of Men's Clothes*.' It was the beginning of a whole new language for Vivienne. She had referenced the past before, but it had been the recent past or an idea of tribalism. It was as if she were working as a theatre designer might, creating a story and an environment that the shop and music would feature too, and that gave context and meaning to an idea of the past. 'When I did the Pirate collection,' Vivienne says, 'I'd seen an engraving of a pirate whose trousers were too big and they were all rumpled about the crotch and I wanted to do that . . . I wanted that rakish look . . . they were interested [in the seventeenth century] in sexuality in a totally different way. And I only found it out by research.

'And I'd have to say that my confidence grew. It had to. I had decided quite consciously to be officially a designer, to do a show and also to look at the past, go into history, and be romantic. That's where other designers got their ideas from, I thought: they'd go to Mexico on holiday and get their ideas from there. I couldn't do that. I was broke and had two boys. But I could look at the past in books, which ended up being romantic. That's when I started thinking pirates. It was an idea of getting off the island – this little island, this moment that I was stuck in – and going into history and into the Third World, trying to find out more about the world we lived in through the Pirate collection, rather than in the tunnel of London, just in the streets with punks. It was exploration and the Age of Wonder. That was the idea. Gold teeth, no more black and chains. If there were chains, then they'd be rusty pirate chains – distressed and New World. The first collection was a combination of inspiration from Geronimo to pirates. It was a combination of those things, along with the French Revolution with all its promise of change, and its violence and sexiness. It's a look that has gone all over the place, reached into theatre and film. You can see it in *Pirates of the Caribbean*, even: Jack Sparrow could have been on the Pirates catwalk.'

The shop at 430 King's Road was kept and remodelled – for the last time – in the spirit of a buccaneers' ship, with a sloped decking floor. It was retitled 'Worlds End', without the apostrophe, as both destination and declaration. The thirteen hours on the Worlds End clock outside have run backwards ever since, and the Worlds End label on the collection sold there still features a pirate's cutlass and the legend 'Born in England'. The Pirate collection went on sale at the revamped 430 'Worlds End'.

Pirates was a first for Vivienne in a number of ways. It was the first time Vivienne was accorded, and accorded herself, the status of

Architect's drawing for the Worlds End clock.

a designer. It was the first time she went onto a catwalk, at Olympia, at the end of a proper collection. 'I had on an old grey school sweater and no make-up, I nearly missed the show, and Malcolm made me go on stage, saying, "They want to see you as you are, they want to see that you have been *working*." It was the first time Malcolm had been able to synchronize properly his fashion and music crossover, getting sponsorship from cutting-edge musical technologists Sony Walkman(!) and showcasing his latest band, Bow Wow Wow, in Vivienne's pirate clothes. And the V&A promptly bought one of the outfits. As John Galliano was moved to say, 'It's impossible to think of the bands, the music and the spirit of both Punk and New Romanticism without Vivienne's work.' It was to be her next claim on fashion posterity. Boy George was at the show, Adam Ant had already followed in the wake of the Healey / McLaren / Westwood pirate look, 'and Steve Strange [the club promoter] named his "Club For Heroes" just as we had called the Seditionaries clothes "Clothes for Heroes" – it was jolly good for business.' Club owners and habitués like Steve Strange and Leigh Bowery enthusiastically bought and wore her clothes. So too did club promoters Michael and Gerlinde Costiff, who attended that first Olympia show. Michael described it as 'the most extraordinary thing you have ever seen – absolutely magical. It was so luxurious, all the glitter of gold, that whole swashbuckling, heroic feeling, it was stunning . . . Vivienne up until then had been very black; to see all that colour, that *gold*!' They were indeed clothes for heroes, as the shop legend had it, and the heroism was, in Vivienne's mind, part of the ongoing punk crusade with clothes: 'I don't believe in closing in. You don't make people want to change things by making them realize how poor and humiliated they are . . . you have to make people feel great before you get change.'

'I'm very literary,' Vivienne repeats to me one morning, 'and I've got literary ideas. The pirate trousers, for instance, are like something from a story. But more than that, even worn denim gives the idea of experience. If you wear old clothes, then you can look like you have the experience, the story that the clothes carry. So it was a big, big design moment when I did those pirate trousers – it was the start of a whole new look. I was searching for something and I found it in historical costume, so it's the beginning too of me looking backwards as well as forwards. And it's important, in a small way also, to acknowledge the issue of "distressed", and "vintage", as it has become. Because that became part of how to tell a story in fashion, and give an idea of experience. Malcolm had been so important to begin with, and was often the initiator of the ideas. But by Pirates, it was all shifting and then, by Witches and Punkature I just didn't want to design with Malcolm at all. He was mainly in the US and he'd pop back and interfere and after a while I didn't want him bossing me about.

'So that was moment where we split, creatively. The Pirate collection. Malcolm named it, you might say, but I gave birth to it; he wasn't around, an absentee father: I did it. He came up with some fabric ideas: the squiggle print, the African block print that has become one of our signatures, but that was on the table of Jean-Charles de Castelbajac, a designer friend of mine, when Gary Ness and I happened to be in his office. But then Malcolm just stopped being creatively involved.

'I'd have to admit now that some part of me wanted to discover if a person like me, not attached to a big fashion brand in any way, could survive on talent, hard work and word of mouth, not just marketing. I had a sort of practical interest to know what fashion, the business, would teach me about the world. It would make me have to survive in the business world. I would have to understand more about the world. So, I did it like that. As an intellectual challenge. And a personal one. I had an ambition, a personal ambition to take advantage of my own designs, and I felt, if I didn't, I would just be some Dolly Daydream. And as well as all of that (and this will sound mad, but maybe I was), you could sort of sum it up like this: apart from the ambition to prove something to myself, there was also, for me, a kind of duty. A duty that I owed to fashion or to myself. That something I *could* do, I somehow *ought* to do. Because if I didn't do it, nobody else would. Just like my politics, really. Just like me as a little girl. "It was me." I don't know. So that's why I did it, and although it was at times a chore, I don't regret it. Just the opposite. I proved what I wanted to prove and I have found real satisfaction in it, as well as a voice. But if somebody had come along to me in 1979 and said, "Look, Vivienne, you're really good but I'm as

good as you are and I can do that job for you. You go off to university,"
I probably would have said, "Oh, all right, OK, I will."'

'There were things to prove about money. And this as well I am at
liberty to explain now, and I hope it will be useful to anyone who has
ever felt done-in commercially, or has suffered, well, fraud. It's not
that I'm bad with money. I was brought up in a shop; it's not that. I am
just too trusting and assume other people are as honest and hard-
working as I am. I can tell you about why Michael Collins got away
with that – with stealing from me for years and years. And I can say it
now. I'm sorry Michael died but we can now be honest. The very first
day he came to the shop he was stealing. He worked for me for at least
eight years and took every spare penny, and I could never understand
why it didn't work, why the books didn't balance, and I thought it
must be because I'm stupid with money. Until Michael worked for
us the shop had done very well. So this very stylish young man came
and I gave him a job. And that first day I took no money. I couldn't
work it out. He said to me, "Oh, this is terrible – so look, I've
got money – I don't actually need to work. I've got this boyfriend."
He was gay, Michael, and he said, "He keeps me. I'll give you the
money you need. What do you need?"

'So, he gave me the money and I just thought, "What a great bloke,"
and of course the shop was newly reopened and I was not at all sure if
it could be a success, so I had no reason to be suspicious, and I trusted
him from that point on and it was always, "Oh, you know, I'll get my
boyfriend to give us a bit of money if you don't have enough." He
was very charming. And I believed him. But it was all MY OWN
MONEY! The boyfriend didn't exist. I was so naive. I wasn't keeping
proper record of stock or anything. That's how we did things. And
believe it or not, this went on for eight years. Eventually a pattern
cutter, Mark Tabard, who was working with me, said, "I can't stand
this any longer. Vivienne: Michael is taking all your money," and
the penny dropped immediately. I feel embarrassed by all that, but
that's how it was.

'Now meanwhile, all through this time, Malcolm had been man-
aging The New York Dolls and then The Sex Pistols and Bow Wow

Wow. I was making clothes for them – the Dolls and the Pistols – and sending the Dolls' stuff to them over in America too. I did sometimes send Malcolm money, in America. So I did have some money, but hardly enough to keep going and I was just working like a maniac all the time. Malcolm started saying, and we would row about it, that because I came from the North of England I was absolutely stupid and too trusting of people, and not responsible regarding business, and only clever at what I did with my hands. That's what Malcolm said, but he wasn't any better. He was hopeless with money. He didn't interfere and say, "What's going on with the money?" or anything, you know. We were both stupid, really. But for years after Malcolm made out that it was all my fault, like I was incompetent and couldn't seem to make any money, but meanwhile I was doing things for him. The financial scamming had gone on for about eight years and Malcolm was busy doing his music thing, living in America, very interested in early hip hop, and with me sending him money and him criticizing the business. So some of the roots of our finally ending were in that, really. And nobody was trying to make it work. Yet every time I'd try to separate, he would sort of drag me back . . .'

In late 1979, Malcolm left Thurleigh Court for the last time. There was no concluding argument or final showdown: as Joe put it, one day he just never came back. Malcolm's sights were increasingly set on the States, but the family finances were in crisis every bit as much as those of the Worlds End shop, which was one reason Vivienne took a lodger in the form of long-time friend and shop manager Gene Krell. Gene and Malcolm had been great pals, and both Malcolm and Vivienne admired what Vivienne describes as Gene's 'great gifts as a salesman'. But Granny Takes a Trip folded, 'Gene was on his uppers,' and so Vivienne offered him both a job and a home. Close witness to the long fallout of the break-up, therefore, was their mutual friend Gene, who admits nevertheless to seeing it all through a haze of heroin addiction, and a tint of grateful love. For he credits Vivienne, despite all her troubles at the time, with saving his life.

'I was addicted to heroin and then I became addicted to alcohol because I couldn't get heroin. Vivienne nursed me through it. She was always very anti-drugs. I have to say, though, with Malcolm, it became very difficult. The level of acrimony when Vivienne and Malcolm split up was unbelievable: people used to spit at me on the King's Road or when I went in nightclubs because they felt somehow betrayed. Like their golden couple had split. Like it was anyone else's business. And Vivienne took complete responsibility for the business and the design. She had a lot on her plate. The press gave the impression we were huge, and we were in PR terms, but there'd be bailiffs coming round. They tried to close the shop, the rent being unpaid, and I refused to surrender the keys, and that could have led to deportation for me. But Vivienne was determined to keep in business, to prove something to herself or to Malcolm. And she stayed at Thurleigh Court and, basically, sewed her way back to life. She became such a recluse that on one occasion a drag queen came in and pretended to be Vivienne. It was a strange time in many ways. We used to get a lot of death threats. Delivered by mail. I don't even know if Vivienne knows this. Basically four kinds. People who supported Malcolm, people who supported Michael Collins and meanwhile there were the bailiffs and there was also this other mail about how we were responsible for the moral decay of the nation. They were more articulate. "Damnation awaits you," addressed to Vivienne, all that stuff. Very personal. Of course, now, you'd take things like that a lot more seriously than Vivienne or I did at that time. But to this day Vivienne probably doesn't know the danger she was in. I didn't tell her: she was going through enough. But it was an extraordinary atmosphere.'

'Mum is always very gracious about Malcolm,' Joe tells me ruefully, 'she's nice that way. But you have to understand that Malcolm left us all with debts: Mum and me and Ben, in that it was our lives and our home too. He not only left us all the debts of the company he had had with Mum, but he left us all the assets of the company, as well. And he left and he went to America. It wasn't a company, it was a partnership, but he left everything. Debts and assets. At the time, with both Worlds End and Nostalgia of Mud, the new shop, it was a risky, risky time. And he didn't just walk away. He smashed it to bits. Tried to. Vivienne went into work one day and Malcolm's new girlfriend was in there wearing her clothes, telling everyone what to do, that she was now the "designer" and that Vivienne wasn't working there any more, and

The Punkature collection programme featured *Blade Runner*-inspired prints.

do you know who had told her to go in there and do that? Malcolm. That's how my "dad" was. Which is why it's so incredibly fucking gracious of Mum to later let him take co-credit: he didn't do it in the first place, she did, and he tried to destroy it as well when she was fighting for her life. He threw it all away and he'd tried to smash it to pieces, and smash Vivienne to pieces. Because he was like that: if he couldn't have it and own it completely, it was trash to be thrown away.

'And so Ben and I started trying to help out, working at Worlds End, and it wasn't because we wanted to have a career in fashion or retail. We just wanted to help our mum. She had nothing. She's our mum. And we're in Clapham with no electric, no phone, no water, no gas, 'cos Malcolm's had them all cut off. I've got my dodgy mates round who know how to jack all the utilities back up and the fucking bailiffs are at the door – even some heavy guys – and eventually I think, "I'm going to call my dad," and I remember calling him on a payphone and he says, from Hollywood, "Don't you people have a telephone?"

'But Vivienne was always very nice about Malcolm. Especially with me. But I knew that she wasn't saying what she really felt. She was saying what she thought wasn't going to upset me. But that's Vivienne. It was fucking hard on her. But we should say it like it is, now. His story became "the only reason Vivienne ever had any success was because of Malcolm McLaren". And he's right, *but* only in the sense that he was the instigator. I think the thing that people forget is that Vivienne *created*: she did the design. All those fucking amazing punk rock T-shirts, I know they are her, because I saw it happen, right there in Thurleigh Court when I was a kid: that was Mum. We had silk-screen machines in our flat and that table, the one she has in her studio now, we ate at it but it was always covered in stuff she was printing. And Malcolm's contribution? To belittle it all: "Oh, doing your potato cutting again, are you?" All those Seditionaries and Anarchy shirts, she made them all. She made them all in our flat – dyed in our bath, printed in our living room. Week in, week out. Making stuff to put into the shop.'

'I should probably explain,' says Vivienne quite out of the blue one day, when we are looking at fabric samples and a vaguely punky graphic design, 'about Malcolm and me. Psychologically and mentally, why I went along with this stormy relationship. Because people do wonder. He would walk out, and then change his mind, come back, walk out again. It was exhausting. Way later, at its worst, I remember Malcolm had a lawyer threatening me, wanting £50,000 . . . and when I eventually found a way to get it, Malcolm refused to accept the money and said "Can't you see? I want you back." All the time he was playing these games with me, not coming home and such. But I did use to get angry. I used to hit Malcolm. One day he hit me back. That's the last time I hit him. But it was me that hit first. But mostly, and I think I'll just say this here properly, Malcolm would make me cry. He had this thing, and it took me a while to work it out, but he had this thing where he couldn't leave the flat until he'd done that. Until he had made me cry.

'But there came a point when I simply stopped crying: I lost the ability. I'd no more tears left. I realized the only way to get rid of him and to get him to stop was to cry – that's what he wanted of me. He wanted to feel bad or something – he was trying to draw blood. He was trying to hurt me all the time. Because he was hurting. That's just what he did, and he couldn't get out of the house till somehow he had gone through that – brought me to tears – and sometimes I used to just get so angry with him for the way he was. So it was simpler to give in; to give way to the tears so he would stop. Real tears have never come back for me. I stopped crying at that point. I haven't cried properly since. I shed all I could. I think in crying that you only cry for yourself, and there came a point when I'd just had enough.'

Joe concurs. The relief for both Joe and Ben when the relationship finally disintegrated is still palpable in what they say and recall from those years, though Joe for one is very clear that his mum was far from a doormat: 'It got to a horrible point in the end. Every morning, just screaming, shouting and screaming. It was like you were just waiting for Malcolm to get out of the house. In the end, every morning, Vivienne sort of made herself cry because she knew when she started crying he'd leave, and that was it, and we could start our day. He was a horrible bully. It was archetypal, a textbook case of a dysfunctional, toxic thing – a sort of codependency where making her cry allowed him to feel . . . whatever it was he needed to feel. Because also you couldn't get Vivienne to snap that easy but, you know, you knew when you'd gone too far. Bloody hell, yeah. I mean Mum can hit to make you see stars. I remember we were on the Tube once, about this time, and I don't know if it speaks of her anger, but anyway she had an office in Camden and the Tube always got stuck between Mornington Crescent and Camden. And I was there, and these girls were all taking the piss out of an Indian woman on the Tube. "It really stinks like curry in here," horrible racist sort of thing. So this Indian lady got up to get off but she can't because the Tube's stuck in the tunnel, and one of these girls picked a huge bogey out of her nose and wiped it on this woman's sari. And this woman turned round and went, "Why are you doing this to me?" And Vivienne stepped in and said, "They're just incredibly badly brought up," and then the Tube moves and we get up to get off and one of these girls stuck their leg out, to trip her up. So Vivienne picked this girl up by the hair, by a full head of hair, and whacked her around the face and she ended up just with this handful of hair. And then she got off the train, just trembling and shaking. But it was good. So yeah, Vivienne can pack a punch.'

'Here's my theory,' continues Vivienne, 'the more pain you invest in a relationship, the more you feel betrayed when it falls down. I had to invest everything in that relationship. Because of Joe, and because I knew Malcolm needed me. And I suppose some element of my love for him was always there. So when I knew it was over, when he left, when at one point he did get another girlfriend who was more than just some fling, I felt betrayed, I felt dead for years. For about four years I was dead inside. Until I found a sort of love with another man – with Carlo. About four years, it lasted. I was just burning with betrayal; somehow, having invested so much pain in the relationship, that's what it was about. That's exactly accurate, that's why. Not for any other reason. Not because I wanted Malcolm back. That's the last thing I wanted. But I felt so upset about his leaving, do you understand? It's funny, you go over and over and over things from your past, and it can drive you almost insane, trying to understand, but one thing I knew: I didn't want him back. Oh no, thank you. And over the years we would bump into each other in public at things, but we didn't see each other in private for a long time, years later. I remember it was ten years later, and he must have been surprised at how pleased I was to see him. I was pleased to see him because I was happy to find I felt no emotion about him. I never stopped liking him, and being interested in him. But it was such a relief when I knew he couldn't hurt me any more. So I found I could be pleased to see him.

'And after we split up, people soon started asking, because it was obvious we were apart, about the importance of Malcolm versus the importance of me on my own. Malcolm was rather jealous of people and he was certainly jealous of me, and always wanted to claim that somehow I was totally nothing. His seamstress, he'd call me, his creation. He was called "Svengali", in terms of The Sex Pistols. And he made that reputation for himself, and that's how he wanted to be seen, regarding punk and The Sex Pistols and regarding his work with me. I really didn't care. I felt contemptuous of him and even sorry for him, because it was pathetic. But also here's the thing: whenever you're doing something creative, I think you're always impressed by what somebody *else* does. I am. And you don't even think that the things that you do – especially if you do them easily – are important at all. And that's the key with Malcolm and me, really. I gave Malcolm all the credit because I was just helping him to do something he wanted to do. And to begin with it was about going back to the look of the 1950s and I was very interested in that, the idea of rock 'n' roll and reselling it. Malcolm had ideas that were great, but he never – he was never, ever able to tell me, "No, this isn't good. Do it that way" – not ever – because he wasn't practical. And there were good friends who said, "Vivienne: Women's Lib would be so ashamed of you – you're making all these things, and there you are still giving the credit back to him – what are you talking about, woman?" "WHY? Vivienne, why do you let him get away with it? You're not crediting yourself with being as clever as you are." But you see, Malcolm was very talented. He was very good on ideas, like putting a bra on top of something as outer-wear. That was his idea. I've been given the credit for that. Gaultier, Madonna, all of that; but that was Malcolm as well as me. Things like that that he did or thought of were really good. Or he might even start me off – he might even send me something; some pictures to be inspired by. That was his way. And he was very good on shoes. Maybe one way of explaining this is the exhibition at the V&A. There was a point in the Witches collection when it credited "Vivienne Westwood & Malcolm McLaren", and in fact Malcolm had done one thing in there, one thing only, which was a little pointy Chico Marx hat. He gave [the curator and catalogue writer for the V&A] – he made her a nervous wreck – she was in tears. Nearly every day she got a letter, couched in legal terms, from him saying, "You're completely mistaken. You're in infringement of my copyright," and everything, "by doing this exhibition because *I'm* the designer of these clothes and it's not Vivienne." He'd refer to me, at the V&A, as his "seamstress".'

Joe concurs that his father had a particular animus about design attribution. It was a story echoed years later when Joe tried to open Agent Provocateur by raising an element of the capital with recreations of his parents' designs. His mum agreed; Malcolm threatened to sue. 'I saw him then for what he was and what he had been like with Mum. He took a perverse pleasure out of trying to belittle people around him, including me and Mum. I Tippexed his name off all the labels. Which was some metaphor. I didn't speak to him for years.'

'He couldn't help it, I expect,' says Vivienne, 'he was even jealous of me and he was jealous of Joe in the end. He went really crazy. He was so needy, when it came to being recognized. It mattered to him more than anything. More than either of us. I've actually bent over backwards to credit him over the years, often more than he deserved, but it made for an easier life at the time. You see, Malcolm was so very protective of all that kind of thing, or the idea of his reputation or posterity. Malcolm ended up wanting to sabotage everything I did. And I've never really spoken much about this, and I've never been able to be honest about this until now, but because he's dead, I don't mind saying this: he behaved incredibly cruelly. Professionally, personally, in every way. But at the end of the day he had real problems, and that still has the power to make me sad. Because once I loved him. And I remained loyal to Malcolm. Until he died.

'I think there comes a point in some relationships where you realize that you have learned all you can from someone. I'd been fascinated by Malcolm, intellectually, but as the years went by, and the attrition was so huge from his temper and his jealousy, the boredom won out. Malcolm never wanted to finish a book. I'd see him read a book in three-quarters of an hour and then decide there was one nugget from it he could sell – just take out something in it that you wouldn't be able to find if you read it yourself! But it was enough for him if he could give a theory to people or tell somebody that he knew something new. He splashed around in the shallows like that. He wasn't interested in truly discovering anything, except things he could just use, to sell or to shock or to impress. And so, inevitably, I got bored with him. I got bored of hearing the same old things, the same approach to everything. It really bored me. People noticed, of course. There's a piece of footage when I was dressed in a Buffalo skirt – so it must have been early 1980s, and we had already split up personally but not professionally – and Malcolm and I were being interviewed, and I was so bored with Malcolm I was just picking at my dress and just thinking, "I do wish he'd shut up." And Simon Barker said afterwards, "Vivienne, were you purposely trying to upstage him, or were you just so uninterested in everything he was saying? That's all you can see up there."

'After I lost interest in him intellectually, in a sense things were doomed, because that was all we had. In the beginning, Malcolm could help me, intellectually, with the things that had given me a problem: political things. How do I find out what's going on in the world? And he did know an awful lot more. He went to art school and they had all these Big Ideas: the underground and the alternative people, and all this stuff that was the beginning of the hippy movement in 1968. But once you had worked out his thing, there wasn't anything more there. He had arrested development: he was stuck in 1968. He didn't dig. He wasn't prepared to try to understand the world he lived in. He'd rather live on the surface and try and manipulate it somehow and manipulate the people around him. I'd nothing more to learn from Malcolm by the end; I knew I couldn't grow with him: the conversation had stopped. Malcolm was more conservative, in a way. I remember him telling me when I did Punkature collection how much better it would have been if I'd done this cotton skirt in silk, and I found myself saying, "Well, Malcolm – it could have been like that. It would have been good. But it's just as good this way, and actually I rather prefer it." He

Invitation to Witches collection, with Keith Haring artwork.

was right only in that it would have looked more couture and I think my collections would have been made out of silks and things earlier if Malcolm had had his way. Which is ironic: you see, Malcolm quite liked posh. But after Pirates I just knew I didn't want to work with him any more – I had these ideas that I wanted to get on with myself. We stumbled on with both our names on the labels, but more and more it was mine. Punkature was the last collaboration. And then Witches was the complete break for me.

'I initiated Witches (autumn / winter 1983) completely. I'd been to New York, and while I was there, I'd been introduced to the work of Keith Haring – and to Keith. Graffiti that looked like hieroglyphs. Symbols. Pictures like a dog barking or a little baby with a light shining round its head – a visual language, it seemed to me, that looked like magic symbols. He seemed terribly flattered when I said I loved his work and I used a lot of those ideas in Witches because he said he was very keen to work with me. I'm not into modern art as such but there are certain things that I think are really valid and I think Keith Haring's work was. You'd have to call him an artist. He was a communicator and his things were very attractive. A year after we met he developed AIDS and died. He was one of the first people. He was ever such a sweet man. Lovely, generous, and really talented. Had he survived I feel sure he would have found other ways to develop his work beyond his graffiti style – he was very talented. So Witches was to some extent inspired by him and his colours: the colour of blue firework paper, you know, that sort of mauveish touchpaper . . . and his graffiti that was fluorescent. And dirty green, near-black – all these colour decisions according to the story, which was in part the story of Keith. And Haring did this face with three eyes. And this square with three eyes. And this is the time of hip hop, as well, so there was a sort of freeze-frame thing going on, dance, that you could mirror in clothes, for instance these trainers with three tongues. I was the very first person to put trainers on a catwalk, but all·of this was done for a reason, you know – part of this animated thing and this graffiti thing that was going on in New York and London, and this cartoon way of dancing and everything, which I told as a fashion story.

'Gradually the confidence began to come back. Number one, I knew by then that I had a talent, a confidence given in part by the fact that I'd seen all this punk stuff that I had originated being shown on Paris catwalks. I saw how it had changed everything. It had changed hairstyles. It had changed *Vogue*. I could see I was being taken seriously. For instance, I'd been to Grace Coddington [at *Vogue* in London]. I went with a suitcase of my things and she was just embarrassed by what I showed her, she wasn't interested, but I remember thinking, well, at least she could see it was good *design*. This little boot, that became the Pirate Boot, that I put on the table in front of her – it was fantastic. You see them all over the world – all over Paris now. But her attitude at the time was, "No, no: go and see another magazine." So I went to *Ritz*, who put me on their front cover, but here's the thing: even as Grace was turning me down, she was wearing a copy of a mohair sweater that *I had designed*.'

According to stylist Caroline Baker, 'an amazing stylist', according to Vivienne, who worked for Westwood but had also worked at *Vogue*, it wasn't until Terry Jones left *Vogue* and helped found *i-D* magazine – concentrating on how street fashions were changing the landscape – that British *Vogue* woke up to what they had missed. 'I loved what was going on at Vivienne's: it seemed a natural and visible manifestation of the chaos that the country was experiencing politically, and insane that *Vogue* and others were ignoring it. My favourite collections of hers therefore were the first two – Pirates and Mud [Buffaloes]. Like the meals she cooked us: delicious, simple, thrown together as if by magic. I turned into a bit of a Rasta girl – which was the look of the Mud collection: big skirts, the Rasta hats and a ragged ringlet hairstyle that we had discovered (ancient ringlet-curling technique wrapping hair around ribbons of cotton). All that was Vivienne.'

'So by 1982–3 I was on my own,' explains Vivienne. 'I had a pattern cutter to help me and one or two other sample machinists. But it was even me who tried on the clothes. I learned there's no substitute for trying things on yourself to get things to fit nicely and to feel right. I still believe that. I just got on with it. But it was a very, very difficult time.

'So I designed on my own, and I owned the company on my own, and it was very, very hard to get the production and everything.

Staff and Vivienne (centre back row) outside the Nostalgia of Mud shop in St Christopher's Place, 1982.

Personally I went through being very, very poor indeed. I was on my own, and even as the press were going mad for what we were doing – right beyond the Mini Crini collection and Harris Tweed, we had ten very, very hard years.'

As the relationship fell apart, the company had tried initially to expand, and Vivienne opened her first West End shop, Nostalgia of Mud, in St Christopher's Place off Oxford Street, named after the French romantic idea of idealized poverty. The interior caused as much comment as the clothes, but matched her palette of earth dyes and voodoo details: a style that poured straight onto the catwalk and indeed into much contemporary British theatre design. 'I was responsible for the look of that shop,' says Vivienne, 'the look of an archaeological dig. Roger Burton and me. The Miss Havisham chandelier, all the bits and pieces I collected in my little mini, and I made scarecrows out of wood and planks and that's how I met Tom Binns. The only other shop I've done is Davies Street. But I loved Nostalgia of Mud and it was very influential.' The shop gave its name to the collection 'Nostalgia of Mud', but the accompanying Buffalo Girls soundtrack and use of sweeping Bolivian skirts mean it has just as often been known as 'Buffalo'. The shop was to last only two years, a victim of the split between Vivienne and Malcolm. The Buffalo / Nostalgia of Mud collection, however, was shown in Paris to huge acclaim. It began a period of creativity, Vivienne's first largely on her own, of almost unprecedented impact on the fashion world. New Romanticism – the billowing shirts and skirts, the sashes and luxurious fabrics – was only the beginning. The Buffalo palette of muddied colours and distressed felts was copied all over the fashion world, and as much on the high street and in clubs as on the catwalk. Vivienne's unfitted look and subtle colouring was much admired by the Japanese, and her tattered 'hobo' style was immediately taken up by Comme des Garçons as their signature look. But it was more fundamental than simply setting a fashion as a result of the intense media interest in her and her partner. She also did radical things with cloth that became, almost immediately, axioms in fashion. Take the tube skirt, for instance. Vivienne recalls, 'I was working in my studio and we had these tubes of double

stockinette that are used for window cleaning. We had made a "kitchen sink" cardigan with Vim-lid buttons for the Punkature collection. So I started wearing a tube of the stuff – it comes as a giant stocking – because I was continually trying on things that I had made.' Vivienne was and remains a British size 10. 'It's just a tube of fabric, and no one had made one before, the idea of a sweatshirt of jersey tube. You could wear it around your body however you wanted it, but I liked it really low, down to your ankles. It became a very important look.'

Vivienne's designs were beginning to have ever wider impact. Take the Witches raincoats (1983) that remain in the Elcho Street Archive. They look complicated and futuristic, but are made of squares of fabric, showing off Vivienne's cutting skills: evidently the work of someone used to laying fabric over bodies and dummies, and not wasting too much by using curves. The raincoat was copied the world over, usually less well. Though Vivienne subsequently became obsessed with Savile Row and with tailoring and eventually corsetry, at the time of Witches her passion was 'the pull and push of garment against the body. I start with the material, I put a couple of slits in a square, make sleeves out of the slits and some gussets to give room, and then I try to see where it touches the body. Where a garment touches the body determines the way you stand and move and what your body can do physically.' It was a radical way for a designer to work and to think, and one of the joys of seeing the progression of Vivienne's work is that in a sense she learned her art and her craft in public: you can see the seams. The tube skirt, the multilayered raincoat, much copied in Japan, with its allusions to kimono as well as sci-fi, the pirate-inspired trousers and blouses, the childlike joy in mud – all these went mainstream so very fast it is sometimes difficult to remember they can be dated to a time and to a person. Vivienne.

'I never wanted anyone to love me,' Vivienne states to me emphatically. 'Love is not essential to me. I am grateful if I am liked. But I have no expectation that that will be. I loved being on my own. The best compliment to anyone that I could give is that being with them is as good as living on your own.' By 1983 Vivienne seems to have had everything that the clamour of the city might offer her, apart perhaps

The Witches raincoat influenced design all over the world.

from financial security, and she had seen her two boys grow strong and begin to leave. But, recalls Gordon, her brother, 'our mum was really worried about her – she said she had never in her life seen anyone work so hard. It was like a mania. It was strange even to be around – working all night, sleeping on piles of material.' Her son Joe explains his mother in their shared language of fashion: 'Half the battle with clothing or making something,' says Joe, 'is knowing how to solve a problem. It is very soothing, because real life isn't like that. Vivienne can tell you a way to make something work. And I've seen her do it to people who've got tailoring in their blood. They know everything about making clothes, and I've seen them fucking around with a problem, trying to make something work for weeks, and twenty samples later, it's still not there. And then Vivienne comes along, and in five minutes she's done it and gone – I'd see her do it at Thurleigh Court – and they're just standing there with their jaws on the floor, going, "Right, how the fuck did she do that?" And that's Mum, you know. I've never seen anything like her after decades in fashion. That's genius – and that's also where she put her heart.'

It is a point worth considering that for most of her adult life, and certainly through the glory years of punk and New Romanticism, Vivienne was often the oldest person in the room, regularly the one Malcolm could cast as 'mother' when he wanted to deride and dismiss her. She was old enough to be Sid Vicious's mum. She found her voice and her proper creative stride perhaps a little late, but was all the better qualified, experienced and grounded to take advantage of what she had learned through nearly two decades around youth cults and fashion when she at last found herself in charge of a burgeoning fashion business, but alone. 'I realized after Pirates that I didn't have to qualify my ideas. I could do anything I liked; it was only a question of how I did it that would make it original. I realized that I could go on for ever.' As is often the case with a traumatic break-up, Vivienne was spurred on to greater and different creativity after the explosive ending of her relationship with Malcolm. What Carlo D'Amario, who met her that year, describes as her quicksilver volatility, 'like a grenade with the pin pulled', was seen by others as part of the dark magic of McLaren, and in a sense his parting gift and his best one.

'Malcolm used to tell us bedtime stories when we were little,' recalls Ben, 'me and Joe, and they were great stories, really exciting. But the thing with Malcolm is that he started off a story, but he could never finish it. He sort of left you to fill in the second half. So I think that's perhaps what his genius and his legacy is: he started something off, especially with Mum, but it was never for him to finish it. She did.'

VIVIENNE WESTWOOD
PRESENTS
CLINT EASTWOOD
WINTER 1984 COLLECTION
WORLDS END

scusa This
invitation is
VERY Horrible

JARDIN DES TUILERIES SALLE PERRAULT
MONDAY 26 MARCH AT 19.00 HRS.
SHOWROOM: 4, RUE FAUBOURG ST. HONORE 75008 PARIS
TEL. 265 25 88
RSVP:
LONDON   DAVID TEL. 434 24 25
PARIS - SYLVIE GRUMBACH TEL. 296 34 81 - 246 10 87
MILAN - ELISABETTA TEL. 837 07 37

MAID IN ITALY

Behind some great women there is a man. I wanted to make Vivienne a queen. But don't write about me. Call me 'Carlo de Seingalt' [Casanova's nom de plume]. 'Carlo D'Amario' is not in this story. He doesn't exist.

CARLO D'AMARIO

I introduced Vivienne to Keith Richards; I thought they'd make a nice couple, and he said to me afterwards, 'Wow, she's a character,' and she said to me, 'Wow, he's a character.' I don't know if they ever got it on. You'll have to ask her. [I did. They didn't.] GENE KRELL

tries to fix up Vivienne and Keith Richards

'When I first met Carlo D'Amario,' Vivienne tells me, looking over my shoulder as if he might be listening, 'he wanted to do my PR in Italy, but when I asked him to be my manager a little later it was in part because of something he had said to me. Sometimes your life can turn on an idea. Carlo said that punk was a battle, and then everything I'd done since had been a battle. That's what he said, the very first time I met him. And here's the other thing he said that really impressed me. He's really interested in old cars. Vintage cars. And he said this to me: "The Establishment is like a car, and it's going a hundred miles an hour. And you want to slow it down. So what does Vivienne do? She throws some rocks at it to try to make it go less fast. But do you know what happens instead? It goes faster: it uses your energy. Don't let it. Don't waste your energy like that – when you, Vivienne, can go two hundred miles an hour instead, and make an impact." And I understood what that meant for me. It meant, don't attack the Establishment. Go faster. Let them catch you up: get the *ideas* out there.'

Vivienne had met Carlo D'Amario – on the brief occasion she refers to – after the Witches collection in Paris in the spring of 1983. Carlo's background included a close friendship with the Italian designer Elio Fiorucci and stints on the hippy trail to and from Afghanistan, Goa and South America, importing ethnic goods and Afghan coats into Swinging London. He speaks in Age-of-Aquarius parables still, to the frustration of those who have to translate him into Japanese for business purposes, but Vivienne credits him as the man who broke the destructive cycle of life with McLaren and laid the foundations for her eventual commercial triumph. In 1983 Carlo offered her more than just the possibility of contracting him or his PR company. Within weeks he had provided her with an introduction to Fiorucci, and the D'Amario home in Milan as a base. 'Elio was very nice,' recalls Vivienne. 'He and Carlo both said you have to produce in Italy, and Carlo agreed to be my manager if I took production there. So he went to Fiorucci and we did a deal.' It was a perfectly timed offer, though Vivienne's absence from the UK for much of 1983 and 1984 was partly what allowed McLaren to undermine her and the Worlds End shop.

'He went as far as calling the factory in Italy, telling them not to work with her,' recalls Bella Freud, Vivienne's later assistant. 'Not only did he break her heart, he also wanted to stop her succeeding.' Even in Italy.

It could all have gone very wrong. America in particular was keen on Vivienne's name, but wary of her business reputation. American *Vogue* might already have cited Vivienne's designs as 'some of the most interesting to come out of England since the sixties,' noting the club-strobe light effect of her angular-cut raincoats and the unprecedented use of trainers on the catwalk – albeit with multiple tongues and built-in lifts – but the orders were thin on the ground. Bloomingdale's took one order to feature her in their windows, and then pulled it for fear they were never delivered. Meanwhile, it had been apparent to Vivienne for some years that her exacting standards of tailoring, combined with unusual patterns and fabrics, bemused her UK suppliers and subcontractors, and that if the business was ever going to leapfrog out of the King's Road / St Christopher's Place boutique into international fashion, she needed to find better, faster and more responsive manufacturers. Carlo persuaded her that Italy could offer her just that.

Leaving Ben in charge of Thurleigh Court, and with sixteen-year-old Joe due to join her after a trip across Europe, Vivienne left England. Her next collection, Hypnos, for spring / summer 1984, was designed whilst living with Carlo in Italy, and learning Italian. Carlo D'Amario is eventually persuaded to take up the story:

'I had just come back from Afghanistan where I ran an office for Fiorucci, importing ethnic jewellery and sheepskin leather – hippy stuff. I'd been doing that for nearly ten years. And I was looking for some new job in London or Paris. And all I heard in Paris was "Worlds End, Worlds End". And I see Vivienne for the first time there. And she is incredible – this punk – this incredible show "Witches". And I remember Vivienne saying, "I want to change the world." Back then in the eighties people still talked about "the system" as if fashion was not part of it. Thatcher was the system. Reagan was the system. Coca-Cola was the system. Not fashion. So we talked about the system. So I go to see her, back in London. And Vivienne was already quite famous back then. This is before McQueen and Galliano – she was the first huge British talent recognized internationally. It was therefore quite a shock when I visited her office, because you could see the business was a disaster and she had no money, and I just thought, "oh fuck." It wasn't a business. It was punk. I used to call it "Bombay", that chaos-factory in Camden. But I saw her, and in one second I made the decision to stay. And this is why. It was like when you are a child and some other child says, "Come inside and play with me," and you know instantly it will be an adventure. It wasn't about the money. It wasn't what people thought or think – it wasn't with an eye on anything. It was just, "Come into my house and play with my toys." So I did.

'The first thing I did: I sold my car. I had driven my Mercedes over from Italy, via the Paris shows, and I sold it. It was just instant for me, like a love affair. I just said to her, "I stay with you, Vivienne."

'The problem was it was messy with Malcolm, personally and commercially. Worlds End, the label as well as the shop, belonged to Malcolm McLaren too. There wasn't "Vivienne Westwood" written anywhere. So I said to Vivienne: "Forget Worlds End, forget Malcolm. Let's call what you are doing what it should be called: let's call it "Vivienne Westwood".

'She'd been like Cinderella, it seemed to me, this woman who did all the real work while Malcolm went to the ball. But here was my different perspective: I was from Italy, and in Italy, Vivienne was already the real name. Italian *Vogue*, for instance, only wanted to talk to Vivienne. People forget, she was more famous outside the UK at that time: Italy and France and Japan discovered her long before the British, in fashion terms if not in terms of punk. This happens. Giorgio Armani was more famous in America than Italy to begin with. But I could see she needed to be out of Malcolm's shadow financially too.

'So, I said I would take her to Italy. I set about trying to improve her name, her standing, individually. First of all, it had to be the end of "Worlds End" – because if everything was done as Worlds End, then half the profit went to Malcolm. Second of all, I arranged a big push for Vivienne personally in Italy – Italian *Vogue* and so on, to profile just her. And so "Vivienne Westwood" began to be an Italian story. Which it has been, to some extent, ever since. Italian TV covered her. We had already started making things in Italy. I offered to pay off Malcolm for Worlds End, to buy him out. And at first he refused. But then in the end it was going under and we took the name. Next, I went to Elio Fiorucci and I said, "You have to help me with this incredible woman, because she has all this talent, and all this potential, but no capital." And he said, "Call Giorgio Armani." So Fiorucci and I call the manager at Giorgio Armani, Sergio Galleotti, the man who built Giorgio Armani. And the next day, I was given an audience with Sergio Galleotti. It was like meeting the Pope. I go to this huge building in the centre of Milan. And they are so nice to me I am suspicious – there's a cappuccino, very good one, and Galleotti says, "So, whaddaza problem?" and I say, "Well, I have this Big Name, Signora Vivienna Westwood, but I need money," and he said, "Vivienne Westwood?!! No problem – how much money do you want?" And I had no idea what to say, so I just blurted out, "Three hundred million; we need three hundred million," – this was in the time of lire, which was then say 150,000 pounds, so, real money. But he just smiled and said she reminded him of how it was with Armani in the beginning. And he gave me the money. And that was meant to be the deal: Giorgio Armani presents Vivienne Westwood. A joint venture. But huge. I told Vivienne and she was so happy. It was going to change everything. And I felt, you know, like the little Dutch boy with his finger in the dyke – is that the word? – holding back the water: that we might just get away with it all. But then what happened was this: Galleotti died – one of the first people in Europe to die of AIDS – and they pulled.

'So there were two things that went wrong or didn't happen in Italy. There was never an Armani / Westwood collaboration in the end. But Galleotti taught me and Vivienne a lot. We learned that the wisest businessman in Italian fashion could have faith that Vivienne could be another Armani. And Galleotti talked about the children we would have (creatively!), Vivienne and me, and about the future. And he taught me and Vivienne to think far, far beyond the Worlds End. But before he died he told us this: the more creative you are, the more you need a structure. The one allows the other. And before this, for me, fashion had been "sex, drugs and rock 'n' roll". I wanted to do it differently, for Vivienne.'

'He's very interesting,' continues Vivienne later that day; 'very full of tall tales, but real ones, unlike Malcolm's, and he said these amazing things. My life had always turned on ideas. And I just loved him when he said, "Outrun the Establishment. Run faster. Have better ideas." I loved that. So I said, "All right: be my manager. I'll come to Italy." We became lovers quite soon after that. But only for a couple of months. Not here in England. In Italy. And that was very good for me, to be with Carlo, because it got me completely over Malcolm, completely free from him and from worrying about him. That was really good for me. And to go to Italy and just make a complete change. So that was that, and we carried on working, me and Carlo. Why did it end as a relationship? Well, he just didn't fancy me any more, I expect. I think that was it. So far as I remember. Although there were problems with it as a relationship from the beginning. For one thing, Carlo blamed me for everything that went wrong. One day he said I was a ball and chain round his leg. But he apologized; well, no, he didn't apologize, he *explained* after: one of his people in Italy had told him, "Carlo; the

English need to suffer. It's just part of their problem." So he had taken that on board as advice on how to handle an Englishwoman, and decided I needed to suffer, by telling me every victory was his and every setback was mine. And so it wasn't very good, as a personal relationship. But as a business relationship, it worked. Things did go wrong, we did have problems with the company and wresting control of it from Malcolm, so to that extent of course Carlo was right. I came with baggage.

'Every few months I'd come back to England to try to see Ben and Joe, and see if I could rescue the shop and our finances, so the longest I was ever in Italy with Carlo was for a couple of months. I would stay in Carlo's house in Milan and he would try to find good production in Italy. So that Hypnos (spring / summer 1984) and Clint Eastwood (autumn / winter 1984) and even Mini Crini (spring / summer 1986), they were all made in Italy. That was our plan and what we were doing. I learned Italian. I had had an Italian boyfriend once, ever so briefly, who went back to Italy and so that was the end of him, but with Carlo I learned Italian. And I had to, really, because in the factory that was all that was spoken.

'And I've loved Italy ever since, and I loved it then and I thought Carlo was wonderful. I thought he was the answer. Because he was such an unusual man, and in those days I was very much in – well, I was *interested* in him. And I found what he had to say stimulating and something I could learn from. That's what attracts me to men, to anybody. I learned from him. I've rejected quite a lot of what Carlo was interested in as I've continued, but it was a stage in understanding things and understanding people and understanding business. But I was never at the point where I was going to move to Italy permanently to be with him. It was clear that was never going to happen. My home was here, London. There was my flat, my boys, though Joe came out to stay for quite a while . . . and so Carlo and I agreed to stay friends. And we have. Mainly. For thirty years.

'But there was another consequence to the Carlo and Italy story. The final break with Malcolm came at the Hypnos collection show, in Paris, in October 1983. Malcolm came over and was making rubber jewellery for the show with Tom Binns. Accessories. I was with Carlo.

'Carlo said, "There's your logo": the royal orb and the future.'

Malcolm realized then that it was true what he had heard. And when that reality struck him, he asked me to go back with him. I just laughed. I remember at the airport, Carlo and I going back to Italy, and Malcolm was there and asked me to be with him and I just laughed in disbelief and I thought, "It's too late, Malcolm." And from then on it turned even uglier.'

'The story went around,' Carlo continues later, 'about Vivienne and me, and I don't really know what to say, except that 99 per cent of the time a designer has a partner, a manager, and at some stage there has been something there, homosexual or heterosexual, and that's normal and that's assumed in fashion . . . and look, it was an heroic time, that's how I think of it. We were on the road. We slept together. We stayed in the same rooms together and we drove the van together. Yes, we shared a bed and this is how it was and how I think of it: we were fighting in the desert together. We were comrades-in-arms. We were not some bourgeois couple, we were soldiers in battle . . . who slept together. And look, we were very different. We were inviting people into our lives, into our house, to invest in us. That seemed more important than anything. Fashion: people think it's like some Hollywood party. But you have to have your house in order, not just some crazy great ideas. So I concentrated on that. It's like a house: it needs a plumber. I am the plumber here. A house that works needs one. People treated this like a new concept. Because before us, nobody had done that: taken someone like Vivienne, a real maverick, and said, "We can make this a business too." But that's what we did. The plumbing.' (As I said, Carlo speaks in parables.)

'There were three people we produced with in Italy,' explains Vivienne, 'first Lorenzo's, then Carlo spoke with Galeotti about Armani and we planned to do Harris Tweed and Mini Crini, but then in the end we made that collection with Chianciano.' 'We created a new company,' Carlo says. 'Casnell. A name off the peg. It was British-based. Nowadays Vivienne Westwood, the company, is partly based in Milan, but not then. Our professional partnership dates from the mid eighties, but I'd be back and forth, a few weeks here, a few weeks putting production into place in Italy. We maintained the structure in London: the Worlds End, and "Bombay" – the workshops in Camden.

But I also got to show Vivienne Italy at that time. The factories and the travelling. Another life. Sometimes in five-star hotels, sometimes sleeping on the floor. We worked with one company, and the company went bankrupt, and we had to escape, Vivienne and me, with all the patterns and everything they had of ours, and we escaped together at night from Rimini to Milan in a Ford transit van I rented. These were heroic times. In one hotel, I remember, we were plotting the future – and this is the other thing where it could have gone so much better and faster. I said to Vivienne one night, here's what we do – we need a cherry on the cake, we call Madonna. We use Madonna for your fashion show. It was for Mini Crini, which was in part all these Minnie Mouse things – sexy but American, very Madonna, and Vivienne says, "Ooooo, no, Carlo, I can't just call Madonna." But you know, we did. And we got through, and an assistant called us back, and puts Madonna on the phone; and it's Madonna, it really is, and I know because it's this accent, like she chews gum, and she says, "Hi, it's Madonna, can I speak with Vivienne Westwood?" and she wants to do something with Vivienne. It's three in the morning. And I am thinking, "Thank *fuck* – it's Madonna – let's do something big with Madonna," and they must be getting on, because next thing Madonna is saying we can use her house in London, her production studio or whatever, to rehearse for the show. But Vivienne says, "Ooooo, Madonna, no, no, no, don't you worry; I have somewhere where we can rehearse," and Madonna is still saying, "Sure, sure." But when we get back to London to rehearse the show for Paris, and try to make contact, she doesn't return our calls. So there are the two things that almost changed everything for Vivienne from Italy: Armani and Madonna!'

Back in London while Vivienne was in Italy, things fell apart. 'We were never actually bankrupt – that's absolutely untrue, what's been written,' asserts Vivienne, 'but it was very, very rocky.'

'We started signing on the dole,' says Joe, 'me and Ben, getting twenty quid a week or something, you know, and we'd got to the point where it's like, well, you ain't going to get any lower. And there's strength in that. The only way is up when you are at the bottom, and that's how it felt. Despite all the press attention there had been. It

wasn't about being bullish. It was just, "This is what we shall try and do." And we did. We got the shop back and we got Mum back from Italy and we started all over again.'

Vivienne's Italian-designed collections include Hypnos, Clint Eastwood – named in honour of the spaghetti westerns that had made Eastwood's name – and the highly influential Mini Crini that redrew the eighties silhouette and launched a new language of undergarments in modern fashion. The Hypnos and Clint Eastwood collections looked set to sell well, but the structure was not in place to profit effectively from them. These collections included stretch fabrics and futuristic motifs that became the mainstay of body-obsessed mid-eighties culture, but the Clint show nearly didn't happen at all after the buckles arrived late and had to be sewn on by the models themselves. Vivienne's fans in the audience, including John Galliano and Alexander McQueen – both just starting out on fashion careers – were kept waiting two hours, but they and the attendant press considered it more than worth the delay.

Vivienne's Italian period also saw the creation of the Mini Crini collection (1985) that is credited with changing the silhouette of women's fashion. It is often credited too, though not by Vivienne, with changing the course of her career. 'That was more Harris Tweed, but actually, at the time, things never feel like they are life-changing. I had been inspired by pictures of the Queen as a little girl, and by a ballerina. I had been to see *Petrushka*, the ballet, and there was this one little bell-like cut-off crinoline, that swung. I knew that was brilliant. And I saved that idea for a rainy day. And that rainy day came in Italy.' The impact of Mini Crini was various. Firstly, it redrew the silhouette: very few women ever adopted the cut-off crinoline itself, but it signalled the death of the eighties shoulder pad as it gave back to the female form the reality of female shoulders by redrawing the waist. It is cited sometimes as the origins of Vivienne's work with corsetry, though more accurately this came just slightly later, in Harris Tweed. But by revealing the details of lacing at the back of the skirt, it began the interest in undergarments as outer garments which was part of the joke of the mini crini in the first place: a parody of Victorian strictures that stressed the latent eroticism of structured clothing. The fact that the

Sara Stockbridge models mini crini and rocking-horse ankle boots.

collection found its way from Italy to the Cour du Louvre at all for the spring / summer collection of 1986 was in part a story of near disaster and of seventeen-year-old Joe Corré and an Italian pal driving it over the Alps. 'I'd left home by then and was living up in Finchley,' recalls Joe. 'It was a great time, hanging out with Guy Ritchie and a lot of those kids I grew up with in south London who later turned to crime or to the media. I wasn't doing drugs particularly, so I saved a lot of money, and I decided I wanted to go travelling and see Mum in Italy. I got the bus and I ended up in Tuscany. And she was staying at this beautiful hotel and I went and stayed there. I'd been sleeping rough on the way there, so it was lovely. Mum was in the final stages of doing "Mini Crini". It was a real turning point for us both. The Worlds End shop had closed down. We were there in Italy. I went with her to Paris, or rather I travelled with the collection in the van over the border with this Italian guy. And we did the fashion show. And it was massive. And she ended up saying to me, after that show, would I help her to re-establish herself in England. Changed my life. But then the Italian company decided they were pulling out: they thought it was too avant-garde for them, too extreme. Even though we got the front cover of *Vogue* magazine as the best collection in Paris that season. So Carlo and Vivienne agreed to send the entire collection to Susanne Bartsch in New York who had a shop there and used to run clubs and things in Manhattan, so that she could do a sort of fashion show in New York.'

The collection consequently had an opening of sorts at the Limelight club in New York, and became, briefly, the height of Manhattan cool within the club world – but Susanne had only the catwalk collection itself to sell, and no prospect of production of more from London or Italy. It nevertheless had its impact simply because of the fast reaction of the Paris and New York fashion press. 'I do know and did know,' recalls Vivienne, 'when things would be a success, and I knew then, with the corset and the crinoline. You have to have a sense of what's right.' The collection is credited further for begetting the brief vogue for puffball skirts, which Christian Lacroix put on the catwalk seemingly in homage to Vivienne. 'It wasn't quite like that,' says Vivienne. 'I was later on a friend of his; he was ever such a nice man, a really good person, and he said, "When I saw your Mini Crini collection, I didn't know what to do because you'd done it already." He was already working on similar ideas. So my name rose with his.'

Down in the archive, released from its pink body bag, and then swinging into perky tumescence courtesy of twenty-year-old rigeline – the Viagra of undergarments – is the original catwalk mini crini. Ablaze with cream dots on blood-red silk, it looks unworn, and Murray Blewett smiles his kindly smile as if someone has just unknotted a handkerchief in his memory. 'So Mini Crini was the thing I wanted to talk about,' says Vivienne. 'You have to put things into context 'cos we're talking about fashion; you have to think of the look of the time. The look of the time was Thierry Mugler, Claude Montana. It was their version of futuristic, their version of space-age. The thing that really interested me is when it's used as an undergarment, when the crini is intended to change the shape of women's clothes. For the last ten years clothes had had shoulder pads and tight hips – the inverted triangle – but I wanted women to be strong in a feminine way. These dresses give you a balletic posture and are very, very elegant . . . it gives you presence and swings in the most sexy way. I started with the silhouette, as you do, which is just a nice, classic silhouette that reminded me of my childhood, and of the little coats that Princess Elizabeth had. But then I also looked at Brigitte Bardot, who was a hero of mine. So it had this fifties feeling, formal and playful. It has a very childish Lolita feeling. It was ideas that I'd had from back in the late seventies, that I had saved. And I was surrounded at the time by people like Jordan, who used to have some ballet references to her clothing, and I was with Carlo, and Carlo had an influence, of course. He had a great passion for Walt Disney, so he encouraged me to look at Walt Disney for inspiration. Which gave me some of the colours and prints. So you see this is how it's made: these three strips of fabric, using the width of the fabric, have been sewn together and then a channel's been inserted on the innards inside, through which the rigeline is inserted which holds it out. But then also the waistband and the fastening is harking back to a drawstring. It reminds us of underwear, and that's harking back to the Pirate collection to some extent. So it's sexy. Playful. That was the whole point: you sit on the Tube with that, it rises up. You can show your knickers just by the way you walk or move or dance. So people loved them because they had this incredibly nice flirty aspect to them.

Dancerly too. Showing and not showing, that's what it's all about. It was worn with a twinset and pearls, so this was a nod to my youth as well, to pictures of the Queen and to Brigitte Bardot in the fifties, and even Jordan, because Jordan used to wear twinset and pearls in the shop. And with it all, unlike today, there were men's things: a Savile suit, which is a long-line single-breasted suit with a smaller more classic shoulder, which was like nothing at the time. Pale-blue or navy wool or this pillar-box red.'

The Mini Crini collection was written of as taking Vivienne in radically different directions, but for her, it harked back to previous work – Pirates, in particular – and forward, in its tailoring and fitted wool jackets, to the Harris Tweed concerns heading her way. What is astonishing is that this collection that had such impact on the silhouette of women's fashion, and that nudged forward the story of shoes (her rocking-horse platforms) and corsetry and undergarment-as-outergarment, was all created just as Vivienne's world was once again imploding. 'All this attention. No money. The clothes in New York,' as Joe puts it, 'so my mum and I ended up coming back to London. Ben had barricaded himself into Thurleigh Court, living in just one barricaded room for fear of the bailiffs who were knocking on the door every day, after the money Mum and Malcolm owed. It was a nightmare. Except for Mum it had seemed like that forever. What was astonishing, looking back, is that she never gave up – she just kept on going. She'd split up with Malcolm. The business had gone down the toilet. It needn't have done – but Malcolm was so vicious and spiteful and fucking horrible to her when they split up that he tried to destroy everything that they had had, and to destroy her with it. I mean, he was really fucking horrible. That's what I think. But do you know what she did? She managed to get this sample collection back from New York – well, some of it – instead of it going back to Italy where it should have gone back to, and we got it to London. And she knuckled under, and reopened the shop to sell it – to sell what she had made. She still didn't own it. And so, we opened the shop again there. And that's where we started. Her and me. By fucking candlelight, to begin with, because the fucking electric had been cut off.'

'The real story,' Vivienne tells me, 'was that Susanne Bartsch in

Vivienne and Holly Johnson (Frankie Goes to Hollywood) in Worlds End, 1986, by Ben Westwood.

New York gave me some money, and an order. So we had clothes for New York half made, cut but not sewn, but Susanne was never able to send the second half of the money, so she kept the catwalk clothes in New York and sold them. I needed £2000 and I just couldn't get it together, to reopen the shop, finish the clothes, pay customs; and Scott Crolla, Georgina Godley's boyfriend before she married Sebastian Conran, they had this great shop and he loaned me the money. And he wasn't rich. He did it out of respect. For me. Such a wonderful thing to do.'

Word spread fast on the King's Road that Vivienne was back, and the already legendary new Mini Crini collection was in the window at number 430. Isabella Blow bought a number of outfits: 'She wore my stuff on planes, which made some impact in those days.' Murray Blewett recalls the clamour up and down the street and the rush to get there to see, and if possible to buy, in the knowledge that the collection would sell out and for fear that Vivienne might go under completely. It was shortly after this that Murray found himself sewing the iconic crown headwear that adorned the next collection but which is often seen in mini crini photo shoots. He has been with Vivienne ever since.

'I was working in King's Road and someone said, "Vivienne's back! There's some new action in Worlds End – it's reopened, with Vivienne's mum working in there, and candlelight." Dora Swire ran the shop – Joe was there too, the summer of 1986, and we all headed down there and spent everything that we could buying these samples up. For Vivienne. Because we loved her and everyone wanted to support her – and it was amazing stuff. People forget, because mainly they noticed the mini crinis, it was really the beginnings of beautiful Savile Row type tailoring for men's suits there as well. Vivienne fitted me herself. I bought one of the 'Savile Suits': single-breasted, lightweight, pale-blue wool, half-lined. Long, thin lapels. One amber tortoiseshell button, with the Vivienne orb on it that's now all over the world. Suits like that changed everything. It was like Roxy Music all over, or Kid Creole. At the Limelight club and places like Heaven, Taboo, Bar Industria, suddenly all the coolest most beautiful people in London were all head to toe in Vivienne,' recalls Murray.

One thing that soon became apparent was that Vivienne needed a logo. 'When I did the Harris Tweed collection,' she recalls, 'I designed a sweater, imagining it would be a sweater for Prince Charles, such as he might wear with a kilt! It had a thistle, a rose, a shamrock, lions rampant. And at the time Ben was really into astronomy. And I liked the idea of something starburst and futuristic. It said "Deep Sky", this sweater. And Carlo said, "There's your logo": the royal orb and the Saturn rings: tradition and the future. Plus, I am a great fan of Prince Charles.'

This logo, representing Britishness and global and future concerns all at once, reflected also some of the duality of the Vivienne Westwood enterprise at the time and since. Vivienne moved more and more into the realms of high-end couture and historical-reference tailoring but at the same time continued to reiterate modernist graphics and formerly punk designs. Murray, moving in to work at the Camden studios, created eighties reinterpretations of classic punk designs, with eighties Day-Glo safety pins, for instance, as well as continuing his work on tailored crowns and corsetry. Not only were they sold side by side at the Worlds End, they were and are still worn together in the heady mix of references and styles that typifies the House of Westwood. 'I think of it as Englishness,' says Vivienne, 'this mix of many references, always some history, always something more.'

By the winter of 1986–7 Vivienne was deep into research for the collection that would consolidate her move into tailoring and indeed into the hearts of the British public: the collection she named simply 'Harris Tweed'. She had worked a great deal already with heavy British fabrics; the worsteds and felts that gave structure to some of the Buffaloes and Punkature clothes. They were exactly the same fabrics that had revolutionized tailoring in the later eighteenth century when Beau Brummell brought cavalry wear and uniform and neo-classical structure into modern fashion. Vivienne was turning to tweed, with its long-standing associations with the British countryside and British aristocracy: ideas and images that would refract in her work for years to come. 'I love to parody the English, and to use British fabrics. We have this amazing tradition: a fabric for fox hunting, another for opening Parliament, another for tiger hunting in the Raj; this is what I use as a designer.'

Meanwhile, back home at Thurleigh Court, Gene Krell noted Vivienne's newfound confidence and buoyancy, and a singular dedication

Original drawings for the Vivienne Westwood Red Label, by Vivienne, 2000.

to making the most of the opportunity to prove herself in fashion. She said she liked being alone (though he tried unsuccessfully to fix her up with Keith Richards, who, she claims, lost her interest after he spent an evening sitting in front of the telly picking his toenails), and she was filling the gap left in her life by the departure of Malcolm in an intriguing manner: by considering a partial move into music herself. One utterly unsung part of the extraordinary career of Vivienne Westwood is her occasional forays into lyric writing, but specifically her creation of a band, long forgotten, that fused fashion, art, ambitious stagecraft and Vivienne's own songs in a manner well ahead of its time. The band was called Choice, eventually, and the search for a singer was part of what had led Vivienne to be calling Madonna from Carlo's Italian hotel room. It was meant to be a fusion project, not unlike The Sex Pistols, in that it was to be about a 'look' (Vivienne's clothes) as much as the music, and it was to be about an idea: the uses of high art in pop culture, along with English folk tunes reimagined and reworded by Vivienne. Her choice in the end for lead singer was the twenty-two-year-old model Sara Stockbridge, who would become the Face of Westwood for much of the rest of the eighties and nineties.

'The idea of the band,' Vivienne explains, 'was about culture. There were all these songs that were stories, and the idea was for amazing videos, and changes of looks, and that Sara would act these songs about the past: about a caveman, about Venus the Goddess of Love.' It was a radical idea, not least as there was no single creative or musical voice. Simon Barker managed the group, and helped turn Vivienne's hummed tunes ('very Hilda Ogden', according to Murray; 'sort of folk tunes, and lovely', according to Sara) into potential pop hits. But it was much more about the look than the sound, and the look was extraordinary, and beautiful. In one, Sara stepped out of a gauze projection of Titian's *Venus*, utterly naked; in another, a giant gold frame arched over the whole band. It was, perhaps, ahead of its time, but for those in the closely related fashion and clubbing scene of the late eighties, Choice became briefly cultish, and could, if it had survived, have taken Vivienne's name and creativity into arena pop and the installation-music events of recent musical history.

'We played the Limelight in New York,' Sara recalls, 'and did a huge AIDS event in New York called the Life Ball, at the Roseland Ballroom.

And that was a huge event with all the international designers partici-
pating, and they were all asked – given five minutes to do whatever
they wanted to do. So Vivienne did Choice.'

'Sara stepped out of a picture frame,' Murray remembers, 'and the
crowd went wild. I played a prince once with a velvet Vivienne suit and
crown; that was at the Kinky Gerlinky club with Leigh Bowery, and we
were asked to Tokyo and the first time we performed abroad was at the
Hamburger Bahnhof in Berlin for three days with Michael Clark, so it
was oddly high-profile considering (a) it's completely forgotten now,
and (b) Vivienne hadn't tuppence to rub together at the time.'

Sara Stockbridge remains a great beauty, and has lost none of her
earthy laugh, ready wit and 'bollocks to that' attitude. The very British
melange of saucy sexiness and slightly old-fashioned good manners
that made her the perfect muse, and indeed actress, in the outré
Vivienne shows of the late eighties, marks her still as she offers me tea
in her Brixton town house. 'Choice was utterly ahead of its time. By
decades,' she opines. 'A different outfit for every song. Like Madonna
would do now or Kylie – and to have me singing in a very English
accent, which everyone does now, but it sounded odd then. But the
songs really were so great, the ideas were so great.' Sara, a woman who
was once on the front cover of every important fashion glossy in the
world and in a league with the so-called 'supermodels' of the era, says
her only regret, now, is that she let Vivienne's Choice disband.

Vivienne's post-Italian dream of playing Malcolm at his own game
and bringing together theatrical tableaux, great costumes and innovative Brit pop, was not to be. But Sara modelled in nearly all the
shows from Harris Tweed to Anglomania and still graces almost every
Vivienne Westwood store, in iconic images of crowns and ermine and
peekaboo jumpers. And Choice and Sara Stockbridge are important
reminders that Vivienne was having great fun, creatively and socially,
as she moved into her late forties, and began to know too that she had
found in Italy not just a country but a man who could secure her the
financial and production base to launch herself into something even
more wildly ambitious than a King's Road boutique or a pop band.

Today, the Vivienne Westwood Group could almost be mistaken
for an Italian company. It is owned and run from London, but the

Vivienne, with Carlo D'Amario in the background. Bustle by Herr Kronthaler.

majority of the production is in Italy, and you are as likely to hear Italian or German spoken around the Battersea headquarters as English. Although much Red Carpet and many wedding dresses and special commissions are made in Elcho Street, nearly all the rest of the production of the House of Westwood is currently based in Italy. Much of it is with Vivienne's close friends Rosita Cataldi and Paola Iacopucci, co-owners of Cataldi, the Italian factory that produces Vivienne's Gold Label, Gold Label knitwear, Unisex and Knitwear ranges. MAN Gold Label and the Anglomania and Red Label ranges are made by Staff International in Italy. This is the 'Carlo' model: according to D'Amario, at least, Vivienne Westwood exemplifies the 'designed in the UK, made in Italy and sold to Asia' paradigm now emerging in fashion. Vivienne shrugs. She is enthusiastic about Italian production and artisanal skills, and the small-is-beautiful aesthetic. 'Sometimes in Italy, you go to the garden shed at the end of the garden, and find this is where some element of luxury and art is being created: it has grown organically, family businesses set up after World War Two.' But it is now shifting again, in part because of Vivienne's passion for ethically sourced and produced fabrics and her determination to reduce her carbon imprint. Vivienne Westwood T-shirts, for instance, are now British-manufactured in order to assure the low ecological impact of production and the use of organically grown cotton. So Vivienne still travels back and forth to Italy on occasional weekends once or twice a year, as she has done since her days with Carlo. Nowadays she stays with Rosita and Paola, preferring real homes to hotels, and so that they can trade English and Italian lessons. 'She makes a deep impression on us and everyone here in Italy,' says Paola, 'she "gets into your soul" as we say in Italian; she enriches you professionally because for her nothing is impossible, which is a challenge and joy to us and to the factory. She challenges our Italian pride and creativity, because she is so exacting and so are her designs. And she swears very well in Italian, which is very useful!'

The main legacy of Vivienne's Italian expedition was and remains Carlo D'Amario. 'He is the other side of the organization,' says Vivienne, cryptically. 'I owe him a great deal, and he risked a lot, in the beginning. People forget, after the split with Malcolm two *Vogue* writers walked out of my show in protest: Carlo had faith in *me*. And he and Andreas get on well.'

Vivienne's links with Italy are therefore more than just the mining of Italian know-how or indeed the Italian management skills of D'Amario. The Italian connection has allowed Vivienne to flourish and expand. What was happening, back in the day, was this. There would be a huge risk coming up to a collection, with Vivienne ordering fabrics worth tens of thousands of pounds, never knowing what was going to sell, but needing to be prepared for orders. This is the classic problem as a designer takes that leap, as Vivienne did, from boutique to international. When most of the production was in England, this was in danger of bankrupting Vivienne every single season. Which was why Carlo suggested introducing another label, another line, which became 'Red Label'. This is a licensed line or what's known as a diffusion line. In other words, it takes its inspiration from Vivienne's main collection, the Gold Label, but the cuts are not so extreme and they are more affordable. This has long been the business model for comparable fashion houses in Italy. And also, this being a licence, Vivienne doesn't carry the risk of having to finance the development. She now sells designs and the risk is taken by the factory in Italy, or the people who produce the line.

Meanwhile, some Red Label is sold in the Vivienne Westwood shops as well, on favourable terms. But the couture Gold Label collection and the Worlds End label you can only get at a Vivienne Westwood shop. 'Alberto Biani's company in Italy, "New York", was very helpful, and then eventually we found Paola and Rosita who are marvellous. Italy has affected everything. Take fine knitwear. I introduced that back into fashion, once we had found the machinery that could do it. And of course we quite simply do the best shoes in the fashion world. And handbags. I could go on.' Later on, a men's line was introduced – Vivienne Westwood MAN, and MAN is also licensed, but everything is developed in England, and almost everything made in Italy.

Vivienne Westwood, the company, has expanded massively over the years. There's a jewellery line, which was always an important part of the collections, but also accessories, scarves, glasses, luggage and leather goods and perfume, which can generate income that far outstrips the fashion that started it all. 'But I see it as very important,'

The Vivienne Westwood MAN collection, launched in 1996.

insists Vivienne, 'that we sell *our* designs. Couture is our lifeblood . . . I am aware that handbags are a very important thing, commercially.' But, as Brigitte Stepputtis says, 'Vivienne has it all in a sense; we are almost unique in being a fashion house that makes profit with fashion, with clothes – it doesn't all rely on franchise, because Vivienne is in control. She is not just out there being a brand-for-sale, but at the same time she isn't at constant risk of exposure financially.'

And lastly, it should be said, the thing which Carlo and Vivienne have done together is to own, rather than rent, property. Worlds End, Davies Street, Elcho Street in Battersea and the Conduit Street HQ. 'Carlo likes to invest in stores, and I like it because we can sell direct from our own space,' explains Vivienne, though one side effect of this has been the revivification of the area around Conduit Street into a Mecca for high-end fashion. Turn left at the top of Savile Row, and there is Vivienne Westwood. It is one further reason the business gets held up as a model, internationally. 'You can take a name like Vivienne's,' says Brigitte admiringly, 'and use it to regenerate a whole area, bring in investment, and make the whole company less vulnerable to the winds of fashion.'

Carlo sums it all up more succinctly, in his favoured mode of parable: 'When Vivienne and I were at Buckingham Palace in 2010 and she became a Dame, I shook the hand of the Queen, and of course the husband, what's-his-name. And the Queen was very like my mama, very Italian mama, very sweet woman, the Queen of England, very sweet. And in this moment, I think, this is it: this is the one second that sums up all my life with my queen, Vivienne. You see, on the last day of the Second World War, the last day of the war in Italy, I should say, a bomber destroyed my family home in Milan: a British bomber. And sixty-five years later and after these thirty crazy, amazing years with Queen Vivienne, I shake the hand of the Queen Elizabeth. And this gives to me the "everything in one second", the alpha and omega of my life. Fashion can do that, it seems: it can take you full circle. From being bombed by the British to giving them a British national treasure, made in Italy. It was a very, very emotional experience. And I wept. In Buckingham Palace. Vivienne didn't, of course not. But then I'm allowed to weep: I'm Italian.'

Vivienne, however, is not always happy with Carlo's version of events. She credits the genesis of her commercial success also to her friend Jeff Banks and her son Joe Corre. 'Without Jeff Banks we might have been really stuffed,' explains Joe. 'To round it up, [here's how I remember it]. After Mini Crini . . . we had nothing. Vivienne and I . . . had to start again from scratch. Carlo went back to Italy. So Dora agreed to lend us about £7,000. We sold samples from the Crini collection and some things that Vivienne and Dora made from home. I assumed control of the business and bit by bit, with Ben helping out on production, we managed to get our heads above water. This was made more difficult because when we reopened the Worlds End shop the creditors from Malcolm and Vivienne's partnership came knocking for their money, which I slowly paid off. Carlo at that time began to help by finding some production for us in Italy and sending us some stock which was paid for from the shop takings. The shop [started] doing really well and . . . we realized that we needed to . . . take advantage of the interest in Vivienne's designs. We needed capital and cash flow. Vivienne got in touch with Jeff Banks and [he] helped us to form a limited company, get an introduction to a bank, loaned us £15,000 and guaranteed another £10,000, [and] enabled us to really get going . . . [eventually] I managed to get all the old debts cleared, pay back Jeff, open the two London shops, buy the freehold office buildings in Battersea, build up the whole team and finally get Vivienne a serious Japanese license deal. That was the time when Carlo wanted to come in. The truth is . . . after working for about nine years for my mum . . . I realized that she needed someone else to take the business I had established up to another level. She chose Carlo. And even though that was a bit traumatic for me [at the time], I was happy in the knowledge that Mum now had an established base to build on, a license deal with guaranteed royalty income, and Andreas to look after her. So it was time for me to leave and do my own thing. Which is what I did.'

PAGAN

V

Vivienne
Westwood

CULTURE CLUB

It is their historical character and the fact that each is unique that gives Mme de Guermantes' gowns a special significance. The woman who wears such a gown assumes an exceptional importance.   MARCEL PROUST, À La Recherche du Temps Perdu

The only thing I really believe in is culture. There has never been an age where people have had so little respect for the past.

VIVIENNE WESTWOOD

There are three parts to the legend of Vivienne Westwood. There's punk. And these days there is activism. And in between is something utterly extraordinary, but also central to understanding her and the link she makes between punk and politics: Vivienne is an unashamed cultural elitist. I don't write that easily, as it may put off those who shrink away from the idea of high art or the importance of history. But Vivienne will be remembered equally for these three closely interconnected areas of her life and creativity. She co-created the look of punk and she has now linked all her work into her campaigns for human and ecological justice. But in between, she brought something unique to the art of contemporary fashion: a passion for the past, and what it might teach us about aesthetics as well as about clothes.

For Vivienne, fashion was never just about clothes – not during punk or afterwards. In the years after Malcolm, she travelled and read and spent an enormous amount of time in art galleries. She still does. To understand Vivienne as an artist in cloth it is useful to follow her on the journey she took, in part with Canadian art historian

Gary Ness, into the rich canvases of the seventeenth and eighteenth centuries. If it was true that you had a much better life if you wore impressive clothes, Vivienne was drawn over and over again to the impression that historical forms and stories might make. From pirates to royalty, and from Van Dyck 'swagger portraits', with their billowing fabrics and empowering physicality, to the tweeds and tartans and toiles and brocades of other former generations, Vivienne began to fuse fashion and art history, winning her admiration across the world, along with the bemusement of some and the antipathy of others. 'The fact that she was able to develop punk into couture,' reflects the model Lily Cole, 'that she weaves those two forces together, reflects her own dichotomies: how brazenly unapologetic she is to be who she is. It is rare in fashion to witness someone so independent of thought and committed in action.' The ebullience of punk segued into the swagger of fine tailoring and lush reference to the past: it looked like a volte-face but to Vivienne was seamless.

Key to this would be the Harris Tweed collection (autumn / winter 1987). Such were the rocky finances as Vivienne first relocated back to England that this opulent yet traditional-looking collection was made almost entirely in Thurleigh Court on Vivienne's original sewing machine. Mark Spye, who came to work with Vivienne at this time, recalls the collection arriving at the Worlds End in black bin bags: 'itchy, thick tweeds: no one was wearing that sort of thing then, but wear them they did'. Named after the Hebridean fabric, and leading eventually to the complete revivification of a dying industry – one reason Vivienne was soon to win a Queen's Export Medal – Harris Tweed consolidated the ideas forged in Mini Crini. Out went the Disney spots and fake wood, and in came rich purples and ermine and of course tweed, modelled by the perky-posh line-up of Patsy Kensit, Sadie Frost and Sara Stockbridge. 'My whole idea for this collection was taken from a little girl I saw on the Tube,' says Vivienne, the dedi-cated follower of public transport. 'She was standing and she had on a school jacket, the sort of thing you could buy in Harrods then, and a bag with a pair of ballet shoes. She looked so serene – and lovely.' The combination of the girlish and dancerly with the tailored and British gave Vivienne the chords she needed for a new cadence in fashion:

Sadie Frost models the Harris Tweed collection.

'I thought of debutantes going to balls but with a Barbour jacket flung over their ballgown; that mix, that ease with chic and tradition.' The fabrics were produced on Scottish looms and in English mills, and the jackets – men's and women's – paid homage to the best traditions of Savile Row, but the essence of the collection and its appeal was a flirtatious parodying of Englishness that appealed almost as much abroad as it did when Vivienne opened the show at Olympia.

'When I did the Harris Tweed collection, that's when I really started to do tailoring. Of course we'd done things before which were very tailored, but I remember the Harris Tweed collection as being the first time I really addressed the business of tailoring with men in mind. Before that, men were always *in* it, but maybe just one perfect pair of trousers. I mean, as far back as SEX we had made zoot suits, but I wanted to establish the idea of tailoring as integral to my collections.'

As well as the purple velvets and heathery tweeds, Vivienne used a tattersall check and red barathea that made a strong impact both on the catwalk and in photographs. The use of a crown, too, as a jokey accessory, and her new logo of orb and Saturn rings, all combined to give a series of striking images to fashion photographers and the press. 'I'm really inspired by the Queen at the moment,' said Vivienne at the time, 'all that pomp and circumstance and Norman Hartnell,' and British *Vogue* commissioned the Queen's former brother-in-law, the Earl of Snowdon, to photograph a red barathea outfit from the collection outside Buckingham Palace, the model surrounded by uniformed horse guards. Vivienne had nearly panicked at the last moment about it all, and had been soothed by her then assistant, Bella Freud. 'What I really loved about working with Bella,' recalls Vivienne, 'was her taste. I put on the crown, late at night in Thurleigh Court, and asked her, "Does this look a joke?" And she said, "Vivienne, how can you doubt? It's the most chic thing I have ever seen." Assistants, you see, like models, they have to love the clothes. Bella was brilliant.'

Harris Tweed went straight to the heart of the British public as much as the fashion press, bemusing, amusing and fascinating in about equal measures. Vivienne's stated position that it was all 'comic, but terribly chic' was not appreciated by everyone. Sara Stockbridge recalls getting laughed at on the streets of London, but literally applauded on the streets of New York, in the same ensemble of Harris tweed jacket and rocking-horse shoes. 'The truth was,' recalls Vivienne, 'I wanted to get Diana to wear one, one of the crowns, in that spirit of the auto-ironic, as I call it.

'We did Harris Tweed from Thurleigh Court – Carlo and me had nowhere else to be making things: me, Bella Freud and Mr Mintos and some outworkers. Some of the things were only finished the day before.' The 'Britishness' of the collection was underlined by the use of traditional Smedley twinsets. These were customized with Vivienne Westwood logos and tailored to a slightly sexier fit than had been Smedley policy until then, but they have become a staple in Vivienne's repertoire ever since, allowing, in typical Vivienne style, an exploration of the latent eroticism within that fantasy figure, the librarian. Quite separately, Vivienne moved the undergarment-as-outer-garment up from the waist to the torso, with a series of modern-twist corsets – 'ready-to-wear' corsets, as she calls them – that have had unparalleled impact in modern fashion. The design provenance is typically Vivienne: the look is straight out of the eighteenth century ('That cleavage had not been seen in 200 years'), but the manufacture was all modern in that it used lycra stretch panels in the sides in lieu of 'stays' or lacing, and the structure is plastic rigeline, not whalebone. The effect was instantly sexy, laden with reference to bodice-ripping, but comfortable, and, at best, empowering, all at once.

'When Sadie Frost undid her coat, with that underneath, there was a communal expiration – all the men in the room sort of sighed, and when Sadie left the catwalk, they shouted after her, "Come back, darlin'!"' recalls Vivienne fondly of the original Mrs Jude Law. 'Actually, I saw her at Kate Moss's last week and I said to her then, "You are so beautiful!"' As Vivienne is keen to point out, this iconic corset also formed the foundation of some of her most expressive designs ever since. 'You can build in any direction if the torso is held in place – and it feels great. This is why I called it the Stature of Liberty corset,' and the making of the rigeline corset became the point-of-entry test for anyone aspiring to work for Vivienne in the 1990s. Down in the archive, the original purple-velvet corset, as worn by Sara Stockbridge, maintains its singular erotic charge and lustrous sensuality: even

Sara Stockbridge in fig-leaf leggings.

encased in plastic, you can see how it moves, how strong it looks and how practical. 'For me, the focus of a woman is the waist . . . You just have to look at Diana's wedding dress,' says Vivienne, recalling the David and Elizabeth Emanuel confection worn by the late Princess of Wales, 'to see how much a dress might be improved by a corset. Everything hung from the shoulders, so everything sagged. I mean it was lovely in its way, a great statement, but from a corset you can build in any direction, but keep this strong, feminine core.

'And this corset we made: it is really, really sexy. Low-cut. It held the waist in. It forced the breasts up. That was the whole point, that it was pushing – that's what those corsets did, they pushed the breasts up. And people just loved it. Three sizes were all we ever needed. It was adored: a real wave-the-flag moment of euphoria. What Andreas now calls a "have-to-have" moment. And I should say,' continues Vivienne, warming to the corset theme, 'I loved it. I never wanted to make women look like victims, but it does the opposite. And of course it's very good for posture. It is a fashion history moment in that it is of course taken from an historical pattern, but the originals were measured by men, laced in by servants. Stretch fabric changes everything – hence the name, Stature of Liberty. It gave breasts back a look they hadn't had in generations. And I loved that it was taken up everywhere else – Gaultier in particular. I loved what he did, it was brilliant.'

Vivienne's next five collections, from 1988 to 1990, cemented her reputation, born of Harris Tweed, as a tailor, designer and couturier. The collections became known as the 'Britain Must Go Pagan' series, as they had a linked agenda of playing, in fashion, with Enlightenment ideas of Greek classical (pagan) sensuality. Some have seen this as demonstrative of a schizoid approach to influences in her designs – at this stage freely mixing traditional forms and fabrics of British tailoring (Prince of Wales check, pinstripes and tweeds) with Greek erotic imagery and playful sexual knowingness. In truth her work was an accurate reflection of the Age of Reason's fascination with the sexual and its imagery in the classical world, which seemed to chime comfortably with our modern age of surfaces. For instance, Sara Stockbridge found herself riding a jockey-trainer rocking horse in a tailored eighteenth-century sack-back dress, turned into a skirt so short it needed what Vivienne describes as 'John Smedley old-lady knickers' underneath. By Pagan V in 1990 Sara (and indeed Vivienne) was wearing a mustard-coloured Harris tweed jacket closely modelled on eighteenth-century hunting jackets, teamed with flesh-coloured stockings with a fig-leaf appliqué on the crotch. It scandalized the British tabloids, in a game that suited both sides well enough – especially when Vivienne posed in the outfit for a photo shoot outside the Natural History Museum in support of striking museum staff – but the concept was entirely in keeping with her revisiting of the Enlightenment. Just as the Incroyables and Merveilleuses had both sampled classical civilization for inspiration, and, like so much of the neoclassical, been inspired by Herculaneum's erotic murals as much as by the precepts of democracy, so Vivienne was simply using the best of what had been done before to imagine a better future. Sex and silliness had always been there in ancient civilization, and had been mined already in the punishingly tight trousers of the Regency, for instance, to which she alluded directly with her fig-leaf riding ensemble. 'Englishness is vital to what I do,' says Vivienne, 'it's about cut, it's about irony and it's about risk-taking. And it's about politics. I remember thinking, I know – I'll do this without skirts, like a man who is perfect, but just lost his trousers because he has been having sex. It was also a trick just to keep those jackets I loved from one collection into the next. Or like in the 1950s when we didn't have many clothes, so we would turn up at weddings in unusual combinations of styles: historical or vintage garments mixed with just a piece of fabric. It's about the mix of ideas. Or like a Savile Row window. All those shirt fabrics. The English have so much to work with, so many styles to mix, and I love that, that Gainsborough nonchalance, the Anglomania of dogs and flowers. That's why the French have so long admired what we've done: what "Anglomania" is all about, it's a French idea. It's like they say, a French painter would arrange the hat on his model; Gainsborough knew his subject would have the confidence to cock the hat herself.'

If fashion is an art, it has as its canvas the human body and those decisions over what pulls and pushes, what is revealed, hidden or emphasized. This has been the game of clothes over the centuries. Some of the finest ideas, necessarily, have been aired already, as some of the essentials of the corporeal canvas are constant. Freedom expressed as sexual freedom had been a theme for Vivienne since, well, SEX. What shifted in the eighties was the inspiration she found in the arts that had celebrated the body for one reason or another already: the worlds of classical statuary, for instance, or eighteenth-century portrait art. She laced all this with a fair amount of humour, which is maybe the singular British addition to the longings of sex, and though the fig-leaf stockings that sold out in hours had obvious allusions to classical nude statues as much as to Mr Darcy trousers, they were also hilarious. 'My happiest memory of those years,' says Mark Spye, 'was hearing Vivienne screaming with laughter – I couldn't think what had happened, but it was simply that she had tried on the fig-leaf trousers for the first time and seen herself in the mirror.'

These were the years that generated for Vivienne Westwood a persona in the British national psyche, somewhere between an operatic diva and a costume historian dominatrix, but which won her also many intrigued followers and fans, amongst whom I would have to count myself. The truth was, her clothes were conspicuously sexy, photogenic and compellingly visual, but there was also a great deal to be written and said about them, because of the research Vivienne had dedicated to their creation. Her collections therefore generated many more column inches than would be considered usual for a British designer, and the imagery, which toyed over and over again with visions of royalty, aristocracy and high art, was published around the world to intrigued acclaim. Some combination of the Sara Stockbridge style end-of-the-pier sexiness, Vivienne's astute eye for historical costume, exquisite tailoring and classical and political allusion combined to propel her work into the headlines year after year. The question that hovered was whether all of this could coalesce into mainstream commercial success.

Whereas previously (and with Malcolm) Vivienne had looked to the creation of a street cult as a means to comment upon society as she saw it, through the 1980s her gaze turned ever more to the history of ideas and the history of art as a means to critique the present. She is generous as ever about acknowledging that this was as a result of an artistic 'conversation' every bit as much as had been the case with McLaren. This time, the person who acted as her counsel and inspiration came from an altogether different mould: a Canadian homosexual aesthete called Gary Ness.

'The biggest influence on my life bar none,' Vivienne tells me, 'was Gary Ness. I would not be the person I am if I had not met him. His ideas were so attractive to me. It was as if I had been nowhere until I met him. He was a very strong character with a heretical view of the world and this illuminated for me his strength. Nobody has ever spoken to me like Gary did. He had an amazing brain and character, very informed by his heroes Aldous Huxley and Bertrand Russell. I had never heard ideas like Gary's, but I knew immediately they made sense. His friendship "explains" or at least structures this part of my life and a great deal of what I have done since, in design terms. Men with different brains to mine are the men I want to talk to. He gave me Huxley's *The Olive Tree* to read. I was, you see, still a freedom fighter. But I needed my head rescrewed on.

'During that time when I was on my own, the important centre of things to me was Gary. He taught me a great deal about art and about history. And without him I would not have been the designer I am. To understand what I was looking for and creating then, and my life before Andreas, you need to know two things. You need to know about culture, and why we should care, and you need to know about Gary.

'It's odd how we met. Gary needed money. He had been a portrait painter, and he gave it up – threw his materials into the Thames at one point: sick of gallery owners, sick of the whole thing. But he kept his hand in. He was always drawing. And his idea was to do an exhibition of portraits, and so he was looking for interesting people to paint. And he came and introduced himself to me in my shop in World's End, and he asked if he could paint my portrait, this very distinguished-looking man – chain-smoking all the time – Gitanes. He was very, very handsome. He was gay. But when I knew him, he wasn't interested in sex. He wasn't that well, actually, for a start, though I didn't know that then. And he said he was working in pastel – he'd pronounce it like the French – and he said, "It's the same technique as oil – it's quite different from watercolour." But really he was doing pastel because he had such a small space to work in, and he said, "You need room to be able to paint proper stuff," to buy the materials and everything. So he did a portrait of me, and he put it on one side and said he would have to begin again. He said, "I can't rescue it. I've made you look too old. I'd have to start again." But we never did that one. He just preferred talking and we just talked and talked, and he never did do another one.

'He was full of funny stories. He'd travelled all over America paint-ing, and spent five years in Franco's Spain, living with English expats in Majorca – a circle of people whose families didn't want them, he used to say – and through all of them he came to know Lee Miller well and Roland Penrose. He was amusing: used to quote silly poems:

Freud
Got annoyed
With sex
So to vex
The world
He unfurled
His Theory.

Gary used to say, "Nobody loves to laugh like the French." Gary's name was really Nelson, but he looked like Gary Cooper, even as a kid, so they called him Gary. And he really could paint. He once did a copy of a Velázquez self-portrait in the Louvre, and he said, "You would not have known it from the original." And that's because he knew the technique of how to paint. He had had Roland Penrose as a sort of patron, and worked on his Picasso book, which, Gary said, was full of howlers about which he had to be a very diplomatic editor. His loyalty lay more with Lee Miller and Ness used to say she was driven to drink by Penrose's womanizing, but be that as it may, after Penrose died Ness was in need of a patron, which was when he came to London. He did feel badly about taking money from people, but he also knew he could be useful. When the Ness family money ran out, Penrose had helped find grants for him towards a book, never com-pleted, due to be titled, "Who the fuck needs Art? By Phyllis Stein, no relation of Gertrude."'

Nelson 'Gary' Ness had been born in Saskatchewan in Canada in 1928, making him a full thirteen years Vivienne's senior. In his late teens he attended a local Canadian art school, but then won a portrait competition that secured him a scholarship to the École Superieure des Beaux Arts on Paris's Left Bank.

Paris in the 1950s had given Gary various gifts: his firm belief that France was the centre of the art world and of culture, a classical over-view that civilization had its origins with the ancient Greeks, and also the happiest years of his life. What found him wandering the King's Road was a move to London and a renewed ambition in portrait paint-ing. He couldn't afford oil, so he worked in oil pastels on paper and card, and told Vivienne and the world that it was the superior medium.

'The portrait wasn't very good,' Vivienne recalls, 'or at least he didn't *think* it was very good, but we got talking and every time I mentioned something that interested me, he would go straight to a shelf and pull out a book that developed my thought, sometimes even turned to a page. I learned. He had the gold I wanted. He got me interested in China, and Chinese art. And in Native American culture. He was a life-giving force. My Manifesto book, for instance, was modelled on the little Pauvert pocket books that he collected. And he was heroic, really. He was very ill. Shingles – and the pain is unbearable – for years. Raw nerves and singed skin. Awful. So I valued and value every minute I spent with him. I learned so much. He completely changed my opin-ion about art. He used to say, "Purpose is a man-made invention; all we know is our own purpose," and "Disassociation of ideas is necessary to think," and, quoting Whistler, "There is no progress in art." He would've been eighty-four now, had he lived.' Vivienne stops and coughs. 'He died about ten years ago. He died at the age of seventy-two or three, actually, which is exactly my age now. One time we were going to meet at the French House in Soho, and I was late. He was fuming. He hated it there, said it was pseudo. Stormed out. But he wrote to me. I never opened the letter, but I kept it. And I opened it recently. And it was the sweetest, sweetest thing . . .

'I saw Gary a couple of times every week all those years that I was "on my own". I was giving him money, even when I was on the dole myself. I got £30 a week and I gave him half of it, because he was a

Sara Stockbridge, 'Choice'.

chain-smoker, and I could manage on fifteen quid. I can survive on nothing. And my sons Ben and Joe were looking after themselves at that point. Before I went to Italy I gave Gary £200 – actually borrowed it from Ben's savings – and said, "That's all I've got. I've got to go and try and get things sorted out, financially, in Italy. I can't look after you any more." But when I came back, his health was gone. He'd done nothing except live on Complan and Gitanes. He was surrounded by bags of dog-ends, this poor man with this genius brain.' In an era, nowadays, when one can get bibliotherapy or have a Kindle reading list assigned based on previous buying patterns, it maybe doesn't seem so strange that Vivienne should have appreciated the mentoring of a French-trained cultural critic who was also an evangelist for the importance of high art and indeed fashion. It was, clearly, a love affair, though perforce a platonic one. Gary appeared both odd and needy to many who knew him through Vivienne, and when it became apparent to Carlo and others in the business that she had put him on a 'retainer' as a sort of cultural consultant, there was both dismay and pique. What was it, exactly, that Gary did?

'Gary helped me most in this,' explains Vivienne, 'in the idea that great art is as alive today as when it was first done. That the past is relevant. It gave me the confidence to say that true culture is not about a break with the past. And people in fashion can get very irritated by this, and by my quoting and making historical reference, but I hated it when I was called anachronistic, because I knew that time was on my side; if art is original it fits into the tradition.'

Gary holds his place as the ideas-man behind many of the historical themes of Vivienne's work and the title-writer of almost everything from Voyage to Cythera (autumn / winter 1989) to Vive la Bagatelle (spring / summer 1997), but he was much more than a copywriter or dramaturge. 'I advise Vivienne on what to read,' he once proudly boasted, and left it at that. But the coded descriptions in the press of Gary as an 'aesthete' and a man with a 'richly draped apartment' and a penchant for 'impeccably manicured fingernails' denote the simple fact that Gary was gay in the quasi-closeted manner of his generation of sophisticates. He found real love, it seems, with Vivienne, in that he discovered a passion for teaching and mentoring. 'I wouldn't want anyone to think other than highly of Gary,' says Vivienne. 'He was a man of real moral grit and intellectual rigour. He adored fabric and he adored art. And he gave me something extraordinary. It is my character to be political. I found through Gary that I could be political through art.'

It is a signal of Vivienne's ongoing quest for knowledge that in the years between Malcolm and Andreas she should turn to Ness for intellectual stimulation unalloyed with physical or romantic intent on either side. Still, he had a profound impact upon her thinking, her taste, her philosophies about art and culture, and about the potential for fashion to be art and for a fashion designer to be a propagandist for culture and ultimately an activist through 'the applied art', as he called it, 'of fashion'.

Gary took Vivienne to a brave new horizon of aesthetic politics – and a respect for high art that has remained at the core of what she believes and what she makes. 'The basic idea,' he later said, 'is that Rousseau – proto-socialist and godfather of the idea of the "noble savage" – is responsible for the damage that has been done to traditional ideas.' In this can be traced the origins of Vivienne's attachment to a 'hierarchy of arts' and to high culture: a disavowal of Romanticism in the political or 'hippy' sense. In other words, Ness, like many of his generation, saw in the political emancipation of the Age of Revolutions the seeds of decay in Western culture. The best things are to be debated and created by an educated elite (an 'elect', as Vivienne would now say), based on clear knowledge of the best of the past. Their fruits should be on offer to all, of course, but they will not be appreciated by all. Which is to say there *is* such a thing as a classic, there *is* such a thing as great art. It can be defined and it can be aspired to. It looked like quite a volte-face for the punk in the 'Destroy' T-shirt, but Vivienne embraced it all.

Vivienne's dedication to the high arts, and in particular to the decorative and fine arts of eighteenth-century France and England, was anathema to many of her associates who had been punks. For Gary there were no more ideas after Picasso and Matisse, no real greats after Manet. But Vivienne achieved something extraordinary in her punkature fusion of what she had done before and what she was in thrall to after Gary. She found a critique for the contemporary world that was the best of the past. This has become her counterpoise to easily marketable tat: high art and a return to the values of other ages, even within fashion. It was, in its way, a punk position. If eccentric viewpoints did not get airtime, it was because 'to get any message across you need a lot of money'. If democracies were failing true values, it was because elections were exercises in marketing. 'The problem is that the marketing people have the same point of view as the Marxists,' Gary was quoted as saying to her, 'they are trying to bring about the dictatorship of the proletariat. Or, at least, they've succeeded in destroying the idea of Taste.' It was why Vivienne and Gary started calling marketing folk the 'Marxisting people'. Gary thus gave Vivienne an absolute rationale for looking backwards and forwards at the same time. Though fashion writers baulked at what they saw as Vivienne-the-teacher preaching about costume history, Vivienne and Gary took this as reflecting only the commercialization of fashion. 'If something is absolutely great,' said Gary, 'it fits into a tradition. Everything else has to readjust, in order to accommodate it. In this way, not only does the past influence the present, but the present readjusts to the past.' Or as Vivienne said more recently, 'We take the best of the past, and their ideals for their future, and make them speak to our present and our hopes for the future. That's what culture is, and what fashion, at its best, can do. My clothes have a story – that's why they have become classics; they keep on telling that story. All fashion designers worthy of the name do what I do in that sense: they create in a bubble, they populate that bubble with people who would live in that better place that they have imagined. Only better-looking.'

Her rationale was in place. Her passions were engaged in a personal journey through the history of art. It could be mined for new statements in fashion. And thus Vivienne entered the most creatively fecund period of her life. Tweeds, wool, twinsets and pearls, pinstripe with giant amber lozenge buttons, blazers and Fair Isle sweaters shared catwalks and collections with Sèvres patterns printed on classical togas, silver- and gold-lamé corsets, floaty Grecian drapery and even tutus. The whole dressing-up box was opened, and the fashion press were sometimes bemused. If there was clarity and focus to the Harlequin and Columbine costumes of Voyage to Cythera [birthplace of Venus], there was confusion when Norfolk jackets, flat caps and plus fours were teamed with medieval armour allusions in the aptly named Time Machine (autumn / winter 1988). Her use of historical themes and literary references, however, as intended, has rendered many of these structured and tailored items 'classics'. Not only do they not date through being unattached to the prevailing winds of fashion at the time, they also maintain their allure by being well made and strongly argued in the first place. Autumn / winter Red Label for 2014 featured tailoring and themes from Harris Tweed (1987) and Anglomania (1993), in tartans and tweeds that have become synonymous with that part of Vivienne's output that is inspired by British history.

Not everyone was impressed. Certainly on home turf her parodying of British style and her unabashed cultural elitism could get a brash reaction. Disastrously in 1988 she accepted an invitation to appear on live teatime TV on the then popular *Wogan* show, hosted in his absence by Sue Lawley. In the long British tradition of mocking the avant-garde and the aesthetic, Lawley appeared to encourage the audience to laugh at the designer and her creations in a moment of excruciating TV later parodied by 'Alan Partridge' and Rebecca Front. Sara Stockbridge recalls, 'She was such a bitch, Lawley. Janet Street-Porter tried to rescue things, but basically Sue Lawley just got the whole audience laughing at me and Michael Clarke and the other model. And for those people who thought Vivienne was ridiculous I fear we probably just cemented that view.'

'You can laugh,' said Vivienne coolly, 'but *look* as well. I remember being on the Tube the next day,' she recalls, 'and I overheard two cockney lads talking about it. So it reached out. And I remember one said, "That Sue Lawley just couldn't handle it," and always afterwards I've thought: you have to remember, it's not about the studio audience, it's about the millions watching. And I must thank Janet Street-Porter, because she stood up and addressed the studio audience and said, "Do you know who this is? Do you realize?" But really, I was just puzzled at the time.'

If it cemented one view of Vivienne in the British public's mind, it was all beyond or indeed beneath Vivienne's concerns at the time. Her confidence as a designer grew over the eighties and early nineties into a systematic approach to designing with constant reference to the past; a crusade, as she has written and said, to civilize through teaching about the best, as she sees it, that human culture has had to offer. Though ultimately this has taken her to explorations of Asian and South American art, for instance, initially her areas of concern would be recognizable to an eighteenth-century *saloniste*: classical form and ideologies, freedom of expression and freedom to explore the sensual universe, the swaggering presentation of self.

'Fashion as we usually think of it,' Vivienne said at the time, 'the fashion of the West, depends on tailored garments, clothes made of specially tailored components: sleeves, bodices, skirts, trousers. These clothes have an ever-changing rapport with the body, as a result of their cut. Sometimes movement is restricted; sometimes liberated, and clothes affect posture and deportment and the movement of the body. The eros of fashion is finding the challenge as well as the defence: the essential woman, choosing to show this, or hide that. You can express yourself with clothes. They talk about the body, and express personality and ideas. Clothes also move in a dynamic way and talk about potential. The convention that comfortable clothes should be loose-fitting is a convention of our time. I feel comfortable when I think I look great, and I couldn't bear to put on shapeless, stamped-out, mass-manufactured clothes. I design clothes in the hope of *breaking* convention. Comfort is to do also with completing a mental image of what you want to look like – what you are and who you are.

'I once had an argument about this with my teenage granddaughter, Cora. We were at the British Museum, and she came in something – well, shall we say it was "comfortable"? And we ended up having an argument, though it was brave and right of her to stand up to me, but I was trying to explain that comfort comes from making the impression that you want to make!

'Perhaps the best example of how I was working at that time, in the late eighties and early nineties, the high point of these ideas about fashion and art, would be the Portrait collection. I wanted to do a

'The eros of fashion is choosing to show this, or hide that.' Vivienne Westwood

collection where I would put together a range of fabrics so rich in scope that it would live up to all the richness of texture seen in oil paintings. From linen to lace, tweeds to velvet. I had to have a go. Red barathea wool was important (I had used it before) because it represented English country life. I even wanted to get the textures of the fields and countryside on my ladies' backs. And I had this idea of a print taken from Boulle furniture, the back of a mirror in the Wallace Collection, and I wanted to get all the things you see in paintings, but also even the furniture. When I arranged these fabrics there was still something missing. It was the paintings themselves. I knew I had to have an actual painting on the clothes. I chose a Boucher, *Shepherd Watching a Sleeping Shepherdess*, from the Wallace Collection – and I chose earrings with drop pearls, as the most obvious from paintings, and used my shoes with extra-high platforms, and this was to put my lady on a pedestal: I wanted her to look as though she'd just stepped out of a painting.'

This led parenthetically to a whole other issue within the iconography of Vivienne Westwood: platform shoes. The story of Vivienne and revolutionary shoe design properly begins with the Hypnos, Eastwood and Mini Crini era 'rocking-horse' shoes, but this led into the era of the Portrait collection and onwards to enormously elevated platforms, that are nonetheless adored by those who wear them. 'Before me, platform and heels were always added to the shoe, like a separate support. I've taken the leather or fabric over the whole edifice, shoe and platform. It's a simple thing but makes them radically more beautiful: an extension of the whole look, and the leg. I'd order leather to cover right down the platform, so it looked a bit orthopaedic, as well – a bit kinky. They have become a classic. A little bit kinky, but also Art, which is very me. Women should be on pedestals. Like art. Sometimes. Or look like they have stepped out of a portrait. I wear them all the time.' (It's true.)

Vivienne has often noted that if she could do it all again, she might have studied art history. She is known in all the London galleries these days not just for imperturbable ease with celebrity-gawkers, but also for the length of time she will stand in front of a canvas. Vivienne is a watcher, and has, no matter what you think of her other gifts, the

Denice Lewis models the Boucher corset.

enviable ability to look. It is the power of the individual in the portrait that seems to have alerted her to the potential of historical reference in clothes. 'My clothes are dynamic,' she said at the time, 'they pull and they push and they fall slightly off. There's more to clothes than just comfort. Even if they're not quite comfortable and slip and have to be readjusted now and again I don't mind, because that's some sort of display and gesture that belongs with clothes.' These are the words of someone who understands how actors use clothes, what they can mean in the theatre, but who has learned this from the theatricalized portraits of the seventeenth and eighteenth centuries. Swagger was all about rendering impact with clothes, though that impact almost invariably used the possibility of uncovering as much as covering, and, like the best fashion always, was in part about sex. 'Mind you,' Vivienne corrects me, 'we do endless fittings. It's about the body of an individual, how people move, which can be very specific. Like Andreas: no one moves like him. So we always say, "How would you walk in this?" "Put your hands on your hips." It's about the clothes *and* the body and movement. Always.'

From Watteau-inspired dresses to Georgian riding coats, from baroque corsetry to neoclassical semi-nudity, the seventeenth and eighteenth centuries have had a profound influence on Vivienne's work. Played out in masks and masquerade, at the theatre and in an apparent stiff formality, the age was alive to the sexual, the revolutionary and the artificial. It was one of the great ages of fashion in that it plundered the past (Greek statuary reimagined as eighteenth-century breeches, images of Arcadia replicated on toiles), and played constantly with hiding and showing and with pretending, or dressing-up if you will – and this would be as true for Marie Antoinette in her *hameau* as for Thomas Jefferson in his slave-built Monticello. Masks, performance, sexual frisson and a moral imperative for art: these have all been part of Vivienne's story in fashion, and it should be said that her relationships have their eighteenth-century spin too – not for her the simple closure of conventional marriage or conventional men. Vivienne, often with Gary's input, had an instinct that the Age of Surfaces (the eighteenth century) would speak to the modern world in the throes of another sort of enlightenment: post sexual revolution, post media saturation, postmodern. Over and over again through the nineties she alluded to Revolutionary France and to the empowered women of the first sexual revolution: especially from Portrait (autumn / winter 1990) to 1997's Vive la Cocotte via 1994's On Liberty. Though some fashion writers felt they were being lectured about the history of fashion – and they were – others were overwhelmed by the sheer theatrical exuberance of it all and the power of the eighteenth century still to shock, provoke and liberate.

This eighteenth-century duality was a comfortable zone for Vivienne: she liked to have it both ways. You can see it in the press cuttings of the time, and her insouciant love of rubbing the British tabloids up the wrong way. Accepting an invitation to Kensington Palace for a Fashion Week event hosted by Princess Michael, Vivienne wore one of her eighteenth-century Boulle-inspired translucent sheath dresses, but no underwear. The papers tutted accordingly. 'It was the lights!' Vivienne protests, 'The pattern was reflective in natural light but under flashes, yes, the cameras picked up my breasts. I covered my face when I saw the papers, but then again the press were very kind about it. And I got a lot of letters of support. It was taken as a protest for womankind, but it was an accident.' Granted an OBE in the Queen's Birthday Honours in 1992, Vivienne did it again. She created a Dior-inspired skirted suit, twirled for the cameras, and again revealed a very eighteenth-century attitude to undergarments. 'I was told by someone at the palace – I can't say who as they are still there – that the Queen thought it was all hilarious.' Her granddaughter, Cora, who was at the Palace when Vivienne was subsequently made a Dame, recalls that the only question anyone was interested in was whether or not her grandmother was wearing anything underneath.

'So what I grew to believe was that to make clothes today, if you want to make something new, you can sometimes go back into the past. Take the Watteau dress, for instance. It's called the Watteau dress because it appears in so many of his paintings, but it's a style that lasted a full seventy years up to the French Revolution. You can see one in the Wallace Collection, the Boucher portrait of Mme de Pompadour, Louis XV's mistress. Luckily for me, the silks from that dress are still

The idea of an eighteenth-century salon, a forum for discussion on arts and ideas, was central to Vivienne and Gary's plans for their shared future.

being produced. So I copied this dress – the "Watteau" dress that is in fact in a Boucher portrait. So silks and suits with swinging backs crept into my collection. We worked with my pattern cutter to bring out this asymmetry, the movement that you can see in the painting, and that inspired cutting for the rest of the collection and it all began to look as if they were being blown by the wind. And we gave them names like "little breeze suit" and "storm jacket" and "squall coat", "hurricane dress". So, while drinking tea one afternoon in my studio, the title came to me: Storm in a Teacup. Clothes that would gift, because of great taste, equilibrium through any storm and all the drama of a crazy world. That was the thought in my head.'

London's Wallace Collection – the finest collection outside France of eighteenth-century fine and decorative arts – became for a while the spiritual home of Vivienne. It features heavily in the *Painted Ladies* documentary she made with her brother Gordon and in the later *South Bank Show* special devoted to her work. In the course of her ascendancy as designer, post punk, it was as much the styles of this collection as the taste of Ness that shaped her world and thoughts. Take for instance the André-Charles Boulle pattern that she admired on the back of a mirror. It was rendered as metallic overlay on lace and on stockings and remains highly influential as a pattern and technique. The fabrics of Jean-Honoré Fragonard's swinging dresses and the bosomy maids so beloved of François Boucher all featured in Westwood collections, like modern riffs on Wallace's taste and eighteenth-century idealism. It was noted, and approved of, that there was a building theme to Vivienne's work and output. In 1990 Karl Lagerfeld approached her about featuring several years' worth of work in *Vogue*, styled by Isabella Blow and titled 'Ich Bin Ein Englander'. 'You need a British mentality to get away with this,' wrote Lagerfeld, paying tribute to Vivienne's inventiveness and homage to the past. Versace was even more direct. 'I had the loveliest thank you from Gianni – did I tell you?' Vivienne suddenly recalls when we are talking eighteenth-century cherubs one day. 'He had started using baroque stuff on his things – you know, all that gold and detailing he did and they still do. He said he wanted to personally thank me for the putti!'

Two events, as the decade turned, set a seal on the ascendancy of

Vivienne through the late eighties: her mainly men's collection 'Cut and Slash', shown at the Villa Gamberaia in Florence at the instigation of Pitti Uomo, and the invitation from Azzedine Alaïa to show at his atelier in Paris from 1991 onwards. 'Azzedine loaned me his space; it was very generous and supportive. I am a huge fan of his work as well.' The first collection at Azzedine's was titled 'Dressing Up' and featured looks from several of Vivienne's past shows: historical references including codpieces, the Tudor fabric 'slashing' of the eponymous menswear show, tartan and other key elements of recent collections – gilded prints, corsetry, the 'love jacket' sporrans, lacy jabots and mackintoshes printed with old masters. This was closely followed by Salon, which was perhaps Vivienne's most consciously eighteenth-century collection. The international – and the British – press paid attention like they never had before. There were a series of rapturous receptions, with the Asian press in particular falling headlong for the reworkings of classics of Western art and the rebranding of an ex-punk as an iconographer in cloth. 'Westwood is probably England's greatest fashion designer this century,' *Vogue* was moved to write about the woman who had been shooed out of Grace Coddington's office a decade earlier. 'She has single-handedly revitalized England's trad-itions of tailoring and creating opulent eveningwear.'

The historic-inspired collections under the influence of Gary Ness, through the late eighties and into the early nineties, are considered some of Vivienne's most influential. They maintain their ravishing beauty, and are the crowd-pullers at her exhibitions every bit as much as the 'Anarchy' T-shirts or platform heels. It was Linda Evangelista in the green silk Watteau dress that became the signature image of the V&A exhibition every bit as much as Vivienne herself, framed in bar-oque gilt and pulling a face for the photographer Rankin.

'I am interested in bodies and sometimes in shocking people, but the most interesting way to do that can be to take things from the past. When you look to the past, trying to copy technique, you start to see the standards of excellence – the good taste in the way things were put together. By the time we were working on Vive la Cocotte in 1995 and Les Femmes in 1996 I was able to create a whole new silhouette, one

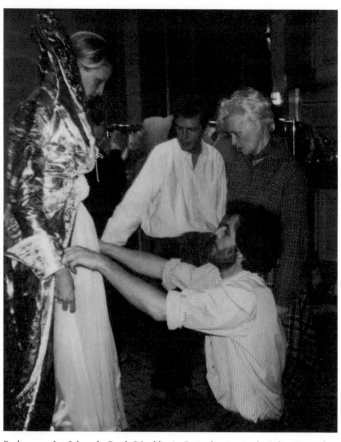

Backstage at Les Salons du Cercle Républicain, Paris, the nineties, by Robert Pinnock.

that hadn't been done before; nor could it have been done because it was a synthesis put together in the present with forms from the past. Our sexy idea of the hourglass figure with a wiggle, taken to an extreme. Coquetry is a part of woman's wisdom. She can be the most beautiful thing on earth and the changing fashion of her clothes creates a perpetual lust for her body and the art of her gestures and the potential in her face. This is one of the things fashion can do, and the thing, at the time, that fascinated me most.'

The world of high culture, brought to Vivienne in part through Gary Ness, is the pivotal point between her original punk past and her punk-activist present, because in using the past to look to the future, she is about her usual business of imagining a culture, or a subculture, that is contingent. More than this, her ideal of a 'hierarchy of arts' allows her to see the moral importance of art and design in a manner that helps explain her right – and her duty, as she sees it – to have political views as an artist. 'Faithfully antique but markedly original,' as Proust had it, writing about Fortuny's Greek-inspired dresses; the past proved to have huge power to inspire the present, and to impress a whole new constituency for Vivienne. Vivienne saw it all as punk. Swagger is punk. And so too is her Climate Revolution. 'Undoubtedly Vivienne has had a massive impact on British culture and fashion, but for me it has always been in a classical way,' her friend the British artist Tracey Emin tells me. Vivienne is specific about the moral agenda: 'We all say we love art. And some of us claim to be artists. Well, without judges there is no art. Art only exists when we know her. Does art exist? The answer to this question is of vital importance, because only if art is alive in the world will there be change. No art, no progress.'

Her historical and royal motifs, her reflections of the latent eroticism of corsetry and swagger, not to mention her patronage of artisanal designs like tartan, certainly secured for Vivienne first of all the curiosity, and gradually the adulation, of the fashion cognoscenti and press. Irrespective of the later awards and titles, Vivienne Westwood's place in the fashion pantheon is likely to be secured by the much-quoted testimonial of John Fairchild, the admired fashion writer, who wrote as early as 1989 that there would be six designers who would be remembered from the end of the twentieth century: 'Yves Saint Laurent, Giorgio Armani, Emanuel Ungaro, Karl Lagerfeld, Christian Lacroix and Vivienne Westwood [because] from them all fashion hangs from a golden thread.'

Fairchild went on to point out that it was only Vivienne who struggled financially, and that 'of the six, Vivienne Westwood is the designer's designer' (an idea quoted directly in the press materials for the later *Sex and the City* film in which Sarah Jessica Parker wears a vastly glamorous Vivienne Westwood wedding dress).

'Of course, at the time, Fairchild was just pointing out that I wasn't selling as well as the others!' He might just as easily have pointed out, however, that Vivienne was unique in this pantheon in one further and vital way: she was the only woman.

DRESSING UP!

Vivienne
Westwood

FRÄULEIN
KRONTHALER

Fashion has an ability to take over people's lives . . . Sometimes it is simply the result of a chance encounter.

MALCOLM MCLAREN

I'm not a jealous person. The Chinese have a proverb that if a horse is yours, it will always come back to you. That's how it is with Andreas. In every way, he's a horse – proud, elusive, electric.

VIVIENNE WESTWOOD

'I was very, very happy on my own. There are great advantages to it.' Vivienne leans forward with a slight air of conspiracy. 'For instance, Andreas is in Italy today, and this morning it was lovely: I woke up at six o'clock and I wasn't tired any more, and if he'd been there I would have hung around in bed for quite a bit longer, pretending to be asleep, instead of which I'm able to just put the light on and do some reading and writing and do what *I* want. You can do more stuff, when you're on your own.'

In July 1991 Vivienne gave a totally uncharacteristic interview to Caroline Phillips of the *London Evening Standard*. It ran in a series called 'My Image and I'. It was a knowing and a sophisticated piece about what it is like to live in the glare of arc lamps, as Vivienne had done for more than a decade. It also caught her at a pivotal point in her life. She had turned fifty a few months earlier but was officially single, statedly happily so, and in the first full flush of real commercial success. 'I think I am going to be quite rich, possibly very rich,' she said with typical Derbyshire candour. Pictured smiling and smoking her then habitual

Gitanes, she went on less characteristically: 'I really like myself physically. I see all kinds of things in my face; secrets and depths. I wouldn't dream of having a facelift.' Her self-confidence would be the envy of any woman, particularly coming from a fifty-year-old woman in fashion whose public profile had been based in part on her photogenic features and provocative sexiness. But Vivienne, at fifty, was very far from retiring into beige or sensible shoes. She was boosted in her own confident womanliness by the critical adoration of the press – abroad, if not at home – and by the growing sense that she was being understood within the industry in the UK, and a series of intimate revelations tumbled out:

'I know I've got these horrible saggy things around my chin,' she complained, 'but I've still amazing confidence in my looks. I still think any man is either mad or stupid who wouldn't prefer me to every other woman in the room – and as for my body, I've always taken pleasure in it . . . I have all the intellectual and sexual advantages of being a fifty-year-old. I think I'm kind. I've got a good sense of humour – and I take pleasure in amusing myself and knowing that what amuses me will amuse others. I like making fun of myself. More than anything at all, really, I am unorthodox – it's completely instinctive – I'm never satisfied to do things the way other people do them. Never was. I am proudly eccentric, proud in that this is an age of conformity, and I am vulnerable and I am shy – until I get in front of people! I am quite happy not to have sex again until the day I die – I can manage without it. They say art and creativity are sublimation of sexual drives – and ·maybe that satisfies me. And you know, where you do it yourself, I find that very satisfactory.'

Notwithstanding this, Vivienne then went on to hint at what was changing in her life, beyond the commercial and artistic confidence that had been gifted to her:

'. . . I don't mind if I don't have a relationship either, because I love to be on my own so much, but I do think sex is brilliant . . . and I do wish men would proposition me more, and that I could proposition men. Though, actually, I have tried a little recently . . . on somebody.'

The somebody in question could not possibly have been guessed at by the *Evening Standard*, or indeed many others outside the immediate circle of Vivienne and her company. But the young Austrian in question could have been either cause or effect of this ebullient sexual self-confidence. His name was Andreas Kronthaler.

Since 1989 Vivienne had taught three days a month at the Vienna Academy of Applied Arts. Her Paris-based friend Jean-Charles de Castelbajac had recommended her for the post as his replacement. 'He couldn't afford to do it! It was a lot of work, and to make it pay you had to live quite frugally, but I decided I would give it a go.' Vivienne made £4000 a month. Her teaching career in fashion went on to include thirteen years back and forth to Berlin after Vienna. 'I adored teaching and I loved Berlin,' says Vivienne. 'Jürgen Frisch became my assistant: a wonderful man, I really miss him, and we set up a brilliant working relationship in Berlin, with him and Gundula Wolter the fashion historian and Iris who is a cutter with me still. And I'd take everybody to the art gallery and the Philharmonic. The Gemäldegalerie is my favourite art gallery in the whole world. Or at least the one I know best. Berlin has real cafe society: people talk about ideas, and it was cheap to live for me, and for my students. At the time. It is a real art city, but small-scale. I was very happy teaching in Berlin, but it all began in Vienna, because Jean-Charles de Castelbajac didn't want the job!'

Vivienne and fashion teaching turned out to be a perfect match. Her later documentary, *Painted Ladies*, gives some insight into her teaching technique in Vienna and Berlin, which involved a great deal of re-creation of historic costume, and a very Arts Council attitude that the best way of learning to appreciate culture is by doing. There was a certain irony, noted at the time and subsequently, that the self-taught cutter and punk seamstress should espouse this very technique-based apprenticeship in historic design and cutting. But there was a further irony of course that the sixties radical and Situationist propagandist should be teaching old-world styles in old world Vienna at all. The story took a further unexpected twist with what happened at the Academy.

'I love teaching and I loved teaching fashion: imparting things to other people. And my only regret is that I never tried to learn German while I was there. The only bits of German that have stuck are from the titles on the paintings in galleries, such is my literary mind maybe:

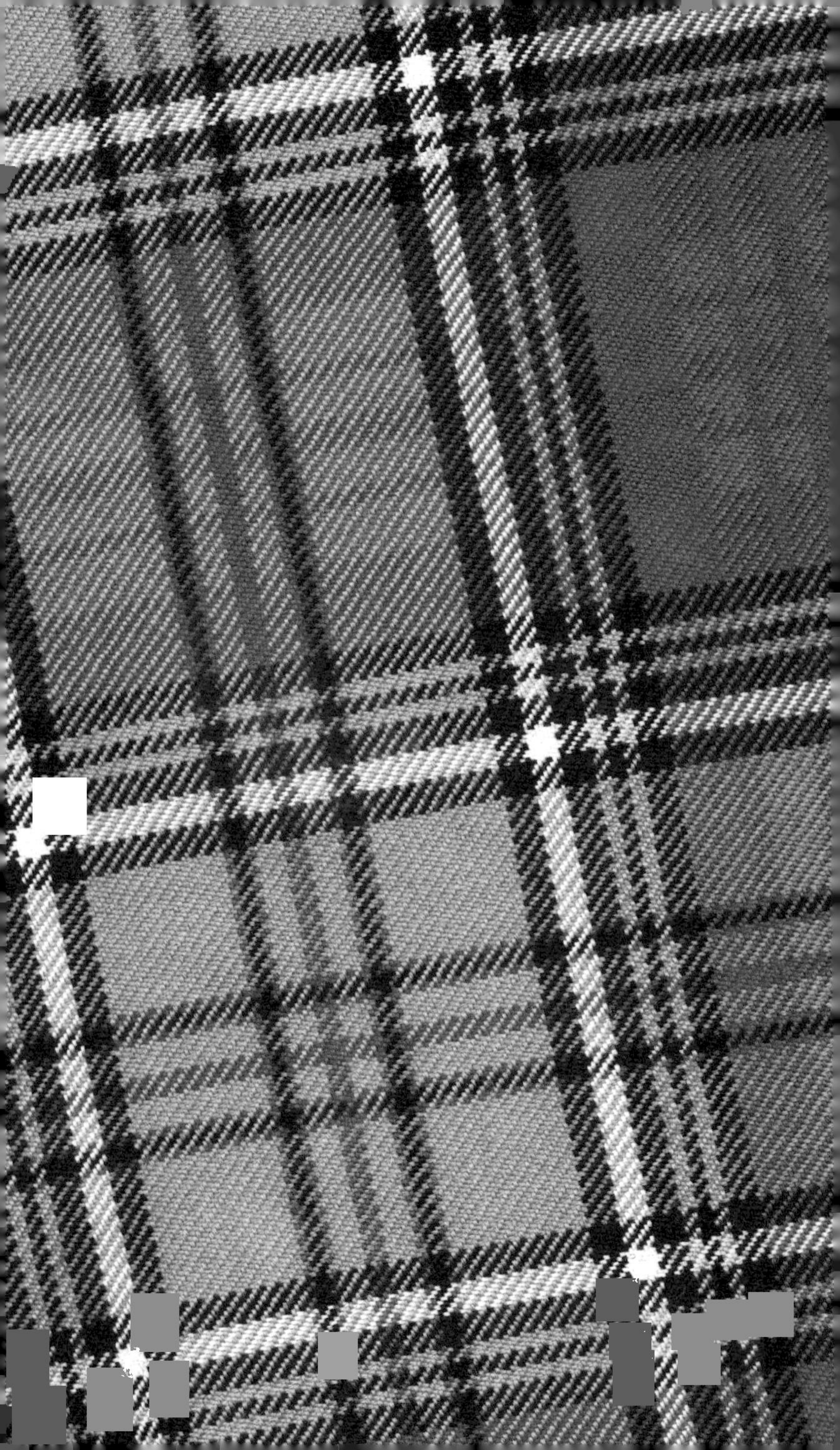

Regenbogen mit Landschaft: "rainbow with landscape", which has not proved very useful in my life with Andreas! There was always a selection process for people who had applied for my course. And this time I asked them to make an animal out of cardboard and paper. And I took them on the basis of what they managed to do, with just cardboard. It's funny. I mean, there was one student who just took a tube of UHU and gave it to me – it was a pun: you see, UHU means owl in German – so he just gave me the glue and I laughed and I took him. And then there was this boy, this man, Andreas Kronthaler. He made a cow. We met over a cow. He had pressed the paper into a realistic model of a cow. It had these eyelashes painted on it as well. God, he was in a mess, he'd got paint everywhere, on his hands and his face, and I asked him why this cow, to him, was the most beautiful creature he could think of, and he looked at me as if I'd asked the most foolish question. It had blue, blue eyes, and these horns, and it was black and white. And Andreas turned to me, with his big eyelashes, and said, "But Vivienne, the cow is the most beautiful animal there is." And that was that.'

Twenty-three-year-old Andreas Kronthaler was selected. Son of a Tyrolean blacksmith and a dairy farmer's daughter, and certain since the age of ten that clothes-designing was all he wanted in life, Andreas had found himself almost by accident in Vivienne's class, and unable, at first, to make complete sense of her Derbyshire accent. He was nevertheless smitten by her style and her aura of fashion-savvy sophistication, and then, soon enough, by the ideas he began to understand her articulating. His memories of their first encounter are also pin-sharp.

'I'd heard of Vivienne Westwood, of course. I saw something a year or two before in a magazine, when I was about twenty, in Italian *Vogue*. I had heard from others that Vivienne was a very good teacher. She's got a great talent for teaching people because she's got incredible patience and at the same time this clarity and force. So here's the story. It was all, to say the least, unexpected. I was a student. I was sitting on the window seat, those high-up window seats, really quite deep, like little cupboards, really; high up, so I was half hidden with my legs dangling down. Watching. And I sat up there at the back, and she came into the room, a big room. The New Professor. And in one second, in

Westwood MacAndreas tartan.

just a second, a split second, everything slowed down. Like in slow motion. Vivienne comes into the room and I thought she was – she is – so chic. Maybe more than anything that was my first impression. My God, this *woman*. And I can see it all now. All I could think was that I'd never seen anybody so good-looking and so well-dressed, and so very, very elegant, and I just found – I still find – that incredibly attractive. I remember she had this very fine Scottish knit with argyle leggings and a matching sweater, and she had on a big plaid shawl on one shoulder, so that, you know, it fell on and off her shoulder. Very simple, very sexy. And I remember she had a little purse made out of wooden beads with a zip on top, terribly nice. And inside it a magnifying glass. So I sort of stop-frame that moment. And then she sat down on a high chair at a table and started to speak. And it was the way she spoke. You know how it is, how can I say this: when you hear somebody speaking out of your soul? How do you say this in English? She gave word to things I had thought and believed all along, but had never heard said before. Which is one meaning of love. And I just knew. I knew I was in love. So, yes, Vivienne Westwood was an eye-opener for me, and quite a surprise, and I remember I just thought, "Well, I wasn't expecting this when I got up this morning. This is going to be interesting."'

Andreas was twenty-three. Vivienne, forty-eight.

'To begin with I just thought he was absolutely great,' recalls Vivienne, 'and the student who interested me the most. I used to fly back and forth, and soon he started coming to meet me off the aeroplane, as well. So straightaway he was, you know, special. Andreas used to say he thought I looked incredible. He's told me that since. The way I looked. Though I thought I was a bit fat, to be frank, at the time; I didn't always like the way I was. And I wore this kilt all the time, which I thought flattered – or hid. But straightaway we really liked each other. And that's how it began. He's very funny. Especially about women. I remember very early on noting the importance he gave to clothes. Take gloves. He showed an outfit: one of the exercises, it was a bathing costume for a girl, and he teamed it with long gloves, and he said, "The arm of a woman: there is nothing more beautiful . . . except the legs, and of course the face . . . everything in-between I don't care about." He is a great connoisseur of women, legs especially – and of our models.

'Andreas is an incredible talent. When I first met him, teaching, you couldn't have given him marks at all, he was totally off the scale. His was just so – such a big talent. Straightaway you could tell. Oh, God, he was amazing.'

In March 1992 American *Vogue* wrote: 'Through the mists of hard times, the fashion genius of Britain is emerging in good shape,' and to illustrate the figurehead of this brave new armada of British talent, *Vogue* had Vivienne pose alone in an ethereal wedding gown. Isabella Blow set it up, and it was due to be photographed by Snowdon. 'It was a one-off: mountains of feather-light tulle, hand-shredded by Andreas and hand-dyed dirty-off-white by me, a dozen dye loads easily.' Someone at *Vogue* subsequently put this iconic dress in a giant box so that it looked from above like packing tissue, and the *Vogue* caretaker accidentally threw it out. If it was meant to look like Greta Garbo in *Queen Christina*, as Vivienne said Snowdon intended, the effect was rather more Miss Havisham in *Great Expectations*. But it posed intriguing questions about how she saw herself within the romances she depicted in cloth, as the relationship with Andreas moved forward.

Though it was several months before their May-to-September romance was consummated, Andreas and Vivienne fell deeply into a mutual obsession, spending many hours closeted together arguing and laughing over art and ideas. 'At times it was difficult,' recalls Andreas, 'she's a very strong woman and to stand up to her or to live beside her or in her shadow is tough. But that was and is also what I found attractive. I enjoyed that. I wanted to be some quiet strength if I could. I'd look at her doing interviews and stuff and I'd always think: "I can take care of her." But I drank a lot in the early days. We both did, but mainly me. Austrians do, when they do. And you see, I'd read that Yves Saint Laurent drank a bottle of whisky every day, and I thought, I'm going to do the same, you know, because that's the route to genius! It turns out it's not. Like I say, I was very young. Vivienne was very forgiving. So I was unsure what to do. Here's somebody who says those things out loud that you've only ever heard in your head. She was also a guru or a mentor for me. It is different, again, to move in with somebody. But it's everything with Vivienne, you know, there are no lines. I loved what she stood for and stands for and what she believes in. I loved the way she sold things: ideas as well as beautiful things. She opened my eyes to so many things, so I grew up very fast. It's very difficult to put my finger on, but here's the thing: I'm flexible. I can bend like a tree. I thought: "I never expected this, but this is my life. And she's just so straight and sticks up for things, and, well, I've never met a person like this before and I feel so lucky to be able to be with this person." So the age gap was never an issue, for me. It's changed, of course, over the years. It has changed. But at the beginning, it was just being in a happy place and not thinking about it too hard. And at one point – and I'm a gentleman and I won't go into details – it just became utter pleasure. Every day became more and more pleasurable and creative and I became more and more happy, just being with her. And I used to say to myself day in, day out, "How happy and how lucky I am to be with Vivienne, to be able to spend time with this incredible woman."'

If young Andreas credited Vivienne with changing his life, the feeling was mutual. 'Andreas was in touch with reality. I don't think I was, or am,' says Vivienne. 'He is very practical. I see things in black-and-white. I'll give you an example. Just today, I said to Tizer, our PA, I would like to be in touch with whoever's running China. I love Chinese painting. I think it's like the high point of human achievement. Traditional Chinese civilization persisted fundamentally unchanged for thousands of years up until 1911, since when you had a revolution and now a copy of the American financial model. I think China could be inspired fully to embrace true human values by switching to a true-value economy. We hear they've already begun. But they had these values in the past and they should return to them. Now Andreas would never think like that. But if I asked him, practically, to help me reach out to China, he would. Instead, do you know what he said? He said, "I've just had the most wonderful day of my life," because he'd seen the work of the designer Charles Worth at the V&A. He was so inspired by it. That's his talent and his eye. That's what I mean by reality: something within his means to deal with.'

'I didn't move in with Vivienne when I first came to London,' explains Andreas. 'It wasn't like that. I stayed for a few months in Camden Town in this studio itself, which I loved. It was like being back in the attic at home with my mother's old clothes: sleeping on Vivienne's fake-fur things as a bed, and piles of fabric. I had to get up in the morning to put everything away before anyone came to work, and wash myself in the studio sink. Or if I got lucky, somebody would take me home and I could have a shower. But what it gave me, once Vivienne and everybody left in the evening, were, of course, all these clothes around and all the boxes full of old clothes and the clothes you are just working on, and I was just studying them and looking at them. Just like when I was a little boy in the attic of the family house, or watching my mother and her dressmaker. Through looking and studying things, you learn.

'And then what happened was, at some stage, I guess Vivienne felt sorry for me – sleeping on the floor. Like I said, for me it was right from the start, it was love at first sight. But maybe it wasn't so simple for her; it was complicated. In some ways it was just a natural progression, because we were spending so much time together. In other ways, it really wasn't acknowledged or official until much later. It was furtive.'

Vivienne recalls it slightly differently: 'He came to work here. I used to have ever such a nice woman called Minnie from Australia, and she did jewellery and accessories and went on to teach at St Martin's. And she was the first one to notice: "Vivienne and Andreas – they're in love," she used to say, like we were all at school, "They're in luurve." And it was the first time I ever heard of it, and it took me by surprise as an idea because I knew that I really liked Andreas, a hell of a lot, but I never, ever, dreamed of having a romantic relationship with him beyond liking him intensely and admiring his talent. We were attracted to each other and sought out each other's company at every opportunity. I'd see his eyes following me in a room and I'd watch him. But there were a number of issues. Because of my age, for one thing. In France they give medals for that sort of thing, but in England you'd get arrested these days. I just was never even thinking of it. "No," I said to myself, "I won't go there: a male student." But then I did. The pursuit came from his side, I should say. Eventually. And there we are. Anyway, so a couple of, you know, sort of accidental things happen, and then you realize that, somehow, there's this sexual thing starting. But I thought I should pull myself together and in no way was I doing that. Dear me, no. In Derbyshire we had a word for it: we called it cradle-snatching!'

The feelings that Vivienne thought she could suppress and the burgeoning love affair that she thought she might hide were all too obvious to those around her. 'They were so very close, right from the beginning,' recalls Brigitte, who moved over from Germany at almost the same time, 'and Andreas would stay at Vivienne's at quite an early stage – within weeks or months, maybe sooner.' In those early months Vivienne and Andreas would discuss things for hours and hours together. 'Art. Fashion. Culture. And eventually they assimilated each other's ideas: that's how it seemed. And then they started cycling in to work together and hid from no one that they went home together. They were very open.'

'I had come to London because Vivienne invited me, and I've never left,' says Andreas simply, 'and after a couple of months, I went back to Vienna to pack my stuff and I moved in. I wasn't involved with anyone else. It was easy just to come. I loved Vivienne and I loved working with her. I jumped right into that and she just gave me all this freedom and also responsibility, and I just, without thinking, just took it on. I was really young, maybe twenty-three. But suddenly, everything fell into place. It wasn't easy – there were people here who found it strange. But I never really minded. And one thing I remember, as well, from Vivienne, quite early on, is that she is incredibly positive. I fell in love with her all over again. The flat, for instance, would get so humid – condensation running down the insides of the windows and it would be pouring with rain outside – so miserable – and she'd look out of the window and say, "How lovely, what a lovely day." And now, I think the same.'

'I think that Andreas came at exactly the right time,' muses Vivienne. 'For one thing, in design terms. Andreas introduced me to the real potential of couture, and in particular to Yves Saint Laurent. The change of the corset into ready-to-wear, for instance, he really encouraged me to do. His dedication to Dior made a big difference in my work too. Vive la Cocotte, for instance, the Metropolitan jacket, that was all in homage to Dior and the Dior jacket they have in the Metropolitan Art Museum. That was Andreas. I learned from him and

The Metropolitan jacket from Vive la Cocotte.

from Iris in terms of letting fabrics speak and do what they want. I might have found a way on my own, but that's how it is with me and relationships: it applies to Malcolm and to Gary and to Andreas. What makes me good is I really appreciate what they can offer, and I can use. With Andreas, his talent was so big, it needed to be anchored. I became the anchor. It's reciprocal. Andreas says taste means never being satisfied. He exhausts himself. He goes in early to do things. He can see qualities and textures that I might miss. I think of him by the time we got the Grand Hotel collection, with Naomi in mauve which so suited her, and Christy Turlington in yellow, and Tatiana in a straw petticoat; these vast dresses that filled whole rooms. They were built on my corsets by Andreas, all that fabric gathered in and held; it's a very practical problem, the sort of thing he is very good at solving. And I think of him throwing all this fabric in the air – he's a big man – and saying, "Things should be as light as air and look as if they are made by angels!"'

A couple of things sealed the relationship from Vivienne's point of view. There was Andreas's evident talent and passion and their easy rapport at work. He was also warmly embraced by her family, especially by Vivienne's mother, and by Joe, who is the same age. 'They all really got on. Andreas really loved my mother. He started going to the pub with her every Friday and he didn't do it out of any feeling of duty to her or anything. He did it out of pleasure in her company – and I dare say it was a break from me, as she didn't really concern herself with politics! And another thing that attracted me, and changed me. Andreas is such a gentle person, but he's also very strong. His gym teacher wanted him to be a professional boxer. He has that thing, in boxing, like his gym teacher said: "You smile when you hit people." He's not aggressive at all but he is powerful in a very physical way. So it surprised me when, one day when we were first discovering each other – and it's not always easy; he was very young, he's twenty-five years younger than me, but God! – he miders. You know what midering is? It means pestering. Mider, mither. Let's call the whole thing off. And Andreas really miders; he still does, and I just said, "Oh, Andreas, JUST FUCK OFF." This was quite early on. And he was ever so quiet and then he said, "Vivienne, you said to me, 'Fuck off,' so I think I should. Run away." Since then I wouldn't dream of telling anyone to fuck off.

Andreas supports Scottish independence with Robert Pinnock (Murray Blewett in the background), 1999.

I realized he had been brought up never being shouted at, never having been slapped. And I've converted to his way – just like Zen!

'And I remember the first show Andreas saw was Portrait – he was still a student – and he wasn't totally complimentary about the collection. And I thought it was very, very good, and so did everyone else, but he had reservations about it and he said so, and I thought, bloody cheek! But Andreas is so passionate about his ideas that everyone listened to him, and he had a very big influence, immediately, towards the next collection. Now as you'd imagine, people like Murray, who'd worked with me for ages, and Mark and one or two other people were a bit taken aback, as well they might be, but straight from early on, they realized that Andreas was really talented, and they were prepared to listen to him. Because, you see, they'd been helping me and they knew I needed somebody to bounce off. I had Mark and Murray, who are completely key members of the design team.But at the time, I know it was difficult for them.'

Robert Pinnock saw the team intermittently, mainly when the collections were coming together. 'Let's put it like this: Andreas is a very strong character. Some equations just work. X element plus Y element. They spur each other on. And he's this very handsome man, coming from this very beautiful place but one that is rather right-wing, so I think it must have been difficult for him, growing up, and he was liberated by Vivienne and the Clapham design studio and you could see he grew and grew in strength and in love. But I think there was jealousy. It's not always easy, a fashion house.'

'What I found I remembered was that I love working in design with a man,' Vivienne says. 'Well, I love working with Andreas, anyway. All the great male designers like Saint Laurent, like Dior, they make women look like goddesses. Aliens, but also goddesses. And I want to dress them to look important, like a hero. I like the great women designers who find chic in playfulness, like Chanel dressing up in her black dress and white collar and cuffs like a housemaid, or costume jewellery or a Tyrolean jacket, which is the ultimate in rustic chic, or street fashion, or your old man's tweeds, or straw boaters on women: a man's hat for a woman. So the combination works with me. Men designers can be outrageous. Andreas certainly is. He wanted to have this false bottom. A bustle. He got his father to make a little cage, because his father is a blacksmith, and the next season the girls all had these false breasts and bottoms. In that particular collection, of course, we had to make two versions of everything; one for the catwalk and one to sell, because I knew people weren't going to fork out on these foundation-undergarments before they'd bought a suit. But I felt so proud that Andreas had introduced that, in my name, and that we had invented together a new silhouette – a new way of celebrating a woman which alluded also to the power of the past. Again, I might have done it just on my own – it was almost a fusion of SEX and Harris Tweed, sort of kinky-history, but it came out of a conversation with Andreas about my underwear and the way women's bottoms move. Art takes a conversation, sometimes a conversation between a man and a woman about sex.'

'It's vital to respect a woman,' continues Andreas, 'and men designers don't always; they put women into shapes they like. When Alexander McQueen was around, I showed Vivienne a McQueen piece, a top: a tube, really, that was constructed so that the breasts were squashed, and Vivienne hated it, said it looked like it would hurt. You have to care – and you really have to care about breasts. I was always intrigued by how things are made. Design plus craft is what makes great work. And if something, say, by Vivienne is not well executed, well, it could make me sad. I cried one time when I saw what had been done. I longed for her things to be beautifully made as well as beautifully designed – like Cerruti. So I think my first "gift" was to help design a summer travelling collection that was so beautifully made and so light you could roll it up, in tiny balls, in vacuum packaging, and it came out looking perfect. I never looked ahead, back then; I lived in the moment. And mainly I remember laughing. I am very curious, adventurous: food and fashion looks . . . not everyone is. But we were on an adventure, it was fun; we could not at the time make the most of it all, but now we do and we can because we were so adventurous then. I was just so inspired when I first knew Vivienne: it was like the weights dropped off my eyelids; it was a revelation.'

*

Quite apart from the burgeoning relationship – creative and otherwise – between Vivienne and her twenty-three-year-old student, there were quite unrelated upheavals in the structuring and personnel at Camden. It was a tumultuous time, because the business was struggling to react to the intense media interest in the brand, and the orders that were coming in thick and fast, from Asia in particular. In the early nineties when Brigitte and Andreas both found themselves, for different reasons, in the close orbit of Vivienne, there were only eight people on the payroll, and there was a recession. Joe was in charge of the company and it was run like a family business. There were only two shops: Davies Street, Mayfair, and Worlds End on the King's Road. And despite major coverage and glossy shoots, Vivienne and all the team still went to Paris for Fashion Week in a van with the last of the clothes, and finished them on the way. But it was an exhilarating time for everyone, not just the unorthodox couple at the centre of it all. The Paris shows in the wake of the Azzedine Alaïa endorsement made the fashion press across the globe, and especially the Far East, go wild.

'I knew the impact I was having, I could see! But I never expected to have any kudos back at home. The tabloids remained interested but not the UK fashion press.' Through the 1990s Vivienne became one of the major draws at Paris Fashion Week. By the time of Café Society and Storm in a Teacup, she had started building up an international clientele – buyers, collectors, couture people. And she became a craze in the world of fashion.

'Everybody wanted to come to her shows,' recalls Brigitte. 'It was outrageous,' remembers Robert Pinnock, who was also toiling backstage, 'a wild and dangerous feeling: like everyone wanted a part of her. Like it was the absolute epicentre of fashion and everyone was watching what she would do next. There were riots outside. Quite literally. We would be working inside but we could hear riots outside, police holding people back who were trying to get in.' And at the same time, and because of all the attention and indeed notoriety, Vivienne started to work with international supermodels, which exposed her yet further to the world's media and increased the buzz of excitement over what she was creating. Sam McKnight, the world-renowned fashion hairdresser, was very influential in this. A long-time fan and friend

Jerry Hall in Storm in a Teacup.

of Vivienne's, he introduced her to Linda Evangelista and Naomi Campbell, but in such a way that they would do her shows for much less than their usual rates. They joined Sara Stockbridge and Jerry Hall on the runway, amongst many others, flaunting the new sexual and artistic confidence in Vivienne's creations. 'It's advertising where models make the most money,' explains Brigitte, 'but you only get advertising if you are "hot", and being in a Vivienne show was as hot as you could get.'

So by the mid nineties – the time of Anglomania, Café Society, On Liberty, Storm in a Teacup, Vivienne found herself the most sought-after designer in the world, and her clothes, worn on the backs of the world's most-photographed women, were becoming recognizable to millions. The British press remained predictably hostile, using Vivienne's shows as an excuse for lazy philistinism, or in order to sell stories about Kate Moss's nipples. Fashion was to be made fun of. But the foreign press were increasingly respectful and kind to Vivienne, which in fashion terms mattered more. 'It's like Oscar Wilde used to say,' quotes Vivienne, '"In France all the bourgeois want to be artists; in Britain all the artists want to be bourgeois." At the time, back home, the press were only interested in writing about Chanel. But then cable TV happened, and then the Internet, and those fashion shows in the nineties: they went everywhere. I became a star on that.' Eventually, the British press, and for that matter the British fashion industry, just couldn't ignore this any longer.

In October 1993 Gene Pressman of Barneys in New York expressed the newfound commercial confidence in Vivienne. 'There are a million ideas there,' he said of her Paris show, Café Society, 'and we'll sell it all.' Orders from German shops that season were up tenfold on the year before. Littlewoods and the French catalogue company Trois Suisse had taken out Westwood collections (in the era before easy on-line shopping). There was suddenly a deal with the handbag maker Braccialini, Swatch watches created the first 'designer' brand watch featuring a Vivienne orb, and there was a licensing deal with Japanese trading company Itochu. Liberty of London bid to make her wedding dresses, Thames & Hudson asked to bring out a glossy coffee-table

Vivienne and Andreas, the night Naomi fell off her platform heels, in her feather boa.

book. *Marie Claire* had a cover shoot of the Paris collection arranged within hours, and Jean Paul Gaultier was reported to be 'ranting in ecstasy'. The supermodels involved – Naomi, Linda, Cindy, Kate – were rumoured to have accepted outfits in lieu of payment in the certain knowledge that, in the end, they would be worth more. Robert Pinnock noted the changes in Paris and the growing confidence of the company, and of Vivienne: 'By the mid 1990s the money started coming in. You could feel it. Biggest ticket in Paris, and all the supermodels – Linda, Naomi – I'd never been interested in fashion, really, till then, but for me and a lot of people, suddenly what Vivienne was doing made sense, accentuating the beauty of a woman. And Vivienne just did it so well. Even for me, who'd grown up around couture, what she was doing was a revelation. And you could feel the excitement. People literally gasped. And we knew it was going very, very well for her ... mind you, you still had to put Carlo in a headlock to get money out of him: we were still paid in clothes!'

The mid nineties became Vivienne's 'moment' in PR terms. Vivienne's creative heritage plus Andreas's influence plus the attention of the world's press, all came together. So too did the attention of Japan – and the business savvy of Carlo D'Amario. 'Of course it was hugely exciting for all of us who worked with Vivienne and Andreas,' continues Brigitte, 'we were working day and night, and even selling the clothes, doing the deals, the day after the Paris show – it was very hands-on.'

'Carlo got a deal with Alberto Biani in Italy,' Vivienne recalls, 'and then turned his attention to what we were doing here in London. Joe left working for me because he found Carlo too bossy. I was very upset – it was the worst day of my life, actually, having to choose between Joe and Carlo, which is what it amounted to. But I hoped it would be good for Joe and of course eventually it was, because he went off and founded Agent Provocateur, and because he was so very young and he was very astute. But I did it for Carlo too. I had to. Because he had sacrificed so much.'

'And soon after that,' continues Brigitte, 'Christopher Di Pietro was put in charge of the marketing side, so we didn't have to do hands-on selling any more, which was a relief. It began to feel like a real business.

But one based on this sincere love for what we were doing.' It was a very exciting but also a very stressful time. 'The company seemed to double or triple its turnover each season, all the way through the nineties, it was just mad.'

Already sailing a favourable wind of press coverage, the 1993 Anglo-mania show in Paris went down in fashion history as perhaps the single most iterated image ever from a catwalk show. Naomi Campbell fell off her Vivienne Westwood platform heels, and the image went onto front pages across the world. It was an accident that helped turn Vivienne's into a household name. 'Oh my gosh,' Naomi giggles when I ask, 'I was *so* embarrassed. I thought: I've let down Vivienne. But when I was actually down on the floor I thought to myself, "So what, girl, I'm down. What do you do? You pick yourself up, things happen. You keep going." Which was fine until I got backstage, and there, oh my gosh, everyone was laughing. Vivienne too. It was hilarious. You can't take life or fashion too seriously and, you know, I won't say any names, but a few other designers actually thought that I did it on purpose, which I want to say now is *absolutely not true*, and they'd ask me if I could do the same for them, to get them press! Because it was huge: it went all over the world.' 'It was, backstage,' recalls Robert Pinnock, 'about the happiest I have ever seen Vivienne. I think everyone knew, instantly, that it would catapult things onto front pages globally, and it did.'

'Paris eventually changed everything for us, during the nineties,' repeats Vivienne. 'You just couldn't ignore the fact any more,' explains Brigitte. 'Vivienne was being talked of as the most influential designer in the world, but most intriguingly, she was becoming one of the most successful European designers selling into Asia. Carlo started selling licences to Japan, but that happened because of Paris too. This has become a big part of the business. Here's how and why: Japan has to be a licence, because import tax in Japan is so high. A British-made Vivienne Westwood outfit would be double the price in Japan. Which is why Japanese customers started spending so much in our shops in England. And Vivienne became enormously influential in Japan at this time. Knowingly or not, she exactly hit all the buttons the Japanese like, and her shops there are very successful. They loved the colours. They loved Vivienne's references to Western culture – to paintings

Vivienne, still knitting. Paris, 1997.

and history – the tartans, the tweeds, they just loved it. So, she had a big client base there by the mid nineties, and a lot of press attention, and that was a big, big help at the beginning and towards a favourable licence deal. And because of all this Carlo D'Amario started concentrating on Japan towards the turn of the century and there are now dozens of shops.'

As business began to boom, Vivienne and her semi-secret lover had a problem. Andreas travelled a great deal – to Italy for production and to the Far East. But Austria wasn't in the EU, and his visa was due to expire. 'The simplest way to tell this story,' smiles Vivienne, 'is that we had problems getting through customs all the time, so I said to Andreas, "There's only one way: you have to marry somebody. We have to find somebody for you to marry." And he just laughed and he said, "But Vivienne, I have to marry you".

'I simply hadn't thought of it. When I was with Malcolm I thought being married was a point for the system. So now it entered my head and I thought, well of course, it's possible. I'm not married to anyone and he's my man. I like being married. The ceremony confirmed my feelings I have for Andreas. I'll stay with him "for better or worse."

'So, that's when we decided to get married. And we didn't tell anybody and I don't know who did find out. I don't know why we kept it a secret, in retrospect.

'My choices are to do with mental stimulation. And I've learned so much from Andreas. What he's learned from me, you'd have to ask him. I'd be interested to know what they are. I think he did tell me, but I wasn't paying attention.'

Andreas smiles too when he recalls their clandestine wedding. 'The age thing never was an issue. It never was. I think it is becoming more significant now simply because, for all she's a tough old bird, as the English say, I am only in my late forties and I'm not slowing down. Just the opposite. But, you see, at first, really it was straightforward. There was this amazing woman, and we were having an amazing time, and the only way I could stay was to marry. But actually, it's the best thing I've ever done. I don't know why we kept it a secret so long. Look – it isn't easy, it hasn't been easy. I did have a very difficult time, on a very personal level, in my mid thirties to mid forties, really. I'm not sure if

Vivienne ever knew. Mine is quite a lonely position. I think the Duke of Edinburgh feels the same way! I will ask him.' 'That's Carlo's name for Andreas, you know,' chips in Vivienne, 'which Andreas doesn't much like, but Carlo called him "Principio Consortio" – the prince consort!' Andreas continues more sombrely. 'Actually, I think the collections from those dark years are great, very special, and now I've got the distance from that time I can see that, as sometimes happens, good work came out of a dark place. And Vivienne and I, we survived. And now I think, we are people in design, and we are often outsiders – like Vivienne, like me. Chanel, also, from the most tiny little village in the Auvergne. Sometimes, people from the most rural, most remote places, they're the most worldly people. It's a freak thing, I think. We are freaks, in fashion! We have that in common too.'

'The mental stimulation is my main reason for staying with Andreas,' says Vivienne one morning, without my asking, 'apart from the fact that I'm committed to him. And whatever he does, I would stick by Andreas. And the way I see it, he can do whatever he wants. And I don't just mean creatively. I like to think for myself. I am proud and I am a rebel. So I would not stoop, ever, EVER, to expect anything from anybody that they didn't want to give me. I would never, ever demand anything from a man. I wouldn't. That is our arrangement and I like it. He can always do what he wants. Andreas can do what he likes. There's a wonderful Chinese proverb. If a horse is yours, it will always come home. And you've got to understand, Andreas is a horse. A wild horse. I am lucky, blessed, I know, to have someone like Andreas. In so many ways. He could easily have been a designer completely in his own name and nothing to do with me. So I was lucky to get him! Secondly, he has these mad ideas to take what I do further, and that's good for me. And Andreas is incredible – extremely talented. I couldn't live without him, at work or home.'

If the mid seventies and punk are the origins of Vivienne's notoriety in the public mind and the foundations of her credibility in fashion, the early nineties when she met Andreas are really the beginning of Brand Vivienne, of the business and the fashion empire that has impressed itself on the world's consciousness. As Brigitte pointed out, there was a

Vivienne and Andreas lark for Karl Lagerfeld in Vivienne Westwood couture, 1997.

happy 'moment' that comprised the international fashion press focusing on Vivienne just when her designs were, arguably, at their most exquisitely photogenic and had the clearest story to tell: old world culture and historical costuming reimagined for the modern woman and man. At one and the same time, the Far Eastern emerging markets gave a confidence to the fledgling company and allowed Vivienne, at long last, to find financial security. It is a small irony, therefore, that one of her last acts of simple financial pragmatism before she became aware, as she stated to the *Evening Standard*, that she might finally be 'very rich', was to take a job teaching in Vienna that found her, unexpectedly, in love with a man half her age – a man who would take the company, and Vivienne, in other happy directions too. 'These days,' she tells me, 'I would like to see Andreas credited more. I am the public face of "Vivienne Westwood". But it's his story too, now. So I worry that people think Andreas is less than equal to me or that I say these things simply because I love him: but the truth is, he is more passionate about fashion than I am, now, for sure; and he is every bit as talented, and at some things (don't tell him) more so.'

So there it is – the story of the Kronthalers: a match made in fashion heaven. Like any couple, their relationship is unfathomable from the outside, and they live enough in the public eye to be wary of giving too much more away. And, because Andreas is twenty-five years Vivienne's junior and in the business he is in, there are rumours of various hues. Tizer Bailey, who lives in their pockets as their PA, was succinct about it from the beginning: 'I'm in awe. You only have to be with them for thirty seconds to see, after all these years, they adore each other. They bicker, obviously. Who doesn't? But if I could have a relationship like that in my life, I'd die proud and blessed.'

'Here's some advice for you on marriage,' Vivienne says alarmingly one day. 'I will always be faithful, I would not ever, ever – I'd never even think of infidelity. But when I met Andreas I was perfectly happy on my own. Still would be. But then I met this perfect man. Well, he's not perfect but he's perfect for me. And I think it's very good if you get the opportunity, to try to stick it out and live with somebody. And so,

I'm 100 per cent committed to Andreas. Now for my side, I wouldn't just wander off and not tell him where I am. I think it's very, very good advice to anybody for a marriage: you yourself, you be totally faithful, loyal, committed to this person. For *yourself*, as well as for him or her. It doesn't mean to say you have to hold hands when you go shopping. Eurgh. But on the other side, let them do whatever they want, and they'll come back to you. That's what I wanted to say. We're both interested in paintings, for instance, and I love it when we go to galleries together because he just gets it. He looks, and he gets it. In one go. A visual person can't always remember the words, and we are different in that sense, he remembers a poem from its imagery. Andreas is a great communicator if he is talking about what he can see. I think he sees me.

西太后
'DOWAGER EMPRESS WEST'

Only time can testify success. Only those who fully pursue their interests will sooner or later meet with the 'originality of the past'.
V I V I E N N E W E S T W O O D

Fashion is like walking a tightrope. You risk falling off into the ridiculous, but if you stay on you triumph. V I V I E N N E W E S T W O O D

Vivienne's name, '西太后' or 'Queen Mother West', is one of the most recognized Western names in Chinese. In Japan, she is included in the top ten most recognized global brands, year on year, up there with Coca-Cola and Disney. In Korea and Taiwan and Hong Kong, her stores and her story have a unique appeal, expressing a series of ideas about what it is to be Western, stylish, British, and a woman. She is the Scotch whisky of fashion, the Jaguar of couture, but she also embodies an idea which has had enormous impact in Asia, and is of longer standing than in the West, perhaps: in the Far East, the Queen Mother of the West is still a punk rocker, still tied to an idea of what the West was, which is why her name in Mandarin, 西太后, alludes also to the last imperial widow, 慈禧太后, the Empress Dowager Cixi. Vivienne, in some variants of the translation, is 'Dowager Empress of the West'.

On 1 April 2004 the Victoria and Albert Museum opened its Vivienne Westwood exhibition. While Vivienne had been persuaded to loan many items from her own wardrobe as well as the Vivienne Westwood archive, the museum was also drawing attention to a significant acquisition made for its permanent collection. The curators had made the bold decision the preceding year to buy the entire collection of nearly

300 early Westwood / McLaren items which had belonged to Michael and the late Gerlinde Costiff. They had been two of Vivienne's keenest early admirers and collectors, wearing her clothes to clubs and Rio carnivals, but also, Michael Costiff recalled, 'in places like the Sudan or Mali or Burkina Faso, where people would point and say "Worlds End!"'. The V&A also bid at the 2001 Christie's sale of Vivienne items, which included shoes and hats, original SEX rubber dresses, and Café Society's 'Bettina jacket with lilac rubber masturbation skirt' [sic]. The entire collection cost the V&A £100,000, nearly half of which has been raised through the museum's appeal to the National Art Collections Fund. It was a scale of honour never before afforded to a living designer.

The V&A were also well aware that Vivienne was likely to be big box office in an age when museums were realizing the vital new footfall from one-off blockbuster exhibitions. Photos of Vivienne, her face contorted in a Rankin pose and framed in baroque gold, appeared on the sides of buses and on Tube lines and brought her image, and that of her 'brand', to many only half aware of her growing cultural impact. The exhibition also sailed on a new tide of interest in fashion and in red-carpet glamour that had become a twenty-first-century leitmotif for Vivienne. Her clothes made waves and made headlines, be they paraded at the Oscars – by Kate Winslet, nominated for her role in *Titanic* – or by Nigella Lawson on the Jay Leno show. Vivienne's clothes have always made an impact, but the V&A exhibition made the point too that they were, at the time, defining a particular sort of confident womanhood and ebullient self-assurance in the theatrical – perhaps best exemplified by the Linda Evangelista green taffeta ballgown that formed the centrepiece of the exhibition. Based on the Watteau dress designs of the French *ancien régime*, it is hardly an easy frock to wear or find an occasion for. But its full-on revelry in the sensual and the historical makes it the grandmother of many of the hoisted bosoms and swagged necklines that have dominated evening wear almost ever since, though Vivienne herself has returned recently to earlier neo-classical column dresses that tend to share red carpet and catwalk space with her more recognizable 'baroque 'n' roll' swagger dresses.

The Vivienne Westwood assault on mainstream consciousness began at this time too – or at least began for newer generations, as other constituencies than those interested in punk. Vivienne's close friend Kate Moss turned up at a party in 2001 wearing original 'Pirate' boots – sampling Vivienne vintage and having her choice noted by the paparazzi as much as the fashion police. Westwood pieces were becoming collector's items by the end of the twentieth century, but between then and the V&A retrospective the trade gathered pace. Sotheby's dedicated an entire sale to the Vivienne Westwood collection of Lady Romilly McAlpine, her friend and dedicated follower, who had worn Westwood to the State Opening of Parliament and introduced Margaret Thatcher to Vivienne's designs. Christie's followed suit with a sale dedicated to vintage Westwood. This period, in turn, gave birth to the global success of the Anglomania diffusion line within the Vivienne Westwood *oeuvre*. 'I don't believe Mrs Thatcher ever wore my clothes,' says Vivienne, raising an eyebrow, 'but she is on record as saying "I'm so glad she's British." Hmm.'

Vivienne's name in the States, meanwhile, has waxed and waned in mainstream popularity, in a market that is perceived internationally as a little cautious, a little wary of shock. She has been known to bemuse the American press and to be openly critical of American foreign and domestic policy, which hardly endears her, though Vivienne credits American *Vogue* with helping her early profile enormously. 'Anna Wintour has a lot of clout in America, of course, and she is famous for helping people and discovering people. What I had forgotten until I saw her at the Met Ball when they were honouring punk last year, is that Anna is so very, very pretty.'

Vivienne's profile in America was raised monumentally as a result of her appearance in the film of *Sex and the City*. It was an unprecedented and unexpectedly high-profile brand endorsement, offering a whole new generation of women – and brides in particular – an introduction to Vivienne's style. The culmination of what amounted to a decade-long education for many on the ways of fashionistas, the film rounded off the story of Carrie Bradshaw, fashion devotee and columnist, played by Sarah Jessica Parker, with her long-anticipated wedding to the man known only as Mr Big. It was clear for many months before that a Vivienne Westwood New York catwalk show would feature in the film; what was not clear was who would be chosen to design the

Gloriana, with safety pin. Invitation to Anglomania (autumn / winter 1993).

wedding dress for a twist in the plot where a designer gives a wedding dress to the Carrie Bradshaw character. 'I would only do that,' says Vivienne, 'if I really liked someone.' Anna Wintour had suggested Vera Wang to the producers. It was not until shooting began that Sarah Jessica Parker personally insisted on wearing a Vivienne dress. 'I was in NYC for ten days filming the catwalk show,' recalls Murray, 'but had nothing to do with "that" dress to begin with – the wedding dress. Sarah Jessica Parker personally selected the dress out of all the ones submitted, and it was chosen above all the other designers who were also asked to submit, which I think was a surprise to many, including Vivienne. I remember thinking at the time, "They will never let Sarah Jessica use this dress, even though she's an executive producer – they'll want to tie it in with an American brand or a massive international fashion house." How wrong was I?! I thought it proof of just how powerful and respected Sarah Jessica was at that time in the world of fashion and how adored Vivienne is, rightly, by those who really know fashion. The film's director, however, was very "on team" in that he was also very clever, really understood fashion and deeply respected Vivienne's work. He was so excited and intrigued by the clothes that were used in the fashion-show segment of the film and really involved himself in understanding the fabrics and forms Vivienne uses. So in that regard, it was quite right that "the dress" ended up being a Vivienne dress.'

'I wasn't sure about the green feather,' says Vivienne, of the bridal headwear, 'but that dress is a divine archetype; it lives, as it were, in Plato's wedding heaven! And I wrote the note in the film, I did do that, pretending it was the real thing.' Her *Sex and the City* appearance, or rather that of her dress, gave Vivienne a bizarre double-sided imprimatur, from both fashion maven Sarah Jessica Parker herself, who remains a fan, and her fictional alter ego, Carrie Bradshaw. It was a drama which had defined for a generation the concept of urban chic, of fashion obsession, and of glamour such that putting a Vivienne wedding dress at the intended point of narrative closure for the Bradshaw character sealed forever Vivienne's reputation in America as the 'designer's designer' and internationally as the ultimate go-to for a certain sort of urban sophisticate.

Angelica Gleason is PR coordinator for Vivienne on the American West Coast, based out of the Vivienne Westwood Melrose LA flagship store on Melrose Avenue and dealing with the crossover between fashion and film that is the LA awards season, culminating in the Oscars. The Sarah Jessica Parker 'endorsement' made a huge impact in America, but Vivienne had long been a favourite of movie stars looking to make an impact. 'In some ways,' Angelica explains, 'this has replaced what Paris couture used to be: these awards dresses are one pinnacle for a designer. Vivienne, the brand, is now so big in America, and she has such a big following, that it's been really fun to be in charge of the press in the US. My world is LA. And to me a celebrity is like a walking billboard for Vivienne and for her ideas. But it's so great to hear who loves the brand. Jennifer Garner, Christina Ricci, Julia Roberts, Matthew McConaughey and Bradley Cooper. Bradley had a coat that I'd never seen on a guy. He told his stylist it was his *favourite* piece of clothing like ever, and he hasn't given it back. (Which I was fine with.) And Sarah Jessica Parker, of course, famously, is a fan. She wore the wedding dress in her movie, which came with a personalized note from Vivienne. And then also in the "Red Label" collection we have a pair of shoes that Vivienne brought back specially for *Sex and the City*. And Sarah Jessica wears them a lot still. But then there's the Oscars, and for Vivienne, the brand, this is a big deal in LA. Here's how it works: every stylist in town is fighting for dresses and every designer is trying to dress people. And, you know, there's a *lot* of designers out there that *pay* celebrities to wear things to the Oscars, but Vivienne doesn't and won't do that. She doesn't need to. So here's what goes on: our couture team flies out to LA from London. I make appointments. The stylists come in and they select dresses for their clients. We are sworn to secrecy. We always hope that we can dress someone who is actually nominated, and, like everyone else in town, we really, really, really want an Oscar, so we're trying to dress someone who's actually going to win!'

Vivienne has also become involved in the Red Carpet / Green Dress movement spearheaded by Livia Firth (wife of Colin) and Suzy Amis Cameron, wife of James 'Avatar' Cameron. 'There was this young man who won the competition that Suzy Cameron organized to come and make a "green" red-carpet dress here with me. The funny thing was it turned out to be very, very difficult to source sustainable fabrics, and he wanted to use sustainable silk, supposedly. And they said, I remember, "The silk worms are still alive and they are allowed to go back to their community", and I said, "What do they do – back in their 'community'?" Instead of gassing the silk worms, the silk is unwound, apparently. But how does this help the environment? The beads were recycled from other gowns, but how "green" is that? It's terribly difficult, especially for the red carpet. Wool is not too hard on the environment, but hardly suitable for all occasions. The only thing we manage very well already is in regard to T-shirt cotton. It's our only bulk order is why, and we order bio-cotton, which is organic. Katharine Hamnett has been very good on this too, and is trying to make a library of eco-friendly fabrics, which I approve of and would use. But she is virulently anti-cotton. Dyes, of course, can be "green" so I do try there too: vegetable dyes can give the most wonderful colours.'

Vivienne's A-list regulars, whether or not they decked in responsibly sourced fabrics, would include Helena Bonham Carter, Helen Mirren, Anne Hathaway, Tilda Swinton and Meryl Streep. Tracey Emin, friend and fellow campaigner and occasional Westwood model, is also often seen in Westwood, as well as newcomers to the red carpet, the actress Olivia Colman or the models Cara Delevingne and Lily Cole. Renée Fleming and Joyce DiDonato, the opera stars, rate her ability to make impact and to be aware of their professional needs, 'and Barbra Streisand wanted my empire-line dresses in order to sing,' recalls Vivienne, 'and ordered a lot of stretch-velvet tops – I remember she said, "Do you have stretch velvet in Europe?" and I wanted to say, "Of course!!"' Cookery writer Nigella Lawson told British *Vogue* that the appeal of Vivienne's designs was personal as well as political: 'I do feel that her clothes understand my body. I can have my shape and not feel bad about it . . . and the structure of the clothes makes me feel safe; I know I won't bulge or slip or need to start tugging at hemlines . . . In a way I feel her clothes are the anti-fashion, which suits me perfectly.' This was an opinion recently echoed in the *Guardian* and is key to understanding Vivienne's ongoing appeal: 'Vivienne designs frocks for women with things like breasts and hips . . . which is generally considered another aspect of her [supposed] lunacy, since every other fashion designer knows that such things as breasts and hips spoil the line of the clothes.'

A certain sort of celebrity endorsement has therefore become part of the story of the Vivienne Westwood Group, not through chasing Oscar nominees so much as allowing those in Vivienne's ever-widening circle to embrace her style and often her politics. From Carla Bruni to Tracey Emin to Pamela Anderson to Jonathan Ross or to the Poet Laureate Carol Ann Duffy, I have seen Vivienne and her eclectic range of friends free-range in conversation between art, poetry, politics and what to wear. Occasionally, these friends end up modelling, because Vivienne is attracted to strong women with strong personalities who also happen to be photogenic. The British artist Tracey Emin would be one such: a friend close enough for Vivienne to worry that she, Vivienne, is puzzled by Emin's art, and close enough too for Vivienne to have persuaded Tracey to tread the catwalk in Paris.

'I met Vivienne at a *Vogue* shoot in the summer of 1999,' Tracey tells me. 'Mario Testino was taking the photos, a group shot including Vivienne and myself. I cadged a cigarette off Vivienne as she was smoking Gitanes in those days; we have been friends ever since. My first impression of Vivienne was that she was quite motherly and kind; showing an interest in me and what I do, which surprised me only because I had known quite a few people who are a bit scared of her. And then she and Andreas asked me to model for them. I said yes, but I felt like I was being thrown out of an aeroplane backwards without a parachute as I was pushed onto the runway – this was around 2000: but Vivienne and Andreas exuded a certain amount of confidence in me and you have to live up to that. I think Vivienne is quite wild, wilder even than she is portrayed. We went there and back on Eurostar and both times got drunk and laughed all the way. She's an inspiration: a real artist. But also passionate about the simple things. And someone you can have a wild laugh with.' 'Actually, as I recall it,' Vivienne deadpans, 'Tracey asked me if she could model.'

In 1997 Vivienne became a mother-in-law – an unlikely role for her, perhaps – having been made a grandmother in 1996. Joe married his long-time girlfriend and business partner Serena Rees, mother of Cora

Vivienne on catwalk, in Active Resistance T-shirt, 2005.

Corré, in a ceremony he describes as 'like the fucking Jerry Springer show'. Serena recalls it more fondly: the Westwood studios made her a white leather wedding dress in less than a week, Andreas corseted her in so tightly she claims still to have scars, and Vivienne, unconventional to the last, made a speech as mother-in-law both 'hilarious and very warm'. 'I remember Dora was sitting in the front row,' says Joe, 'and Malcolm rocked up and I'd asked him to say something and he was like, "Get someone else to do it." But he got up and he was just horrible – to Dora, to Ben – and I just thought, fucking hell, I'm not having this. So I go, "Listen, don't you fucking talk about my brother like that, all right? I love my brother." And then Ben stood up and said, "Yeah, it's his fucking wedding," and then Mum pitched in and made a speech. Pure Jerry Springer. I don't think she'd intended to.'

The volatile wedding led to a marriage that has not lasted, but Serena lends a unique perspective to the story, a major player in the fashion world herself having co-founded with Joe the internationally successful Agent Provocateur. She still sees a lot of Joe's family and is a staunch supporter of her former mother-in-law, as role model and businesswoman. 'Vivienne was quite pleased, I think, when she knew she was going to be a grandmother, and I'd have to confess I was surprised she felt that way,' says Serena. 'I used to think that she wouldn't be too bothered because, you know, babies haven't got an opinion and they don't wear very interesting clothes! But Vivienne came up with Cora's name, after some pretty funny suggestions. And Malcolm gave her "Honeysuckle" as her middle name.'

Malcolm, unsurprisingly, was an absentee grandfather as he had been an absentee dad, leaving Vivienne to play a newfound role as punk grandmother, even proudly putting the four-year-old Cora on the catwalk with septuagenarian supermodel Verushka. 'I never really saw my grandfather Malcolm at all,' says Cora, picking at imaginary lint in a manner identical to her grandmother. 'I remember calling him grandpa once and he hit the roof. "I'm not your grandpa, I'm Malcolm." But I call Vivienne "Grandma Vivienne", and she likes that. I think. When I was younger I was quite a big reader, which obviously she loved, and my favourite memory of her is sitting in bed with her for a whole day, the entire day, just reading *Of Mice and Men*, because I had to do it

ACTIVE ☒ᴀᴿ☒ RESISTANCE TO PROPAGANDA

Manifesto Vivienne Westwood #2

Vivienne's Manifesto cover, as modelled on Gary Ness's pocket books.

at school, for an exam. And she'd stop all the time and say things like "Do you know what that means?" and then she'd go off on a tangent and it took a whole day! But I did really well on that book. And each year, for my birthday, I'd get an outfit from Grandma Vivienne, like a book of me growing up, in clothes. And Mum would say, "Grandma Vivienne's coming over, let's put this lovely dress on that she's made." And I'd just freak out and scream "No!!" because I was like that. But they're *beautiful* and we've kept all of them, and then, finally, for my sixteenth birthday I got given this – oh, this dress! – I'd never even thought about wearing such a thing – but I saw this dress, and I literally fell in love. A couture dress. For my sixteenth birthday! I felt like Cinderella. And now it's my most prized possession, my Red Dress from Grandma Vivienne.

'Christmas is the best with her. She wears a paper hat. She likes a game, Grandma Vivienne, silly party games and she is very, very competitive, and the only time I've ever seen her scream at Andreas was when we were playing a game of Rizla, you know, where you have to put the name of somebody famous on your forehead, or, like, something Christmassy. Uncle Ben was cheating, looking in the mirror. Andreas struggles because of his English – or ours – and they lost, because he had "Turkey" and couldn't get it. And I thought Grandma Vivienne would explode; I have never seen someone so angry with a game in my whole life. But it's always fun – and Grandma Vivienne does like that sense of family and that sense of occasion. You don't expect her to, but she actually does like Christmas. And she's a very good cook. We have this normal Christmas . . . except, I suppose, for what Vivienne and Andreas are wearing . . .'

If some of the British press still insist on characterizing Vivienne as eccentric and disinclined to profit by her name, the figures as the company moved into the twenty-first century simply failed to match the thesis. Her sales, backed up now by several Queen's Export Awards, belie this and so too do repeated accolades, such as Designer of the Year – consecutively in 1991 and 1992 – or the Women's World Fashion Award presented to her by President Gorbachev. Meanwhile her activism has only fed interest in the brand, and tends to theme her output without denting her profitability. The Propaganda collection (autumn / winter 2003) was inspired by Aldous Huxley's assertion that organized lying was the basis of all modern evils. She followed this with AR (Active Resistance to Propaganda), which she terms a synonym for culture: think for yourself, don't get sold stuff. Her signature ballgowns and fine tailoring now regularly share catwalk space, to great effect, with slogans and radical T-shirts. Her 'I am not a terrorist' T-shirts and indeed babygros, developed with Shami Chakrabarti's Liberty organization, remain bestsellers (though ill-advisedly worn at airports).

Every occasion now is an opportunity for Vivienne to make a point or to raise a question. In this spirit, she gamely accepted the secret invitation, late in 2005, to be put on the Queen's New Year's Honours List and be made a Dame of the British Empire. It had its ironies for the woman who had stuck a pin through the Queen's lip back in 1977 and who had twirled knickerless for the photographers the last time she had made it to a Palace investiture. This time it was Prince Charles who was pinning the medals, having himself become a firm friend of Vivienne's through their shared ecological concerns. Vivienne wore silver customized devil's horns in her hair, took her granddaughter and her mother for the shindig, and then asked Shami Chakrabarti what she should gen up on for the Andrew Marr / David Frost show the next day, where she had no intention of talking queens, punk or fashion, but rather wanted to appeal for a restitution of habeas corpus. There's a Dame who knows how to play the system, or, indeed, outrun the Establishment.

In May 2006 New York's Metropolitan Museum of Art Costume Institute unveiled its new blockbuster exhibition, quoting Vivienne and Gary Ness in its title, 'Anglomania', and featuring the Alexander McQueen David Bowie jacket as its key poster image – its period detailing, punk reworking of the Union Jack and distressed fabric owing a clear debt to Vivienne. So too, of course, did the Met's follow-up 'Chaos to Couture' exhibition in 2013 on the history of punk. Attending this, with its loving recreations of the Worlds End shop and dozens of her designs, Vivienne acknowledged the continuing impact of her work. 'It was amazing. Andreas and I arrived with Lily Cole as our

Grandmother and activist. These items are not advised for air travellers.

guest, and she was wearing a dress made of rubber from the rainforest, a sustainable rubber charity she supports, and made by Andreas. And I wore a *Free Bradley Manning* sort of poster in a plastic envelope pinned on my dress, so that when the fashion press said "What are you wearing?" I could talk about my jewellery, meaning Bradley. And then we went to go up the stairs, up this red carpet; it was all lined with the entire staff all dressed as punks, and suddenly everyone was applauding. And I assumed at first they were doing that for everyone as they arrived, but when we got to the top of the stairs there was Anna Wintour, greeting her guests, and she told me: she said, "Vivienne, they are doing it for you, you know." I sort of turned and bowed and thanked them all. I was really grateful. It was very kind. And then I spoke to this punk boy who was standing at the top, about Bradley Manning. He didn't know who I was talking about.'

'I think my favourite memory of Vivienne was that,' recalls Julian Assange from his refuge in London's Ecuadorian Embassy. 'Vivienne was the only person at the ball who had anything to do with the origins of punk, and she also performed the only punk act. And people couldn't handle it. This really brought home to me that we have to draw on the veteran radical movements for thinking about the style in which political activism is done. She's a sartorial agitprop artist!'

It fell to Vivienne's old friend Gene Krell to tell her that Malcolm had died, in a Swiss clinic, in early 2010. He rang not expecting to get through, having heard the news, and spoke to Vivienne before even her family had. Gene had been talking to McLaren, about the semiotics of iPhones, of all things, only days before, and both Joe and Ben, alerted to the severity of McLaren's disease, had flown out to be at his bedside. Vivienne, as ever, was at the time tied to deadlines on the latest collection.

'I was so sorry he died. I had heard that he was ill. Either Joe or Ben had told me, but Malcolm at first said it wasn't true. He was diagnosed a second time, and he called Ben, not Joe. And Ben played me the message he had left: "this fucking thing", he called his cancer, but you could hardly even make out what he was saying.' Malcolm died of mesothelomia, a very rare cancer often associated with exposure to asbestos. It has been suggested that one likely site of his exposure, if such was the cause, was the ceiling of the Worlds End shop, through which he created a bomb-blast hole above his giant photos of 'Dresden' and an upturned Piccadilly, but Vivienne pooh-poohs the idea. 'There was no asbestos in the shop. My theory is that, like Donna Summer, he was affected by visiting the rubble of the Twin Towers. But who knows. Steve McQueen had the same. It's a horrible disease.'

Malcolm was only sixty-four. 'I am an artist without portfolio,' he used to say, 'my career has been a brilliant act which deserves to be seen as art.' His dying words – Ben was at his bedside – were in tribute to Vivienne and her causes. It's unclear whether he muttered last 'Free Leonard Peltier' or 'Who Killed Bambi?' – ideas and songs of Vivienne's that danced in his head at the end.

'On this bleak, bleak day,' Vivienne intoned shakily on the day of his funeral in London, 'I want to say a few words about Malcolm,' – but she barely managed to, mired in her own attempt at an overview of his cultural impact and heckled unexpectedly by an 'anarchist' objecting to her supposed 'sell-out'. 'I didn't recognize him at all – it was Bernie Rhodes, from back at the World's End. He was quite justified in what he said, in that I was talking too much about me and about my ideas. I had been wanting to use the opportunity to explain something. "The Age of the Consumer." "That Nobody is Thinking." "There are No Ideas Any More." That was the subject of my address. I wanted to try not to be complacent about punk. Because it had ended up being a marketing opportunity. I wanted to say, "I am not here to praise Malcolm for giving us punk. But I do think he was an exhilarating experience." That's what I wanted to say.' It was a rough day on her, as on the family and friends, though studded with occasional flashes of humour and a stellar turnout. Adam Ant was there, seated with the family, Alan Yentob, Bella Freud, Bob Geldof and Boy George, Edward Tudor Pole, Jarvis Cocker, Jean-Charles de Castelbajac – who spoke eloquently and at length – Robert Pinnock, and quondam banshee Siouxsie Sioux. 'He was Danton, Robespierre and the French Revolution rolled into one,' Adam Ant opined memorably, while Geldof, as ever, was yet more loquacious: 'I'm a Paddy, and I talk, but he out-talked all of us here. He was endlessly fascinating, endlessly interesting

Vivienne and Malcolm (Ben Westwood in the background). 'Malcolm had something special. He's gone, I thought, but he was happy.' Vivienne Westwood

... and I know that sounds wanky, but I think there is almost a tangibly physical gap in the cultural fabric. He's gone, and he feels gone, and I feel sad that I realize he's gone.' Vivienne was at his Highgate graveside after the cortège had wound its way through Camden, Malcolm's coffin bearing the legend they had created: 'Too Fast to Live Too Young to Die'. Yet both Joe and his mum have said since that their loss was offset, as is sometimes the way with the complicatedly bereaved, by a sense of freedom. Without Malcolm's jealousy of them both, there could be a reckoning, both personal and historic, of which this book is one part. 'He really broke something in me,' says Joe, 'and I don't think it ever really healed. I knew not to trust him.' Vivienne tends towards regret, not anger at all: 'It's just very sad. And it's sad because he was a human being who lit up people's lives: mine too. But actually I liked Malcolm's funeral. I liked seeing Annabella again, of Bow Wow Wow. I'd hardly seen her since she was fourteen. The whole day was full of nice people. Malcolm had something special. He's gone, I thought, but he was happy. My mum said she saw him on the telly a little while before, and he was talking about Paris, and of all things shopping for a chicken and then showing you how to cook it, and Dora said for the first time ever he seemed, to her, likeable.'

Vivienne has about her, increasingly, the 'I-shall-wear-purple' insouciance of a much-loved grandmother. National treasures get away with almost anything, and Vivienne takes full advantage. Not 'playing the game' in PR terms, however, sometimes brings its own victory, and Tizer and also Laura McCuaig in the press office no longer worry about it. 'It's expected and allowed,' says Tizer. 'I only wish she would keep gifts sometimes – or not send them back to children saying she doesn't need things . . . or criticizing their drawings.' I have been begged repeatedly by her friends and acquaintances to make clear that her occasional brusqueness is in stark counterpoint to her astonishing big-heartedness and generosity (she will ask me to cut this bit), from her generous financial support of good causes to her frequent habit of enquiring after, and sending gifts for, unwell friends and colleagues. Her gestures are legendary in the industry as well, where she is able, as head of the 'brand', to offer gifts of great munificence to those she finds are fans, or simply those, like Tizer, who found themselves in need of undarned tights one day, and love. 'I do always try to be open and honest in all my dealings. Though it is astonishing sometimes what people write, after you think you have been very nice. Mainly I don't give a fuck. I try to think, after some speech I've been paid to give, for instance, "Well, that just made £10,000 for the rainforest," and sort of shrug. Mainly I am just grateful for the attention for the cause. There's potential cynicism about that. There's rudeness when you think you've been nice. But recently, I've noticed, mainly they've been kind. And often I am relieved: the press were very nice about me forgetting my knickers at Buckingham Palace, and I was ever so grateful for that.'

Beau Brummell, who knew a thing or two about fame and about fashion, and through whom in a sense Vivienne and I met back at the V&A exhibition, pointed out that the rise to glory or indeed notoriety is often more intriguing than what comes later. So don't go thinking that I, or Vivienne, have shirked the business of writing about later decades. In Vivienne's case, the potential ennui of having 'made it' can only have been exacerbated by what I now realize is the stultifying, Ground Hog Day repetitiveness of the industry of fashion. Year in, year out, the House of Vivienne Westwood produces two collections for Gold Label, two for Red Label, two for MAN, as well as the constant iteration of ideas through diffusion lines – Red Carpet, Worlds End and so on, not to mention accessories, perfume, jewellery and quite separate international franchises. On and on it goes. It may not be surprising, therefore, that Vivienne's memory seems to be acute for details of her tumultuous years with Malcolm, but her interest less attuned to the nuance between Ultra-Femininity (spring / summer 2005) and World Wide Women (autumn / winter 2011). She is after all the wife who failed the Home Office tests with Andreas because she couldn't recall much about their life together. Such is the nature of creative happiness, perhaps. And the further challenge of heading a great fashion house is not to innovate constantly, or to change the world every season, as appeared to be the case in the late eighties and early nineties, but rather to be creative and reactive to the world within the terms of the style and business that works. Lines, ideas and graphics repeat, sometimes as signature pieces, sometimes as the distinctive 'look' of a Vivienne Westwood creation. And there is another game to play, which is the establishment of Vivienne Westwood as a brand of international renown, and, indeed, of sufficiently authentic and recognizable voice to survive beyond the life of the woman who currently runs it and whose name it bears. There was a time when the thesis ran about Vivienne that she was some sort of creative genius constantly struggling to stay in business. But as the world has turned, Vivienne has come to seem prescient when she says, 'I always knew time was on my side.' And there is now, for anyone intrigued by this story or by her shops and clothes, much more than the promise of something finely made. There is the whole iconography of a story. There is a narrative: a woman and a series of ideas. When you buy Westwood you buy something backed with a story, like a recipe with true history. Something anti or something ante, as it was described to me at Elcho Street; something with the scent of her learning and her story, her reading and her picture-gazing, her rows with the Establishment or indeed with Malcolm; something wrought with human graft. Vivienne has achieved a longevity in fashion unprecedented since Coco Chanel. Piloted by Carlo and now Andreas she has achieved that rare navigation: expanding without diluting her reputation. It is now as if Vivienne is trying to get to the purest Vivienne. And it takes immense strength of personality not to give in to the pressure of constantly having to come up with the next trick. 'It's like when I went to Dior,' explains Vivienne, about being headhunted for the top job at the Paris house. 'I thought I should put my hat in the ring because I might be the only one who would respect Dior enough to continue his name. I was so relieved when Galliano got it, when he went over from Givenchy. You see, even Yves Saint Laurent had had businessmen over his head, looking at what he did, which is how it would have been at Dior. I've ended up with all the advantages of heading things myself. I have what I want.'

Vivienne's creative life, even more than her personal one, has been played out in the public eye. In this she resembles a pop star as much as

Vivienne's Tree of Life.

a designer, an actress as much as an artist. Although she says of punk, 'I am proud to have been part of it. It was heroic at the time,' she shares with all artists an allergic yawn when asked about past work, and on this particular patch of past, of course, she had said all she meant to say, before being grilled by me. As anyone would tell you who has had cause to go through her press cuttings, Bradley Manning the whistle-blower, or climate disaster, are more likely to be the answers given to respectful questions about fashion or to anything one asks about punk, because Vivienne's world is a perpetual 'now', marking her out not only as an instinctive artist, but also a working one. Fashion, as she once said, is like a 'nostalgia for the future' – looking to the past to feel most present in the moment. 'I am trying to put intelligence and humanity back into the technological process,' she once said of her patterns, and women and men respond to this – to the cut and feel of her creations, as much as the Big Ideas they either shout or whisper.

One constant truism would have to be Vivienne's lack of hunger for commercial success, though arguably Carlo has plenty, and Andreas too. It's not that Vivienne does not enjoy her status, wealth and the platform it affords her to talk about art and politics. She does. And she knows that her platform totters on the high heels of commercial fashion. But historically, many of her most marketable ideas had not been capitalized upon. The customized T-shirt – a Vivienne and Malcolm idea; the tube skirt – a Vivienne original; and printed and slashed denim (Cut and Slash: Vivienne and Andreas) were potentially enormously marketable, but the profits of these fashion tropes have not been hers. 'I've never cared one way or the other about failure, or about having to fold the business,' she claims, with all the brio of a woman who has survived penury and bounced back. 'For thirty years,' she said in 2003, 'I've been the judge; it's me that had to like it. First you have to have aptitude. Talent. I have that. That incredible need to just question everything. I have to do it another way. I'm making something new all the time – the technical, physical fact of doing it introduces me to other possibilities all the time . . . Chanel designed for the same reasons that I do, really; a certain perversity and irrita-tion with orthodox ways of thinking.' But Vivienne has also emulated Chanel in continuing to head up a couture house subsidized by the mass market. Her creative and political freedom is supported by her diffusion lines and accessories and her back catalogue of classic designs.

What is it, then, that makes Vivienne Vivienne in design terms? There's the historicism, there is punk, there is her utterly non-conformist view on most things – especially the visual – and there is her unique ability to see afresh and reinvent. But more than any of this, Vivienne's overriding gift to fashion and the real argument for her as an important cultural figure is her conviction that clothing can change how people think. Fashion as agitprop. In this, as her son Joe pointed out, she remains rooted in the world of punk – it is the wellspring of her credibility within fashion, and it is also one of the very few moments in the history of dress (or music) when the language of a culture was shifted by clothes. And yet she has enormous, and ultimately, I find, infectious faith in the personal as well as the political, and one can't get much more personal than what one wears. 'I think the real link that connects all my clothes is this idea of the heroic,' she stated boldly for the purposes of the V&A retrospective; 'clothes can give you a better life.' Vivienne has said that her clothes 'allow someone to be truly an individual', which, from a clothes designer, sounds like the perfect contradiction in terms. But Vivienne pirouettes on contradictions all the time. It is her essential dandy-pose, as mesmerizing as it is frustrating. Her 'individuals' are co-opted in the cause of a sartorial revolution that also plays its part, she hopes, in a wider revolt. By offering an alternative, and by espousing hope and protest for a generation mired in hopelessness and inaction, her clothes and her ideas do seem forever heroic, and forever punk. It hasn't been for a long time a question of tackling the Establishment, but rather, quoting Carlo D'Amario, of outrunning it.

'The first impact you should have in fashion is about making beauty, it's about the beautiful woman. It's about clothes that suit. That's what chic means. It's you. You can tell without the signature that it's right . . . My work is rooted in English tailoring . . . and in the past: when you look to the past, you start to see standards of excellence, the good taste in the way things are done and put together, formed. By trying to copy technique you build your own technique.'

Vivienne's fusion of inventiveness and practicality, her fascination with silhouette, historical cuts and with fabrics, often British – tweeds, tartans, silk taffeta – combine the fearless unconformity of her punk years with a sense of tradition and with the verve and wit-in-sexuality that is pure Brit. As she said first in her years at Seditionaries, and re-iterated more recently when talking about taffeta ballgowns, 'You have a much better life if you wear impressive clothes.' Who would want to argue with that?

Fashion, as a fine or an applied art, has its story to tell. Art in the modern city shifted in Vivienne's lifetime, and fashion, for a while, did not. Vivienne has been much exercised by this. Art, largely as result of the camera in the nineteenth century and of cinema in the twentieth, was robbed of its representational function and came to be a discussion, broadly, of the rules of the formation of an image. The world as it should be and the world as it is forms the dialogue of art. In fashion, there was a necessary lag because, like much representative art, fashion obsesses upon the human form. Unlike art, to some large degree it always will and must. 'Fashion is alive,' says Vivienne, 'because it has to relate to the limited; the limits that are the human body. Fashion is alive and well today because of these practical limitations. Which is not the case in some other areas of the arts.' By the time Vivienne was hanging out with Malcolm and Gordon and their art-school friends, there was an easy acceptance within contemporary art circles that representation was over and so too, possibly, was minimalism and post-minimalism: art that dwelled on the impossibility of its own being, on the numinous. But clothes and fashion, even at their angriest and most polemic, were always bound to loop back to pleasure and to sensuality: as Vivienne says, no one enjoys looking crap or looking *at* crap. The shocking in fashion had to be shocking *and* attractive to be worn. 'The cult of the body, which we practise today, is only part of the story. The Greeks wanted clothes, like art, to express more than physical beauty. Beauty, virtue, morality – clothes were meant to express it all. If clothes can't express our higher aspirations as human beings then they are not doing their job.'

*

Vivienne at home in Clapham, with insignia, 2000.

There was a party at the Wallace Collection in 2011 to mark her for-
tieth year working professionally in fashion – taken from the 1971
opening of her Worlds End shop. Vivienne wore one of her Active
Resistance creations and an elaborate ballgown decorated with recycled aviator sunglasses. The Vivienne Westwood company, idea, and
person, are largely unrecognizable from the primary-school teacher
selling ersatz-ethnic jewellery at a market stall. In the eighties, the
company had meant one line, one shop, one owner (Vivienne), one
seasonal collection. Now there are whole books' worth of activity, and
hundreds of staff. But some things are exactly as they always were.
Vivienne, complex, demanding, questioning, at its core – one of the
last fashion houses standing with its eponymous creative force at
work every day.

Forty years into fashion she remains inspirational, and inspired not
just by politics but by the entire three-dimensional world around her.
She can still be ravished by beauty: in paintings, in clothes, in humanity and in ideas. Instinctively frugal, she is lavish in her designs and in
her generosity. She remains a fantasist and an idealist long after many
have apostatized into conventionality. This is a woman who does not
own a mobile phone (in fashion!) nor a television, yet who attains a
mindfulness about the present that would surpass most teenage bloggers. As she comments, 'It's very unusual for people to work in three
dimensions the way that I do. Cutting is what I have changed in fashion. It has changed clothes everywhere. I can see it in the little shop
next door here in Clapham. Everywhere. The principles came from
ethnic clothes, and older patterns. Like that very first T-shirt I started
with that used the whole width of the cloth. All in rectangles. Nothing
wasted. Very "utility". Very historical. But making fabric turn around
a corner, you get volume that way. Working like Vionnet did. Keeping
it simple, for manufacture. That's the thing I am most proud of, in
fashion: cutting. Historically, that is what I have contributed to the
fashion vocabulary.' To which, she could rightly have added:

And the slogan-printed T-shirt.

And detritus, collage and DIY in fashion.

And the 'in' and 'out' group list on a T-shirt.

And fetish-wear as fashion (with Malcolm, we should say).

And the reintroduction of the corset.

And that stretch corset as the foundation of formal gowns.

And the whole approach of looking to historical patterns.

And the historical costume in fashion.

And the 'English' mix and match of historical reference.

And the resurrection of tweed ('it's like butter, you can't go
wrong with tweed').

And the platform 'pedestal' shoe.

And undergarments as outer garments.

And the tube skirt.

And fine knitwear on the catwalk.

And the hourglass figure.

And asymmetry on the catwalk.

And unisex fashion garments.

And punk – which has become, quite simply, part of the
English language.

'My clothes,' Vivienne tells me, 'have a story. They have an identity. They have a character and a purpose. That's why they become classics. Because they keep on telling a story. They are still telling it.'

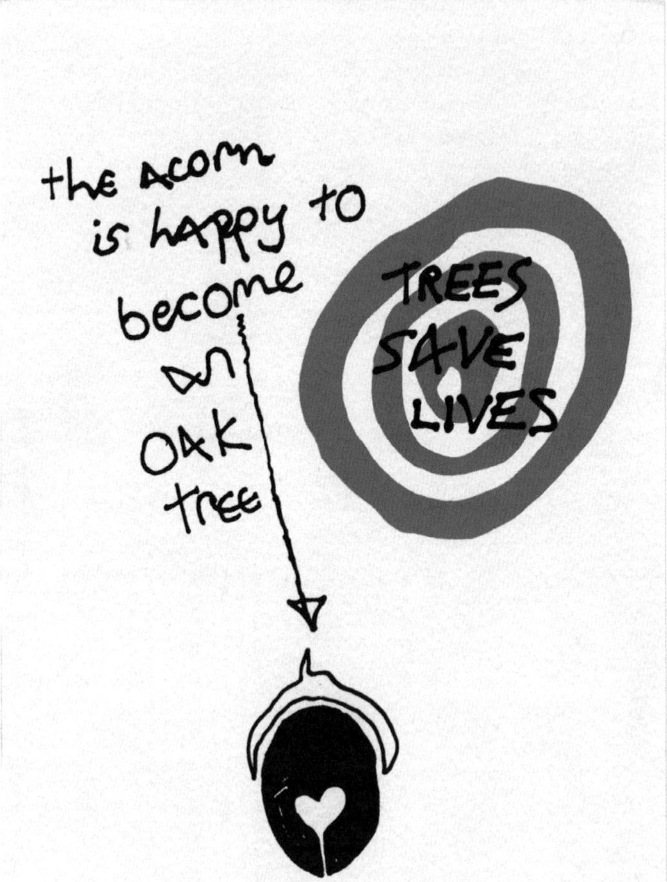
the acorn
is happy to
become
an
OAK
tree
TREES
SAVE
LIVES

CLIMATE
REVOLUTIONARY

Imagine if you and your family wished to fly somewhere and there was only one plane in the world. Imagine this plane had things wrong with it and you were told that if anything malfunctioned it would cause a chain reaction, and that the plane would crash. Would you fly? Why don't we call the engineer NOW? VIVIENNE WESTWOOD

If we don't save the rainforest there is no hope of saving the planet and Cool Earth has the best plan to halt the destruction. 'Be Reasonable: Demand the Impossible', we used to say, but this is possible.
VIVIENNE WESTWOOD and MATTHEW OWEN of Cool Earth

In some circles Vivienne is more famous now as an activist than as a fashion designer. What has happened since the turn of the millennium has been a gradual eclipsing of one crusade centred on fashion and culture by another, focused on humanitarian and ecological activism, which nonetheless inspires collection after collection on the catwalk. Vivienne is a patron of Reprieve, campaigning for victims of injustice and prisoners on death row, and also of Liberty, which campaigns for civil liberties in the UK. She supports Amnesty International, the Refugee Council, PETA, the Environmental Justice Foundation and Friends of the Earth. She is a long-time advocate of freeing Native American Leonard Peltier, and once told her PA Tizer Bailey that 'Leonard is the priority here, not fashion writers.' Her personal attachment to the cause of US whistle-blower Bradley Manning led her to wear his image at the 2013 New York Metropolitan Art Museum Costume Institute Ball, held partly in her honour, celebrating punk in fashion. She is in regular contact with Julian Assange for the same reasons and visits him in the Ecuadorian Embassy where he is seeking asylum as I write. She backs the Greenpeace Arctic Campaign and in 2009 personally donated £1 million to rainforest charity Cool Earth. Activism as much as design has come to dominate Vivienne's life.

There are a few theses on why this has come to be. One is that it is all connected, and always has been. Another is that this is what keeps her going, and keeps her inspired. Vivienne's former daughter-in-law Serena Rees, another woman in the fashion business, perhaps best explains the simple synthesis that Vivienne has found of politics and design: 'It brings her a sense of purpose, and fashion, on its own, just can't after a while. It's complicated because on the one hand she's got this very successful global company and it's like a machine that you can't stop. That's hard for Vivienne. The best you can do within your situation is all we can strive for. But beyond any of that, she is making people aware and making the next generation aware: she's talking to different generations and a wider audience, one that wouldn't normally take any notice. So it's not just "keeping Grandma Vivienne busy": she's reaching places no one, absolutely no one else could.' Lily Cole, the young British model and activist, describes how Vivienne works the fashion / activism crossover: 'When we went to the Met Ball together in 2013, all Vivienne cared about was a photograph of Bradley Manning she was wearing with TRUTH written across it, pinned to her dress. When we arrived, a reporter asked her about her outfit. Vivienne launched into a lecture on Manning and walked away buzzing. "Well, *now*," she said, "now it was worth coming all this way."'

'People think it's because I'm a grandmother,' says Vivienne, 'that I suddenly thought forward, but it's not and I'll tell you why not. Of course I love my granddaughter Cora, and all my family, but I've always treated my own kids like people, not so much like children, and I don't feel that I can make my children or grandchild a special case. So it's not that I'm thinking of Cora or her future exactly. I'm thinking of this little kid – it's an image from the past but also from the future – this little black girl probably, this pretty, pretty thing, so beautiful, this perfect child of about four or five crawling with a flower that she is trying to give to somebody so they would give her something in return. Water, I imagine. And she is crawling but she is too weak to walk about, you know. That's who I think of, this nightmare of the future. And then I think, my God. What did I do? *What did I do? What am I doing?*

'But now my two areas of work, fashion and activism, they help each other. Here's in part how it began for me. I read an interview with James Lovelock in the *Guardian* in 2005. He wrote that by his estimate, by the end of this century, the twenty-first century, by 2099 there would only be one billion people. One billion people left. That's all. I was so shocked, that it might happen that quickly. Even if one person thought it could happen that quickly I could imagine the unimaginableness of it all, the horror, the impossibility of being able to help one another. Everywhere hot. People on the move, trying to find food. It's unimaginable. But we must try and imagine. The end of the planet – that it could come so quickly and that we could destroy this rich, this one-off thing.'

James Lovelock's Gaia hypothesis is at the core of Vivienne's environmentalist thinking. 'Our economic system,' she says, 'is run for profit and waste and based primarily on the extractive industries, and it is the cause of climate change.' At around the same time Vivienne wrote her manifesto, 'Active Resistance to Propaganda', a text peopled by everyone from Ancient Greek philosophers to Disney cartoon characters to inspire an interest in learning and culture, in place of indiscriminate consumption – and to help link in her own mind as much as others' her twin crusades towards a better culture and a rescued planet. The manifesto and the collections inspired by her campaigns began to alert the world's media and the fashion-buying public that there was something new going on at the House of Westwood that was not exactly punk and not exactly culture either – though for Vivienne, climate revolution is both. 'It's like Andreas says, if people made real choices and only bought beautiful things, that's Climate Revolution too, because buying less and choosing well wouldn't hurt the environment so much.'

Vivienne is perfectly aware that all this begs the question: how can a fashion designer, a woman at the forefront of a globally recognized

Invitation to Save the Rainforest (autumn / winter 2014).

fashion business and one that until recently has worked to Carlo's mantra that only constant expansion guarantees success; how can such a woman possibly point the finger at anyone without also incriminating herself?

'Guilty,' Vivienne tends to say, sometimes even literally holding up her hands. 'One answer is that you have to start from where you are. Another is that I reach people – people who read fashion magazines, for instance – who would never have heard about some of this otherwise. My main point, though, is quality rather than quantity. What I'm always trying to say is: buy less, choose well, make it last; though sometimes I might as well say, "buy Vivienne Westwood"!'

Climate change, and the real prospect of catastrophic global warming, has galvanized Vivienne into a determination to reach the widest possible audience with a message of 'climate revolution'. It is most simply expressed in this handwritten appeal I found in Vivienne's archive from March 2012, though its concerns predate then. It is addressed to Vivienne's friend and collaborator, the supermodel Naomi Campbell:

Dear Naomi,

I have wished for so long to tell you properly what I am doing and to ask for your help.

The best thing is to list a set of bullet points:

- *We have till 2050 to stop Climate Change (CC) and start coming down from the present peak by 2020. By 2020 we will know if we can stop CC or if we will have Runaway CC meaning we can do nothing about it and there will be accelerating loss of habitat and massive extinction of the human race – you would be a witness. Me – not. (Statistics: end of the century, 1 billion people left)*
- *Almost every scientist agrees on the dangers but governments are doing very little*
- *Hope lies with the thousands of NGOs, charities and individuals who are doing stuff. This in itself is helping and will help to hold back the problem but the great hope is that this will raise public awareness re urgency and that this in turn will put pressure on governments*

- *The very process of stopping CC will mean that all our structures would have to change and the focus of our values would become human values – and a more secure, healthy and happy world – not based on competition, cheap labour, depletion of natural resources, and profit*

- *What I am doing is working with the charity Cool Earth to save the Rainforest. This is a bottom-up programme, working with the indigenous people and if it can save the three great forests of the equator by stopping illegal logging it will protect the forest. It is a practical plan, already working and it will cost an incredibly small amount compared to the enormous benefit. Indeed if we save the rainforest we might save the planet and if we don't – forget it. We need 7 million in the next three years, and then, to achieve the completed plan, we need just over another 100 million by 2020*

- *My plan. (1) I give my own £. (2) Fundraise. (3) Get models to help form a nucleus of avant garde engaged citizens. (4) Promote publicity to raise public awareness and engagement with the world and the future. This is really urgent and important – without public support / opinion, nothing is possible. (5) Put pressure on government*

- *My target. Storm Model Agency and Harpers are organizing an event in August (not sure if it will be a dinner, an auction, a conference). The event will focus on 'Cool Earth' and raising awareness and publicity.*

I hope to announce that we have raised an extra ½ million pounds. I am trying to get donations of £10 thousand from some models who can afford it, and less, but something, from ones who can't and I am trying also for large donations (e.g. some people who have an art gallery have promised me £100 thousand). Ideal would be 10 x £10 thousand from models – we have £50 thousand so far, and 4 x £100 thousand from big donors. Therefore Naomi I am asking you if you can spare £10 thousand and / or if you can help in other ways. I ask this even though I know you do a lot besides. I think you are so important to have in support.

I hope to present the models who are engaged in this as aspirational people. I am arranging to go to the art galleries with them. We are dangerously short of culture, because culture is the antidote to propaganda and consumption (I have a manifesto about this). The idea is 'Get a Life': you get out what you put in. And if people (models) get a life right now by being engaged with the world (and human genius from the past) they can hopefully get a life in the literal sense for the next generation.

I thought it was a great idea to ask people for £ and not only to put their face to our cause.

I am asking a lot.

(heart) Vivienne

She wrote in similar vein to Marc Jacobs in December 2011, but with added emphasis, from one designer to another, on how activism was in turn renewing her energy for fashion.

I am especially happy at the moment because I feel that everything is coming together – that I can use fashion as a medium to express my ideas to fight for a better world; and because of the credibility fashion gives me a voice, and this in turn helps the fashion and keeps me stimulated and inspired ... I hope you are happy and that your busy life is exciting and that you too are enjoying your work as much as ever.

She ends (after asking for money for Cool Earth) with the suggestion of a get-together in Paris: 'It would be exciting to see you this side of Christmas, but I am having a knee operation on the 13th – fell on the Tube escalators in mad platform shoes! Oh Marc! What a life!'

'Oh my gosh, I remember all that!' Naomi tells me when we talk. 'With Vivienne and me, it always was just about ultimate trust. Trust her vision. Trust her. I mean, I've known her all my adult life – my first castings in '87, '88, and what she's trying to get at, whatever issues, I've trusted her 100 per cent and wanted to help get her vision to come to life. She's an extraordinary lady. She's so passionate. She cares about so many people and so many issues. I mean, she's got the biggest heart, Vivienne, but yet she's very astute. She doesn't take nonsense, from me or anybody, and I love that about her too. She'll say to me, "*Use* who you are to help others, and this is how." Things that I wasn't even *aware* of, she'd make me aware of. *Use* your celebrity.'

An ability to recruit high-profile names like Naomi's to her causes is part of what makes Vivienne an effective campaigner and fundraiser. However, her brand of activism is more than celebrity endorsement. She puts the full force of her personality and creativity behind the causes she espouses, and, increasingly, she focuses the House of Westwood onto these causes too.

'So here we go: let me explain what I do and how it started. After reading James Lovelock, I phoned up my brother and he is the ex-husband of Cynthia King. She's a wonderful human being. She's a producer and he's a film-maker – a very good film-maker. So I phoned him up and I said, "I've got to do a television show. Some sort of show where we try and get this across to people," and so we did. We went to Ravensbourne College, which is where he had studied, and did this pilot thing. It didn't work out and here's why: I was trying, in my head and in what I said, to deal with *culture* at the same time as dealing with the *environment*, which is difficult, but if you get it right – and I try to – you can make sense of so much. It was in the form of a chat show, and though it worked in getting the audience to ask questions about the environment, I couldn't find a way for us to discuss culture. It looked like two separate programmes. I try to link it and I need to link it – culture and the environment, the physical and the ethical environment, and I am better now at linking it all, because, of course, it's all connected. One of the key tent poles, if you will, of trying to overcome climate change and have a better world is to link culture and climate change. We're talking *quality*. The quality of life, which very much involves culture. It's about a sort of mindfulness, if you like: paying attention to what you are doing and creating and how you are living. I believe at present we've not got true culture. We've got a pseudo-culture, which is sometimes called "popular culture". I wanted to involve people, but I said to Cynthia, "We don't have time for TV programmes; we've got to do something else." So there were two things that happened. In the course of making this pilot, this little TV programme about the climate, we had met Cool Earth; and we'd interviewed Matthew Owen for the pilot. About the same time, I had been invited to Brazil. I went to Brazil for a fashion show with Andreas, and Matthew said, "Would you like a trip up the Amazon?"'

Gordon recalls Vivienne's enthusiasm. 'They offered her a trip up the Amazon, she took it and they explained the rainforest. Now Vivienne has this ability to just switch focus and she simply said, "Well, the rainforest is more important than anything." And that was some of the beginnings of what became Climate Revolution.'

'The specific other thing that happened was this,' continues Vivienne. 'Matthew who operates Cool Earth enormously impressed me, as did his work, and so then what I did, I went to our company and I said, "I'm going to take a million pounds out of this company, and I'm going to give it to Cool Earth."' How did that go down with Carlo? 'Well, I can do what I like: I'd never had any big money out of the company. I was able to do that, so that's what I did. That's how I started Climate Revolution, by giving money to Cool Earth, and then beginning this diary. A blog. That was part of trying to get across to people what I was thinking – this diary about the environment, and it was a way to talk about the true culture as well. And I did it because I thought the information about the environment, the exhortation to try and *do* something, would be easier to assimilate in the form of a diary. And I put in a bit about fashion! And I do believe that if people read this they will get a point of view that they won't find anywhere else today. I am, however, very careful not to use it as a way to sell fashion or my brand. That's not the point. It's more of a way to let them know what my daily life is like. I know that I have a lot of credibility within fashion and I wanted to be an inspirational person, to inspire people to listen. The diary is now part of the Climate Revolution website. En route to that I came up with the idea of this campaign called Climate Revolution, that we were going to involve people in Climate Revolution. People don't demonstrate much today. That's bad and good: I mean, you can influence events and you can influence politics through social media. You can challenge the status quo, just as Wiki-Leaks challenges the status quo. These things can only happen on the Internet. So that was part of it, to be part of the online revolution, but very much with the idea of wanting to work with other NGOs and link everybody as best we can, because everything is connected, and the main message that I want to get over is that the environmental crisis is a crisis caused by the rotten financial system. These are the snakes that eat each other's tail. The shit financial system has caused the environmental problem. But also the fact that we are exploiting the earth to the extent where we're going to destroy it, is what's also causing the financial crisis. Cause and symptom. And so that's one major way in which everything is connected, because I thought if you can get through to people about the money in their pockets and you can start to understand the connections then you're going to have them on your side for the environment too. Hence our slogan "What's good for the planet is good for the economy. What's bad for the planet is bad for the economy."'

The specific area of ecological concern for Vivienne has been the rainforest. It has become an area where even cynics have had to admit she has made real impact, and taken a personal journey in every sense, and made personal sacrifice, in order to put her money where her mouth is. Matthew Owen, Director of Cool Earth, the pioneering NGO that creates rainforest shields by working with indigenous communities in the Amazon, Congo and Papua New Guinea, cites Vivienne now as their most effective, as well as most high-profile, supporter. He and Vivienne met in 2010 and have worked together on Cool Earth since 2011.

'I was at a talk by James Lovelock – author of *Gaia* – at the Institute of Directors in London. He was lambasting the audience for thinking that they could rely on renewable energy to halt climate change. Vivienne asks direct and pertinent questions and she demanded to know what people should be doing and, as always, Lovelock said, "Save the rainforest." She had been doing lots of research into what made the biggest difference in preventing climate catastrophe and came to the conclusion that Cool Earth's – this charity's – way of halting deforestation was the best hope we have. Vivienne is very smart and very honest. She asks the questions that everyone wishes they had the guts to. This makes her a commanding presence in any meeting, and one-to-one she's just as curious and thorough. This initial impression hasn't changed a bit. She's a wonderful travelling companion – we have literally been up the Amazon together – and is more resilient camping in 100 per cent humidity than people half her age. And it could be tough, even for a less than seventy-year-old! We took a rest

The 'Free Leonard Peltier' winged phallus, disseminating his innocence.

under some shade on a long walk to a remote village, and without knowing it perched Vivienne on a bullet ant nest, and she was covered. Still no complaints from Vivienne; she is bulletproof. But no conversation with Vivienne is a walk in the park. I remember one meeting with Peru's Minister of the Environment in Lima in November 2012. Vivienne had just come out of a week living with an Ashaninka community in the central forest. We all felt exhausted and it looked as if we had taken a two-hour detour for a handshaking exercise. Out of nowhere Vivienne made a perfect speech, charmed the whole room, and we walked out with an agreement for the government to use the Cool Earth model across all of Peru's rainforests. She saved a million acres of rainforest in an instant. If nothing else, I'd love people who read this book to know that. I don't know anyone else who could have done that. Though I'd have to say almost as happy a memory of that trip was swimming in the Rio Mamiri – a black-water tributary of the Amazon – with Vivienne, Andreas and about a dozen children from the village drifting in and out of the current. The kids were completely beguiled by them and a nine-year-old orphan called Cladys was Vivienne's constant companion. Vivienne is the kind of supporter that any cause dreams of. I know Reprieve, Greenpeace and PETA would say the same. She is a very substantial contributor to all of Cool Earth's projects and she has wrangled her friends into backing us. But even more valuable is her radical common sense that gets the message across better than anyone else: "We must save the rainforest if we are to save the planet." I fear there has been this lazy tendency to use Vivienne as either the poster designer for extreme fashion or a shorthand for punk royalty. But I can't think of many other businesses from the late seventies that are as global or as creative as hers. And Vivienne has been as prescient on human rights and the environment as she has been on fashion. I think the public knows this, and the press have had to raise their game.'

Cool Earth has ever since been one of the mainstays of Vivienne's activism, and the clearest example of her putting her money, time and energy where her mouth is. It has taken her from the Brazilian rainforest to 10 Downing Street, and has brought her the friendship of many people involved in the same area, from Sting to Prince Charles to Pamela Anderson. 'I have been told by my team,' wrote the Prince of Wales to Vivienne in 2009, 'that as a result of your appearance on the Jonathan Ross show, we acquired a further 30,000 sign-ups to the cause . . . [supporting] the fight against climate change by stopping destruction of tropical forests . . . which is just incredible! It was completely wonderful of you to mention my project on such a popular platform, and it certainly seems to have had the desired effect . . . Your support and influence cannot come at a better time as we try for a final push to encourage as many people as possible world-wide to sign up.' It was a typical example of Vivienne's campaigning: turning up on a popular TV show, largely eschewing the chance to talk fashion or punk history, and instead use her platform to reach a new demographic. 'It really does make all the difference,' continued the Prince in another letter to Dame Vivienne, 'to have the support of iconic designers such as yourself, and I could not be more grateful [for] your public support of my Rainforests Project.'

Pamela Anderson, who describes herself as an 'activist, art lover, actress and friend of Vivienne's', has bonded over the last decade with both Vivienne and Andreas, sharing a number of eco-political causes. 'We are of similar minds on social justice and climate revolution,' Pamela tells me. 'Vivienne invited me to a fashion show where I became more interested in her manifesto than in the fashion. I adore her clothes but I was fascinated by her connection to the planet and to . . . art. We spoke after the show, she said she "didn't have to draw me a map", and was happy that I used my position in life to champion causes I believed in. She is inspirational. Now when we are in the same city we go to galleries and museums [and then to] a good veggie restaurant.' One result of this unlikely pairing – the Baywatch babe and Vivienne – has been a series of dramatic Jeurgen Teller shoots and Pamela's appearance on the catwalk as well as in photo shoots, and when on the West Coast – for the opening of Vivienne's Hollywood store, for instance – Vivienne and Andreas are often in Pamela's company. 'We were together when Obama was elected,' Pamela tells me, 'and were *so* hopeful. She is a real force in our family; my oldest son Brandon gets reading lists from her – *Of Mice and Men*, Anatole France . . . whenever I see Vivienne I make sure I have paper and pen: I take notes. I am so grateful to her for how she paints the world but also for her personal interest and admiration. It doesn't matter what anyone thinks of me: Vivienne understands me – enough said.'

'You can save the rainforest for £100 million,' Vivienne states simply. 'It's not that much money. It's the advertising budget of Samsung. They could protect the rainforest for that budget and would get so much publicity out of it if they chose to do that . . . I should speak to them.' In 2009 Vivienne was invited to 10 Downing Street by Steve Hilton, former advisor to David Cameron, specifically to discuss this subject. 'I couldn't believe it. A Conservative government that was interested in saving the rainforest. I thought that was brilliant. He was brilliant. Then he left. I don't hate David Cameron, but all politicians are just so . . . delayed.' Vivienne faces all obstacles with her belligerent ingenuousness: she has no time, and nor, she believes, does the planet.

'The best first thing I can do is to be efficient reorganizing my company. I heard that people come out of Primark with carrier bags of T-shirts that cost as little as £1. That's bad for the planet and for people, for farmers and for factories of cheap labour, and it's bad for the people who buy it; they're just consumers, suckers-up with their washing machines and landfill. Why can't we recycle old clothes as paper? The best paper used to be rag paper! Everything has its cost – its effect. It is all subsidized by the planet, by the despoiling of the planet. And just in the same way, fashion is subsidized if you are not mindful with it. It actually costs less than it should do, often. In my company, everything costs less than it should. It should cost more! I know it's shocking and I know it's only fashion. Here's a better example: a chicken costs less than it actually costs. It can be done because the earth is carrying our subsidy, our debt. The whole way that the earth is run is because it's run on the idea of debt. You can make small amends by paying attention, and you can operate a company ethically, and with regard to quality. The first thing to say is that if people only bought beautiful things, we would perhaps be able to manage our carbon footprint. I know, I know, but if people really did have quality of life, instead of non-stop distraction and consumerism, sucking up rubbish, we would be in a better place. I think fashion that is really, really good, and this isn't easy to say, but clothes that cost more, means people would buy less and that's how it should be. The central banks print money out of air by pressing buttons on a computer. This is lent to governments and becomes a debt to be paid back by the taxpayer and also through consumption. The banks make enormous profit from the interest; the more debt, the more profit. This is the money system, and it causes ecological crisis. It's what money pundits mean by growth. The world runs on debt in order that a very, very small minority can suck up the profit, and the creating of debt is an important part of how they can do that. That's how it works.

'Personally, we do what we can do. Switching lights off. Trying to have a plastic-bottle-free building. Recycling paper. Rubbish-sorting for recycling. Trying not to use plastic bags. Hangers that are reused. Trying to cut down on air flights. Sometimes it can be a hands-on and business-integrated issue.'

In 2011 Vivienne travelled to Africa for the first time, at the invitation of the International Trade Centre of the United Nations. She has set up a scheme to help alleviate poverty in Kenya. Over 250 women are now employed to produce bags and handcrafted items under the Vivienne Westwood label using a range of recycled materials. 'This is not just a charity,' says Vivienne, 'it's better than that; it's work.' 'It's a brutal environment,' explains the Kenyan model Ajuma, 'and I would know; there has been real impact, as well as real gratitude.'

'So I began the Climate Revolution campaign with the Worlds End shop – right back to the beginning. That was always my forum for politics, that shop; it's a crucible of ideas. I love that shop, so it was right that it was based there. And in terms of the look, it fits with Climate Revolution because for years it has been about a kind of recycling, and, as the name suggests, the end of the world. So we use it for classics, where we've done all the costings so you don't have to charge people again for something that you've got as a stock design, if you like, that has become a classic. You've got your money back on the design so you don't have to pay for the invention of it any more. It's revolutionary, climate-change chic, and a bargain, in a sense, because once upon a time it took six months to do it, but you're not paying for that any longer, because it's a classic.'

Vivienne's activism is not limited, however, to environmental

Climate Revolution invitation to Red Label (spring / summer 2013).

concerns, though that tends to be the over-riding issue. Her work with Liberty was explained to me by the head of the organization, Shami Chakrabarti:

'Vivienne cares a lot about the planet, but she cares a lot about human rights as well, and when you spend time with her you find she's a visionary on this. I think it's partly the mother and the grandmother in her. She's looking to the future and I think it's telling that she cares about human rights and about climate change and she sees the connection. I think she sees the physical and the constitutional environment as equally important as the one protects the other. These are the two causes that she's been most associated with in recent years, and not everybody has straddled those two worlds and I think we all need to do it more, because it's all about the future. It's all really about our kids and our kids' kids and what kind of world they're going to inherit from us. Both in terms of their rights to the freedoms which safeguard a quality of life, but also in terms of the planet that they're inhabiting. There's got to be clean water to drink and there's got to be food for everyone to eat and there ought to be a beautiful planet to inhabit. But equally, who wants to live in paradise as a slave? You've also got to have free speech and fair trials *as well as* rainforests and clean water. And I think that Vivienne is somebody who gets that, and gets that they are connected, and can talk about these things at a high level, because sometimes we do need to lift our heads high. It's the job of some of us to drill down into the detail of this particular legal case, or that particular international convention, be it on human rights or on the planet. But we do also need the big-picture people, the visionaries, the storytellers who inspire, and I would put Vivienne in that category.

'Vivienne's involvement with Liberty began in 2005. I had already been Director for two years. Liberty, also known as the National Council for Civil Liberties, is the UK's domestic campaign for human rights, looking at human rights violations here in the UK. Though Vivienne also, of course, is heavily involved with Reprieve and Amnesty, which deal with similar issues, globally.

'I think I wrote to Vivienne to enlist her help and to ask for a signature for a petition, and just said, "If you are ever interested in, you know, coming to the office and finding out more about our work you'd be more than welcome." And she came over with her bicycle clips on, on her own, and sat with me for many hours asking questions about human rights. And I explained exactly what we were doing. My point is, ours is not a popular cause. It's not animals. It's terror suspects and asylum seekers and it's naughty kids who've got an ASBO and it's not sexy and it's not fashionable. What was and is extraordinary about Vivienne for me is twofold. There's her incredible hunger for learning and enthusiasm for things that she cares about, many of which I care about too. But what's really special about Vivienne and what I was struck by straight away was she's the sort of person who will ask any question and not worry about whether she seems naive. But when you speak to her, you're conscious that you're speaking to a woman of a certain age and of huge experience. But also when you speak to her you could be speaking to a knowledge-hungry sixteen-year-old girl, or a six-year-old girl, because of the openness and the humility and the "no question is too simple". She's never afraid – she's never worried that you will judge her if she doesn't know something, so long as she's asking an honest question. And in my experience of "celebrities" and people in the public eye, that's almost unique. Vivienne reminds me of something Thomas Hardy wrote about Tess of the d'Urbervilles, that she was several ages. Sometimes she was the little girl and sometimes she was the woman. You spend time with Vivienne and you see the little girl and sometimes you see the punk rebel, this young woman, and sometimes you see the grandmother, and she's all of those things. None of them afraid of what you might be thinking.'

Vivienne states emphatically, 'All human beings have a passion for justice. Envy comes from the same root, a feeling that things aren't fair, but in this case the feeling comes when someone overvalues their own worth. Shami tells me that, like other human rights lawyers, she was inspired in her choice of career by *To Kill a Mockingbird.* Shami and I know "it could be me". I believe there are many innocent prisoners and especially political prisoners, and I am thinking about Guantanamo, and their luck is down to being in the wrong place at the wrong time: a convenient solution to a frame-up.'

'I don't think you can separate Vivienne's politics and her activism from her art and her fashion,' continues Shami. 'She's a mother and a grandmother and I think that very much affects her passion for the planet, and she's been ahead of the rest of us in connecting the constitutional environment with the physical environment; she's a human rights activist and a climate change activist and these worlds, these two worlds, aren't always as well connected as they should be. Vivienne does that. She has this "brand Vivienne" that has grown up around her artistic talent but the thing is she's not afraid to use it for these other passions which are all now intimately interconnected.

'The other thing I should say about Vivienne is that she is not at all like other so-called "celebrities". They can be high maintenance, capricious, go off the ranch, say things that they've made up. This simply does not apply in Vivienne's case. She asks for briefings. She is a team player, which is not what people would necessarily expect of someone who is *a)* so famous; *b)* so successful; *c)* such an individual. There's nothing frivolous about her at all. At base, Vivienne gets that human rights are there so that people can be human and can celebrate their expression, whether it's through their clothing, or their music, so I think it's dangerous to ever denigrate anyone for being supposedly in the "wrong" industry to have an opinion. I think the opposite. Here she is, having gained a position in the world and yet she wants to use this position to make a contribution to really important debates, and to get people thinking.'

The personalities and causes that have associated themselves with Vivienne might seem an eclectic mix, but there is a clear rationale behind the comrades-in-arms attachment of names as diverse as Pamela Anderson and the Prince of Wales. There is also an obvious link between the causes of Leonard Peltier, in prison in Florida for a crime several courts acknowledge he did not commit and for which there is no evidence extant, Bradley Manning, the American soldier and WikiLeaks source who is now known as Chelsea Manning, in prison for a crime many see as an act of heroism, and even Julian Assange in his confinement. Vivienne believes in making the political personal, and has signed up to help these individuals. 'We met at my forty-first birthday party in Norfolk while I was under house arrest without charge,' Assange tells me. 'Vivienne really carried an aura with her but I think her charisma comes from her convictions, from her passionate commitment to justice and truth. She designed and produced a T-shirt to raise funds for WikiLeaks but she first showed the T-shirt at her show held in the Foreign and Commonwealth Office, which was poignant as this is the institution' – Assange alleges – 'preventing my safe passage to Ecuador and contravening international law by doing so. Vivienne is effective because she can see through dogma. She is inconvenient; people cannot handle the consistency and seriousness with which she sticks to her politics. They are made uncomfortable by the way she injects politics into everything. But politics is everywhere, and if we didn't have bloody-minded people just like Vivienne, we'd have no chance of changing our world for the better.' Like many, Vivienne believes that access to information is key to the proper functioning of democracy and indeed climate awareness, for which reason the actions of Manning and Assange are in her eyes fully justified. She has featured both their faces on T-shirts and graphics, usually with the legend *Truth* boldly asserted underneath. She has no truck with quibblers on these, or the other personal struggles she has adopted, and the frank gratitude of those whose causes she espouses is clear from their supporters and themselves. This, from Leonard Peltier, writing to me from Coleman State Penitentiary in Florida:

My number is 89637-132. I am a Lakota / Anishnabee Native American from North Dakota. I was thirty-three years old when they brought me in and I am sixty-nine years old now! Over the years, Miss Vivienne has led the charge with various projects to try to help win my freedom, at great risk. She has enlisted her friends, colleagues and dignitaries to my aid. Some of the most creative ideas have come from Miss V, like her ad campaigns and the sewing of 'Leonard Peltier is innocent' (I am) right into the very label of her designs. I am not a writer, but I speak from my heart, so please believe me. I am an innocent man. I am so thankful for people like Vivienne Westwood who can identify with the oppression other people face and take measures to bring world attention to that oppression. Miss Vivienne has demonstrated great courage and the heart of a Warrior. I do not use words like 'courage' lightly. These kinds of fights are never easy and can jeopardize your friendships, your life, your career,

Julian Assange models his Vivienne Westwood / Julian Assange T-shirt, 2012.

Vivienne unfurls her Climate Revolution banner. A still from footage of the closing ceremony of the London Paralympics, 2012.

your own personal health. An old saying among my people is this, 'You
can identify the stature of a person by the size of their enemy.' Miss V is
one of the bravest women I know. Miss V has often given me the gift of
laughter through the stories she tells me about her life and experiences.
At times I have laughed so hard my side literally ached for days. Laughter
is a rare commodity inside this hell. My heart desperately tries to find a
way to truly show her the gratitude I have. So I write this. It takes brave
souls to fight for freedom. Stepping up to the plate and offering your
name and signature and reputation is an act of bravery. That is the
modern version of a battle warrior's way.

It was the cause of Leonard Peltier that first introduced Vivienne to
the American actress Pamela Anderson. It became apparent, subsequently, that Anderson was a fan of Vivienne's designs and often wears
her creations, and that they shared an interest in ecological issues that
manifests itself in Anderson's case more in the cause of animal rights.
But as a result of Peltier and of Climate Revolution, Pamela has become
a stalwart supporter and friend of Vivienne and of Andreas and starred
in three advertising campaigns. 'Pam really puts herself out there,'
Vivienne tells me, 'the sort of person who, every time she travels, she
seizes the opportunity to make a point or try to help one of her causes
locally.' Typical of their relationship would be this apparently breezy
note that passed over Vivienne's desk when we were talking one day:
'I am doing the *Ellen* [DeGeneres] show on 16th,' she wrote in October
2013. 'Can you dress me in all the political things you can? Tights,
T-shirt, climate change assange [*sic*], chelsea manning please. Something wild funky cool punk rock. Maybe you know a great hairstylist
that could give me a big Mohawk?!: Free Leonard Peltier! Anything
that works!!!! Any ideas. PAM xxx' It is a simple tribute to Vivienne
that she can hold together these disparate causes and agendas, the
ersatz of Hollywood and the macrocosmic political issues of our
times, and attempt to find synthesis, communication and a positive
outcome. 'I never get depressed about it,' she says one day, a little after
a further setback in the Manning case and just before helping to
launch the latest Ecocide debate. 'We can only try to be our best selves
and do the best we can. Else why get up?'

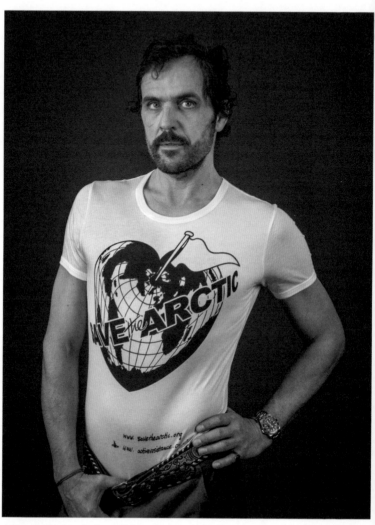

Andreas in the Save the Arctic T-shirt, photographed by his and Vivienne's friend Andy Gotts.

The crowning moment of Vivienne's latter years as a campaigner was her appearance in the closing ceremony of the London Paralympics in 2012. Though many had recognized already that activism was her main *raison d'être*, notably in the UK after her Jonathan Ross show appearance where she spoke barely a word on fashion and a great deal on climate change, it was the Paralympics that sealed the new image of a national treasure rebranding herself. Her designs had already been seen in the opening and closing ceremonies of the main Olympic games, with punks featured in the Danny Boyle sequence on the history of modern Britain, and Vivienne's designs themselves included in a closing sequence on modern British fashion designers (the others were Burberry, Victoria Beckham, Christopher Kane and Alexander McQueen). But the Paralympics offered a different opportunity for her, as she was asked to appear at the stadium in person. 'Joe Rush of the Mutant Waste Company works a lot with festivals and his work involves creating with scrap metal. And he had been asked to design the Closing Ceremony. There was a giant fly, I remember, made out of a helicopter, and there was a giant fish, like Mardi Gras festival floats made out of scrap. And then there was to be a chariot. And it was all to take place at night. He is a real artist. I suspect people missed some of the true effect of it, on TV. And when Joe Rush asked me to be this Boudicca in a chariot, at first I said no. I thought, "Get a model." No one needs me up there. But he wanted me and I thought, well, if I do it, how do I *use* it? Because this is how I deal now with publicity requests, for good or ill, as you may have noticed. And I came up with this idea of launching the Climate Revolution at that point, at the Paralympics, to the widest possible audience. It was an apposite moment. Four years before, after the Copenhagen conference on climate change, it had been said, "We have 100 months." Prince Charles and I both spoke of this. He was part of the awareness campaign. We'd have 100 months to stop climate change. To halt it. Otherwise we had no chance. Every four years is half of 100 months, forty-eight months to be exact, so launching it at the Paralympics, it was halfway through our allotted 100 months. In other words, by the next Paralympics, or Olympics, we're supposed to have halted climate change. It's a very short time. Of course, the timescales shift. Scientists say, "We might have a bit more time than we think we have and nobody really knows," but most scientists agree we may well be on the precipice already. I had to deceive everyone because I had this thing printed inside my dress and I knew they'd have checked. They'd have asked: "Have you got any branding?", "Is there any nudity?" I didn't feel that guilty because, you know, if I'd told them what I was up to they'd be duty-bound to stay on the safe side and not allow me to do it.' Once the cameras were rolling and it was too late for anyone to pull back, Vivienne revealed herself as Boudicca, the British warrior queen, riding a chariot of sorts but enfolded in a giant cape emblazoned with her call to arms: 'Climate Revolution!' Proud, defiant, a little bit naughty and jarring all at once, it is a classic Vivienne image and moment. If James Lovelock is as right as Vivienne believes and the earth really is like a pleasure boat drifting in the eddies above Niagara Falls, it is clear that Vivienne at least is determined that it won't be a quiet ride.

In October 2013, Greenpeace activists protesting against Russian oil exploration in the Arctic were arrested and charged first with piracy and then with possession of illegal drugs. Vivienne was asked to represent Greenpeace ('an absolute honour . . . I hope I get it right!') on Channel 4 News, opposite a spokesman for the Russian government. Pitched against her simple and emotive admonition that there were two global priorities for humankind to avoid extinction: saving the rainforest and saving the ice caps, the Kremlin diplomat looked flummoxed. And although his grasp of the figures and facts (the Greenpeace activists had already been warned, the threat of terrorism to oil rigs etc.) was impressive, Vivienne's ingenuous passion had its trumping power, as, too, does her history of activism. When the Russian suggested that no one was protesting against American interference in foreign lands, Vivienne could reasonably pipe up with, 'Well, I am.'

'That's classic Mum,' says Joe, 'she has this disarming honesty about her. It just comes out; there's no hidden agenda with Mum, it's just out. And Vivienne's like that. She's got this naive quality about her, very childlike quality, but it's so fucking charming and truthful, you know? Charming, and devastating. And I think because of that quality she's found a unique strength. She has a way of thinking things through that can get to the heart of the matter. You can get through all kinds of problems with that sort of attitude and that kind of childishness. That's what I've learned from her. Dora had it too: a kind of childlike quality, but I think she probably always had that. I think if anything Mum becomes more like Dora, more childlike, these days. It serves her well – and her causes. And she's not slowing down, you know: she's gearing up!'

WAR X

Peace Yes

www. activeresistance . co. uk/getalife

THE RIVER FLOWS ON

Her face was not soft; it was controlled, kindly. Her hazel eyes seemed
to have a big calm and understanding. She seemed to know, to accept
and to welcome her position. Ma Joad, described in John Steinbeck's
The Grapes of Wrath

What's the best accessory? A book. Vivienne Westwood

No alarms go off at Vivienne's house in Clapham Old Town. Vivienne
often wakes early and her passion and her routine is to read in bed.
Most mornings she will do this for more than an hour, while Andreas
heads down for his yoga routine, to make tea and to write his journal.
Vivienne has a flask of hot water by her bed always, and drinks this
through her first hour or more at her books. It's a large house, by London standards, Grade 1 listed and Queen Anne era, and an expression
of Andreas's interest in interior decor and architectural history (it
retains a lot of original eighteenth-century panelling). Vivienne could
live anywhere. Her creativity faces outwards always. But together they
have made it comfortable as well as darkly beautiful. And everywhere,
there are books.

'In the morning, because we often might have somewhere to go
in the evening, we find ourselves talking about what to wear. Coco
Chanel used to have somebody who looked after her clothes, and they
were numbered in outfits, so you'd just say, "I want Chanel Number 1."
I don't have that. I've got Andreas. I don't want to be wasting time
worrying what goes with what. Andreas takes longer to dress, I could
decide on my own, but it's ever so much better with him. He'll have

got something from the archive for me. And he asks me what to wear if he's going out on his own. Well, actually, I'm just there as a sounding board, really; he usually decides for himself. But every now and then I do have to state a preference – just to get him out of the door, really.' 'That's not quite true,' objects Andreas. 'But I do help Vivienne because she has good ideas in the morning and I don't. So we just talk about what to wear. She never has any clothes; it's ridiculous. She's Vivienne Westwood. She doesn't own anything.' 'Actually,' corrects Vivienne, 'I've too many clothes. I don't want to keep things. I borrow things from the press collections.'

These days, Vivienne and Andreas tend to cycle together to the Battersea HQ of Vivienne Westwood in the late morning. It takes about fifteen minutes. There is a general understanding that late nights are from time to time a necessity in the fashion business, so the early morning is sparsely attended at Elcho Street. Cynthia King is often there. She beavers over the website and the latest ecological campaigns and leaves earlier than some of the fashion crowd. Vivienne is on first-name terms with almost everyone in the building, though it's difficult to keep track of the international interns that come and go for odd months at a time, but she says hello to whoever's turn it is to be on reception (usually an Italian or German, to cope with all the languages on the switchboard) and heads up by lift to her penthouse studio. The Brits address her as Vivienne. To some of the fashion interns from abroad she is 'Madame'.

There are three main floors to the Vivienne Westwood building and a glass-wrapped penthouse studio where Vivienne, Andreas and Tizer Bailey, their PA, work. Most of the roof of the building is taken up with the urban garden planted by Andy-the-Gardener (who also models for Vivienne), where meetings occasionally take place in the summer, where Vivienne grows vegetables and fruit, and where Jackie Onassis, Dora's dog, pees.

Vivienne heads quickly through reception, famous for not often quite replying to a 'hello' or 'how are you?' She can give the impression of being preoccupied, but her colleagues are inured to it. The ground floor houses the online department, stock warehouse and a jewellery vault. Vivienne rarely visits. The unheated archive, however, with examples of nearly everything from Harris Tweed onwards, and items from the early years at Worlds End as far back as Let It Rock, is occasionally trawled by Vivienne: 'not memory lane, I hate that – but for work'. The archive is worth many, many millions of pounds, but at the same time it is a design resource for the company. Items are loaned out to exhibitions and for photo shoots. Cara Delevingne has just been shot in some Mini Crini collection for *i-D* magazine, Julia Roberts has requested another gown for the Golden Globes made from a previous Gold Label collection, but it is also a resource for Vivienne, Murray, Mark and Brigitte in particular. Classic items are reworked for the Anglomania and Red Label collections, and the Gold Label archive is used to inspire both bridal wear and ideas for movie stars wanting something specific for the awards season. Rafael Gomes is in charge in the deep chill of the archive, though it is Murray who knows it best, touching each garment with a loving hand having had input in almost everything as far back as the Pagan collections. There is also, next to the archive, a permanent white colorama studio, a backdrop and lights on standby for shooting 'looks' or individual items for, say, online shopping. Ben Westwood does quite a bit of this.

The first floor of Elcho Street is proper rag trade. Seamstresses and cutters work here in brightly lit studios, some with windows, amidst vast swathes of luxurious fabrics and with the space to deal with formal gowns and wedding dresses. Vivienne bustles by, head down usually, a swatch of fabric in her hand, a thought to deliver to Alex in graphics or Cynthia in Climate Revolution. But the first floor is where your dress will be made if you are a Vivienne Westwood couture bride or attending the Academy Awards in one of her creations. 'These people are gigantically talented and just so, so good at what they do,' says Vivienne. 'Real artists – Alex Krenn too – a genius, and Brigitte and the fabric buyers and jewellery and shoes – we are so lucky to have been able to recruit so many wonderful people over the years.'

They say one sign of a happy company is the state of its canteen. The Vivienne Westwood building, being a fashion house, has a kitchen largely denuded of food, but it's pristine, chat-filled and dotted, like many of the corridors, with a complicated array of recycle bins. The first floor houses too the company's human resources staff and accountants, and also Ben Westwood, who runs the Worlds End website from here. There is no regular day for Vivienne, but today she goes straight to Climate Revolution, as is her wont, to check in on the response to her press conference about Ecocide, and to input text for her blog. 'I think I've got to tell you what I mainly do in the company. I do Climate Revolution, that's me, and Cynthia. The ideas, the whole thing, you know. And Joe, of course, our computer graphics genius; he operates the site but is also very involved intellectually with the content.'

The second floor at Elcho Street is more crowded and is awash with colour and artwork. There may be no sewing machines here, but there are cutting tables and the 50-per-cent-size mannequins on which Vivienne has always designed, and there is the team who head Red Label and Anglomania and MAN. Various special projects come and go here as well: today, the Vienna Opera New Year's Day concert dresses and the sharp uniforms Vivienne and Andreas and Gail are designing for Virgin Airways. This is Mark Spye's kingdom. Alex Krenn is based here too, designing graphics and images and patterns for Vivienne Westwood fabrics and the items – ties, scarves, handbags – that might use them. The third floor has corner offices for Carlo and Christopher Di Pietro and between them are the ranks of marketing and social media folk who fret at screens with the air of a stock exchange. But even here, there is design. Shoes and bags, belts and accessories, the vital world of Vivienne Westwood jewellery, with refreshed ranges every season and constant reworkings of the iconic orb logo, which also adorns the perfumes that are licensed from this office too. Vivienne walks in and out, back and forth between the different concerns of her day and her company, head down, not one for small talk, leaving the big speeches come retirements or birthdays to the loquacious Italians and to Andreas.

The glass penthouse at Elcho Street is an oasis of calm atop the whirring sewing machines and loud Italian laughter on the floors below. Andreas works at McLaren's old army surplus desk, bought for the Oval flat and long pressed into the design business, surrounded by art books and fabric samples. Opposite is Tizer's office, where the phone rings constantly. 'I am a bit in awe of them still,' says Tizer, 'in

Sewing at Elcho Street, 2014: Gold Label, wedding dresses, Red Carpet.

awe, that is, that two such talented individuals are married and work together so closely. I am always enchanted to watch two people who adore one another, and I'm ever so privileged to feel the intensely personal connection they have with each other. It's very real. And very rare.' Tizer's love for both her 'bosses' is palpable, and long-standing. She met Vivienne when she was a seventeen-year-old model employed as the house model in Camden in the days when there were only nine people working there. 'I was able to walk in the platform court shoes, which was why the job stuck,' say Tizer with typical self-deprecation, 'though I became a little bit famous [she went down the catwalk topless with Susie Bick, causing another tabloid paper-storm for the House of Westwood].' But it was years later that she and Vivienne became friends, when pregnancy and single motherhood had put her out of work and Vivienne spotted her one day in old clothes and holed shoes and took her to the Davies Street store to kit her out. 'I walked away with bags of beautiful clobber, but of greater value at the time: a warmed heart. I will never ever forget that generosity – how much it meant to me.' Every day, Tizer tells me, Vivienne tries to respond first not to the agenda of the brand and the business, but to her causes. Leonard Peltier and Bradley Manning get her regular contact first, as well as her campaigning zeal. She will be unable to visit them in prison the way she regularly did Louie McManus (whose fondest memories of prison life, perforce, were the frequent visits of Dame Vivienne Westwood in full couture at Wormwood Scrubs). Next she attends to Climate Revolution, Cool Earth, to Liberty, Reprieve and so on. Vivienne also responds swiftly to specific requests and invitations for press events related to her causes: today, for instance, a press conference about the campaign to have ecocide –the deliberate endangering of the ecosystem – recognized as an international crime. Next her time is taken up with the myriad decisions of design. Collections at differing stages of creation, from pattern doodles to fabric choices, to cuttings and fittings. Mainly, decisions and samples are brought to Vivienne in the studio. Sometimes, it can feel very Coco Chanel. Mainly, it feels like the HQ of a radical student magazine.

Here's how it works. Vivienne may draw something in the studio after a lunch of salad she has brought in – a detail, a line, a doodle. She and Andreas will collect images and pictures and stick them onto a window in the penthouse: Edwardian corsets, medieval manuscript, Brigitte Bardot. Vivienne has a half-size dummy at her side. She drapes calico, cuts and pins and allows shapes to evolve as a sculptor might, in three dimensions. There is a constant flow in and out of swatches of fabric, some the size of postcards, some cut from the whole length of the roll. These are chosen, or not chosen, to make up the designs, full size, after the calico originals. The calicoes themselves have been made with Andreas or Vivienne, Iris, Brigitte, Mark or Murray in attendance, and the designs are then rendered in two dimensions by pattern cutters. The collections are usually a combination of classical tailoring, like suiting, jackets, trousers, skirts and historical-influenced garments, and then also experimental pattern cutting, working with basic geometrical shapes and coming to new results. It's a long and continuous chain of decision-making, small steps which build little by little into a direction and theme and a design that ultimately Vivienne and Andreas will tweak, assess and accept.

'I have various ambitions at the moment, in design terms,' Vivienne tells me. 'Worlds End: I love that shop and I love that concept and I want to build that up again. I like the recycling of classics and direct selling – back to basics. I like reusing surplus fabrics and not wasting – that's so important. I even sell toiles at Worlds End and even Gold Label things that haven't worked elsewhere, maybe remade in less lavish fabrics. I want Worlds End to be more than a place for fashion pilgrims; I want people to bring their mums there for something utterly chic and unique. That's today's plan!'

Up in the studio, there is a call from the Lady in Waiting to the Duchess of Cornwall, who will be wearing a Vivienne Westwood creation to a gala event, and an enquiry from Julia Roberts' stylist, put through to Brigitte, about remaking a Red Carpet dress in her favoured petrol blue, for the Oscars. It's a busy time of year. Lily Cole arrives for a fitting for the dress she will wear to open the new Red Label collection. Usually, special fittings take place at Conduit Street. Friends of Vivienne's who wear her special creations sometimes come to Elcho Street - Tracey Emin, for instance, or later today, the opera singer Joyce DiDonato.

'I met Vivienne first when I was making a documentary,' Joyce tells me when she arrives. 'It was one of the most stimulating hours of my life, and utterly fascinating! I'll never forget at the end of our interview, the cameras had been turned off, and she took a pair of scissors into her hands to show me how she first came up with the pattern for the corset that was to be the foundation of my dress. It was watching a true artist reach back into her roots and I felt it was a magical moment.' Vivienne frequently offers to design dresses for friends and women she admires. I saw her do this at a literary event with Carol Ann Duffy, the Poet Laureate, while Noreena Hertz, the radical economist, was approached by Vivienne after a Royal Society Lecture, they became friends and Vivienne made her wedding dress when she married BBC supremo Danny Cohen. For Vivienne, making the political personal is sometimes a return to where it all began: making clothes for girlfriends.

The end of the day is sometimes dictated by the fading light in the studio. Vivienne and Andreas often work late in the weeks coming up to collections, but during other months are as likely to leave at six if Tizer has a ballet ticket for them stuck in the diary, or if there is a function or opening. Once a week Vivienne goes to yoga: 'It's the best tip I could give anybody: do yoga!' Mostly, Vivienne's idea of luxury is an evening at home with a book.

'Vivienne cooks,' Andreas tells me, 'and we have got Elia from Chile who cleans and also cooks a couple of times a week, which makes a big difference because we can go home and we can sit down at a table and eat and talk instead of spending another hour cooking. I like cooking, but she's better. Mind you, one thing always annoys me – it's never all ready at the same time. Coordination, she can't do that.'

'That's not fair,' chimes in Vivienne, 'it's because I am always rushing.'

'Vivienne still loves designing more than anything,' says Andreas, 'but now she's driven by these other needs. She was always very environmentally conscious, but to be this actively engaged in the politics of climate change these last years, our collaboration allows her to do that. It's what, at the end of the day, we give each other.'

Vivienne doesn't watch television. Andreas has a little television. right on the top floor for the news. 'We very rarely go to see films,'

Vivienne and Alexandra face the rain at Clapham Old Town, 2000.

Andreas laments. 'We go to concerts and the ballet and the theatre a lot.'

'The theatre is so important,' says Vivienne.

'Our love,' Andreas continues, 'is different now. It's the reverse of what it was in the beginning but in a good way: I held on to her at the beginning for guidance, for ideas, for strength, and now, I hope, she's holding on to me. If she really asks me something, it is with an intensity I need to respond to. And then I have to stop and give her my full attention. That's Vivienne's way. She always did that. She listens like no one else I know.'

Tonight Vivienne is throwing a small party for workmates and friends, a gathering of the troops. A debrief after the Red Label collection for London Fashion Week, I had assumed, or a meal to spur us all on towards the next Paris collection. The Gold Label team are already working regularly till midnight, taking it in turns to cook food. This evening, we all bring a picnic of sorts – it's still very DIY at the House of Westwood. But Vivienne has arranged something unusual: a screening of Steinbeck's *The Grapes of Wrath* in the Doodle Bar by Elcho Street. Most of the team are there. Alex and Georg, Benedikt and Rafael. Cynthia King, formerly Mrs Gordon Swire, is there representing Climate Revolution. Linda Watson the *Vogue* fashion writer is there, and Ben Westwood and Tomoka, Sara Stockbridge and her new husband, just back from honeymoon. Louie, too, who lives at Thurleigh Court. Friends. Family. The Team.

'It's all about books, actually,' Vivienne gets up to announce, throwing half a smile at me. 'This is what I wanted to say. There's a lot to do, and the work carries on. But I think we should all read more. And not just anything. *The Grapes of Wrath* is very good on monopolies and how they work. It reminds me rather of Arundhati Roy's *Broken Republic*, about the havoc wreaked by monopolies and their support by political rulers in India. Nothing has changed. Our rulers are still our oppressors. The world is still run for cheap labour and private ownership of its bounty. "Pray God someday kind people won't be poor. Pray God someday a kid can eat," as Steinbeck says. This is one of my favourite books, *The Grapes of Wrath*. I've never actually seen the film. It won't be as good as the book. Films never are. They tell you too much, and don't let your imagination work. Like the difference between a painting and photograph, really. You can only live it, I think, if you read it. I've led so many lives. And they've been great. And are great. But most of the lives I've lived I lived through reading. Richer than my own life. You only live once if you don't read. If you read books, you can live a hundred lives. More. So. There it is.' And she takes her seat.

The lights dim, and the screen flickers into its sepia story. The dust bowl. The preacher man. The ex-con, Henry Fonda, rescuing his family – and himself along the way – on an odyssey across the American West. Towards a Utopia that does not exist. It's sentimental in its way, and dated, of course; a little theatrical. But it shocks still to see the American Depression on film: another America, the curdled dream. Vivienne is sitting next to me, her attention rapt, but serious. She doesn't laugh at the comedy grandpa. But then she knows he is going to die. She doesn't flinch at the violence, even though the death of the preacher who has lost his faith in God is harshly realistic. But then Fonda has to leave his mother. Ma Joad thinks she will never see him again, and he tells her, carefully and hopelessly, that she will see him in every angry man, and every fighter for justice, every raised fist. Vivienne, the woman who told me she learned with McLaren never to cry again, blinks and stares forward.

'Being a woman is different,' Ma Joad explains in the closing moments of the film. 'Man: he lives in jerks,' she says, 'baby born and a man dies, an' that's a jerk – gets a farm, an' loses his farm, and that's a jerk.' But women are different. They continue on in spite of everything: 'Woman: it's all one flow, like a stream, little eddies, little waterfalls, but the river, it just goes right on. Woman looks at it like that,' she says.

'My continuity is what I think and what I read,' Vivienne tells me late that night, 'and I only judge myself by recognizing that something is new to me. A new idea. That makes me happy. *Cogito, ergo sum.* I think, therefore I am. That is my, you know, "sum it up". My identity is there. And that's all I know, that's the only way I know myself. I'm not interested in the "self" as such, and I don't think I'm unusual in that. I see everything from outside. I do know we can come to some

sort of enlightenment through being interested in self, but I don't do that at all. I just can't. I'm not interested in things for myself. I am not materialistic. Ideas make me happy – and making things, I suppose, making beauty out of ideas. But the ideas are more important, and increasingly, of course, the ideas are huge: the end of humanity. I think of my family a lot. And my friends. I do want to say, as well, and it's a sort of apology, with regards to the people I love, that I know I am *difficult*. I am not an easy person or an ordinary person – my life is not an ordinary life. I don't have time to see my friends or, you know, go and make jam or just ordinary things, you know, that grandmothers do. And sometimes I wish I did. And I do think it is to do with me always thinking, "I will try and solve this thing." I think it's to do with that, more than anything else. But at the same time, this instinct made me who I am. I get myself into situations.

'The best guide for living, Ian? That would be *The Adventures of Pinocchio*. It's a philosophy of life. A way to live. So naughty. So wild. But he's got a heart of gold. And that, of course, that's what saves him. Andreas left before me for work this morning and he said, "I'm in a bad mood." So I asked why and he said, "There's just too much to do." So I said, "You have to do one thing at a time, yes. But don't forget, in between, we are getting things done, step by step. We'll get there."

Vivienne on the 'We Need to Talk About Fracking' tour, June 2014.

CHRONOLOGY
A LIFE IN FASHION AND ACTIVISM

1979	Shop name is changed to Worlds End
Mar 1981	Pirates collection (autumn / winter 1981)
Oct 1981	Savage collection (spring / summer 1982)
1981	McLaren and Vivienne split. Their business partnership continues
Mar 1982	Nostalgia of Mud (Buffalo) collection (autumn / winter 1982)
Oct 1982	Punkature collection (spring / summer 1983)
	Vivienne opens second shop, Nostalgia of Mud
1982	Vivienne meets Carlo D'Amario
Mar 1983	Witches collection (autumn / winter 1983)
Oct 1983	Hypnos collection (spring / summer 1984)
	Westwood / McLaren partnership ends
	Vivienne moves to Italy
1983	Vivienne is asked to be part of Best Five (Western designers) along with Calvin Klein, Claude Montana, Gianfranco Ferré and Hanae Mori, in Tokyo
Mar 1984	Clint Eastwood collection (autumn / winter 1984)
1984	Collaboration with McLaren formally ended
	Deal agreed with Giorgio Armani
Oct 1985	Mini Crini collection (spring / summer 1986)
1985	Vivienne's father, Gordon Swire, dies
1986	Carlo D'Amario appointed as managing director of Vivienne Westwood
	Vivienne returns full time to London and reopens Worlds End
Mar 1987	Harris Tweed collection (autumn / winter 1987)
Oct 1987	Pagan I collection (spring / summer 1988) – Britain Must Go Pagan series
Mar 1988	Time Machine collection (autumn / winter 1988)
Oct 1988	Civilizade collection (spring / summer 1989)
Mar 1989	Voyage to Cythera collection (autumn / winter 1989)
Oct 1989	Pagan V collection (spring / summer 1990)
1989	Vivienne meets Andreas Kronthaler while teaching at Vienna Academy
Mar 1990	Portrait collection (autumn / winter 1990)
Oct 1990	Cut, Slash and Pull collection (spring / summer 1991)
1990	Vivienne named Designer of the Year at the British Fashion Council awards
	First complete menswear show in Pitti Uomo in Florence
Mar 1991	Dressing Up collection (autumn / winter 1991)
Oct 1991	Salon collection (spring / summer 1992)
1991	Vivienne awarded Designer of the Year for a second time by the British Fashion Council

Mar 1992   Always On Camera collection (autumn / winter 1992)
Oct 1992   Grand Hotel collection (spring / summer 1993)
1992   Vivienne Westwood is made an Honorary Senior Fellow of the
               Royal College of Art
           Vivienne Westwood awarded OBE
           She introduces wedding gowns to her spring / summer range
Mar 1993   Anglomania collection (autumn / winter 1993)
Oct 1993   Café Society collection (spring / summer 1994)
1993   Vivienne marries Andreas Kronthaler
           She creates her own tartan, Westwood MacAndreas. Lochcarron
               of Scotland officially recognizes the clan, a process that normally
               takes 200 years
           Red Label launched
Mar 1994   On Liberty collection (autumn / winter 1994)
Oct 1994   Erotic Zones collection (spring / summer 1995)
1994   Vivienne Westwood wins the first Institute of Contemporary Arts
               Award for outstanding contribution to contemporary culture
Mar 1995   Vive la Cocotte collection (autumn / winter 1995)
Oct 1995   Les Femmes collection (spring / summer 1996)
1995   Vivienne Westwood company moves to Elcho Street, Battersea
Mar 1996   Storm in a Teacup collection (autumn / winter 1996)
Oct 1996   Vive la Bagatelle collection (spring / summer 1997)
1996   Vivienne Westwood MAN label is launched
Mar 1997   Five Centuries Ago collection (autumn / winter 1997)
Oct 1997   Tied to the Mast collection (spring / summer 1998)
Mar 1998   Dressed to Scale collection (autumn / winter 1998)
Oct 1998   La Belle Helene collection (spring / summer 1999)
1998   Vivienne Westwood Limited is awarded the Queen's Award for
               Export
           Anglomania label launched
Mar 1999   Showroom collection (autumn / winter 1999)
Oct 1999   Summertime collection (spring / summer 2000)
1999   Opening of first US store on Greene Street, New York
Mar 2000   Winter collection (autumn / winter 2000)
Oct 2000   Exploration collection (spring / summer 2001)
Mar 2001   Wild Beauty collection (autumn / winter 2001)
Oct 2001   Nymphs collection (spring / summer 2002)
2001   Collaboration with Wedgwood
Mar 2002   Anglophilia collection (autumn / winter 2002)
Oct 2002   Street Theatre collection (spring / summer 2003)
Mar 2003   Le Flou Taillé collection (autumn / winter 2003)

Oct 2003 Blue Sky collection (spring / summer 2004)

Mar 2004 Exhibition collection (autumn / winter 2004)

Oct 2004 Ultra Femininity collection (spring / summer 2005)

2004 The Victoria and Albert Museum hosts a Vivienne Westwood retrospective exhibition to celebrate thirty-four years in fashion – the largest exhibition ever for a living British fashion designer

Vivienne Westwood is awarded the Women's World Fashion Award by former president Mikhail Gorbachev in Hamburg

Mar 2005 Propaganda collection (autumn / winter 2005)

Oct 2005 Active Resistance collection (spring / summer 2006)

Mar 2006 Innocent collection (autumn / winter 2006)

Oct 2006 I am Expensiv collection (spring / summer 2007)

2006 Vivienne Westwood is made a Dame in the Queen's New Year's Honours list

Mar 2007 Wake Up Cave Girl collection (autumn / winter 2007)

Oct 2007 '56' collection (spring / summer 2008)

2007 Vivienne Westwood is awarded Outstanding Achievement in Fashion at the British Fashion Awards in London

Mar 2008 Chaos Point collection (autumn / winter 2008)

Oct 2008 Do It Yourself collection (spring / summer 2009)

2008 Vivienne Westwood receives a distinction from the Royal College of Art for her services to fashion

Dora Swire, née Ball, Vivienne's mother, dies

Mar 2009 +5° collection (autumn / winter 2009)

Oct 2009 Get A Life collection (spring / summer 2010)

Mar 2010 Prince Charming collection (autumn / winter 2010)

Oct 2010 Gaia The Only One collection (spring / summer 2011)

2010 International Trade Centre (United Nations) collaboration to create the Ethical Fashion Initiative in Kenya, producing handbags

Vivienne Westwood receives special commendation from Prince Philip at the 2010 Prince Philip Designers Prize in November

Malcolm McLaren dies

Mar 2011 World Wide Woman collection (autumn / winter 2011)

Oct 2011 War and Peace collection (spring / summer 2012)

2011 Collaboration with Comic Relief to produce T-shirts for Red Nose Day

Vivienne Westwood joins forces with *Marie Claire* International and works with them to produce a rainforest supplement to be printed in over twenty-seven editions of *Marie Claire* worldwide. A T-shirt is also produced and sold in conjunction with People Tree to raise money for indigenous tribes within the rainforest

	Vivienne Westwood becomes the patron of Reprieve – a human rights charity organization
	She begins campaigning for environmental charity Cool Earth
Mar 2012	London collection (autumn / winter 2012)
Oct 2012	Climate Revolution collection (spring / summer 2013)
2012	Vivienne Westwood unfurls the Climate Revolution banner at the London 2012 Paralympics closing ceremony to announce her environmental agenda
	She gives £1 million to rainforest charity Cool Earth
Mar 2013	Save the Arctic collection (autumn / winter 2013)
Oct 2013	Everything is Connected collection (spring / summer 2014)
2013	Vivienne Westwood collaborates with the English National Ballet on their rebranding campaign
	She designs and launches the official Save the Arctic campaign logo to stop drilling and industrial fishing in the area
	The Metropolitan Museum of Art, New York, opens annual fashion exhibition entitled 'Chaos to Couture' which displays over twenty pieces of Vivienne Westwood's work from the 1970s to today. The exhibition marks punk's influence on the history of fashion
	Vivienne Westwood redesigns Virgin Atlantic's new uniform as part of a ten-year long-term partnership
Mar 2014	Save the Rainforest collection (autumn / winter 2014)
Oct 2014	End Ecocide collection (spring / summer 2015)
2014	Vivienne publishes her authorized biography, written with Ian Kelly
Mar 2015	Unisex collection (autumn / winter 2015)
2015	Vivienne receives a lifetime achievement award from SCAD Museum of Art and launches her Politicians R Criminals Campaign
	Vivienne and Greenpeace launch the Save the Arctic Campaign at Waterloo station in London

Continuing Work & News

climaterevolution.co.uk

350.org
amnesty.org.uk
coolearth.org
ejfoundation.org
facebook.com/jointheclimaterevolution
foe.co.uk
greenpeace.org.uk

liberty-human-rights.org.uk
monbiot.com
talkfracking.org
thebrooke.org
twitter.com/climate_rev
viviennewestwood.com
worldsendshop.co.uk

ACKNOWLEDGEMENTS

This book is the product of the many hours Vivienne and I have spent together in the last years and our conversations, mainly taped, during that period, along with interviews conducted with her family, friends and colleagues. First thanks therefore must go to all of them, and in particular to the main men in Vivienne's life: Andreas, Ben, Joe and her brother, Gordon, for their time, patience, warm reminiscences and toleration of the literary invasion of their lives.

Some elements of the book are also based on a manuscript, part typed, part handwritten, that Vivienne began with Gary Ness and has added to from time to time ever since; it resides with her papers in Clapham and Elcho Street.

The book would not have happened without the original impetus of Christopher Di Pietro, Carlo D'Amario and Ivan Mulcahy, and I owe a debt of gratitude too to the work and research of Matteo Guarnaccia. All of them have shown a faith in me as well as an affection for Vivienne that is reflected, I hope, in this work.

The collaboration of friends and family and the many whose lives have been touched by Vivienne around the world would never have been possible without the support and warm efficiency of Vivienne and Andreas's personal assistant, Tizer Bailey, to whom Vivienne and I therefore owe thanks beyond measure. I would like to acknowledge my gratitude to HRH the Prince of Wales for permission to quote from private correspondence between himself and Dame Vivienne Westwood, and to Dr Grahame Davies, Assistant Private Secretary to TRH the Prince of Wales and Duchess of Cornwall, for all kind assistance.

The whole team at Vivienne Westwood in London and in Paris and

Italy, especially all involved in the Gold Label collection spring / summer 2014, warrant our warmest thanks, in particular Maiwenn Le Gall and the Maiwenn Models casting agency, Kiko Gaspar, Rafael Gomes and Ajuma. The detailed input of Vivienne's long-standing creative collaborators Mark Spye, Murray Blewett, Alex Krenn and Brigitte Stepputtis has saved me from many fashion and historical errors; the ones that remain are my own. To all, my thanks, and also to my hosts who made the Parisian chapter possible: Jean and Françoise Pepin-Lehalleur, and Dominique Lapierre.

Of those who donated time and attention in terms of taped interviews or guidance on sources, or who sent personal letters or emails, I would like to thank especially Gene Krell of *Vogue* Japan and Claire Wilcox and Kate Bethune at the Victoria & Albert Museum, whose support and wise counsel on this project were invaluable, as was also the entire 'Vivienne Westwood' V&A cuttings archive which was loaned to me for the purposes of researching this book.

Vivienne and I would like to express our thanks to the many who gave time for recorded interviews, or who emailed or wrote: Pamela Anderson, Julian Assange, Rosita Cataldi, Naomi Campbell, Shami Chakrabarti, Lily Cole, Cora Corré, Joe Corré (thanks also to his assistant Carmen Christensen), Sharon Dechi Palmo, Joyce DiDonato, Terry and Louise Doktor, Tracey Emin, Renée Fleming, Bella Freud, Francine Galea, Bob Geldof, Jerry Hall, Debbie Harry, Noreena Hertz, Andy Hulme, Paola Iacopucci, Neneh Jalloh, Cynthia King, Teddy Kronthaler, Angie Kurdash, Sharon Lishman, Daniel Lismore, Sam McKnight, Louie McManus, Giselle Menhenett, Kate Moss, Matthew Owen, Sarah Jessica Parker, Leonard Peltier, Serena Rees, Lisa Reynolds at Worlds End, Philip Salon, Iris Steidle, Susan Sutton, Gordon Swire, Olga Watts and Ben Westwood. I would like to thank separately Robert Pinnock, for his time and also his photos, and also Sara Stockbridge for her key insights and warm positivity on this project. Past and present colleagues at Vivienne Westwood who gave further advice and input include Cristiana Benini, Marta Grande, Giordano Capuano, Francis Lowe, Giuseppe Aragoni, Victoria Archer, Nuria Gavalda, Andrea Austoni, Benedikt Sittler and Giorgio Ravasio: to all, my thanks, but especially to Laura McCuaig, Roberta Minaldo,

Jessica Moloney, Jessica Evans and Michael Pegrum and all the press and marketing teams: you have made me feel very welcome and made a tough job look fun, and indeed stylish. I would also like to thank Janet Chan for Chinese translations and explanations, Peppe Lorefice for Italian translations, and Ingrid Waasenaar for correcting my French, as ever.

Of those whose previous studies have pointed me in helpful directions, I should acknowledge the work of Claire Wilcox, Aileen Ribeiro, Anne Hollander, Jon Savage, Paul Gorman, Robert O'Byrne, Linda Watson, Ian Macleay, Deborah Orr, Alix Sharkey and Jean-Marie and Letmiya Sztalryd – who graciously allowed me to quote from their film – and also Jane Mulvagh. Thanks too to Denise Elsdon, Judith Woods and Maisie Hulbert, and the team at Alphabet Transcription Services. For more general thanks in terms of accommodation, guidance, encouragement and friendship on this project I would like to thank Philip Hoare, the late Sebastian Horsley, Don Krim and David T. Russell, Andy and Louise Chater, Lisa Darr and Brian Valente in Los Angeles, Lisa Hilton, Jane Willacy, Fleur Britten, Lindsey Clay, Matthew White and Elia Pinaud, Victor Wynd and the Last Tuesday Society in London and Gary Rowland and Olivia Pomp, Stephanie Cohen, Lauren Crowe, Janie Jenkins, Marilynn Scott Murphy, Dan Crowe, Heston Blumenthal and Suzanne Pirret, Erica Wagner, Samantha Conti, Eric Akoto and Steve Hindle, along with all the staff of the Huntington Library, Pasadena, California, and Rosie Apponyi and all at Brody House in Budapest.

At Picador Pan Macmillan in London I would like to thank Paul Baggaley for his faith in this project and his friendship, and likewise Kris Doyle for his dedicated hard work on text and images, along with Laura Carr, Dusty Miller and all the Picador team. I would like to thank Clare Skeats for designing the book, and Joe and Beata De Campos and Alex Krenn at Vivienne Westwood for their invaluable contribution to these beautiful designs and layouts. Ben Westwood and Juergen Teller deserve special thanks and admiration for internal and cover photography respectively.

The following people contributed photographs from their archives or otherwise helped with sourcing and supplying the images in this book; I would like to offer grateful thanks to them: Daniel Picado, Miguel Domingos, Ugo Camera, Juana Burga, Martina Kobesova at Elite Model Management London, Bob Gruen, Sarah Field, Jamie Reid, John Marchant at Isis Gallery, Dennis Morris, Isabelle Chalard, Robert Pinnock, Andy Gotts and Ki Price.

Personally and singly I must thank Vivienne and Andreas Kronthaler. Their instinctive sense of privacy was put to one side in a joint project they did not originate but which has graced me with their friendship, wisdom and kindness. Vivienne's trust in me as writer and friend has been humbling and has challenged me to write something without guile or cynicism in a reflection, I hope, of her spirit and Andreas's.

Last thanks, as ever, I would wish to go to Claire and my immediate family and friends who have graciously borne all absences, actual or mental, and to Michael Codron and Richard Eyre and also George Gibson at Bloomsbury, New York, who have borne my absence from our quite separate projects as a result of this book, and especially to my two children, Oscar and Celia, who have borne all of the above, but have also borne me turning up at the school gates in complete Vivienne Westwood 'MAN' (loaned).

PICTURE ACKNOWLEDGEMENTS

© Vivienne Westwood Limited: 8, 16, 24 (top), 35, 40, 64, 83, 88, 102, 148, 149, 154, 162, 214, 230, 234–5, 244, 251, 260, 267, 278–9, 285, 288, 307, 312–13, 320, 324, 331, 348, 352, 359, 376, 380, 387, 392, 404, 461, 464

Courtesy Vivienne Westwood Archive: 37, 43, 46, 51, 56, 61, 68, 71, 75, 78, 122, 132, 137, 179, 181, 182, 187, 227, 233, 238, 254, 270, 291, 294, 300, 309, 342, 369, 397, 398

© Ben Westwood: 24 (bottom), 118, 222, 256, 275, 282, 372, 409, 412

Courtesy Ben Westwood Archive: 91, 94, 98, 108, 127, 217, 365

© Robert Pinnock: 316, 317, 333, 337, 339, 357

© David Parkinson: 115, 142

© Barry Plummer: 192, 204–5

Photo by Daniel Picado: 13

Photo by Miguel Domingos: 29

Photo by Ugo Camera: 32

© REX / David Dagley: 159

© Alain Dister: 167

© Bettmann / CORBIS: 171

Photo © Bob Gruen / www.bobgruen.com: 173

Jamie Reid, courtesy Isis Gallery UK. Copyright © Sex Pistols Residuals: 176

© Hulton-Deutsch Collection / CORBIS: 197

© Dennis Morris – all rights reserved – www.dennismorris.com: 201

Michael Roberts / Tatler © The Condé Nast Publications Ltd.: 211

Photo by Karl Lagerfeld, courtesy Vivienne Westwood Archive: 345

Photo by Cindy Palmano, courtesy Vivienne Westwood Archive: 362

© Andy Gotts MBE 2014: 400

Photo by Kri Price Photography: 416

© Sam Chick: 459

NOTES ON SOURCES

Most of Vivienne's words are taken from interviews recorded in 2013 and 2014 at Elcho Street, Battersea, Clapham Old Town and in Paris. Other interviews, emails, letters and conversations are noted by initial:

AK Andreas Kronthaler	LM Louie McManus
BF Bella Freud	LP Leonard Peltier
BG Bob Geldof	MB Murray Blewett
BS Brigitte Stepputtis	MM Malcolm McLaren
BW Ben Westwood	MO Matthew Owen
CC Cora Corré	MS Mark Spye
CD'A Carlo D'Amario	NC Naomi Campbell
CDiP Christopher Di Pietro	PA Pamela Anderson
CK Cynthia King	PoW Prince of Wales
DH Debbie Harry	RC / PI Rosita Cataldi & Paola Iacopucci
FG Francine Galea	RP Robert Pinnock
GK Gene Krell	SC Shami Chakrabarti
GS Gordon Swire	SL Sharon Lishman
JA Julian Assange	SR Serena Rees
JC Joe Corré	SS Sara Stockbridge
JD Joyce DiDonato	TB Tizer Bailey
JH Jerry Hall	TD / LD Terry & Louise Doktor
LC Lily Cole	TE Tracey Emin

Manuscripts, Press Cuttings and Vivienne Westwood Personal Archive
Tizer Bailey (PA to Dame Vivienne Westwood), Vivienne Westwood personal archive, including:
Guarnaccia, Matteo, 'Vivienne Westwood', unpublished manuscript, Italy, 2007
Swire, Dora, manuscript note, April 1941: birth announcement
Westwood, Vivienne, *Active Resistance: The Manifesto*, privately published by The Vivienne Westwood Group, 2002; together with manuscript notes

Westwood, Vivienne, 'Alice and Pinocchio', unpublished drama adapted by VW from her manifesto 'Active Resistance' for live reading / performance

Westwood, Vivienne, 'My Life', fifty-page manuscript (birth to early 1980s – incomplete draft prepared with Gary Ness, multiple handwritten insertions and addenda)

Westwood, Vivienne, essay on 'Style' – notes for article planned for *Venti Quatro Ore*, November 1992

British Library

McLaren, M., 'Sex Pistols on Stage, or London's Outrage', manuscript, collage, McLaren, M., ed., Rough Trade Records, BL Manuscripts YD.2005. b860, 1977

Victoria and Albert Museum Fashion Archive: Vivienne Westwood:

Cuttings file including articles from *Blitz* magazine, *Daily Mail*, *Daily Telegraph*, *Elle* magazine, *ES Magazine*, *The European*, *Express*, *The Face*, *Guardian*, *Harper's Bazaar*, *i-D* magazine, *Independent*, *Independent on Sunday*, *International Herald Tribune*, *Liberation*, *London Evening Standard*, *Mail on Sunday*, *Marie Claire*, *Ms London* magazine, *New York Times*, *New York Times Fashion Magazine*, *Observer*, *Sunday Express*, *Sunday Telegraph*, *Sunday Times*, *The Times*, *Vogue* (US, UK, Italian and French editions), *Vogue l'Uomo*, *Women's Wear Daily* and *W* magazine. Also Brenda Polan interviewing VW in *Tatler*, August 1992; Jane Mulvagh in the *Spectator*, Vol. 281, issue 8878, 1998, pp.46–47

Multimedia

Any Questions, BBC Radio 4 (panel includes Michael Portillo, Ken Livingstone and VW), 8 January 2011

Arena, BBC2, August 1995

'Do it Yourself' written by Jean-Marie Sztalryd, dir. Letmiya Sztalryd, Arte Films (Film documentary – a year in the life of Vivienne Westwood, 2010. Unreleased as of 2013)

The Filth and the Fury, A Sex Pistols Film, dir. Julien Temple, 2000

The Great Rock 'n' Roll Swindle, dir. Julien Temple, 1980

Painted Ladies, written and presented by Vivienne Westwood, Channel 4, 1996

Tommy Roberts interviewed by Anna Dyke, BL REF C1046/12A, section 2, track 29

South Bank Show, ITV, March 1990

Vivienne Westwood, Audio Tour, V&A Exhibition, 21 October 2004 (V&A transcript)

climaterevolution.co.uk
viviennewestwood.com
worldsendshop.co.uk
activeresistance.co.uk/ar/?p=1690
activeresistance.co.uk/ar/?s=painted+ladies
youtube.com/watch?v=BK70-kkz4Pg (*Drama Queens*, with Joyce DiDonato)

Select Bibliography

Arnold, Matthew, *Culture and Anarchy, An Essay in Political and Social Criticism*, London 1893

Bell, Eugenia (ed.) (introd. by Andrew Bolton), *Punk: Chaos to Couture*, exhibition catalogue, New York Metropolitan Museum of Art, 2013

Bloom, H. (ed.), *John Steinbeck's The Grapes of Wrath*, Chelsea House Publishing, New York 2007

Breward, Christopher, Conekin, Becky, and Cox, Caroline (eds.), *The Englishness of English Dress*, Berg, Oxford and New York 2002

Bromberg, Craig, *The Wicked Ways of Malcolm McLaren*, Omnibus, London 1991

Burchill, Julie, and Parsons, Tony, *The Boy Looked at Jonny: The Obituary of Rock and Roll*, Faber and Faber, London (reissue, 1987)

Chomsky, Noam, *Media Control: The Spectacular Achievements of Propaganda*, 2nd edition, Open Media Books, New York 2006

Clark, T.J., *The Painting of Modern Life: Paris in the Art of Manet and his Followers*, Thames and Hudson, London 1984

Colegrave, Stephen, and Sullivan, Chris, *Punk: A Life Apart*, Cassell, London 2001

Connolly, Sean, *Vivienne Westwood*, Heinemann Library, Oxford 2002

de la Haye, Amy (ed.), *The Cutting Edge: 50 Years of British Fashion 1947–1997*, exhibition catalogue, V&A Publications, London, 1996

Gorman, Paul (foreword by Malcolm McLaren), *The Look: Adventures in Rock and Pop Fashion*, Sanctuary Publishing, London and New York 2001. Revised second edition, Adelita, London 2006

Holden, Jack, *A Very Special School: Glossop Grammar School 1901–1965*, Teckno, Glossop 1994

Hollander, Anne, *Seeing Through Clothes*, University of California Press, Berkeley 1993

Kilfoyle, Mark (ed.), *Vivienne Westwood, A London Fashion: The Collection of Romilly McAlpine* (exhibition catalogue), Museum of London, Philip Wilson Publishers, London 2000

Krell, Gene, *Vivienne Westwood*, Universe / Vendome, New York and Paris 1997

Laver, James, *Style in Costume*, Oxford University Press, London and New York 1949

Lovelock, James, *The Revenge of Gaia: Why the Earth is Fighting Back and How We Can Still Save Humanity*, Allen Lane, London and New York 2006

McDermott, Catherine, *Vivienne Westwood*, Carlton, London 1999

MacInnes, Colin, *Absolute Beginners*, Allison & Busby, London 2011 (first published 1959)

Macleay, Ian, *Malcolm McLaren: The Sex Pistols, the Anarchy, the Art, the Genius*, John Blake, London 2011

Mulvagh, Jane, *Vivienne Westwood, An Unfashionable Life*, HarperCollins, London 1998

O'Byrne, Robert, with Worsley-Taylor, Annette (consultant), *Style City: How London Became a Fashion Capital*, Frances Lincoln Publishers, London 2009

Rayner, Geoffrey, Chamberlain, Richard, and Stapleton, Annamarie (eds.), *Pop! Design, Culture, Fashion 1956-1976*, ACC Editions, London 2012

Ribeiro, Aileen, *Dress and Morality*, Berg, Oxford 2003

Ribeiro, Aileen, *Fashion in the French Revolution*, Batsford, London 1988

Robb, John, and Craske, Oliver (eds.), *Punk Rock: An Oral History*, Ebury, London 2006

Savage, Jon, *England's Dreaming: Sex Pistols and Punk Rock*, Faber and Faber, London 2005 (originally published 1991)

Scapp, Ron, and Seitz, Brian (eds.), *Fashion Statements: On Style, Appearance and Reality*, Palgrave Macmillan, New York 2010

Sheridan, Jayne, *Fashion, Media, Promotion: The New Black Magic*, Wiley-Blackwell, Oxford 2010

Simon, Marie (epilogue by Vivienne Westwood), *Fashion in Art: The Second Empire and Impressionism*, Zwemmer, London 1995

Sladen, Christopher, *The Conscription of Fashion: Utility Cloth, Clothing and Footwear 1941-1952*, Scolar Press, London 1995

Steele, Valerie, *Women of Fashion: Twentieth-Century Designers*, Rizzoli, New York 1991

Steinbeck, John, *The Grapes of Wrath*, Penguin Modern Classics edition, London and New York 1992 (originally pub. 1939)

Stern, Jane and Michael, *Sixties People*, Knopf, New York 1990

Stewart, Tony (ed.), *Cool Cats - 25 Years of Rock 'n' Roll Style*, Eel Pie Publishing, London 1981

Taylor, Paul, *Impresario: Malcolm McLaren and the British New Wave*, New Museum of Contemporary Art, MIT Press, New York 1988

Teller, Juergen, *Election Day*, Steidl, Göttingen 2009 (distrib. Thames & Hudson in UK)

Townsend, Chris, *Rapture: Art's Seduction by Fashion since 1970*, Thames & Hudson, London 2002

Vermorel, Fred, *Fashion and Perversity: A Life of Vivienne Westwood and the Sixties Laid Bare*, Bloomsbury, London 1997

Watson, Linda, *Vogue on Vivienne Westwood*, Quadrille Publishing, London 2012

Wilcox, C., *Vivienne Westwood*, V&A Publications, London 2004

Wooldridge, Max (foreword by Malcolm McLaren), *Rock 'n' Roll London*, New Holland, London 2002

NOTES

EVERYTHING IS CONNECTED

page:

9   **Never dance without a story** VW quoting Nureyev in Kavanagh, J., *Rudolph Nureyev*, Penguin, London 2007, p.317.

10   **the Coco Chanel of our times** Alexander McQueen.

20   **You need to know, this is a great place to be** Christina Nahler to IFK, Paris, September 2013.

20   **We tell a story** AK to IFK, Paris, 27 September 2013.

21   **I adore working with Vivienne** Val Garland to IFK, Paris, 26 September 2013.

21   **all calm and respect** Maiwenn Le Gall to IFK, Paris, 26 September 2013.

22   **She's my biggest supporter in the industry** Ajuma to IFK, Paris, September 2013.

23   **This is the main message** Press release (original), *Everything is Connected*, Paris, 27 September 2013, p.2.

25   **It has to be last minute** AK to IFK, Paris, 27 September 2013.

26   **It's been the way, this last decade** Rafael Gomes to IFK, Paris, 27 September 2013.

26   **I am going to call the show "Everything is Connected"** Press release (original), *Everything is Connected*, Paris, 27 September 2013, p.2.

38   **It's like when you make a collection** *Any Questions*, BBC Radio 4 (panel includes Michael Portillo, Ken Livingstone and VW), 8 January 2011.

39   **"Once upon a time"** 'Alice and Pinocchio' by VW. TB archive.

THE GIRL IN THE UTILITY DRESS

41   **The patterns which life assumes** Putnam, S., *François Rabelais: Man of the Renaissance: A Spiritual Biography*, Jonathan Cape, London 1930, p.140.

41   **It was all about "Do It Yourself"** 'Do It Yourself' (film documentary – a year in the life of Vivienne Westwood), written by Jean-Marie Sztalryd, directed by Letmiya Sztalryd. Arte Films, 2010 (unreleased as of 2014).

47   **My mother was very proud of me** 'Do It Yourself' (film documentary – a year in the life of Vivienne Westwood), written by Jean-Marie Sztalryd, directed by Letmiya Sztalryd. Arte Films, 2010 (unreleased as of 2014).

47   **My mother, Dora Ball, came from the village of Tintwistle** VW manuscript memoir, VW archive.

48   **Dora and my father Gordon were in bliss together all their lives** VW manuscript memoir, VW archive.

48   **It was all about family** VW manuscript memoir, VW archive.

49   **Jelly and blancmange** VW manuscript memoir, VW archive.

50   **We were very free** GS to IFK, 30 October 2013.

53   **When I saw the Crucifixion for the first time** VW manuscript memoir, VW archive.

53   **I was so shocked** VW manuscript memoir, VW archive.

53   **as a child I became very tied emotionally to the love of Jesus** VW manuscript memoir, VW archive.

54   **this sensation of being different** VW manuscript memoir, VW archive.

54   **there was this boy at school** VW manuscript memoir, VW archive.

54   **I went with my daddy far afield over the snow** VW manuscript memoir, VW archive.

55   **Olga followed me around a good deal** VW manuscript memoir, VW archive.

57   **We were encouraged to make, more than read** VW manuscript memoir, VW archive.

59   **I drew and I studied nature and I read** VW manuscript memoir, VW archive.

LET IT ROCK

66   **Everything shifted for me around that age** VW manuscript memoir, VW archive.

66   **We moved from Millbrook** VW manuscript memoir, VW archive.

66   **We were bang in the middle between Hyde and Glossop** VW manuscript memoir, VW archive.

67   **I was still wonderfully silly at fifteen** VW manuscript memoir, VW archive.

67   **And as for shoes – well, it was such an exciting time** VW manuscript memoir, VW archive.

67   **not much exposure to anything one might call "high art"** VW manuscript memoir, VW archive; 'Do It Yourself' (film documentary – a year in the life of Vivienne Westwood), written by Jean-Marie Sztalryd, directed by Letmiya Sztalryd. Arte Films, 2010 (unreleased as of 2014).

69   **Mr Bell, the art teacher, was quite a dramatic presence** VW manuscript memoir, VW archive.

70   **the fundamental rule of law embodied in habeas corpus** SC to IFK, 30 October 2013, quoting Vivienne's letter to Liberty, December 2004.

72   **Everything that has happened subsequently for me . . . I can date to 1958** VW manuscript memoir, VW archive.

72–3 **I suppose they were ambitious . . . so when they saw an opportunity, they took it** GS to IFK, 30 October 2013.

73   **eventually that took us to London** GS to IFK, 30 October 2013.

76   **Meanwhile, I became a "Trad"** VW manuscript memoir, VW archive.

77   **travelling to the museums in South Kensington** VW manuscript memoir, VW archive.

79   **the reason I left that summer** VW manuscript memoir, VW archive.

82   **Because Teddy Boys . . . society was born** Colin Woodhead quoted in Gorman, P., (foreword by Malcolm McLaren), *The Look: Adventures in Rock and Pop Fashion*, Adelita, London 2006, p.25.

84   **grey worsted trousers** Ian Dury quoted in Stewart, T., (ed.) *Cool Cats – 25 Years Of Rock 'n' Roll Style*, Eel Pie Publishing, London 1981.

84–5 **just look at what people like Jack Kerouac** Malcolm McLaren quoted in Gorman, P., 2006, p.22.

85   **sticking-out winkle-pickers** Nik Cohn quoted in Gorman, P., 2006, p.22.

85   **deliberately archaic** Nik Cohn quoted in Gorman, P., 2006, p.22.

87   **Long hair . . . with long fringes** MacInnes, C., *Absolute Beginners*, Allison & Busby, London 2011, p.86.

87   **Trad became corny** Tommy Roberts quoted in Gorman, P., 2006, p.24.

MRS WESTWOOD'S WEDDING DRESS

92   **Derek was an apprentice toolmaker when we met** VW manuscript memoir, VW archive.

92   **I remember Derek was a really good dresser** GS to IFK, 30 October 2013.

96 **I made my wedding dress myself** VW manuscript memoir, VW archive.

100 **For instance, Nigel Waymouth . . . Hapshash and the Coloured Coat**
Rayner, G., et al. (eds.), *Pop! Design, Culture, Fashion 1956-1976*, ACC
Editions, London 2012, p.6-7.

101 **"we were searching for identity"** Malcolm McLaren quoted in
Gorman, P., 2006, p.34.

THE DIRTY-TURQUOISE SKIRT

103 **When I met Malcolm and I fell in love, I thought he was
beautiful** Macleay, I., *Malcolm McLaren, The Sex Pistols, the Anarchy,
the Art, the Genius*, John Blake, London 2011, p.51.

103 **Malcolm was like a small boy, lost in a forest** Funeral of Malcolm
McLaren, DVD, private collection of Joe Corré, 2010.

104 **Mum's credibility is derived originally from punk rock** JC to IFK,
5 December 2013.

106 **The effect of growing up in a family** MM to Ginny Dougray, *The
Times*, quoted in Macleay, p.4.

106 **Rose was a woman who created her own world** Savage, J., *England's
Dreaming, Sex Pistols and Punk Rock*, Faber & Faber, London 2005,
p.15.

107 **No matter what else you might say about Malcolm, he changed
lives** GS to IFK, 30 October 2013.

109 **Just being alongside him you would realize how "possible" the
world is** GS to IFK, 30 October 2013.

109 **Vivienne used to laugh** GS to IFK, 30 October 2013.

109 **His wildly unconventional grandma, whose mottos included,
'To be good is bad'** Macleay, p.ix.

110 **Vivienne met Malcolm through me** GS to IFK, 30 October 2013.

111 **I left home and ended up sharing a flat in Clapham** GS to IFK,
30 October 2013.

111 *No way* **was I attracted to Malcolm** VW manuscript memoir, VW
archive.

113 **After three or four weeks I decided to feign being sick** Savage, J.,
England's Dreaming, p.21.

113 **Malcolm was a hyperactive kind of person** BW to IFK, 18 October
2013.

113 **I suddenly realized that they were an item** GS to IFK, 30 October
2013.

113 **Malcolm hadn't had a girlfriend at all before then** GS to IFK,
30 October 2013.

113   **Malcolm was like a contemporary, a lad, my best friend** GS to IFK,
           30 October 2013.

114   **I was actually on my way to get an abortion** VW manuscript memoir,
           VW archive.

114   **Malcolm was fascinating** VW manuscript memoir, VW archive.

116   **Malcolm was heavily influenced at that time by the work of the
           French Situationists** VW manuscript memoir, VW archive.

116   **He loved clothes** VW manuscript memoir, VW archive.

116   **I was utterly committed and that's what mattered to me**
           VW manuscript memoir, VW archive.

119   **it was still snowing when I came out of hospital** VW manuscript
           memoir, VW archive.

119   **he had no intention of getting trapped into family life**
           VW manuscript memoir, VW archive.

120   **I couldn't ask him for help at all** VW manuscript memoir, VW archive.

124   **anarchy, agitprop and radicalism were heard continually** Rayner, G.,
           Chamberlain, R., Stapleton, A.M., (eds.), *Pop; Design, Culture, Fashion,
           1956–1976*, ACC Editions, London 2012 (introduction, p.12).

124   **potentially the greatest primary-school teacher** Fellow student Peter
           Silverstone, quoted in Mulvagh, J., *Vivienne Westwood, An
           Unfashionable Life*, HarperCollins, London 1998, p.42.

128   **so he wouldn't be brought up in a narrow, working-class way** Ibid.,
           p.41.

128   **Malcolm tried to excuse himself for the dad he'd been** JC to IFK,
           5 December 2013.

129   **I used to be quite scared of Malcolm** BW to IFK, 18 October 2013.

129   **Me and Joe used to hear the rows** BW to IFK, 18 October 2013.

130   **She had that look a full year before** *Ziggy Stardust* Simon Barker,
           quoted in Mulvagh, p.48.

SEX AT THE WORLDS END

133   **I am now proud of my role as a punk** VW manuscript note for New
           York Metropolitan Museum of Art 'Chaos to Couture' exhibition,
           TB archive, Elcho Street.

138   **Their victory, Mum and Malcolm, was that they found each other**
           JC to IFK, 5 December 2013.

139   **populated by people 'economically, politically, socially and
           theologically, in a mess'** Quoted in Savage, J., *England's Dreaming*,
           p.4.

139   **an American car** Malcolm McLaren quoted in Gorman, P., 2006, p.10.

139   **which at one time sported a giant gorilla** Malcolm McLaren quoted
           in Gorman, P., 2006, p.11.

139   **was noted for selling the first used blue jeans** Malcolm McLaren
           quoted in Gorman, P., 2006, p.11.

139   **All of these stores . . . were the street's visual answer to the musical
           pop culture** Malcolm McLaren quoted in Gorman, P., 2006, p.11.

140–1   **It opened at maybe one o'clock** BL REF C1046/12A, Tommy Roberts
           interviewed by Anna Dyke: Roberts, Tommy (speaker, male;
           interviewee; fashion entrepreneur) (section 2) Track 29.

141   **a pretty druggy reputation** Gorman, p.83.

141   **Are you cool? . . . fucking freezing** Lloyd Johnson quoted in Gorman,
           P., 2006, p.83.

141   **Trevor Myles fell in love with a Swedish model** BL REF C1046/12A ,
           Tommy Roberts interviewed by Anna Dyke: Roberts, Tommy
           (speaker, male; interviewee; fashion entrepreneur) (section 2)
           Track 29.

141   **as you do, or certainly as you did then . . . very wealthy girl who had
           split from her man** Trevor Myles quoted in Gorman, P., 2006,
           p.124.

143   **Malcolm and I searched markets for old rock 'n' roll records**
           VW manuscript memoir, VW archive.

143   **could have the keys . . . walked away** Trevor Myles quoted in Gorman,
           P., 2006, p.124.

144   **You felt, you know, that you could go in there** Steve Jones quoted in
           Gorman, P., 2006, p.131.

144   **dominated by Odeon wallpaper** Savage, J., p.46.

145   **Entering the shop felt like entering the set of a fifties B-movie**
           Steph Raynor quoted in Gorman, P., 2006, p.131.

145   **The place where music . . . my artist's studio** Malcolm McLaren
           quoted in Gorman, P., 2006, p.130.

145   **I [had been] counting on an unexpected moment** Malcolm McLaren
           quoted in Gorman, P., 2006, p.10.

145   **Malcolm would get very excited** V&A archive. Transcript source
           material for V&A exhibition, interview with VW and Claire
           Wilcox.

146   **In those days, at 430 King's Road there wasn't a toilet** GK to IFK,
           Paris, October 2013.

146   **Soon enough there was media attention** Savage, J., p.47 and Gorman,
           P., 2006, p.130.

147   **Trevor Myles had gone broke so I said to Malcolm and Vivienne to**

have it BL REF C1046/12A, Tommy Roberts interviewed by Anna Dyke: Roberts, Tommy (speaker, male; interviewee; fashion entrepreneur) (section 2) Track 29.

150 **£3.50 a day ... On Saturday mornings, you'd turn up late** Glen Matlock quoted in Gorman, P., 2006, p.132.

152 **McLaren, typically, later denied ... Bernie Rhodes** Gorman, P., 2006, p.137.

153 **A favourite of Paul Cook** Gorman, P., 2006, p.138.

155 **I'd be doing my homework in the corner** BW to IFK, 18 October 2013.

155–6 **the inverted cross on the swastika / Destroy T-shirt** BW to IFK, 18 October 2013.

156 **My job then and my job always was to confront the Establishment** Wilcox, C., *Vivienne Westwood*, V&A publications, London 2004, p.12.

157 **The sexual morality that inhibits the will to freedom** McLaren, M., 'Sex Pistols on Stage, or London's Outrage', manuscript, collage, McLaren, M., ed., Rough Trade Records, BL Manuscripts YD. 2005. b860, 1977, p.2.

157 **The only reason I am in fashion is to destroy the word 'conformity'** VW manuscript note for Met 'Chaos to Couture'. TB archive, Elcho Street.

158 **It didn't look, inside or out, like a boutique at all** Wilcox, p.12.

158 **I thought I couldn't look any better** VW manuscript note for Met 'Chaos to Couture'. TB archive, Elcho Street.

158 **one of the all-time greatest in history** Wilcox, p.12.

160 **She was like a goddess** Wilcox, p.12.

160 **That was what was attractive about them** Mulvagh, p.74.

160–1 **Black expressed the denunciation of the frill ... between life and death** Malcolm McLaren quoted in Gorman, P., 2006, p.10.

161 **act as a catalyst for the musical tastes of the time** Malcolm McLaren quoted in Gorman, P., 2006, p.10.

161 **It had started with an interest in any form of youth revolt** McLaren, quoted in Wilcox, p.12.

NEW YORK DOLL

166 **We loved to dress up** Savage, p.59.

166 **No, man, I'm trisexual** Savage, p.60.

168 **It became my *raison d'être* to be in New York** Macleay, p.93.

169 **a sort of feeding frenzy** DH to IFK, July 2014.

170   so awful that it crashed through into the other side Savage, p.62.

174   he wanted to shock VW quoted in Wilcox, p.14.

174   you put that on, and basically you are insulting yourself Bell, E., (ed.)
      Punk: Chaos to Couture, Exhibition Catalogue for PUNK: Chaos to
      Couture, Metropolitan Museum of Art, New York, 2013
      (introduction by Bell, A., p.22).

175   You started to see the early stirrings of a real artist GK to IFK, Paris,
      October 2013.

GOD SAVE THE QUEEN

177   the punk "look" evolved in our shop at 430 King's Road VW
      manuscript note for Met 'Chaos to Couture'. TB archive, Elcho
      Street.

180   The look . . . spread throughout the world Jon Savage quoted in
      Wilcox, p.13.

180   a declaration of war . . . an explosion of the body Malcolm McLaren
      quoted in Gorman, P., 2006, p.10.

183   The clothes needed the groups . . . the biggest plus you can have
      Malcolm McLaren quoted in O'Byrne, R., Style City, Frances
      Lincoln, London, 2009 p. 81.

186   she'd lock Malcolm in a cupboard Mulvagh, p.93.

189   I don't think [punk] was intentionally offensive GK to IFK, Paris,
      October 2013.

191   We all, in Blondie, loved to go down to Worlds End DH to IFK,
      July 2014.

191   I first met Vivienne at SEX JH to IFK, 2013.

191   All the characters I met at 430 King's Road were just as fascinating as
      Jerry GK to IFK, Paris, October 2013.

199   It was one of the best feelings, the next day, when you saw the paper
      Savage, p.260.

199   an unidentified find of Malcolm's MB to IFK, 18 October 2013.

202   [Glen] had been growing apart from them for some time Savage,
      p.308.

203   the Pistols were a contagious disease *London Evening Standard*,
      17 March 1977.

208   These clothes are about survival in London John Krevine quoted in
      Gorman, P., 2006, p.150.

210   The majority of the kids that came in GK to IFK, Paris, October
      2013.

212   "My God – she's world famous" GS to IFK, 30 October 2013.

THURLEIGH COURT

216   **suddenly my parents were Public Enemy Number One** *Observer*, 2 May 2009.

216   **That's when I changed** *Observer*, 2 May 2009.

218   **Vivienne is a *practical* feminist** SC to IFK, 30 October 2013.

218   **I was never worried and I enjoyed myself** BW to IFK, 18 October 2013.

219   **"Wow. My mum's great"** BW to IFK, 18 October 2013.

219   **Mum did need space to create** BW to IFK, 18 October 2013.

219   **Malcolm had gone and got these bollock weights** JC to IFK, 5 December 2013.

219   **We were brought up to be very adventurous** JC to IFK, 5 December 2013.

220   **Not critical enough to think** BW to IFK, 18 October 2013.

220   **We never ever had Christmas there** JC to IFK, 5 December 2013.

221   **Vivienne drinking whisky and dancing** RP to IFK, 9 August 2013.

221   **my mum asked if I would be interested in going to boarding school** BW to IFK, 18 October 2013.

223   **Boarding school was a trauma** JC to IFK, 5 December 2013.

223   **I knew Mum and Malcolm were trying to do the best thing** JC to IFK, 5 December 2013.

223   **I just went from one school to another** JC to IFK, 5 December 2013.

224   **I didn't even really think about clothes growing up** *Observer*, 2 May 2009.

224   **Ben was different, or rather punk and everything hit at a different time for him** JC to IFK, 5 December 2013.

225   **Mum sent me off to a different London museum every day** BW to IFK, 18 October 2013.

226   **My personal involvement in the shop began in the eighties** BW to IFK, 18 October 2013.

PIRATE PRINCESS

231   **Leave everything to me** Westwood, V., *Active Resistance: The Manifesto*, 2002.

236   **Malcolm just wasn't around** VW manuscript notes pre-second draft, May 2014.

237   **I'd seen an engraving of a pirate** Wilcox, p.16.

239   **It's impossible to think of the bands . . . without Vivienne's work** Wilcox, p.16.

239   **you have to make people feel great** Wilcox, p.16–17.

242   **I was addicted to heroin** GK to IFK, Paris, October 2013.

243   **Vivienne took complete responsibility for the business** GK to IFK, Paris, October 2013.

243   **Mum is always very gracious about Malcolm** JC to IFK, 5 December 2013.

246   **It got to a horrible point in the end** JC to IFK, 5 December 2013.

247   **I remember we were on the Tube once** JC to IFK, 5 December 2013.

253   **I loved what was going on at Vivienne's** Caroline Baker to IFK, email, 2013.

257   **the pull and push of garment against the body** Wilcox, p.18.

258   **Half the battle with clothing or making something . . . is knowing how to solve a problem** JC to IFK, 5 December 2013.

258   **I realized after Pirates that I didn't have to qualify my ideas** Wilcox, p.17.

258   **Malcolm used to tell us bedtime stories** BW at Malcolm McLaren's funeral.

MAID IN ITALY

261   **Behind some great women there is a man** CD'A to IFK, 27 July 2013.

261   **I introduced Vivienne to Keith Richards** GK to IFK, Paris, October 2013.

262   **He went as far as calling the factory** Mulvagh, p.183.

262   **some of the most interesting to come out of England** Watson, L., *Vogue on Vivienne Westwood*, Quadrille Publishing, London 2012, p.56.

268   **We created a new company** CD'A to IFK, 8 November 2013.

269   **We started signing on the dole** JC to IFK, 5 December 2013.

272   **It was a great time** JC to IFK, 5 December 2013.

273   **You have to put things into context** MB and VW in archive, 15 January 2014.

273   **I wanted women to be strong in a feminine way** Wilcox, p.20.

273   **a nice, classic silhouette** MB and VW in archive, 15 January 2014.

273   **a great passion for Walt Disney** MB and VW in archive, 15 January 2014.

273   **It reminds us of underwear** MB and VW in archive, 15 January 2014.

274   **It was worn with a twinset and pearls** MB and VW in archive, 15 January 2014.

274   **All this attention. No money** JC to IFK, 5 December 2013.

CULTURE CLUB

FRÄULEIN KRONTHALER

327   At times it was difficult AK to IFK, 15 January 2014.

327   She was also a guru or a mentor for me AK to IFK, 15 January 2014.

330   I had come to London because Vivienne invited me AK to IFK, 15 January 2014.

330   she is incredibly positive AK to IFK, 15 January 2014.

334   Andreas is a very strong character RP to IFK, 9 August 2013.

336   Everybody wanted to come to her shows BS to IFK, 20 December 2013.

336   It was outrageous RP to IFK, 9 August 2013.

338   It's advertising where models make the most money BS to IFK, 20 December 2013.

340   ranting in ecstasy Independent, Friday, 15 October 1993.

340   By the mid 1990s the money started coming in RP to IFK, 9 August 2013.

340   Christopher Di Pietro was put in charge of the marketing side BS to IFK, 20 December 2013.

341   The company seemed to double or triple its turnover each season BS to IFK, 20 December 2013.

341   I was *so* embarrassed NC to IFK, 29 October 2013.

341   You just couldn't ignore the fact any more BS to IFK, 20 December 2013.

344   I think the collections from those dark years are great AK to IFK, 15 January 2014.

344   we are often outsiders AK to IFK, 15 January 2014.

西太后 'DOWAGER EMPRESS WEST'

349   Only time can testify success Matteo Guarnaccia, 'Vivienne Westwood', quoting T. S. Eliot [Italian manuscript, 2002].

349   Fashion is like walking a tightrope *Painted Ladies*, written and presented by Vivienne Westwood, Channel 4, 1996: activeresistance.co.uk/ar/?p=1690

350   people would point and say "Worlds End!" Mulvagh, 2004 edition, new preface, p.xi.

350   Bettina jacket with lilac rubber masturbation skirt Christie's Sale Catalogue, Tuesday, 4 September 2001, p.11.

354   this has replaced what Paris couture used to be Angelica Gleason to IFK, Paris, 2013.

355   Vivienne designs frocks for women with things like breasts and hips Watson, p.138.

356   I met Vivienne at a *Vogue* shoot TE to IFK, email, 2014.

358   **like the fucking Jerry Springer show** JC to IFK, 5 December 2013.

358   **Vivienne was quite pleased . . . when she knew she was going to be a grandmother** SR and CC to IFK, 30 October 2013.

363   **she also performed the only punk act** JA to IFK, 2014.

364   **On this bleak, bleak day** Funeral of Malcolm McLaren, DVD, private collection of Joe Corré, 2010.

366   **He really broke something in me** JC to IFK, 5 December 2013.

370   **I am proud to have been part of it. It was heroic at the time** Marion Hume, *Vogue*, September 1994, p.194.

370   **I've never cared one way or the other about failure** Ibid., p.194

371   **The first impact you should have in fashion** Ibid., p.9.

373   **you have a much better life if you wear impressive clothes** VW, quoted in Wilcox, p.9.

373   **The cult of the body** Westwood, *Painted Ladies*.

CLIMATE REVOLUTIONARY

377   **Imagine if you and your family wished to fly** In response to *Guardian Weekend*, 'What would you ask the Prime Minister?', email, 29 June 2011, VW in TB archive, Elcho Street.

378   **It brings her a sense of purpose** SR to IFK, 30 October 2013.

378   **When we went to the Met Ball** LC to IFK, 27 February 2014.

383   **It would be exciting to see you** VW letter, Saturday, 3 December 2011, in TB archive, Elcho Street.

385   **They offered her a trip up the Amazon** GS to IFK, 30 October 2013.

388   **Vivienne had just come out of a week living with an Ashaninka community** An indigenous tribe that lives in the Western Amazon and works in partnership with Cool Earth to protect over three million acres of the world's most endangered rainforest.

388   **Out of nowhere Vivienne made a perfect speech** MO of Cool Earth to IFK, 2014.

389   **as a result of your appearance on the Jonathan Ross show** Letter from HRH The Prince of Wales to Dame Vivienne Westwood, 24 August 2009.

389   **It really does make all the difference** Letter from HRH The Prince of Wales to Dame Vivienne Westwood regarding the opening of 'Wool Modern', 18 September 2011.

389   **We are of similar minds on social justice and climate revolution** PA, manuscript notes to IFK, April 2014.

389   **We were together when Obama was elected** PA, manuscript notes to IFK, April 2014.

389   **She is a real force in our family** PA, manuscript notes to IFK, April 2014.

391   **It's a brutal environment** Ajuma to IFK, Paris, October 2013.

393   **Vivienne cares a lot about the planet** SC to IFK, 30 October 2013.

393   **Vivienne's involvement with Liberty began in 2005** SC to IFK, 30 October 2013.

393   **I wrote to Vivienne to enlist her help** SC to IFK, 30 October 2013.

394   **I don't think you can separate Vivienne's politics and her activism from her art and her fashion** SC to IFK, 30 October 2013.

395   **she is not at all like other so-called "celebrities"** SC to IFK, 30 October 2013.

395   **We met at my forty-first birthday party in Norfolk while I was under house arrest** JA to IFK, 2014.

396   **My number is 89637-132** LP to IFK, 2014.

399   **I am doing the *Ellen* [DeGeneres] show on 16th** PA to VW, email, 11 October 2013.

402   **Vivienne was asked to represent Greenpeace** *Channel 4 News*, 10 October 2013.

402   **she has this disarming honesty about her** JC to IFK, 5 December 2013.

THE RIVER FLOWS ON

405   **Her face was not soft; it was controlled, kindly** Bloom, H. (ed.), *John Steinbeck's The Grapes of Wrath*, Chelsea House Publishing, New York 2007, p.103.

406   **She never has any clothes; it's ridiculous** AK to IFK, 15 January 2014.

408   **I am a bit in awe of them still** TB to IFK, October 2013.

413   **Vivienne cooks** AK to IFK, 15 January 2014.

413   **Vivienne still loves designing more than anything** AK to IFK, 15 January 2014.

413   **Vivienne doesn't watch television** AK to IFK, 15 January 2014.

413   **We very rarely go to see films** AK to IFK, 15 January 2014.

414   **Our love . . . is different now** AK to IFK, 15 January 2014.

414   **I have to stop and give her my full attention** AK to IFK, 15 January 2014.

415   **Being a woman is different** Bloom, H., p.108.

417   **The best guide for living** 'Alice and Pinocchio' by VW. TB archive.

INDEX

IAN KELLY is an award-winning writer and actor.
His previous works include internationally acclaimed
biographies of Beau Brummell, Casanova, Samuel Foote and
Antonin Carême. He lives in London and Suffolk.

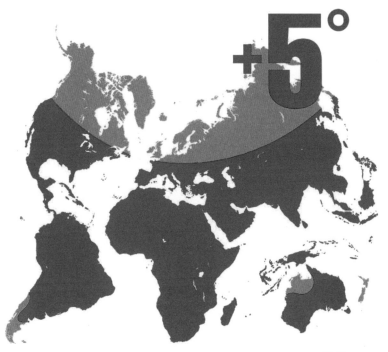

RED = <u>Uninhabitable</u> <u>Land</u> at +5°
Past +2° can't ~~stop~~ → goes to +5°

End Monopoly Capitalism

Everyone is talking about the end of capitalism together with how we transfer to a post-carbon economy. We have no choice. The answer is simple: what's good for the planet is good for people.

I wish quickly to explain how capitalism runs the world and why it must come to an end. To give you a perspective. If you hold on to this perspective then you can work everything out for yourself, even down to the detail. Know what you should do. Everything is connected.

I've written everything down because I want to get it right. One step at a time.

Central Banks: We have to start with the central banks which control the world's economy. They do this by creating <u>debt</u>. (It's actually a global Ponzi scheme.)

The central banks are <u>private banks</u>. The US Federal Bank is one. They are organized by the Bank for International Settlement (BIS) in Zurich.

These central banks print money. Today they do this by pressing buttons. They create virtual money out of nothing.

This money is loaned to other banks, monopolies and governments. It has now become a debt.

The central banks prefer it if the loans are never paid because what they want is the interest – which accumulates out of all proportion to reality.

This means they always have fantastic amounts of money to lend and they don't have to print virtual money except in an emergency.

It also means that the central banks come to own everything – because they own the debt. How often have we heard of a poor country selling its assets and natural resources just to keep up with the interest payments on the debt it has been forced to borrow?

Monopolies: The monopolies work this system for the central banks. The monopolies do the actual job of wrecking the planet and exploiting its people (cheap labour). They suck up small businesses.

Capitalism: This economic system is called capitalism. Capitalism began 200 years ago and is now global. It is coming to an end. It is not possible to continue indefinitely using up the world's resources. Capitalism is run on fossil fuels – which are more difficult to get and running out. You can't have capitalism without fossil fuels. It began with coal and ends with oil and gas.

Environment: The conventional supplies of fossil fuels which are easily accessible have all been discovered. They are finite. Science tells us that we must leave 80% in the ground. Otherwise, runaway climate change is inevitable.

We are in a trap: we can't suddenly stop using these fuels but we must phase them out, as soon as possible, in exchange for sustainable energy.

Sustainable energy: Sustainable energy is cheap and infinite. It will be a base for a different economy, a fair economy founded on true human values. We will develop the world we want.

Don't forget that capitalism is a war economy: it profits from war. Its aim is to own everything.

We would prefer cooperation and community. Capitalists prefer competition and death.

Governments: Governments serve the central banks and the monopolies. Together they form a triad. This triad is desperate to hold on to capitalism. They have resorted to extreme measures, e.g. fracking.

Now that capitalism is ending, the fact that it is a Ponzi scheme is more clearly exposed. Governments help the central banks to conceal this by imposing austerity; pretending that we can control the debt.

The debt accumulates and <u>it can never be paid back.</u> A child unborn already owes an enormous IOU. Debt is simply a promise to pay in the future. Austerity is a proof of government contempt for people: <u>They</u> will suffer, <u>we</u> will continue.

Meanwhile the central banks are showing their hand by printing emergency money. They bailed out the commercial banks to keep the system going. They might as well print more virtual money and tell governments to stop the austerity. It won't make any difference. If capitalism continues, it will crash. The dollars will be useless. All money will be useless.

Democracy: Governments do not care about people. They care only for their own power and that lies within the triad. In England this applies to all the main parties. There is nothing to choose between them. There's no point in voting for any of them. That's why I say there is no chance of immediate democracy in England. Old people vote from habit. Young people – we have to build the minority parties. The Green Party has a sane and practical agenda.

Fight the main political parties. Everything they say is rubbish. Everything they do is dangerous.

Capitalism is at an end; it can't continue. We have no choice but to change to a green economy, starting with renewable energy. The sooner the better. <u>Urgent!</u>

Demonstrate: Time is running out. Come out and be counted. Numbers = People Power. We want a government that's on our side. Oppose present governments to get the government we want.

It's great that we have identified the common enemy as capitalism itself.

Every demonstration is a fight against capitalism against the government and against austerity. Everything is connected.

Capitalism is the enemy of the bees, capitalism is the enemy of human rights. Everything is connected.

And when Occupy says 'We are the 99%' that means that the 1% is Capitalism.

Vivienne Westwood

www.climaterevolution.co.uk
www.facebook.com/jointheclimaterevolution
https://twitter.com/climate_rev